W. (William) Sanday

**Inspiration**

Eight ILectures on the Early History and Origin of the Doctrine of Biblical Inspiration

W. (William) Sanday

**Inspiration**

*Eight ILectures on the Early History and Origin of the Doctrine of Biblical Inspiration*

ISBN/EAN: 9783337179984

Printed in Europe, USA, Canada, Australia, Japan

Cover: Foto ©Lupo / pixelio.de

More available books at **www.hansebooks.com**

# EIGHT LECTURES

ON THE

EARLY HISTORY AND ORIGIN OF THE DOCTRINE
OF BIBLICAL INSPIRATION

*Being the Bampton Lectures for 1893*

BY

W. SANDAY, M.A., D.D., LL.D.

DEAN IRELAND'S PROFESSOR OF EXEGESIS
FELLOW OF EXETER COLLEGE, OXFORD

*SECOND EDITION*

London

LONGMANS, GREEN, AND CO.

AND NEW YORK: 15 EAST 16TH STREET

1894

[*All rights reserved*]

### Oxford
HORACE HART, PRINTER TO THE UNIVERSITY

## Ecclesiae Maiori Anglicanae

SCILICET OMNIBUS QUI EX GENTE ANGLORUM ORIUNDI

QUOCUMQUE SUB NOMINE

CHRISTUM EX ANIMO COLUNT ET VENERANTUR

## Ecclesiae Maiori Anglicanae

CUI ET MINOREM ILLAM

CUIUS IPSE SACRA FERO ET FILIUS AUDIO

DUCEM ET QUASI SIGNIFERUM ESSE VELLEM

## Ecclesiae Maiori Anglicanae

QUAM INTER SPEM ET SOLLICITUDINEM

SED SPE MAIORI QUAM SOLLICITUDINE

SINGULARI AMORE PROSECUTUS SUM ET PROSEQUOR

HAS CONTIONES QUALESCUMQUE

DEDICO

PRECATUS UT SIBI SE NON IMPAREM PRAESTET

SED ANTIQUA PIETATE NULLATENUS REMISSA

AD NOVA MUNERA, NOVAM RERUM CONDITIONEM

DEO ADIUVANTE

SE FORTITER ET FELICITER ACCINGAT

# EXTRACT

## FROM THE LAST WILL AND TESTAMENT

OF THE LATE

## REV. JOHN BAMPTON,

CANON OF SALISBURY.

——"I give and bequeath my Lands and Estates to the "Chancellor, Masters, and Scholars of the University of "Oxford for ever, to have and to hold all and singular the "said Lands or Estates upon trust, and to the intents and "purposes hereinafter mentioned; that is to say, I will and "appoint that the Vice-Chancellor of the University of Ox- "ford for the time being shall take and receive all the rents, "issues, and profits thereof, and (after all taxes reparations, "and necessary deductions made) that he pay all the re- "mainder to the endowment of eight Divinity Lecture Ser- "mons, to be established for ever in the said University, and "to be performed in the manner following:

"I direct and appoint, that, upon the first Tuesday in "Easter Term, a Lecturer be yearly chosen by the Heads "of Colleges only, and by no others, in the room adjoining "to the Printing-House, between the hours of ten in the "morning and two in the afternoon, to preach eight Divinity "Lecture Sermons, the year following, at St. Mary's in Ox- "ford, between the commencement of the last month in Lent "Term and the end of the third week in Act Term.

"Also I direct and appoint, that the eight Divinity Lecture "Sermons shall be preached upon either of the following "Subjects—to confirm and establish the Christian Faith, and "to confute all heretics and schismatics—upon the divine "authority of the holy Scriptures—upon the authority of "the writings of the primitive Fathers, as to the faith and "practice of the primitive Church—upon the Divinity of our "Lord and Saviour Jesus Christ—upon the Divinity of the "Holy Ghost—upon the Articles of the Christian Faith, as "comprehended in the Apostles' and Nicene Creeds.

"Also I direct, that thirty copies of the eight Divinity Lec-"ture Sermons shall be always printed, within two months "after they are preached; and one copy shall be given to the "Chancellor of the University, and one copy to the Head of "every College, and one copy to the Mayor of the city of "Oxford, and one copy to be put into the Bodleian Library; "and the expense of printing them shall be paid out of the "revenue of the Land or Estates given for establishing the "Divinity Lecture Sermons; and the Preacher shall not be "paid, nor be entitled to the revenue, before they are printed.

"Also I direct and appoint, that no person shall be quali-"fied to preach the Divinity Lecture Sermons, unless he hath "taken the degree of Master of Arts at least, in one of the "two Universities of Oxford or Cambridge; and that the "same person shall never preach the Divinity Lecture Ser-"mons twice."

# PREFACE

THE Bampton Lectures are preached before an audience which has some parallels in this country and America, but few, if any, upon the Continent. It is a rare thing for the Continental theologian to be brought into such direct contact with the class of highly trained and intelligent laity who are engaged in the teaching of secular literature and science. We may count it as one of the happiest of English traditions, and in fact as the main compensation for the backwardness of much of our theology proper, that this class has never ceased to take an active interest in all matters connected with religion. It is ready to listen even to what are practically monographs on theological subjects; and many of the best volumes which the series has produced have been more or less of this nature.

The present lectures can lay no claim to the character of a monograph. Their aim has been rather to furnish a general view which shall cover as far as possible the data, at once new and old, which go to determine the conception which thoughtful men would form of the Bible.

If it is thought that this is to attempt too much, and that a satisfactory treatment of all parts of the subject was not possible within the compass of eight lectures, the writer can only assent to the criticism. It seemed however to be more important that the subject should be presented, if only in outline, as a fairly complete and coherent whole, than to work out in detail any one of the parts. That can be done afterwards; and in fact it is being done every day.

Another drawback has been the limited time which is allowed for the preparation of the lectures. Between the election of the Bampton Lecturer and the delivery of his first lecture is an interval of at most ten months. For one who holds, as the present writer does, a double office with double duties, this interval is curtailed still further. In his case nearly three months more had to be deducted for illness, a loss which however was largely made up to him by the kind indulgence of his College. For the timely relief thus accorded to him he cannot be too grateful.

All this time books came pouring from the press at a rate with which it was difficult to keep pace. Many of them were of high value, and of some he wishes that he could have made a more extended use. He hopes that his obligations in various directions will have been sufficiently acknowledged. But he ought perhaps to single out in particular the

## Preface. xi

*Introductions* of Driver and Cornill to the Old Testament and the third edition of Holtzmann's *Introduction* to the New, with the works on the Canon by Ryle, Buhl, and Wildeboer in the one case, and by Zahn and Harnack in the other. In one instance he fears that he has done less than justice. The main reference to Dr. E. König in Lecture III consists in part of criticism; and this makes it all the more incumbent upon the writer to say that the leading idea of this lecture, and indeed one of the leading ideas of the whole book, is to the best of his belief derived ultimately from Dr. König. It is becoming almost a commonplace to say that our conception of what the Bible is should be drawn in the first instance from what the Biblical writers say of themselves. This idea took a strong hold of the writer some years ago, as he believes indirectly rather than directly through the emphatic statement of it by Dr. König. Yet when he came to read the *Offenbarungsbegriff des A. T.*, along with its independence and ability he could not help being struck by what seemed to be an element of arbitrariness and exaggeration. This however has been a diminishing quantity in later books by the same author, notably in his recent *Introduction to the Old Testament*, which he wishes had reached him a little earlier.

The writer is conscious of having criticized most freely (especially in Lecture I) some of those for whom he has the highest respect. This applies particularly to some of the German scholars whose names deservedly carry the greatest weight in England. There are none to whom he is himself more indebted; but he does not wish them to impose upon his countrymen by the weight of authority views which do not seem to be borne out by the evidence.

The parts of these lectures which relate to the Old Testament should be taken with the qualification expressed on p. 119 f. The writer cannot speak in this part so much at first hand as he can in the case of the New. If, in spite of this, the result seems to work out somewhat more positively in the former case than in the latter, this is due in part to the clear-cut form in which modern critical theories relating to the Old Testament are presented. Perhaps also it would be true to say that in recent years stronger work upon the whole has been done upon the Old Testament than upon the New.

In view of this body of Old Testament criticism the writer's own position is tentative and provisional. He does not think that the great revolution which seems to be expected in some quarters, from the Tell-el-Amarna tablets or otherwise, is probable; at the same time his impression is that the criticism of the near future is likely to be more conservative in its tendency than it has been, or at least to do fuller justice to the positive data than it has done.

In regard to the New Testament he has tried to state the case as objectively as possible. He has thus been led rather to understate than to overstate the results which seem to him to have been attained so far. But he believes that there is much still to be done; and he hopes most from the spirit which is not impatient for 'results,' which does not suppress or slur over difficulties in the critical view any more than in the traditional, which lays its plans broadly, and is determined to make good the lesser steps before it attempts the greater.

Besides his large debt to books the writer is also under obligations to friends who have done him the kindness to read through the proofs as they were passing through the press. He owes much to the criticisms and suggestions which he has received in this way, especially from Dr. Plummer, Mr. Lock, and Mr. A. C. Headlam. He wishes that his book were better than it is; but he can truly say that in writing it he has gained for himself a deepened and a strengthened hold on the principles to which he has given imperfect expression.

The Synopsis of Contents was issued separately at the time of the delivery of the lectures, and has been allowed to retain the form given to it for that purpose.

MARCHFIELD, OXFORD,
*August*, 1893.

# SYNOPSIS OF CONTENTS

## LECTURE I.

THE HISTORIC CANON.
ESTIMATE OF THE NEW TESTAMENT BY THE EARLY CHURCH.

Subject and method of the proposed inquiry. Two lectures to be devoted to analysis of main points in the conception of the Canon; the succeeding five to an attempt to sketch constructively the process by which that conception was reached; the last to retrospect and summary. . . . . . . . . pp. 1-4.

Idea of a Canon extended from O. T. to N. T. Two landmarks in the history of the N. T. Canon, about 400 A.D. and 200 A.D. pp. 4-6.

I. *Contents of N. T.* (1) *c.* 400 A.D. Practically the same as our own over the greater part of Christendom. This result very partially due to Synodical decisions (African Synods of 393, 397, 419 [Council of Laodicea *c.* 363], Trullan Council of 692); far more in the West to the influence of the Vulgate, in the East to that of leading Churchmen (Athanasius, Cyril of Jerusalem, Amphilochius, Gregory Nazianzen).

Only considerable exception the Syrian Church which recognised no more than three (two) Epp. Cath. and rejected Apoc. These books wanting in Peshitto, but added in later Syriac Versions. pp. 6-12.

*Contents of N. T.* (2) *c.* 200 A.D.: approximate date of Muratorian Fragment. Solid nucleus of four Gospels, thirteen Epp. Paul., Acts.

Divergent views on this subject. It is questioned (i) that the Four Gospels were everywhere accepted; (ii) that Epp. Paul. stood on an equal footing with Gospels and O. T.; (iii) that Acts formed part of the collection. In each case with but slight real support from the evidence. . . . . . . . . . pp. 12 23.

*Writings struggling for admission to the Canon*: 1 Pet., 1 Jo. all but fixed—Heb., Jac., Apoc.—2 [3] Jo., Jud., 2 Pet. . . . pp. 23-26.

*Writings which obtain a partial footing but are dislodged*: Evv., sec. Heb., sec. Aegypt., sec. Pet.—Epp. Clem., Barn. *Didache*, *Pastor*— Leucian Acts, *Predicatio Petri, Acta Paul. et Thecl.*, &c.—Apoc. Pet.
pp. 26 28.

II. *Properties ascribed to the Canonical Books.* The N. T. is (1) a sacred book; (2) on the same footing with O. T.—a proposition questioned but true; (3) inspired by the Holy Spirit, or bearing the authority of Christ; (4) this inspiration is even 'verbal' and extends to facts as well as doctrines; (5) it carries with it a sort of perfection, completeness, infallibility; (6) the N. T. Scriptures are appealed to as (*a*) the rule of faith, (*b*) the rule of conduct; (7) they are interpreted allegorically like a sacred book, and complaints are made of perverse interpretation. . . . . . . . . . pp. 28-42.

Yet along with this high doctrine there are occasional traces of (1) the recognition of degrees of inspiration; (2) a natural account of the origin of certain books (*e.g.* the Gospels). . . . . pp. 42-47.

III. *Criteria by which books were admitted to the New Testament.* (1) Apostolic origin; (2) reception by the Churches; (3) conformity to established doctrine; (4) conformity to recognised history; (5) mystical significance of numbers. . . . . pp. 47-58.

Note A.—*The Canons of the Quinisextine Council, of Carthage, and of Laodicea.* . . . . . . . . . . pp. 59-61.

Note B.—*Harnack's Theory of the Growth of the New Testament Canon.* . . . . . . . . . . pp. 61-63.

Note C.—*Debateable Points relating to the Alogi.* . . pp. 64-65.

Note D.—*The use of the New Testament by Clement of Alexandria.*
pp. 65-69.

## LECTURE II.

### THE HISTORIC CANON.
### ESTIMATE OF THE OLD TESTAMENT IN THE FIRST CENTURY OF THE CHRISTIAN ERA.

The critical period in the history of the Bible is the forming of Canon of O. T. Our first clear view of an O. T. Canon is obtained in the century which follows the Birth of Christ. For this we have Philo, N. T., Josephus, supplemented by the Talmud. . pp. 70-72.

I. *Properties ascribed to O. T. in these writings.* O. T. (1) is a sacred book; (2) is inspired by God—difference in this respect between Philo and Josephus; (3) has a normative value; (4) is interpreted allegorically; (5) prophetically determines the course of future events; (6) has a minute perfection which implies, at least in the case of Philo, an inspiration that might be called 'verbal.' . . pp. 72-90.

II. *Contents of O. T.* Many other religious books of Jewish origin in circulation during first century besides the Canonical. Distinction between so-called Palestinian and Alexandrian Canon not so much

## Synopsis of Contents. xvii

geographical as between popular and learned or official usage. Both Philo and Josephus have wide views of the range of inspiration and yet treat the Canonical Books only as authoritative. So too in N. T., though there are traces of acquaintance with Apocrypha. With Josephus and the Rabbis of the end of first century the Canon is really complete. There is however still some hesitation as to certain books, especially Cant., Eccles., Esther. . . . pp. 90-98.

Divisions of Jewish Canon point back to circumstances of its origin. Traceable from soon after 132 B.C., and correspond to so many stages in the formation of the Canon : (1) the Law, 444 B.C.; (2) the Prophets, probably in third century B.C.; (3) the Hagiographa or *Kethubim*, c. 100 B.C. . . . . . . . . . pp. 98-105.

III. *Criteria by which books were admitted to the Canon.* History of the word 'Apocrypha': (i) milder Jewish sense, = not read in public ; (ii) stronger sense, increasingly common in Christian circles, = 'heretical.' Discussions in the Jewish Schools mainly concerned with fitness of books for public reading. In Philo, Josephus and the Talmud the leading positive principle was Prophecy. The closing of the Canon supposed to coincide with cessation of prophecy. Symbolism of numbers as applied to O. T. . . . pp. 105-115.

Before entering on larger inquiry it is right to explain the attitude adopted to the criticism of O. T. The critical theories come with great force, though they seem open to qualification in certain directions. They are assumed here hypothetically and provisionally, as a *minimum*. The data which they supply for a doctrine of inspiration cannot well be less and may be more. Leading points in the critical position. . . . . . . . . pp. 115-122.

Note A.—*On the Date of the Formation of the Jewish Canon.* p. 123.


## LECTURE III.

#### THE GENESIS OF THE OLD TESTAMENT. THE PROPHETIC AND HISTORICAL BOOKS.

Belief in Inspiration postulates belief in a Personal, or in Hebrew phrase, 'Living' God. Granted such a God, and it is not strange that He should put Himself in communication with man. pp. 124-128.

I. *The Prophets.* The prophetical inspiration is typical of all inspiration, and is the form in which its working can be most easily traced.

Yet the Hebrew prophets are not without large analogies in other religions. Examples from the Books of Samuel and Judges. The prophetic order. Prophecy as a profession, with professional failings; half-hearted prophets and false prophets. . . . pp. 128-135.

A comparative glimpse of the religion of a kindred race supplied by the Moabite Stone. This has much in common with the religion of Israel, but it has its dark side, human sacrifice and consecrated licentiousness. The problem is, How did the prophetic religion escape this immixture of evil? Most easily answered by what we call Inspiration, *i. e.* the hypothetical cause of that which is distinctive and superior in the religion of the Bible. . . . pp. 135-140.

There is a 'purpose of God according to selection' (Rom. ix. 11): among nations, Israel; in Israel, the prophetic order; among the prophetic order, the higher prophets are chosen to be organs of revelation. Yet the lower prophets, and even the so-called 'false prophets,' also had their function. . . . . pp. 140-143.

Characteristics of the higher prophecy. The prophets only in a secondary degree statesmen or social reformers; before all things preachers of religion. . . . . . . pp. 143-145.

Whence did they derive their authority? They claimed to speak in the name of God. We believe this claim to be true; that in a real objective sense, God *did* cause the prophets to say what He willed should be said. . . . . . . pp. 145-147.

For these reasons: (1) the strong assurance of the prophets themselves, and the clear testimony as to their own consciousness which their writings reveal to us; (2) the general recognition of the claim by their contemporaries; (3) the remarkable consistency in so long a line of prophets, not easily compatible with hallucination; (4) the difficulty of accounting for the prophets' teaching as the product of ordinary causes, whether in (i) the prophets themselves, (ii) their race, (iii) the constitution of the human mind; (5) by the immense permanent significance and value of the prophetic teaching.
pp. 147-155.

II. *The Historical Books*: called by the Jews 'The Former Prophets.' The earlier historians of Israel for the most part prophets. To understand the way in which they worked we must get rid of modern associations, and remember (1) that Hebrew history-writing is as a rule anonymous and involved no idea of literary property; (2) that it was carried on not so much by individuals as by successions of individuals often belonging to the same school or order; (3) that the histories were propagated by single copies which each possessor might enlarge or annotate. . . . . . . pp. 155-160.

Where lies the inspiration of the Historical Books? Double function of the historian, to narrate and to interpret. Hebrew narrative varies in value: it has some special merits, but also some defects. The inspiration lies rather in the interpretation of the Divine purpose running through the history. . . pp. 160-165.

Note A.—*Modern Prophets.* . . . . . pp. 166-167.

## LECTURE IV.

### THE GENESIS OF THE OLD TESTAMENT.
### THE LAW AND THE HAGIOGRAPHA.

I. *The Law.* Different estimate of the Law at different periods: (1) with the Jews; (2) in N. T.; (3) by modern criticism. But though from the critical point of view it may be better to start from the Prophets, the work of Moses is prior both in time and in importance.
pp. 168-173.

In the Law as it has come down to us there are three elements: (1) an element derived from Moses himself, indeterminate in detail but fundamental; and the development of this (2) by prophets, (3) by priests. The cultus not to be undervalued. Though a temporary system, it secured the devoted attachment of many psalmists, and embodied principles which find their final realization in Christianity. It was also a safeguard to the revelation. . . . pp. 173-188.

II. *The Hagiographa.* Inspiration of the writers of these books not primary like that of lawgivers and prophets, but mediate and secondary. Expressive of the intense hold which the principles implanted by lawgivers and prophets took on other classes. A prophetic nation. . . . . . . . pp. 188-191.

*The Psalms.* Date of the Psalter important, but as yet *sub judice*. Made up of a number of smaller collections; analogous to our hymn-books. Prophetic element in Psalter: perhaps more literary than strictly prophetic, but an instance of the way in which different forms of inspiration shade off into each other. Permanent significance of Psalter as the classical expression of religious emotion.
pp. 191-199.

*The Wisdom-Literature.* The 'wise men' as a class by the side of prophets and priests. *Proverbs*, like the Psalter, highly composite; made up of collections which contain the contributions of many minds: cc. xxv-xxix probably earliest, and cc. i. 7-ix latest, at least of main divisions. We thus get an ascending scale of doctrine. The Wisdom-teaching in its basis common to Israel with surrounding nations, esp. Edom. Shrewd observations on life. These with Heb. centre more and more in religion, and at last rise from detached comments on conduct and morals to a comprehensive view of Divine Wisdom as seen in the creation and ordering of the world: a conception momentous in its influence upon later theology, the foundation of the Christian doctrine of the Logos. . . . pp. 199-204.

*Job.* Struggles with a problem—the sufferings of the righteous—to which it does not give a complete solution. Still marks a great advance. Full of deep lessons which are not the less prompted by

God because they are reached in natural sequence. The central impulse comes from that vital grasp upon God and religion which marks the presence and energy of the Spirit. . . pp. 204-207.

*Ecclesiastes.* Pessimism, but religious pessimism. Well that such a book should be included in the Canon. The saving clauses in Ecclesiastes psychologically probable and not interpolations.
pp. 208-211.

*Song of Songs.* As now understood, an idyll of faithful human love, and nothing more. Not quoted in N. T. or inspired in any sense in which the word has been hitherto used. Still a Providential purpose may have been served by its inclusion in the Canon. Another proof of the catholicity of Scripture. And the associations which have gathered round its language justify to some extent its mystical application. . . . . . . . . pp. 211-212.

*Esther.* The most doubtful book in the Canon: Jewish rather than Christian; like Cant. not quoted in N. T. Gained its place mainly by acquiescence in Jewish usage. . . . . . pp. 212-214.

*Daniel.* The use of ancient names became common in later Jewish literature: an innocent device (cp. esp. Eccles.) growing out of (i) the absence of any idea of literary property, (ii) prophetic instinct seeking to clothe itself with authority in a non-prophetic age. Daniel is not to be taken as history, but that it had a really prophetic character is proved by its influence upon Christianity. . . . pp. 214-220.

Note A.—*The Pre-Mosaic History in the Pentateuch.* pp. 221-222.

Note B.—*The Religious Value of the Book of Esther.* pp. 222-223.

Note C.—*The Origin and Character of Pseudonymous Literature among the Jews.* . . . . . . . . pp. 224-225.


## LECTURE V.

### THE GROWTH OF THE OLD TESTAMENT AS A COLLECTION OF SACRED BOOKS.

I. *Transition from Oral Teaching to Written.* This transition, however momentous in its consequences, made no difference in the essential character of the teaching: it was just as authoritative before as after. . . . . . . . . . pp. 226-227.

When did the transition take place? On the critical view, (i) for the Prophets, with Amos and Hosea, *c.* 750 B.C.; (ii) for the Law, with Deuteronomy, *c.* 621 B.C. . . . . . pp. 227-228.

1. For Prophecy the date assigned may perhaps be accepted, though much prophetic writing in the form of history had preceded, and though there is nothing tentative about the earliest written prophecy either as literature or as religious teaching. pp. 228-231.

## Synopsis of Contents. xxi

2. For the Law there is really a chain of connected events: behind Pent. is Deut.; behind Deut. the Book of the Covenant; behind the Book of the Covenant the historic tradition of Sinai preserved in twofold form and pointing far backwards. The idea which underlies the Canon is present from the first.  pp. 231-236.

II. *Transmission and Collecting of Sacred Books*. Transmission of legal writings comparatively regular, through priests; that of prophetic writings more precarious, through disciples. Gradual growth of reading public. The synagogues. Concurrence of causes which led to fully formed Canon, of Law (444 B.C.), of Prophets (third century B.C.). . . . . . . . . . pp. 236-247.

Collection of *Kethubim*: (i) of Wisdom Books; (ii) of Psalter. Remaining books probably added by 100 B.C. The work of scribes.
pp. 247-253.

III. *Final Determination of O. T. Canon*. Principles followed in this. Consciousness of cessation of prophecy. Criteria applied somewhat vague. Probable reasons for inclusion and exclusion of particular books. . . . . . . . pp. 253-257.

The Canon of history and the Canon of doctrine practically identical: a common bond among Christians. Some Deutero-canonical Books (Ecclus., Wisd.) make a claim, which may be allowed, for a certain degree of secondary inspiration.  pp. 257-262.

IV. *Conception of Inspiration associated with the Canon*. That a laxer view of inspiration prevailed at first, appears not only from such claims as these, but also from the state of the text of the LXX Version. The interpolations in this (many of them included in our Apocrypha) show with what freedom it was treated.  pp. 262-263.

As the Canon is more clearly defined the view of inspiration becomes stricter. Attributes which originally belonged to certain books, or parts of books, extended to the whole O. T. Idea of plenary or verbal inspiration derived from Law and Prophecy. Attributes of prophets speaking or writing prophetically assumed to exist where they are not writing prophetically. Need of distinctions.
pp. 263-269.

Note A.—*The inferior Limit for the Date of the Psalter.* pp. 270-273.
Note B.—*The use of the term Deuterocanonical in the Roman Church.*
pp. 273-276.

## LECTURE VI.

THE GENESIS OF THE NEW TESTAMENT. THE GOSPELS AND ACTS.

I. THE GOSPELS. 1. *Their Composition*. A starting-point supplied by Luke i. 1-4, written probably 75-80 A.D. Presupposes much previous collecting of materials, oral and written. Did these include our First and Second Gospels? Evidence of Papias.   pp. 277-281.

The Synoptic problem extremely complicated and difficult, and has not yet reached a solution. It may, however, be safely affirmed that the mass of Synoptic material is older than 70 A.D. Because of (i) the number of allusions to a state of things which came to an end at or before that date; (ii) the compact and consistent character of the terminology of the Gospels, almost unaffected by later developments; (iii) direct indications of the date of composition as not far on either side the Fall of Jerusalem.   .   .   .   pp. 281-293.

Peculiar conditions under which the earliest forms of Gospel were written and copied. Signs of great activity on each side of the year 70. Functions of editor and copyist confused. Freedom in the handling of the text. Number of early interpolations.   pp. 294-298.

2. *Early History*, 80-140 A.D. Freedom in treatment of text continues. Origin of Western Text. Phenomena of quotations in Apostolic Fathers. How accounted for. Catechizing. Prominence given to 'Words of the Lord.'   .   .   .   .   pp. 298-304.

From c. 125 A.D. the Four Gospels begin to stand out. (i) Evidence of Tatian, c. 165-170. (ii) Heracleon's commentary on the Fourth Gospel. Use of this Gospel by Valentinians and probably by Basilides. (iii) Supposed trace of Four Gospels in Hermas. (iv) Use of Four Gospels in Ev. Pet. probable, though marked by freedom characteristic of the period.   .   .   .   .   .   pp. 304-314.

3. *Period* 140-200 A.D. Use of Canonical Gospels becomes more exclusive. Influence of public reading. At first the Canonical Gospels were primarily histories, though religious histories; but towards the end of this period they are treated more as Sacred Books. The potentiality of this is contained in the name 'Gospels.' But St. Luke's preface has all the character of a history: the sacredness is derived from the subject-matter.   .   .   pp. 315-318.

II. THE ACTS. Naturally goes with Third Gospel. Here too the main questions are still open. Criticism of the Acts has been almost entirely in German hands, and has some special defects. An unreal standard applied.   .   .   .   .   .   .   .   pp. 318-320.

Four charges made against the author: (i) that he did not understand the antagonisms of the Apostolic age; (ii) that his statements conflict with Epp. Paul.; (iii) that the Acts of St. Peter are artificially balanced against the Acts of St. Paul; (iv) that the differences between St. Paul and the other Apostles are minimized. Much exaggeration in all of these, and even where true they do not detract seriously from the value of the book as history.   .   pp. 320-329.

Acts certainly composite like the Gospels, and the first step must be to discriminate sources. Valuable data supplied by Prof. Ramsay.
pp. 329-330.

## LECTURE VII

### THE GENESIS OF THE NEW TESTAMENT.
### THE EPISTLES AND APOCALYPSE.

The Apostolic age a great manifestation of the supernatural. The outpouring of the Spirit a reality of which the evidence meets us everywhere. It has left a permanent deposit in the N. T.
pp. 331-334.

I. THE EPISTLES. 1. *Their Origin.* The Epistles arose naturally out of the wants of the newly founded Gentile Churches. There was some precedent for giving to such writings a theological character. This was largely developed by St. Paul. Epistles attributed to him probably all genuine. . . . . . . . pp. 334-343.

Epp. Cath. formed upon this model. An argument against the early date often assigned to Ep. Jac. Bearing of Prof. Ramsay's researches on 1 Pet. Genuineness of 2 Pet. very doubtful; but also doubted in early Church. Effect of this upon the Canon.
pp. 344-350.

2. *Their Inspiration.* St. Paul strongly claims what we call inspiration (Gal. i. 11-17, 1 Cor. ii. &c.). Yet his inspiration consistent with individual characteristics and some weaknesses: it has degrees. Other Apostles wrote with full authority. . . . pp. 350-359.

3. *Their Early History.* Reading of Epp. in public worship. Collection of Epp. Paul. before 117 A.D. On same level with other books by end of century. From the first invested with all the personal authority of Apostles. . . . . . pp. 359-369.

II. THE APOCALYPSE. Recent theories which ascribe a composite origin to this book seem to be giving way to a reaction in favour of its unity. Question of date still outstanding: A.D. 69 or 95? Many points in the problem wait solution. . . . . pp. 369-374.

Apocalypse a prophetic work, and claims the full measure of prophetic inspiration. This is not inconsistent with the fact that some of the symbolism in which it is clothed has proved to be transitory. . . . . . . . . pp. 375-378.

Note A.—*A new Theory of the Origin of the Catholic Epistles.*
pp. 379-382.

Note B.—*On the Genuineness of 2 St. Peter.* . . pp. 382-385.

Note C.—*The Claim to Inspiration in certain passages of the Apostolic Fathers.* . . . . . . . . . . . p. 386.

Note D.—*Early Patristic Comments on 1 Cor. vii. 10, 12, 25, 40.*
pp. 387-390.

## LECTURE VIII.

#### RETROSPECT AND RESULTS.
#### TRADITIONAL AND INDUCTIVE THEORIES OF INSPIRATION COMPARED.

I. Two competing theories of inspiration: (1) the traditional; (2) the inductive or critical. The inspiration implied by the latter quite as real and quite as fundamental as that implied by the former. It is possible to trace the links by which the one has passed into the other.
pp. 391-401.

II. Yet the measure of inspiration is not only the consciousness of the persons inspired. We must add to this the proofs of a Higher Providence at work in the Bible. This is apparent (i) in the impulse which led to the committal of prophetic utterances to writing, and the way in which the occasional letters of Apostles supply a basis for Christian theology; (ii) in the course of Messianic Prophecy; (iii) in that ordering of things by which certain books or parts of books are capable of application by analogy in senses which did not originally belong to them. . . . . . . pp. 402-406.

III. How far did our Lord sanction either view? There are two classes of passages: (i) some showing supreme insight into and sovereign command over the principles of revelation; (ii) others in which the current view is allowed to pass unchallenged.
pp. 406-414.

But apart from any deeper explanation which may be given of these, (i) there is in Revelation what may be called a Law of Parsimony, by which no revelation is given to any age but such as is suited to its wants and capacity, and this law governs the teaching of our Lord Himself; (ii) we must expect to find some analogy between the method of God and of Christ in revelation and in the ordinary government of the world. It is a law of the Divine action that intellectual truth comes late in time. There is a chain of natural connexion between the operation of the Eternal Word, the character of the Incarnate Word, and the constitution of the Written Word. Vindication of the argument from analogy . . . pp. 414-431.

Note A.—*On St. Matthew xii. 40 and St. John x. 35.*   pp. 432-433.

## APPENDIX.

Chronological Table of Data for the History of the Canon.
pp. 435-455.

INDEX . . . . . . . . . . . pp. 456-464.

# LECTURE I.

### THE HISTORIC CANON. ESTIMATE OF THE NEW TESTAMENT BY THE EARLY CHURCH.

'Every Scripture inspired of God is also profitable for teaching, for reproof, for correction, for instruction, which is in righteousness.'
1 *Tim.* iii. 16.

My subject is our Christian Bible. I propose to ask, and to do what in me lies to answer, the question, What it is which gives our Bible its hold and authority over us, and how the conception of that authority grew and took shape in the Christian consciousness.

We must recognise the fact that a change has come over the current way of thinking on this subject of the authority of the Bible. The maxim that the Bible must be studied 'like any other book' has been applied. For good or for evil, the investigations to which it has given rise are in full swing, and it would be hopeless to attempt to stop them, even if it were right to do so. Truth has this advantage, that any method that is really sound in itself can only help to confirm it.

It was a natural reaction which caused the first throwing open of the gates to perfectly free and unfettered inquiry to lead, or seem to lead, to somewhat extreme consequences. As at the close of the Middle Ages there was a rush of the human spirit, long confined in what were felt to be narrow channels, in the direction of Naturalism in all its forms; so now again that there is a new removing of barriers, we cannot be surprised if the current sets through them strongly, and, as at first sight it may seem, destructively.

We know now, I think it may be said, the utmost limits to which destruction can go. It is impossible for any theory that can be started in the future to be more thoroughly Naturalistic than many of those which we have already before us. But again there is beginning to be a certain reaction, a certain reconstructing of the old edifice upon newer lines. When once it was decided that the Bible was to be examined like any other book, it lay near at hand to assume that it must be like any other book; and this assumption has consciously or unconsciously influenced many of those who have taken up the study of it. And yet it is, to say the least, premature. It is better to let the Bible tell its own story, without forcing either way. Let us by all means study it if we will like any other book, but do not let us beg the question that it must be wholly like any other book, that there is nothing in it distinctive and unique. Let us give a fair and patient hearing to the facts as they come before us, whether they be old or whether they be new.

In order to do this in regard to the Bible, it is necessary, as in most other inquiries of a like kind, not only to go straight to the origins and form such conceptions as we are able about them, but also to see what conceptions were formed as a matter of fact in the period immediately subsequent to them. In order to determine how much of our present ideas is valid the first thing to be done is to trace them back to their roots.

The authority of the Bible is derived from what is commonly called its 'Inspiration.' This then is the subject for our more immediate consideration. I propose that we should examine together the history of this doctrine during its really formative period, with a view to ascertaining how far it rests upon a permanent basis apart from tradition. The formative period of which I speak may be said roughly to close about the year 400 A.D. The modifications which the doctrine has undergone since that date are of minor importance, until we come to our own time, when it is thrown again into the crucible, with what result remains to be seen.

I have thought that it would be conducive to clearness and soundness of procedure if I were to endeavour to combine in these lectures the analytic method with the synthetic; first starting from our *terminus* the year 400, and setting out very briefly some of the landmarks which meet us as we work our way backwards to the origins; and then conversely beginning with the origins and seeking to work forwards with more of an attempt at construction. I believe that two lectures will be found enough for the first half of this process, which will deal mainly with facts and avoid for the most part all that is speculative and controversial in the interpretation of those facts. The next five lectures will be devoted to the attempt to follow the genesis of the doctrine; and the last lecture will naturally take the form of retrospect and summary. In both cases the distinction of Old and New Testament makes a dividing line of itself.

When we approach the question of the Canon of the New Testament we have to remember that the conception of a Canon was not a new one. There was a Canon of the Old Testament before there could be a Canon of the New. The process of the forming of a Canon of the New Testament is really the process by which the writings of the New Testament came to be placed on the same footing with those of the Old. It may be true that the Canon of the Old Testament was not complete until the first century of our era. That is one of the questions on which we shall have to touch; but it is really a question of detail, and of subordinate detail. We only have to look at the way in which the Old Testament is quoted and used in the New Testament to see at once that the conception of a Canon was already there—not tentative and struggling, but fully formed and universally accepted in all those circles out of which the New Testament itself sprang. Whether Ecclesiastes or the Song of Songs or Esther were rightly included in the Canon might be, and no doubt was, an open question. But that did not in the least affect the great mass of the books, the Pentateuch, or the Prophets, or the Psalms. The authority ascribed to these books in the New Testament could not well be higher: nor could, upon the face of it, a more exalted dignity be sought for the writings of the Apostles and Evangelists than that they should be placed upon the same level with them. The whole question as to the nature and kind of authority claimed for the books of either Testament will occupy us later. All that it is well to bear in mind at starting when we begin, as we are for the moment doing, from what is really the end of the process, is that so far as the New Testament was concerned the idea of a Canon was not a new idea. In the case of the Old Testament it was a new idea. The mould itself had to be formed as well as the body of writings to be fitted in the mould. In the case of the New Testament the mould, the fully formed conception, was already in existence, and the only question was, what writings should be put into it and why they should be put there.

The unsatisfactory character of the method which we are now pursuing would be apparent at once, if it were meant to be the dominant method of our inquiry. What we want is to realize to ourselves imaginatively the genetic process by which the conception of a Canon grew, and the conception of certain writings as belonging to it. For the present we take the results of this process for granted. Only for the sake of clearness and in order to have certain fixed points well set before our minds, we start with the cut and dry notion of a Canon and Canonical Books, and we seek to mark out some of the salient features in its history.

In so doing, we may endeavour (I) to note some of the main landmarks of growth and change in regard to the extent of the New Testament Canon; (II) to ascertain what was meant by the Canon, or, in other words, what special properties were ascribed to the books included in it; (III) to discover the grounds on which some books were included in it, and others not.

I. Roughly and broadly speaking, there are two main stages in the history of the New Testament Canon. By the year 400 we may regard the New Testament as practically fixed in the form in which we now have it. It was not fixed in any strict sense. No oecumenical council had as yet pronounced upon its limits. In fact we may say that at no time was such a decision ever pronounced at all effectively. It is true that the Quinisextine or Trullan Council of 692, itself recognised only by the Greeks and not by the Latins, sanctioned in a wholesale way the Acts of two local Synods, one of which (that of Carthage in 419[1]) actually

[1] The Synod of Carthage of 419 is the last of a series of African Councils over which hangs some little obscurity. At the first, which was held at Hippo in 393, St. Augustine was present as presbyter; at the second and third, which were held at Carthage under the presidency of Aurelius, bishop of that city, he was present as bishop; in all three he was probably the moving spirit. Each of the later councils ratified the canons of the earlier. At one or other of them a canon was passed prohibiting the reading of any but canonical books

## The New Testament about 400 A.D.

contained and the other (that of Laodicea about the year 363[1]) was supposed at the date of the Trullan Council to contain lists of the sacred books, and that it sanctioned also the so-called Apostolic Canons which contain a list, and no less than three lists put forward by leading Fathers. But the lists in question are not identical[2]. The lists of Athanasius and the Council of Carthage include, while those of Gregory Nazianzen, Amphilochius of Iconium[3], and the Council of Laodicea omit, the Apocalypse; and Amphilochius speaks doubtfully about the four smaller Catholic Epistles. The Apostolic Canons are still more divergent, not only omitting the Apocalypse, but adding the two Epistles of Clement. No attempt is made to harmonize these discrepancies.

But really synodical decisions had less to do with the final constitution of the New Testament Canon than the drift of circumstances set in motion by indi-

(*Ut praeter scripturas canonicas nihil in ecclesia legatur sub nomine divinarum scripturarum*), and a list of these was given, but it is not quite certain at which. Augustine refers (Ep. lxiv. 3 *ad Quintianum*) to a decision on the subject of the Canon at the Council of 397, but his language would be satisfied if this was not a new decision, but an old one repeated and ratified. On the whole subject see especially Zahn, *Gesch. d. Neutest. Kanons*, ii. 246 ff.

[1] On the date of this Synod see especially Westcott, *Canon*, p. 432, ed. 5; Zahn, ii. 194-196.

[2] See Additional Note A: *The Canons of the Quinisextine Council, of Carthage, and of Laodicea*.

[3] Dr. Westcott refers the lists of Gregory and Amphilochius to the influence of Eusebius (*Bible in the Church*, p. 167). He would make the omission of the Apocalypse the characteristic distinction between the Canon of Constantinople derived from Eusebius and that of Alexandria (*Ibid.* p. 165).

vidual leaders of the Church. The Synod of Carthage doubtless had an authority which was not confined to Africa. Provision was made that its resolutions should be communicated to Boniface, the contemporary bishop of Rome; and the fact of its being, along with Sardica, the only Western Council mentioned in the Trullan Canon shows that it carried especial weight. Still the West owes the form of its New Testament probably more to the gradual predominance of the Vulgate. By degrees Jerome's version drove out all others. And this version embodied the tradition of the East; so that East and West fell happily into line together [1].

And when we turn to the Eastern Canon itself, there we see individual influence at work rather than any corporate action. The Canon as we have it arose through the agreement of a few leading authorities. The growth of controversy had turned men's minds to the standard of final appeal, and accordingly most of the great Church leaders in the fourth century put forth Canons. Those of Athanasius and Epiphanius agree exactly with our own not only in contents but in the order of the books. Those of Cyril of Jerusalem and Gregory Nazianzen differ from it only by the omission of the Apocalypse.

Of all these lists that of Cyril of Jerusalem is the earliest. And it is natural to connect this with the fact that in all alike the group of Catholic Epistles

---

[1] The Carthaginian list however differed from Jerome's only in the order of the books.

## The New Testament about 400 A.D.

is headed by the Epistle of St. James. In no Church would it be so likely to have that place assigned to it as in the Church of Jerusalem. So that we are tempted to conjecture that the Catholic Epistles were first brought together as a complete group in that Church[1]. If we were inclined to pursue the conjecture a step further, we might go on to connect it with the library which Alexander, bishop of Jerusalem, had founded there in the preceding century[2]. The founding of this library fell just at that critical moment when the sacred books were being transferred from the smaller rolls of papyrus, which seldom held more than a single work, to the larger *codices* of vellum shaped like our present books, in which it was usual to combine a number of cognate texts and where they soon acquired a definite order.

The only considerable exception to the unanimity which reigned as a whole throughout the East was the Church of Syria. By Syria is meant especially the regions stretching to the N., N.E., and N.W. of Antioch, for the tradition of Palestine is wholly Greek. The characteristic features of the Syrian Canon are the recognition of three only of the Catholic Epistles, St. James, 1 St. Peter, and 1 St. John, and the rejection of the Apocalypse. This is

[1] *Cf. Studia Biblica*, iii. 253.
[2] There is reason to think that the great libraries (*e.g.* of Pamphilus at Caesarea, of Cassiodorus at Vivarium, of Benedict Biscop at Wearmouth and Jarrow, of Egbert at York, and Alcuin at Tours, &c.) had an effect on the course of literary history which should be more closely investigated.

the Canon of Chrysostom, Theodoret, and Severianus of Gabala[1]. Theodore of Mopsuestia and his follower Junilius go a step further and reject also the Epistle of St. James. The limits to the prevalence of the Syrian Canon westwards are well marked by Amphilochius of Iconium, who mentions both traditions without deciding between them so far as the Catholic Epistles are concerned, but asserting that the majority of suffrages are against the Apocalypse.

But in the Syrian Church, as in the Latin-speaking Churches, the most potent influence, so far as general usage was concerned, was no doubt the vernacular version, commonly called the Peshitto, which held the field wherever Syriac was spoken, just as Jerome's version did in the West. The Peshitto from the first contained only three Catholic Epistles, St. James, 1 St. Peter, and 1 St. John. It has recently been proved, chiefly by the researches of Dr. Gwynn of Dublin[2], that the four remaining Epistles, and we may now perhaps add the Apocalypse, were first included in the so-called Philoxenian version of the year 508, which served as the basis for a further revision by Thomas of Harkel (or Heraclea in Cyrrhesticé), known as the Harclean version in 616. But by this time the Syrian Church was broken up into three

---

[1] *Ap.* Cosmas Indicopleustes (Zahn, *Gesch. d. K.* ii. 23).

[2] *Transactions of Roy. Irish Acad.* xxvii. p. 288 ff.; *Hermathena*, 1890, p. 281 ff.; arts. 'Polycarpus' and 'Thomas Harklensis' in *Dict. Chr. Biog.* iv. 432 f., 1017–1020; and for the Apocalypse, letter in the *Academy*, June 18, 1892.

## The New Testament about 400 A.D.

mutually antagonistic bodies; and as the versions in question were both Monophysite in their origin, and in the first instance perhaps intended for private rather than for public use, their circulation must have been limited. As late as the middle of the sixth century the merchant-theologian Cosmas Indicopleustes refers to the usage of the Syrian Church as recognising only three Epistles; and far down into the Middle Ages the list of the Nestorian bishop Ebed Jesu does not exceed this number. What this means is just that the usage of a Church is determined by its Bible, and the Syriac Bible happens to have been translated just at that stage in the history of the local Canon when three only of the Catholic Epistles had an established footing, while the rest were still outside though beginning to knock for admittance.

The end of the fourth century was a time of consolidation and ratification of existing usages. But along with the ratification of books which had made good their title there was a corresponding elimination of others which were not so fortunate. Here again the fourth century, or at least the latter half of it, was not the real period of struggle. It did little more than register results already secured. A scholar like Jerome might study apocryphal works, but rather as literary curiosities than as claimants for a place in the Canon. And the noble volumes (like Codd. Sinaiticus and Alexandrinus) which have come down to us from the fourth and fifth centuries might still give a lingering harbourage to books no longer recognised; but this was only because they were copied from older originals and so perpetuated the conditions of a bygone time.

We may now turn the page and glance at the more stirring movements of that elder time. Once more we take a rough date, the year 200 A.D. This is approximately the date of the so-called Muratorian Fragment, the oldest list of the Books of the New Testament, which if not exactly typical or normal is not far removed from the general usage. This usage, we may say, had a solid nucleus —the four Gospels, the Acts, and thirteen Epistles of St. Paul. To these we might add for the greater part of Christendom, though the evidence does not quite permit us to say for the whole, 1 St. Peter and 1 St. John.

Let us pause for a moment on this solid nucleus before we proceed to speak of other books the position of which was more tentative. We are confronted at the outset by conflicting views. One of the most energetic and original of living theologians has recently put forward the contention that the Canon as such, so far as there was a Canon, sprang suddenly into existence about the year 170. In the time of Justin (*c.* 150 A.D.) it is non-existent. In the time of Irenaeus, thirty years later, it is in full strength. Therefore it must have grown up in the interval. And in fact the formation of a Canon at that date was one of a series of deliberate measures taken by the allied Churches of Asia Minor and

Rome to check the inroads of Gnosticism or Montanism[1].

Such is the theory: and there is probably this amount of truth in it, viz. that the controversies with these sects did bring out into clearer consciousness the idea of a New Testament Canon, and did lead to greater stress being laid upon it. It is indeed the chief weapon with which Irenaeus and Tertullian fight their battle. But to suppose that there was any great and sudden change between Justin and Irenaeus is to draw an inference from the writings of Justin which they certainly will not bear. We have from Justin two treatises, both of the nature of apologies, one addressed to the pagan emperors, the other directed to the points at issue with the Jews. In neither of these was it at all likely that he would appeal to Christian books as authoritative in the sense which we call canonical. If his Compendium (Syntagma) against Heresies, or the treatise against Marcion, had come down to us, we might have had a very different state of things. But Justin had hardly any contemporaries whose writings are now extant; so that for the period 140–175 A.D. we have in reality extremely little evidence. But this absence of evidence must not be confused with negation of the facts for which evidence is sought. It is just here, as so often (I cannot but think) in what is called the critical school, that Harnack makes his mistake. Because we suddenly find traces of a Canon, say from about 175 A.D.

[1] See Additional Note B: *Harnack's Theory of the Growth of the N. T. Canon.*

onwards, it by no means follows that its origin was really sudden.

On the contrary, when we go back beyond the gap and look at the literature, which though still far from copious is a little more copious, in the so-called Sub-Apostolic Age, ranging from about 95 to 140 A.D., we find a state of things which really points forward to that in the last quarter of the century. Development there is, but continuous development, development in a straight line. The break in the evidence involves no corresponding break in the facts.

For proof we may appeal both to the Gospels and to the Pauline Epistles. It is true that upon these Harnack largely rests his case; but in regard to neither are his contentions really tenable. It is extraordinary how much a very short period of time has added to the evidence that our present collection of four Gospels, singled out from among the rest, goes back, not as had been very commonly maintained to the year $\pm 170$, but a full generation earlier. The different items of the evidence may differ somewhat in cogency, but they converge in a way to make a case of great strength. I shall have occasion to return to this point in a later lecture, and therefore will not enlarge upon it here.

The main argument against the validity of the fourfold Canon of the Gospels is derived from the Alogi, a party whose name, given them of course by opponents (Epiphanius, or possibly Hippolytus), is a punning play upon their rejection of the Gospel of the Logos, along with the other Johannine writings, or at

## The New Testament about 200 A.D.

least the Apocalypse. This party was so small that Dr. Salmon believes it to be reducible to the single person of the Roman writer Caius[1]. That perhaps is hardly probable: but it was in any case a party which consisted of a few educated and critically minded persons; it took no root, and gained no popular following.

In the first instance it would seem that the opinion had its rise in the reaction at once against Gnostic speculation and Montanistic enthusiasm. The Gnostics and the Montanists both appealed to the Fourth Gospel; and a short method of cutting away the ground from under them was to deny the authority of the Gospel. But the opposition to the Johannean writings was not based on any divergent tradition or ecclesiastical usage, but only upon such *prima facie* critical difficulties as might be put forward to-day[2]. These can weigh but little against the general consent of the rest of Christendom.

Thus much however the instance of the Alogi does go to prove—not that the Canon of the Gospels did not exist, but that it was maintained in a less exclusive and dogmatic spirit than it was subsequently. For it does not appear that they were excluded from the orthodox communion as Marcion and Valentinus were. This is the main difference between the year 400 and the year 200. At both

---

[1] *Hermathena*, 1892, p. 185. Against this view see Zahn, *Gesch. d. K.* ii. 1021 f.

[2] Our knowledge of these difficulties is derived from Epiphanius, *Haer.* li.

dates there were but four Gospels acknowledged as authoritative; but whereas at the later date no one would have thought of questioning any one of the four, or if he had done so would at once have put himself outside the pale of Catholic Christianity, at the earlier date it was still possible for persons otherwise orthodox to raise a doubt as to whether a particular book had been received by the Church on sufficient grounds [1].

Along with this difference there went another: the use of other Gospels—and indeed we may say, speaking of the Canon generally—of other writings, than the Canonical. An illustration of this is supplied by an incident in the history of the document, a portion of which has been so lately and so unexpectedly recovered, the Gospel of Peter. Serapion, bishop of Antioch from about 190 to 209, found this Gospel in use among the Christians of Rhossus, and at first was disposed to tolerate it, until it was proved to him that it contained heretical (Docetic) doctrine. Apart from this he had been willing to let it be read as a narrative of the Gospel story. At the same time it does not at all follow that he regarded apocryphal writings as on the same footing with Canonical. He makes this clear at the outset of his letter, which Eusebius has preserved [2]. 'We, brethren,' he writes, 'receive Peter and the other Apostles as Christ Himself, but the forgeries

---

[1] See Additional Note C: *Debateable Points relating to the Alogi*.

[2] *H. E.* vi. 12.

current in his name we reject, knowing what they are, for none such have been handed down to us.'

The use of extra-canonical works was doubtless freer in some Churches than in others, and especially in Alexandria as compared with the Churches of the West. Conspicuous examples are afforded by the Homily attributed to Clement of Rome and by the writings of his namesake of Alexandria. But the Alexandrian Clement was heir to the large-hearted traditions of Philo, and it is perhaps hardly right to treat him as an average specimen of the Church to which he belonged. His are the only writings which are certainly Alexandrian of this date, and there is always danger in arguing from isolated cases.

The Book of the Acts is one of those for which direct evidence does not begin until the last quarter of the second century, so that we have no proof of its acceptance before that date. But as soon as the stream of Christian literature begins to run more copiously we have full and explicit testimony to it; in Gaul from Irenaeus and the Churches of Vienne and Lyons, in Italy from the Muratorian Fragment, in Africa from Tertullian, and in Egypt from Clement of Alexandria[1]. Everywhere it is treated as a book

---

[1] It is urged that Clement of Alexandria used the *Acta Johannis* of Leucius, the 'Paradoses' of Matthias, and the *Predicatio Petri* indifferently with the canonical Acts (Harnack, *N. T. um* 200, p. 51). So might Serapion too have used the Gospel of Peter, if he had not found in it heretical doctrine; but it would not follow that he placed it on a level with the canonical Gospels. And in like manner Clement himself refers to the Gospel according to the Egyptians, but expressly distinguishing it from the Four Gospels. If any conflict of testimony

the position of which is established. There is nothing to hint that it was but newly won [1]. It was indeed difficult to dissociate it, on the one hand from the Gospel of St. Luke and on the other hand from the Epistles of St. Paul. The most natural supposition would be that it circulated in the first instance along with the Gospel. Both were not only by the same author but addressed to the same individual, so that they were in the first instance probably made public together. But the Gospel and the Acts are so like in their historical character that the authority which attached to the one would pass over to the other [2].

Still less possible is it to think of the Pauline Epistles as but just recognised as the last quarter

had arisen, he might have made his estimate of the apocryphal Acts plainer. But on the whole question of Clement's treatment of the Canonical Scriptures see Additional Note.

[1] Harnack indeed declares that 'there can be no doubt that the flourish of trumpets with which the Western Fathers accompany the book is to be regarded as the overture (Einführungsmusik) which introduces it into the Church collection' (*N. T. um* 200, p. 53). I have read through the passages to which appeal is specially made (Tert. *De Praescript.* 22, 23; *Adv. Marc.* i. 20; iv. 2–5; v. 1–3; Iren. *Adv. Haer.* lib. iii), and have entirely failed to detect anything of the kind. On the contrary, the way in which the reference is made seems to me to be in all cases perfectly easy and natural, not made with any view to glorify the Acts, but in prosecution of the main argument on the lines laid down by both writers, that of an appeal to acknowledged 'Scriptures.' In referring to those who do not receive the Book of the Acts (*Praescr.* 22) Tertullian probably alludes to Marcion, but for himself it is as much an established authority as the Gospels.

[2] I strongly suspect that the Gospels and Acts were translated into Latin at the same time and by the same hand; but as the proof of this is not quite complete, I do not press the point.

of the second century began. About the year 140 Marcion the Gnostic put forward his collection of ten of St. Paul's Epistles. He omitted the three Pastorals (1 and 2 Timothy, and Titus), which were questioned, as we shall see, by others besides himself, not on the ground that they were not St. Paul's, but in all probability because they were addressed to private individuals, and therefore did not seem so suited for a 'Bible' as the letters addressed to Churches[1]. But it is not merely an assumption of his opponents that the Catholic collection was older than Marcion's. This appears partly from the titles to the Epistles where the general agreement is thrown into relief by the variant 'To the Laodiceans' for 'To the Ephesians[2]'; partly also from the fact that the type of text which he had before him was certainly not that of the original but a secondary text elsewhere current; and lastly from the equal certainty that passages which he is known to have omitted were no later interpolations but part of the genuine letters as they left the hand of St. Paul[3]. The inference thus drawn from Marcion's Ἀποστολικόν, as he called it, is confirmed by the use of the Epistles which

[1] This is clearly the ground of the apologetic language of the Muratorian Fragment, and a like objection is implied by Tertullian, *Adv. Marc.* v. 21; compare Jerome, *Praef. ad Ep. Philon.* (Zahn, ii. 999), Theod. Mops. *in Epp. Paul.* ii. 259 (ed. Swete).

[2] Zahn thinks that Marcion found πρὸς Ἐφεσίους in his copy and altered it on critical grounds to πρὸς Λαοδικέας, Dr. Hort that he had πρὸς Λαοδικέας before him, but in any case Marcion's collection was already provided with titles.

[3] For details see Zahn, *Gesch. d. K.* i. 633 ff.

is made by Ignatius, and still more in the letter of Polycarp to the Philippians [1].

It is maintained that the Pauline Epistles, though generally accepted towards the end of the century, were on a lower level of authority than the Gospels and the Old Testament. Of the latter we shall have occasion to speak presently. But in both instances the inference is again wrongly drawn from the facts. There may be an element of truth in Harnack's assertion that the term 'Scripture' is applied less freely to the Epistles than to the Gospels, and less to both than the Old Testament, though a larger induction would be necessary to make it good [2]. But in any case this would be only a natural survival of old-established usage, and would prove nothing as to a deliberate difference of estimate. We shall see presently what evidence there is for regarding the Old Testament and the New as on the same footing. Two arguments in particular are brought forward to prove the inferior position of the Pauline Epistles. One of these, taken from the Acts of the Scillitan Martyrs (180 A.D.), turns largely upon a mistranslation [3]. And the use which is

---

[1] See Lecture VII, p. 362 *inf*.

[2] *N. T. um* 200, p. 36 ff. The first idea may be dismissed. Harnack, as usual, quotes the *De Aleatoribus* as Victor's, but it is almost certainly later; see Miodoński's edition (Erlangen und Leipzig, 1889), Wölfflin in *Archiv für lat. Lexikographie*, v. 487 ff.; Haussleiter in *Theol. Literaturblatt*, 1889, cols. 41 ff., 49 ff., 225 ff.; *Class. Rev.* iii. (1889) 127, &c.

[3] Harnack's reasoning is based on the Greek Text of the Acts published by Usener in 1881. Since that date a Latin Text has

## The New Testament about 200 A.D.

made of Clement of Alexandria is also untenable[1]. It is quite possible to refine too much and in the wrong place. And where the evidence is too scanty to admit of any deductions at all it is better simply to say so than to strain the little that there is[2].

been discovered (see the Cambridge *Texts and Studies*, i. 106 ff.) which many hold to be the original of which the Greek is a translation. Waiving that point, for I am not sure that both are not contemporaneous and of equal authority, I still cannot admit Harnack's inference. The martyrs are asked what they have in their case (*Quae sunt res in capsa vestra?* Ὁποῖαι πραγματεῖαι τοῖς ὑμετέροις ἀπόκεινται σκεύεσιν;). They answer, '[Our] books and the Epistles of Paul, a [the] righteous [holy] man' (*Libri et epistulae Pauli viri justi;* Αἱ καθ' ἡμᾶς βίβλοι καὶ προσεπιτούτοις ἐπιστολαὶ Παύλου τοῦ ὁσίου ἀνδρός). Harnack (*N. T. um* 200, p. 38) lays stress on τούτοις (πρὸς ἐπὶ τούτοις) as in agreement with σκεύεσιν; but it should clearly be combined with the prepositions as an adverbial phrase—'besides,' 'in addition.' The separation of the βίβλοι and the ἐπιστολαί does perhaps mark an early stage in the history of the New Testament as a collection; but there is more significance in the fact that both are contained in the same case (*capsa* sing., interpreting the ambiguous σκεύη). The epithets given to St. Paul show the estimation in which his writings would be held.

[1] See Additional Note D: *The use of the New Testament by Clement of Alexandria.*

[2] This is not I think an unfair comment on Harnack's treatment of the evidence relating to the Church of Antioch and Syria (*Dogmengesch.* i. 284 f. ed. 1, 319 f. ed. 2). He adds apologetically, 'Es könnte nun allerdings gewagt erscheinen, auf Grund des dürftigen Materiales, welches Theophilus liefert ... den Schluss zu ziehen,' &c. Certainly such a procedure is 'gewagt,' and the reasons alleged do not justify it. But where the master states his case with some qualification, the disciple follows and states it baldly as if it were all admitted truth. Here are some sentences from Dr. Karl Müller's *Kirchengeschichte* (Freiburg i. B. 1892), an able work, which however in the earlier chapters treads too closely in the steps of Harnack. In regard to the Gospels: 'Vielmehr haben andere Asiaten ... künftig

## I. The New Testament in the Early Church.

But indeed the whole case for the sudden emergence ('plötzliches Auftauchen') of the Canon only needs to be stated to refute itself. Let us take Harnack's own words: 'And yet the collection of writings for Irenaeus and Tertullian is closed; it is already thrown in the teeth of the heretics that this or the other book is not recognised by them; their Bibles are measured by the standard of the Church collection as the elder, and this is already employed just like the Old Testament. The assumption of the inspiration of the books, their harmonistic interpretation, the conception of their absolute sufficiency on every question which can arise and in regard to every event which they relate, the right of combining passages *ad libitum*, the assumption that

nur noch die vier, heute kanonischen, Evangelien zulassen wollen, alle anderen Darstellungen des Evangeliums ausgeschlossen. Im übrigen *Morgenland ist dies noch nicht geschehen*, wohl aber in Rom und im Abendland überhaupt' (p. 84). If stress is laid upon the negative side of this proposition, it may be just covered by the case of Serapion; otherwise Clement of Alexandria is the only evidence for the whole of the East—a writer as to whom it is doubtful whether his witness extends beyond himself! Then as to the Epistles: 'Sie galten nicht als γραφή' [How does Dr. Müller know this? They were γραφή for Marcion], 'wurden vielleicht auch nicht regelmässig im Gottesdienst verlesen' [Possibly, but again where is the evidence?] 'und sind da wo sie benutzt werden, entweder unter dem Namen ihrer Verfasser oder überhaupt nicht citirt' [What of Ignatius, Polycarp, and 2 Clement?]. Again: 'eine dritte Klasse von heiligen Schriften entsteht "Die Apostel." Sie verrät die Neuheit ihres Ursprunges dadurch, dass man sie auch in grossen Gemeinden der "Schrift" und dem Herrn zunächst noch nicht gleichwertig achtet (so noch Bischof Viktor (?) von Rom in *De Aleatoribus* um 190 (?); Märtyrer von Scili in Numidien, 180).' Surely we may double the two notes of interrogation, and add a third to the martyrs of Scili!

# The New Testament about 200 A.D.

nothing in the Scriptures is indifferent, and finally allegorical exegesis, are the immediate result of canonization, the proof of which is present from the first[1].' It is an advantage to have to deal with a writer who has so complete and thorough a knowledge of his subject. But he asks us to believe that all this is a *sudden* product, accomplished within the manhood of Irenaeus himself, and without his betraying the slightest consciousness of it! Such changes—and to this writer they are all changes— are not really wrought in a day.

We have spoken so far only of the solid nucleus of accepted writings. Outside these there were the two other groups, on the one hand of writings which were working their way to eventual recognition, and on the other of those which, beginning with a certain measure of acceptance, finally lost it and were excluded from the Canon. It is remarkable that some of the books omitted in the Muratorian list were among those which enjoyed the earliest attestation as writings. The Epistle to the Hebrews is quoted in what is probably the earliest extra-canonical work still within the limits of the first century (1 Clement). The Apocalypse is not only referred to very early, having been apparently commented on by Papias[2], but is one of the first books to be quoted with the name of its author[3]. And the Epistle of St. James appears to have left

---

[1] *Dogmengesch.* i. 276, ed. 1.
[2] The express statements of Andreas and Arethas of Caesarea more than outweigh the silence of Eusebius.
[3] Justin, *Dial. c. Tryph.* 81.

## I. The New Testament in the Early Church.

traces of itself in Clement of Rome, the *Didaché*, and Hermas[1]. This proves that the books in question at least go back to the Apostolic age, if that age is measured by the lifetime of St. John. But after enjoying—two of them at least—a considerable amount of popularity at this early date, they seem to suffer a sort of eclipse: Hebrews apparently from the doubt as to its authorship; the Apocalypse from the opposition among the more cultured Christians to the Millenarian views which it was thought to foster; the Epistle of St. James more probably from the peculiar circumstances of its original destination and early transmission. All three books, except in so far as Hebrews was attributed to St. Paul or included among his writings, had the disadvantage of circulating singly and not under the safeguard of a collection. Hebrews was saved by the value set upon it by the scholars of Alexandria[2]; the Apocalypse by the loyalty of the

---

[1] See the instances newly collected by Dr. J. B. Mayor, *The Epistle of St. James*, p. l. ff. Dr. Mayor's lists are put together with great care, but they seem to me to err on the side of excess. I could not feel sure that all even of the passages marked with asterisks were really allusions to the Epistle.

[2] Overbeck (*Zur Gesch. d. Kanons*, Chemnitz, 1880, pp. 12–17) has the perverse ingenuity to maintain that Hebrews originally began with a paragraph of salutation containing the name of the writer, but that this was deliberately amputated and the concluding verses (xiii. 22–25) added, to make it pass for St. Paul's. If it were so, we might ask, why did not the redactor boldly substitute St. Paul's name for that which he found? And why did he proceed in the one case by subtraction, in the other by addition? Further, the amputation, if it took place, must have taken place very early; for Tertullian knows the Epistle as the work of Barnabas (and the name of Barnabas would have served the purpose as well as that of St. Paul), and

## The New Testament about 200 A.D.

West; and the Epistle of St. James by the attachment of certain Churches in the East, especially as we may believe that of Jerusalem.

As to the two smaller Epistles of St. John, it is somewhat curious that for a time we find traces of the Second only, without the Third[1]. This may however be only accident. When the Third Epistle joined the Second both were naturally accepted together. Some hesitation there probably was on account of their diminutive size, the seeming unimportance of their contents, and the ambiguous character of their address, which might be only to a private person. The like objection appears to have been taken to the Pastoral Epistles of St. Paul. Traces of

Clement of Alexandria has a story derived from his teacher, Pantaenus, already treating the Epistle as St. Paul's (Eus. *H. E.* vi. 14). This would throw back the mutilation to a date when I should not imagine that Overbeck would allow that there was any thought of a Canon at all.

It is significant that Harnack (*Dogmengesch.* i. 279 n. ed. 1, 312 ed. 2) refers to Overbeck's essay as if it had settled the matter once for all. This is the way in which myths get currency, like the other myth about 'Victor, *De Aleatoribus.*' It is impossible not to be struck by Harnack's great powers, but he sorely needs to learn to weigh degrees of probability and not to build upon pure conjecture as if it were certain.

As to the opening of the Epistle, we may remember that these early Christian Epistles hover between the idea of a letter and a homily; so much so that a writing (2 Clement) which is clearly a homily almost from the first took rank as an Epistle. The writer of Hebrews frankly gave his work the homiletic form.

[1] So in Irenaeus, the Muratorian Fragment (apparently), in the debates of the Council of Carthage (*Sentent. Episc.*) of the year 256, and also, so far as we can be quite certain, in Clement of Alexandria: see *Stud. Bibl.* iii. 250 f.; Harnack, *N. T. um* 200, p. 55 ff., &c.

controversy on this point are perceptible in the Muratorian Fragment. The doubts however in both cases were overruled.

The Epistle of St. Jude has good attestation in proportion to its importance, in the Muratorian list, Tertullian, and Clement of Alexandria. 2 St. Peter has, as is well known, the scantiest support of any book in the New Testament Canon. The evidence for it begins with Origen [1], who however expressly mentions that it was doubted. But fresh light has been thrown upon this Epistle by the newly discovered Apocalypse of Peter, the significance of which we shall attempt to estimate later.

There are many indications that at the end of the second century the claims of these various writings were being weighed and considered. The Muratorian list is one of such indications; Tertullian's comparison of Hebrews and the Shepherd of Hermas is another [2]; still more his striking statement about the synods at which the latter work was formally rejected [3]. Then again Clement of Alexandria, followed by Origen, on

---

[1] Coincidences with the Epistle have been pointed out in writings earlier than Origen. Probably the strongest is the group of passages Barn. xv. 4, Justin, *Dial.* 81, Iren. *Adv. Haer.* v. 23. 2, 28. 3, which contain the idea of 2 Pet. iii. 8 μία ἡμέρα παρὰ Κυρίῳ ὡς χίλια ἔτη. Clearly this was a common idea among the early Christians, but the passage in 2 St. Peter may be one expression of it and not the source. See below, p. 381.

[2] *De Pudic.* 20.

[3] *De Pudic.* 10: *Sed cederem tibi si scriptura Pastoris, quae sola moechos amat, divino instrumento meruisset incidi, si non ab omni concilio ecclesiarum etiam vestrarum inter apocrypha et falsa judicaretur, adultera et inde patrona sociorum.*

## The New Testament about 200 A.D.

the Epistle to the Hebrews; the many discussions on the Apocalypse; and Hippolytus' defence both of it and of the Gospel of St. John. The end of the second century is the true turning-point in the history of the Canon. We are rightly reminded [1] that the forming of the Canon was not only a process of collection and accretion, but even more a process of reduction and contraction. What a number of works circulated among the Churches of the second century all enjoying a greater or less degree of authority, only to lose it! In the way of Gospels, those according to the Hebrews, according to the Egyptians, according to Peter: in the way of Acts, the so-called 'Travels' (περίοδοι) of Apostles, ascribed by Photius to Leucius Charinus [2], the Preaching of Peter, the Acts of Paul, the original form of the Acts of Paul and Thecla: in the way of Epistles, 1 and 2 Clement, Barnabas: an allegory like the Shepherd of Hermas; a manual like the *Didaché*; an Apocalypse like that of Peter. Truly it may be said that here too the last was first and the first last. Several of these works had a circulation and popularity considerably in excess of that of some of the books now included in the Canon. It is certainly a wonderful feat on the part of the early Church to have by degrees sifted out this mass of literature; and still more wonderful that it should not have discarded, at least so far as the New Testament is concerned, one single work which after-generations have found cause to look back upon with

---

[1] By Harnack, *N. T. um* 200, p. 111.
[2] *Biblioth.* 114 (p. 90, ed. Bekker).

any regret. Most valuable, no doubt, many of them may be for enabling us to reconstruct the history of the times, but there is not one which at this moment we should say possessed a real claim to be invested with the authority of the Canon.

II. We are now brought face to face with our second question, What was it that the Church determined by declaring certain books to be Canonical? It decided that they were possessed of certain special properties or attributes, and we now have to inquire what those attributes were [1].

It was agreed upon all hands that the Scriptures were in some sense 'divine.' From the first moment that we possess Christian literature of any volume expressions which imply this abound. The term 'holy Scriptures' (αἱ ἅγιαι γραφαί) followed by a quotation from St. John begins with Theophilus of Antioch (c. 181 A.D.)[2]; 'sacred writings' (ἱερὰ γράμματα) of the New Testament with Clement of Alexandria [3], who also uses αἱ βίβλοι αἱ ἅγιαι [4]; 'sacred books' (ἱεραὶ βίβλοι) with Origen [5]. The 'divine word' (ὁ θεῖος λόγος), introducing a quotation from St. Paul,

---

[1] In what follows use has been made of the collection of *Testimonia* in Routh, *Rell. Sacr.* v. 235-253, and occasionally of references in Zahn and Harnack; compare also the very ample materials in Bp. Westcott's *Introduction to the Study of the Gospels*, Appendix B.

[2] *Ad Autol.* ii. 22.

[3] *Strom.* i. 20. § 98; ii. 11. § 48. Note also the expanded phrase, ἱερὰ γὰρ ὡς ἀληθῶς, τὰ ἱεροποιοῦντα καὶ θεοποιοῦντα γράμματα (*Protrept,* 9. § 87).

[4] *Paed.* iii. 12. § 97.

[5] *De Princ.* iv. 9.

## Properties ascribed to the New Testament. 29

is found in Theophilus of Antioch[1]; 'the divine Scriptures' (γραφαὶ θεῖαι, αἱ θεῖαι γραφαί), apparently about this date the commonest of all expressions, begins (for the New Testament) with Clement of Alexandria; γραφὴ θεϊκή occurs in an anonymous writer quoted by Eusebius, αἱ γραφαὶ τοῦ θεοῦ in a fragment of Caius[2]; θεία παράδοσις belongs to Clement of Alexandria[3]; θεῷ πειθαρχεῖν, as an equivalent for 'obeying the Scriptures,' to Hippolytus[4]; *Dei voces, Scriptura divina, divinum instrumentum, divina literatura, sacrosanctus stilus* are phrases of Tertullian's; *divini fontes, divina magisteria, praecepta divina, divina et sancta traditio* are characteristic of Cyprian: another word which is rather frequent in the Latinity of Cyprian's time is *deificus* (*scripturae deificae*, &c.), probably only in the sense of 'divine'[5]; *sancta et adorabilia scripturarum verba*[6] is a phrase which shows the reverence with which the Scriptures were regarded. Cyprian defines the Scriptures as *illa quae Deus loquitur*[7]; and Tertullian sums up the authority to which the Christian appeals, *Dei est scriptura, Dei est natura, Dei est disciplina; quicquid contrarium est istis, Dei non est*[8].

---

[1] *Ad Autol.* iii. 14.
[2] *H. E.* v. 28. 13, iii. 28. 2.
[3] *Strom.* vii. 16. § 103.
[4] *Contra Noet.* 6.
[5] Miodoński on *De Aleat.* p. 107; Rönsch, *Semas. Beiträge*, ii. 8; otherwise Westcott, *Canon*, p. 413.
[6] Lucius, bishop of Thebeste, at the Council of Carthage in 256 (*Sentent. Episc.* § 31).
[7] *Ad Fortun.* 4.
[8] *De Virg. Vel.* 16.

## I. The New Testament in the Early Church.

The Scriptures of the New Testament are placed by the end of the second century entirely on the same footing with those of the Old. This is admitted on all hands for the West—for Irenaeus and Tertullian and the Muratorian Fragment (which equates 'prophets and apostles,' besides in its whole tenor implying for the New Testament the full prerogatives of Scripture), for Hippolytus, Cyprian and Novatian. It is allowed[1] that when Melito made a special journey in the East to ascertain the exact number and order of the 'books of the Old Testament' (τὰ τῆς παλαιᾶς διαθήκης βιβλία) he presupposes a like collection of books of the New Testament. Origen seeks to establish his teaching by testimonies from what Christians 'believe to be the divine Scriptures, as well of that which is called the Old Testament as of that which is called the New[2].' And even more expressly he says that it was the same Spirit proceeding from the one God who determined the elder revelation and that of the Gospels and Apostles[3]. A doubt however is raised about Clement of Alexandria. He repeatedly combines or contrasts the New Testament or Covenant with the Old; but there is of course a certain ambiguity in these phrases. It may be the two dispensations which are coordinated with each other, or it may be the writings belonging to the dispensations,

---

[1] *E. g.* by Harnack (*Dogmengesch.* i. 275, n. 2, ed. 1; p. 308, n. 2, ed. 2).

[2] *De Princip.* iv. 1 (= *Philocal.* 1; Lommatzsch, xxi. 485 f.; xxv. 1).

[3] *Ibid.* 16 (Lommatzsch, xxi. 509: these references give Origen's own words, and not merely the Latin of Rufinus).

## Properties ascribed to the New Testament. 31

not the two Covenants but the two Testaments. This ambiguity applies to some of the passages in Clement, but by no means to all: there are some in which the idea of the dispensation seems to pass into that of the written documents, and others in which the reference to these documents is clear. And apart from that, there is abundant evidence to show that Clement really assigned to the New Testament an authority equal to that of the Old [1].

That which gives to the Scriptures this authoritative and sacred character is more particularly the fact that they are inspired by the Holy Spirit. This too we find declared in set terms and evidently implied all through the Christian literature from the beginning of the last quarter of the second century onwards. The epithet πνευματοφόροι applied to New Testament writers occurs twice in Theophilus of Antioch [2] (181 A.D.): in the first place he expressly includes among the πνευματοφόροι the Apostle St. John, proceeding to quote the first verses of his Gospel, and in the second he affirms that the writings of Prophets and Evangelists agree 'because all the πνευματοφόροι have spoken by one Spirit of God.' Irenaeus speaks of the Apostles after they had been clothed with the power of the Holy Spirit descending upon

[1] See Additional Note D, p. 65 f.
[2] *Ad Autol.* ii. 22; iii. 12. There is also a very strong passage in which, with reference primarily to the prophets of the Old Testament, he explains what is contained in this term πνευματοφόροι: οἱ δὲ τοῦ Θεοῦ ἄνθρωποι, πνευματοφόροι Πνεύματος ἁγίου καὶ προφῆται γενόμενοι, ὑπ' αὐτοῦ τοῦ Θεοῦ ἐμπνευσθέντες καὶ σοφισθέντες ἐγένοντο θεοδίδακτοι καὶ ὅσιοι καὶ δίκαιοι (ii. 9).

them from on high as being fully assured about all things and possessing perfect knowledge[1]; he also describes the Gospels as, in spite of their fourfold form, being 'held together by one Spirit[2].' In like manner the Muratorian Fragment speaks of the leading facts of the Lord's life as declared in them 'by one sovereign Spirit' (*uno ac principali*[3] *Spiritu declarata*). Tertullian describes the Sacred Writers as having their minds 'flooded' (*inundatos*) with the Holy Spirit[4]. Clement of Alexandria refers a saying of St. Paul's (1 Cor. iii. 2) to the Holy Spirit in the Apostle 'using mystically the voice of the Lord[5]'; and he describes St. John as led to the composition of his Gospel 'under the *afflatus* of the Spirit' (Πνεύματι θεοφορηθέντα)[6]. Origen defines the process of inspiration still more elaborately: he says that 'the Sacred Books are not the works of men,' but that they 'were written by inspiration (ἐξ ἐπιπνοίας) of the Holy Spirit, at the will of the Father of All, through Jesus

---

[1] *Adv. Haer.* iii. 1. 1 : *de omnibus adimpleti sunt* (clearly = ἐπληροφορήθησαν) *et habuerunt perfectam agnitionem*.

[2] *Ibid.* iii. 11. 8 : ἔδωκεν ἡμῖν τετράμορφον τὸ εὐαγγέλιον, ἑνὶ δὲ πνεύματι συνεχόμενον.

[3] The reference seems to be to ἡγεμονικῷ πνεύματι, Ps. l. 14 LXX (li. 12 Heb.); in regard to which Origen (or Rufinus) says that there are many spirits, *sed in his principatum et dominationem hunc Spiritum Sanctum, qui et principalis appellatur, tenere* (*Comm. in Rom.* vii. 1; Lommatzsch, vii. 86; cf. also Tertullian, *Adv. Hermog.* 4; *De Anim.* 15, quoted by Hesse).

[4] *Apol.* 18.

[5] *Paed.* i. 6. § 49 : διὰ τοῦτο ἄρα μυστικῶς τὸ ἐν τῷ ἀποστόλῳ ἅγιον Πνεῦμα τῇ τοῦ Κυρίου ἀποχρώμενον φωνῇ 'γάλα ὑμᾶς ἐπότισα' λέγει.

[6] *Ap.* Eus. *H. E.* vi. 14. 7.

## Properties ascribed to the New Testament. 33

Christ¹.' Somewhat similar is the language of Hippolytus, who speaks of the Sacred Writers as 'receiving the inspiration, or *afflatus*, of the Father's power.' (τῆς πατρῴας δυνάμεως τὴν ἀπόπνοιαν λαβόντες) ². The word θεόπνευστος applied to the New Testament appears first in Clement³, then in Origen⁴ and Eusebius⁵, and even in the address of the Emperor Constantine to the bishops assembled at Nicaea⁶.

Another way of describing the source of inspiration is, not to refer it directly to the Holy Spirit, but to regard the writer as invested with the authority of Christ Himself. Thus in a passage which has become very familiar of late, Serapion, bishop of Antioch at the end of the second century, identifies the authority of an Apostle with that of Christ: 'We, brethren, receive Peter and the other Apostles as Christ Himself⁷.' Clement of Alexandria speaks of obeying the Scriptures as 'obeying the Lord⁸.' He repeatedly gives to both Testaments the title κυριακαὶ γραφαί⁹, and refers alike the teaching of Prophets, of Evangelists, and Apostles to Christ¹⁰. Irenaeus in like manner describes those who prophesied of the Coming of Christ as receiving their inspiration from

---

[1] *De Princip.* iv. 9; Lommatzsch, xxi. 498.   [2] *Cont. Noet.* 11.
[3] *E.g. Strom.* vii. 16. §§ 101, 103; *cf.* p. 28, n. 3, *sup.*
[4] *E.g. De Princip.* iv. 8; Lommatzsch, xxi. 496.
[5] *H. E.* iii. 4. 7, &c.
[6] Theodoret, *H. E.* i. 6 (ed. Schulze, 5 ed. Vales.).
[7] *Ap.* Eus. *H. E.* vi. 12. 3.   [8] *Strom.* vii. 16. § 101.
[9] *E.g. Strom.* vii. 1. § 1 ; 16. § 94.
[10] *Strom.* vii. 16. § 95: ἔχομεν γὰρ τὴν ἀρχὴν τῆς διδασκαλίας τὸν κύριον διά τε τῶν προφητῶν διά τε τοῦ εὐαγγελίου καὶ διὰ τῶν μακαρίων ἀποστόλων.

the Son Himself[1]. Origen assumes that the true sense or mind of the Gospels is really the mind of Christ[2]. And a later writer quoted by Jerome takes up St. Paul's phrase 'Christ speaking in me' (2 Cor. xiii. 3) as a mode of expressing the process of inspiration[3]. The Epistles of St. Paul prepare us for the equivalence of the two phrases, 'Christ speaking in me' and 'the Spirit of Christ speaking in me.' Those who used them no doubt meant exactly the same thing.

Testimonies to the general doctrine of inspiration may be multiplied to almost any extent; but there are some which go further and point to an inspiration which might be described as 'verbal.' Nor does this idea come in tentatively and by degrees, but almost from the very first. Both Irenaeus and Tertullian regard Inspiration as determining the choice of particular words and phrases. For instance, Irenaeus in view of the Gnostic separation between the man Jesus and the aeon Christus, the descent of which they postponed until the Baptism, says that the Holy Spirit, foreseeing these corruptions of the truth and guarding against their fraudulent dealing, said by the mouth of Matthew, 'Now the birth of Christ was on this wise[4].' This is the more noticeable, because the

[1] *Adv. Haer.* iv. 7. 2 : *Qui . . . adventum Christi prophetaverunt, revelationem acceperunt ab ipso Filio.* Compare iv. 15. 1.
[2] *De Princ.* iv. 10 ; Lomm. xxi. 499.
[3] *Comm. in Ep. ad Philem. prol.*
[4] *Adv. Haer.* iii. 16. 2 : *praevidens Spiritus Sanctus depravatores et praemuniens contra fraudulentiam eorum per Matthaeum ait, Christi autem generatio sic erat.*

## Properties ascribed to the New Testament.

reading which Irenaeus assumes, though very possibly and perhaps probably the right one, is not now found in a single Greek MS. And in like manner Tertullian speaks of the Holy Spirit as foreseeing that some would claim unlimited licence for bishops, and therefore laying down that they were to be the husbands of only one wife [1]; and in more places than one he speaks of the 'foresight' (*providentia*) of the Holy Spirit cutting away the ground from heretics [2]. Tertullian, like Irenaeus, quite adopts the formula of St. Matthew and other New Testament writers as to the Spirit of God speaking 'through' the human author. Origen, adopting another phrase from St. Matthew's Gospel, expresses his belief that 'there is not one jot or one tittle but is charged with divine lessons [3].' Inspiration may attach even to a number. Thus the author of *Computus de Pascha*, a contemporary of Cyprian's, refers St. Paul's estimate of the length of the period of the Judges expressly to the teaching of the Holy Spirit [4]. And as inspiration is here invoked on a question of numbers, so elsewhere in regard to the facts of history; Moses was indebted to the teaching of the Holy Spirit for the older history from the Creation to the times of Abraham, and in like manner it was He who informed the Evangelists of the wondrous sign which happened at

---

[1] *De Monog.* 12.   [2] *De Jejun.* 15; *Adv. Marc.* v. 7.
[3] *Comm. in Ev. Matt.* xvi. 12; Lomm. iv. 39: ἐγὼ μὲν οὖν ἰῶτα ἓν ἢ μίαν κεραίαν οὐ πιστεύω κενὴν εἶναι θείων μαθημάτων.
[4] *De Pasch. Comp.* 11: *Secundum Pauli b. apostoli sermonem, qui Spiritu Domini edoctus retulit eos implesse annos ccccl.*

the Baptism[1]. The four Canonical Evangelists were not like others who attempted to write Gospel narratives, they really wrote them at the prompting of the Holy Spirit[2]. Dionysius of Alexandria says that 'the Holy Spirit, imparted severally to the Evangelists, describes the whole mind of our Saviour by the words of each[3].' And Archelaus, bishop of Caschara in Mesopotamia, makes the Holy Spirit vouch for the accuracy of a saying ascribed to our Lord in the Gospel of St. Matthew[4].

We cannot wonder if this high doctrine sometimes takes the form of asserting the absolute perfection and infallibility of the Scriptures. We saw that Irenaeus attributes to the Apostles 'perfect knowledge[5].' Elsewhere he is still more explicit, asserting that the Scriptures must needs be 'perfect, as having been spoken by the Word of God and His

---

[1] *Contra Cels.* i. 44; Lomm. xviii. 83 f.: "Ἄλλος δ' ἄν τις εἴποι, ὅτι οὐ πάντες τοῦ Ἰησοῦ ἤκουσαν ταῦτα διηγουμένου οἱ ἀναγράψαντες τὰ περὶ τοῦ εἴδους τῆς περιστερᾶς καὶ τῆς ἐξ οὐρανοῦ φωνῆς· ἀλλὰ τὸ διδάξαν Μωϋσέα Πνεῦμα τὴν πρεσβυτέραν αὐτοῦ ἱστορίαν, ἀρξαμένην ἀπὸ τῆς κοσμογονίας μέχρι τῆς κατὰ τὸν Ἀβραὰμ τὸν πατέρα αὐτοῦ, τοῦτ' ἐδίδαξε καὶ τοὺς γράψαντας τὸ εὐαγγέλιον, τὸ γενόμενον παράδοξον κατὰ τὸν χρόνον τοῦ βαπτίσματος Ἰησοῦ. A similar idea occurs in Josephus, *c. Apion.* i. 8 : μόνον τῶν προφητῶν τὰ μὲν ἀνωτάτω καὶ παλαιότατα κατὰ τὴν ἐπίπνοιαν τὴν ἀπὸ τοῦ Θεοῦ μαθόντων.

[2] *Homil.* 1. *in Luc.*

[3] Migne, *Patrol. Graec.* x. 1389 : Τὸ οὖν Πνεῦμα τὸ ἅγιον εἰς τοὺς εὐαγγελιστὰς κατανεμηθέν, τὴν πᾶσαν τοῦ Σωτῆρος ἡμῶν διάθεσιν ἐκ τῆς ἑκάστου φωνῆς συντίθησιν.

[4] *Sed et Spiritu* (*Spiritus* cod.) *Evangelista Matthaeus diligenter significat Domini nostri Jesu Christi sermonem: Videte ne quis vos seducat,* &c. *Acta Disp. S. Archelai cum Manete* (Migne, *ut sup.*, col. 1485; Routh, *Rell. Sacr.* v. 131).

[5] *Sup.*, p. 32.

## Properties ascribed to the New Testament. 37

Spirit[1]. An anonymous writer against the Montanists guards himself against being supposed to be ambitious of supplementing the Gospels to which no good Christian could add anything and from which he could not take away[2]. Heracleon, the Gnostic, is convicted of this audacity, inserting qualifying words in the prologue to the Gospel of St. John, which entirely pervert its meaning[3]. Clement of Alexandria asserts that 'not one tittle' of the Scriptures (in which he has included just before the Epistle to the Romans) can pass away, because they are spoken by the Holy Ghost[4]. Methodius, bishop of Olympus, lays down that there can be 'no contradiction or absurdity in holy writ[5].' Origen starts from the premises that the Gospels having been composed with the cooperation of the Holy Spirit the writers cannot have had any lapse of memory[6]; and elsewhere that the Evangelists 'cannot have made a mistake or set down anything falsely[7],' so that two

[1] *Adv. Haer.* ii. 28. 2: *rectissime scientes, quia Scripturae quidem perfectae sunt, quippe a Verbo Dei et Spiritu ejus dictae.*
[2] *Ap.* Eus. *H. E.* v. 16. 3: δεδιὼς δὲ καὶ ἐξευλαβούμενος, μή πη δόξω τισὶν ἐπισυγγράφειν ἢ ἐπιδιατάσσεσθαι τῷ τῆς τοῦ εὐαγγελίου καινῆς διαθήκης λόγῳ, ᾧ μήτε προσθεῖναι μήτ' ἀφελεῖν δυνατὸν τῷ κατὰ τὸ εὐαγγέλιον αὐτὸ πολιτεύεσθαι προῃρημένῳ.
[3] Orig. *in Ev. Joan.* ii. 8 (Lommatzsch, i. 117).
[4] *Protrept.* 9. § 82.
[5] μηδεμία ὑπεναντίωσις ἢ ἀτοπία ἐν τοῖς θείοις λόγοις (*De Resurrect.* 48; ed. Bonwetsch, i. 155).
[6] Εἴπερ ἀκριβῶς πιστεύομεν ἀναγεγράφθαι συνεργοῦντος καὶ τοῦ ἁγίου Πνεύματος τὰ εὐαγγέλια, καὶ μὴ ἐσφάλησαν ἐν τῷ ἀπομνημονεύειν οἱ γράψαντες αὐτά (*Comm. in Ev. Matt.* xvi. 12; Lomm. iv. 36).
[7] μηδενὸς σφαλλομένου τῶν εὐαγγελιστῶν μηδὲ ψευδομένου (*Comm. in Ev. Jo.* vi. 18; Lomm. i. 228).

sayings with a slight variation must really have been spoken at different times. And Novatian, who although the author of a schism was a very orthodox writer, says roundly that the Scriptures are infallible (*nunquam fallunt*) [1].

The object of the appeal to Scripture is to establish the rule of faith or the rule of conduct. Irenaeus calls the written tradition as well as the oral teaching of the Apostles 'the foundation and pillar of our faith.' He lays himself out to prove his whole position by the Scriptures, and treats this method as one universally recognised [2]. Indeed on both sides, the side of doctrine and the side of practice, the authoritative use of Scripture—the New Testament equally with the Old—underlies the whole of the Christian literature of this period. Not only might we quote for it page after page of Irenaeus, Clement of Alexandria, Tertullian, Hippolytus, Origen (with the single exception of the Apologies, where the method would have been out of place), but—what is of even more importance—the method is shared alike by orthodox writers and heretical. It had been used by Basilides and Valentinus and their followers; and the great Church-writers fought them with the same weapons; they authenticate Scripture by Scripture, Gospel by Gospel, and Epistle by Epistle—for in dealing with many of the Gnostics the Old Testament was out of court. This usage is really coextensive with the

---

[1] *De Trin.* 30.

[2] *Adv. Haer.* ii. 35. 4; cp. iii. 4. 1, 2: the written tradition forms the first line of evidence, oral tradition the second.

## Properties ascribed to the New Testament.

Christian name, and arises very soon after the first traces of a Christian literature outside the New Testament.

How high the authority was which is ascribed to the Scriptures comes out from the stress which is laid upon their interpretation. It appears equally from the methods of interpretation adopted by orthodox writers and the jealous watch kept over those who were not orthodox. Only in a book which is regarded as possessing peculiar sacredness and authority is the attempt likely to be made to elicit another sense from the words than the obvious and literal one. Now in the earliest known commentary on a book of the New Testament, that of the Gnostic Heracleon on St. John, which is probably not later and may even be some little time earlier than 170 A.D.[1], the allegorical method is already full-blown. It is notorious to what lengths it was carried by Clement of Alexandria and Origen. It may not be used quite to the same extent for the New Testament as for the Old, but it is used quite as unequivocally, and for the Epistles as well as for the Gospels[2]. It may suffice to note the fact of the use of allegory for the present. We shall have occasion to return to the subject in the next lecture, where we shall be brought to closer quarters with the origin and first application of the method.

---

[1] See Mr. A. E. Brooke in the Cambridge *Texts and Studies*, i. 4. 34. The evidence relates perhaps rather to the teaching of Heracleon generally than to the Commentary on St. John, but the date given (c. 170) is probably not far wrong.

[2] See Additional Note D, p. 68 f.

Complaints of the perversion of Scripture by the heretics are exceedingly common, and perhaps commonest in the second century. The earliest reference to such perversion in the case of the New Testament is probably the allusion in the Second Epistle which bears the name of St. Peter to the Epistles of St. Paul, 'which the ignorant and unsteadfast wrest (στρεβλοῦσιν) as they do the other Scriptures[1].' We must only take this passage with the uncertainty which attaches to the genuineness and date of the Epistle in which it occurs. There were two methods of tampering with the Scriptures. One was the interpolation or mutilation of the text; the other was the perversion of its meaning. It is now pretty generally understood that the accusations which we are constantly meeting under the first of these heads are for the most part groundless. One such attempt we certainly do know, the attempt of Marcion the Gnostic to adapt to his own purposes the Gospel of St. Luke and ten of St. Paul's Epistles. But he did so simply by excision of the passages to which he objected. The charge of altering the text of the portions which he received, generally speaking[2], breaks down. The supposed alterations are in so many cases demonstrably nothing more than various readings which he found in his copy as to give rise to considerable presumption that the same would be true of the remainder. There are other well-known

---

[1] 2 Pet. iii. 16.

[2] This must not be taken to exclude slight consequential changes due to the omissions.

examples[1] in which not only does the Catholic writer wrongly accuse his opponents of falsifying the text, but in point of fact it is his opponents who have the right reading, and he himself who is misled by a wrong one[2].

The other means of commending error by perverse interpretation was no doubt far more common. Tertullian[3] and Irenaeus[4] with equal vehemence accuse the Valentinians. An anonymous writer quoted by Eusebius accuses the rationalizing Monarchians[5]. Hippolytus urges his readers not to 'force' the Word of God[6].

And yet it must be admitted that the 'forcing' was not all on one side. Both the orthodox champions and the heterodox employed such methods as were current, and there was probably no great difference between them so far as these methods were concerned, though the mind of the Church was doubtless governed by an instinct which was nearer the truth

---

[1] See (*e.g.*) the various readings on John i. 13; iii. 6; vii. 53–viii. 11; Luke xxiii. 44; and perhaps Matt. i. 18.

[2] Compare Hort, *Introd.* p. 282 : 'It will not be out of place to add here a distinct expression of our belief that even among the numerous unquestionably spurious readings of the New Testament there are no signs of deliberate falsification of the text for dogmatic purposes.' And again, *Appendix*, p. 66: 'Notwithstanding the random suggestions of rash or dishonest handling thrown out by controversialists there is no tangible evidence for the excision [except by Marcion] of a substantial portion of narrative for doctrinal reasons at any period of textual history.'

[3] *De Praescr. Haeret.* 38.      [4] *Adv. Haer.* i. 3. 6.

[5] *H. E.* v. 28.

[6] *Contra Noetum*, 9: μὴ βιαζόμενοι τὰ ὑπὸ τοῦ Θεοῦ δεδομένα.

than any argument that could be put into words. *Securus judicat orbis terrarum.* There were questionable points in the exegesis of Irenaeus and Hippolytus as well as in that of Basilides or the Valentinians; there were questionable points in the exegesis of Athanasius as well as in that of Arius; but it is possible to admit this and yet to think that Irenaeus and Hippolytus on the one hand, and Athanasius and his fellows on the other, represented more truly the real sense of Scripture than the Gnostics or Arians.

And yet the right is sometimes on the side of the minority. On this very matter of the inspiration of Holy Scripture we come across isolated sayings from time to time which show a greater insight into the real facts of the case, and would have formed a wholesome corrective to the current views if more attention had been paid to them. Even a writer who holds so high a doctrine as Tertullian yet points out that St. Paul recognises different degrees of inspiration, sometimes speaking in his own name and not in the name of Christ [1]. The same passage which put him upon this also caught the eye of Origen, and is more than once used by him in support of a wider view in regard to an ascending and descending scale of inspiration. Origen saw that there was a difference

---

[1] *De Exhort. Cast.* 3 : *In primis autem non videbor irreligiosus, si quod ipse profitetur, animadvertam, omnem illam indulgentiam nuptiarum de suo, id est, de humano sensu, non de divino praescripto induxisse.* The apologetic language in which this opinion is introduced reveals a consciousness that it ran somewhat counter to general feeling. Any seeming depreciation of Scripture was as unpopular even then as it is now.

between the inspiration of Christ and all other inspiration [1]. The inspiration of the prophets was given them at particular times and for particular purposes; they had visitations of the Spirit which ceased when they had served their turn. Only upon Christ did the Holy Spirit abide continually [2].

We may probably trace the influence of Origen, though it is certainly not Origen himself who is speaking, in a remarkable criticism to which Jerome refers in the preface to his commentary on the Epistle to Philemon. He says that some who refuse a place to this among the other Epistles of St. Paul urge that all the Apostle's utterances were not made by 'Christ speaking in him' because the weakness of human nature could not endure the constant indwelling of the Holy Spirit (*unum tenorem Spiritus Sancti*), nor yet could the ordinary functions of the body be always discharged under the presence of the Lord. There must have been times when St. Paul could not venture to say 'I live, yet no longer I, but Christ liveth in me' (Gal. i. 20), or 'do ye seek a proof of Christ that speaketh in me' (2 Cor. xiii. 3)? 'What sort of proof of Christ is it, they ask, to be told "The cloak which I left at Troas with Carpus, when thou comest, bring with thee" (2 Tim. iv. 13), or in Galatians (v. 12) "I would they were even cut off" (or 'were mutilated,' *excidantur*?) "that trouble you," and in this very Epistle, "But withal prepare me also a lodging"(Philem. i. 22)? They say that this was the case not only with

---

[1] *Hom. in Num.* xvi. 4; *in Ev. Jo.* i. 5 (Zahn, *Gesch. d. K.* ii. 1002).
[2] See the passages quoted by Zahn.

the Apostles but with the Prophets; so that we often find it written, "The word of the Lord came to Ezekiel" or to any other of the prophets, because when the prophecy was finished the prophet resumed his ordinary self and became like any other man, and except our Lord Jesus Christ the Holy Spirit abode permanently with no one. And that this was the sign which John the Baptist had received, that on whom he saw the Holy Spirit descending and abiding upon him he might know to be the Christ (John i. 33). A proof that the Holy Spirit descended indeed upon many, but it was a peculiar distinction of the Saviour that it abode upon him. On these and other like grounds,' says Jerome, 'they decide that the Epistle to Philemon either is not St. Paul's, or, even if it is his, it contains nothing that tends to edification, and they say that it is rejected by many of the ancients as being only a letter of commendation and not for the purpose of teaching [1].'

We may differ from this ancient critic in our estimate of the beautiful little Epistle to Philemon, with its touches of nature which appeal to the common heart of mankind. We may have different ideas as to the true dignity of an inspired writer. And yet we must admit that he has hit upon truths in regard to the nature of inspiration which have by no means always been remembered, and which it is important to keep in sight.

There are not wanting other indications that side by

[1] *Comm. in Ep. ad Philem., prol.* (ed. Migne, vii. 637; ed. Vallarsi, vii. 742 f.).

side with the high and strict doctrine of which we have given illustrations, there was a sort of under-current, sometimes perceptible in the very same writers, which took more account of human infirmity and was in closer contact with the facts. There was not indeed any hard and fast dogma of inspiration imposed upon the whole Church. Men formed a high idea of it, and they clung to that idea, largely we cannot doubt from a sense of the preciousness of the Scriptures to themselves. But this did not prevent them at other times and in pursuance of other trains of thought from giving the reins to a freer and more candid observation, and allowing the facts to tell their own story in a simpler and more natural theory.

Quite of this simple and natural character is the account which Papias gives of the origin of St. Mark's Gospel, put together from notes of the occasional preaching of St. Peter, and therefore incomplete though careful as far as it went[1]. This is in perfect keeping with the language which St. Luke uses in the preface to his own Gospel, which again describes a purely natural process based upon the human virtues of research and care, but without claim to anything beyond. In like manner the Muratorian Fragment, while apparently repeating a tradition similar to that of Papias about St. Mark[2], lays stress upon the extent to which St. Luke was an eye-witness of the events recorded in the Acts, and St. John of those recorded in his Gospel.

[1] Eus. *H. E.* iii. 39. 15.
[2] This part of the Fragment is mutilated, but the words which remain point to this conclusion.

Origen in the context of a passage already quoted implies that in his day there were persons who thought it possible that the discrepancies in the Gospels were due to inaccuracy and failure of memory[1]. Origen himself, as we have seen, rejects this explanation; but in another place he admits the possibility at least of clerical error. This is in his comment on St. Matt. xxvii. 9[2], where a quotation from Zechariah is attributed to Jeremiah. The passage is a touchstone to ancient commentators. Eusebius[3], like Origen, gives an alternative: either clerical error, or that the original of the quotation had been fraudulently removed from the copies of Jeremiah. Augustine first rejects, by a piece of really good textual criticism[4], the reading *per prophetam* only (without *Jeremiam*) which he found in some MSS., but then goes on to say that St. Matthew was inspired to write 'Jeremiah' in order to bring out the completeness of the agreement between

---

[1] *Comm. in Ev. Jo.* vi. 18; Lomm. i. 228 f.: οὐ γὰρ περὶ τῶν αὐτῶν, ὥς οἴονταί τινες οἱ ἀπομνημονεύοντες διαφόρως ἠνέχθησαν, μὴ ἀκριβοῦντες τῇ μνήμῃ ἕκαστον τῶν εἰρημένων ἢ γεγενημένων.

[2] Lommatzsch, v. 28: *suspicor aut errorem esse scripturae* [*Scripturae*, Lommatzsch, which is surely wrong] *et pro Zacharia positum Jeremiam, aut esse aliquam secretam Jeremiae scripturam, in qua scribitur.*

[3] *Demonst. Evang.* x; ed. Migne, iv. 745.

[4] *Sed utatur ista defensione cui placet: mihi autem cur non placeat, haec caussa est, quia et plures codices habent Jeremiae nomen, et qui diligentius in Graecis exemplaribus consideraverunt, in antiquis Graecis ita se perhibent invenisse: et nulla fuit caussa cur adderetur hoc nomen, ut mendositas fieret; cur autem de nonnullis codicibus tolleretur fuit utique caussa ut audax imperitia faceret, cum turbaretur quaestione quod hoc testimonium apud Jeremiam non inveniretur.*

the prophets, so that sayings of Zechariah might be claimed by Jeremiah and *vice versa*[1]. Jerome has not only heard of but seen an apocryphal work of Jeremiah in which the words quoted occur: he does not however adopt that solution, but simply remarks that the passage is not in Jeremiah but expresses the sense of a place in Zechariah[2]. The *Breviarium in Psalmos*, which is printed with the works of Jerome[3], treats together of St. Matt. xiii. 35 (with the reading 'Isaiah') and xxvii. 9, and ends with the frank avowal of a mistake, but apparently on the part of the scribes not of the Evangelist, in both places (*Videlis ergo quia et hic error fuit sicut ibi*).

III. But now we have reached the third and last of our main questions. We have traced backwards the process by which the New Testament received its present dimensions, and we have endeavoured to define what was understood by the New Testament as a Sacred Volume. It remains for us to ask by what criteria the several books were admitted to their place in that volume, or in other words what were taken to be the tests of the presence or absence of inspiration.

The general test which determined the place of a book in the New Testament was no doubt *Apostolicity*.

[1] *De Cons. Evang.* iii. 29, 30; ed. Benedict. iii. 2. 114 f.
[2] *Comm. in Ev. Matt.* ad loc.; ed. Migne, vii. 213; ed. Vallarsi, ii. 228.
[3] Ed. Migne, vii. 1108.

When the writer of the Muratorian Fragment declares against the admission of the Shepherd of Hermas into the Canon, he does so on the ground that it is too recent, and that it cannot have a place 'among the Prophets whose number is complete, nor yet among the Apostles in these latter days.' As 'the Prophets' here stand for the Old Testament, so 'the Apostles' are practically equivalent to the New [1].

This agrees with the whole tendency of the age in which the Fragmentist was writing. As there grew up round the Church in the second century a crowd of tentative theories for the explanation of the universe into which Christianity was worked with more or less of modification, and as among Christians who were unaffected by these external theories different shades of doctrine began to prevail, it was necessary to fix upon some standard by which competing views might be judged and verified. It was natural that this standard should be sought in the teaching of the Apostles as the best interpretation of the mind of Christ Himself. 'We walk,' says Tertullian, 'by that rule which the Church has handed down from the Apostles, the Apostles from Christ, and Christ from God [2].' There was a double guarantee for this tradition, the written Word and the historic continuity of the Apostolic Churches. The heretics, according to the argument which Tertullian wields with so much forensic skill, were really debarred from appealing to the Scriptures because

---

[1] So Kuhn, *ad loc.*

[2] *De Praescr. Haeret.* 37. Compare Serapion as quoted above, p. 33.

they stood outside the Churches which were the proper guardians of those Scriptures. Tertullian claims to be himself 'heir to the Apostles' by his loyalty to the faith which they had bequeathed. The Apostles had disinherited and repudiated the heretics who were not true to that faith but struck out new ways of thinking of their own.

Before Tertullian Irenaeus had taken up substantially the same ground. He too lays down that the 'plan of our salvation' (*dispositionem salutis nostrae*) had only become known through those who first preached the Gospel and then handed it on to us in the Scriptures [1]. With these the oral tradition transmitted through successors of the Apostles is wholly consonant [2]. The double tradition, written and oral, is a storehouse of truth which the Apostles have formed from which every one may take as he will [3]. The preaching and the writings of the Apostles along with those of the Prophets and the teaching of the Lord supply the premises for his argument [4]. And even Clement of Alexandria adopts a similar line of reasoning. He appeals to the Scriptures as carrying with them the authority of the Prophets in the Old Testament, and of the Lord and the Apostles in the New [5]; and he too, like Tertullian, claimed first that the tradition derived from the Apostles is one and the same, and secondly that it proves its truth by its priority to the heresies [6].

But this tendency to appeal to the authority of the

---

[1] *Adv. Haer.* iii. 1. 1.
[2] *Ibid.* 3. 1.
[3] *Ibid.* 4. 1.
[4] *Ibid.* ii. 35. 4.
[5] *Strom.* vii. 16. §§ 95, 97.
[6] *Ibid.* §§ 106, 108.

Apostles can really be traced much further back, in fact to the confines of the New Testament itself. The now famous *Didaché* is put forward in the name of the Twelve Apostles. Ignatius would 'have recourse to the Gospel as the flesh of Christ, and to the Apostles as the presbytery' (or 'governing body') 'of the Church [1].' Clement of Rome refers the Corinthians to the Epistle which the blessed Apostle Paul wrote to them under the influence of the Spirit ($\pi\nu\epsilon\upsilon\mu\alpha\tau\iota\kappa\hat{\omega}s$) [2]. And Justin, though he is not writing for Christians and therefore does not need to lay stress on the point, yet calls the Gospels 'Memoirs of the Apostles,' and is careful to note that the Apocalypse is the work of an Apostle [3].

We observe however that in the Muratorian Fragment there is still a healthy feeling that the authority of the Apostles is not merely of the nature of dogmatic assertion. In all that he says about the Historical Books the writer insists on the personal qualification of the authors either as eye-witnesses, or as careful historians [4].

The Fragmentist takes his stand on the position of the Canon in his own day, and it is that position of which he gives an account. But the idea of Apostolicity did not exactly cover the contents of that Canon. Three of the Historical Books just mentioned were not by Apostles. And in the debates relating to the

---

[1] *Ad Philad.* 5.  [2] *Ad Cor.* 47. 1.
[3] *Apol.* i. 66, 67 ; *Dial. c. Tryph.* 88, 101, 103, 104, 106 ; and for the Apocalypse, *Dial.* 81.
[4] See above, p. 45.

## Criteria applied to the New Testament.

Epistle to the Hebrews the same difficulty was evidently felt. There were two ways out of it. One was to regard the works in question, if not directly Apostolic, as vouched for by Apostles; the Gospel of St. Mark going back virtually to St. Peter, the writings of St. Luke to St. Paul, and the Epistle to the Hebrews deriving its substance, if not its actual words, from the same Apostle. This expedient was adopted very early [1]. The other was to lay stress, not so much on Apostolic authorship as on reception by the Churches. This was a parallel line of argument all through the history of the Canon. Reception by the Churches clearly admitted of degrees [2], and reception by the Apostolic Churches took the next place as an argument to certainly Apostolic origin. In the later stages of the history ecclesiastical usage proved decisive. It is the principle which runs through the Canon of Origen, and after Origen still more distinctly through that of Eusebius. St. Augustine lays it down very

---

[1] Tertullian, *Adv. Marc.* iv. 5: *Marcus quod edidit evangelium Petri affirmatur, cujus interpres Marcus. Nam et Lucae digestum Paulo adscribere solent.* Cf. for St. Mark, Eus. *Demonstr. Evang.* iii. 5 (ed. Migne, iv. 217): for St. Luke, Iren. *Adv. Haer.* iii. 1. 1, 14. 1; Tert. *Adv. Marc.* iv. 2; Orig. *ap.* Eus. *H. E.* vi. 25. 6, Eus. himself quoting common report, *H. E.* ii. 4. 8, &c. Tertullian takes a rather different line in regard to Ep. to Hebrews. He places it a step, but only a single step, below the writings of the Apostles: *Volo tamen ex redundantia alicujus etiam comitis apostolorum testimonium superducere, idoneum confirmari de proximo jure disciplinam magistrorum. Extat et Barnabae titulus ad Hebraeos, a Deo satis auctorati viri, &c.* (*De Pudic.* 20).

[2] Tertullian uses the comparative *receptior apud ecclesias* of the Epistle to the Hebrews as compared with the *Shepherd* of Hermas (*De Pudic.* 20, as above).

explicitly. 'In regard to the Canonical Scriptures let him follow the authority of as many as possible of the Catholic Churches, among which of course are those which are of Apostolic foundation or were thought worthy to have Epistles addressed to them. He will therefore follow this rule as to the Canonical Scriptures, to prefer those which are accepted by all the Catholic Churches to those which are not accepted by some; and among those which are not accepted by all to prefer those which the greater and more important Churches accept to those which are supported by fewer Churches or those of less authority[1].' Jerome supplements this, with a scholar's instinct basing his individual opinion more upon the verdict of eminent and ancient authors. Writing with something of the freedom of private correspondence, he says that 'it does not matter who is the author of the Epistle to the Hebrews, as in any case it is the work of a Church-writer (*ecclesiastici viri*) and is constantly read in the Churches[2].' As the Latin Churches reject Hebrews so the Greek Churches reject the Apocalypse, but Jerome himself accepts both on the ground that they are quoted by ancient writers as canonical. I do not know that there is any instance in which Apostolic authorship is so expressly abandoned as a necessary condition of Canonicity. We have at the same time brought out another factor which also runs through the whole of

---

[1] *De Doct. Christ.* ii. 8. § 12.

[2] *Nihil interesse cujus sit, quum ecclesiastici viri sit, et quotidie ecclesiarum lectione celebretur* (*Ep.* cxxix. *ad Dardanum*; ed. Migne, i. 1103; ed. Vallarsi, i. 971).

the history, the influence of leading individuals, whether of bishops or scholars, in determining the usage of the Churches. It is in this way that Irenaeus appeals to the 'presbyters,' that Clement appeals to Pantaenus[1] and Origen to the ἀρχαῖοι ἄνδρες[2], and that Eusebius also rests his judgment on that of leading Churchmen (οἱ ἐκκλησιαστικοί)[3]. The further back we go the more weight such individual opinions doubtless possessed. The usage of particular Churches would be determined, especially at the earliest and most critical stage, by those of its members who carried the greatest weight whether invested with formal authority or not, but especially when invested with such authority, or at least through the direct intervention of those who possessed it[4]. The judgment of individuals would thus pass into and be lost in the judgment of the Society; and the combined judgment of these societies would be the verdict of the Catholic Church.

The whole process was checked at each step by an active and jealous sense of what was Catholic in doctrine. Just as under the Old Covenant the message of a prophet was to be tested not merely by the success of his predictions but by the agreement of the substance of his prophecy with the funda-

---

[1] *Ap.* Eus. *H.E.* vi. 14.
[2] *Ibid.* 25.                    [3] *Ibid.* iii. 25.
[4] Instances in which learning was on one side and episcopal authority on the other would be Origen and Demetrius at Alexandria, or Hippolytus and Zephyrinus with his successor Callistus at Rome; but there would be many other examples of the opposite state of things where the bishop took the advice of his leading presbyters.

mentals of Israel's religion, so also under the New Covenant it is clear that writings which came with any claim to be considered canonical were judged by the nature of their contents. The Muratorian Fragmentist will not have 'gall mixed with honey.' He rejects with decision the works of the heretics; just as Irenaeus and Tertullian and writers as far back as Agrippa Castor in the time of Hadrian reject them[1]. It is often objected that this is an argument in a circle, because the Scriptures are used to establish Church doctrine, and then Church doctrine is used—not as the only test but as one of the tests— to determine what is Scripture. But there is not really a *petitio principii* here any more than there was in the testing of a prophet's message. There was enough New Testament Scripture, as there was enough Old Testament teaching, established on a firm and unshakeable basis to be used as a standard in judging of the rest. There were writings as to the authorship of which the early Church had not a shadow of doubt, and those writings continued to speak with the same personal weight with which their living authors had spoken. Here was a fixed standard to which doubtful writings could be referred. On the strength of it was drawn up before the middle of the second century that short summary of Christian Doctrine which formed the basis of what is known to us as 'the Apostles' Creed.' And round the outskirts of this there grew up a larger Church consciousness, fed and nurtured upon the unquestioned

[1] Eus. *H. E.* iv. 7. 6, 7.

## Criteria applied to the New Testament. 55

documents, which became itself a touchstone to decide what was the 'analogy of the faith.' I do not say that it was an infallible touchstone. I only say that it was one which did exist, and which was applied by the men of those days according to the best of their lights, and without any clear logical fallacy.

The standard thus obtained worked in two directions. On the one hand it excluded any writing which did not satisfy it in regard to doctrine; and on the other hand it also excluded, or had a tendency to exclude, any writing which clashed with those already received in matters of history. This was the objection brought by the Alogi against the Gospel of St. John[1]. It gave force to the charge brought by Apollinaris against the Quartodecimans that by their practice they made the Gospels conflict with one another[2]. And Origen treats it as a principle accepted by most if not by all that the Gospels cannot disagree.

There remains one more test which the ancients applied, and of which it is all the more incumbent on me to speak, because it has been the subject of much ridicule and has helped perhaps more than anything to bring the work of the early Canon-makers into discredit. I refer to the use of numbers, of which we have conspicuous examples in Irenaeus and the Muratorian

---

[1] Epiph. *Haer.* li. 4: οὐ συμφωνεῖ τὰ αὐτοῦ βιβλία τοῖς λοιποῖς ἀποστόλοις.

[2] *Chron. Pasch.* i. p. 13 (ed. Dindorf). *Comm. in Ev. Matt.* xvi. 12 (Lommatzsch, iv. 36): Ὁ μὲν οὖν τῇ ἱστορίᾳ ψιλῇ παριστάμενος, καὶ μὴ βουλόμενος διαφωνεῖν τοῖς εὐαγγελισταῖς, compared with what follows, Εἴπερ γὰρ ἀκριβῶς πιστεύομεν ἀναγεγράφθαι, κ.τ.λ.

Fragment, but which was employed equally in regard to the Old Testament and in regard to the New[1]. According to Irenaeus, there must be four Gospels, as there are four quarters of the globe and four cardinal winds[2]. Even Origen compares the Four Gospels to the four elements[3]. And the Muratorian Fragmentist makes out, as he can do indeed without forcing, that St. Paul wrote exactly to seven Churches, as St. John also in the Epistles attached to the Apocalypse. In this stress on the number seven there is clearly an allusion to the idea of universality, the seven Churches in each case symbolizing the Church universal. The idea is no doubt connected with the revival of Pythagoreanism and the doctrine of the value of numbers[4]. It is of course not at all a specially Christian idea, but is simply an application to Christian subjects of intellectual methods current at the time. The estimate of these methods belongs to the general history of culture, and in a very subordinate

---

[1] It is perhaps true (as Mr. Lock suggests to me) that this use of numbers was more often a symbolical interpretation of the facts after the settlement of the different parts of the Canon than a means employed in that settlement, I suspect however that it had something to do with predisposing men's minds to accept the Epistle to the Hebrews as St. Paul's and so making up a total of 14 Epistles (2 × 7), and also perhaps in determining the number of the Catholic Epistles. We should thus have a complete system of sevens. St. Paul and St. John wrote alike to 7 churches (*cf.* Fragm. Mur.); Epp. Cath. are 7, and Epp. Paul. twice 7.

[2] *Adv. Haer.* iii. 11. 8.

[3] *Comm. in Ev. Joan.* i. 6; Lomm. i. 13.

[4] See Dr. C. Taylor, *Hermas and the Four Gospels* (Cambridge, 1892), p. 20.

## Criteria applied to the New Testament. 57

degree to the history of Christianity. In order to be fair to them we need to place them alongside of those wonderful guesses at the constituent elements of the universe made by the early Greek philosophers. Let us realize for a moment the chaos in which thinking must have been involved before the invention of numbers, and realize also the impression which must have been made upon men's minds after their invention as day by day new properties were discovered in them, and we shall not I think be surprised if a mystic power sometimes seemed to attach to them, and if they were applied as a key to the solution of problems to which they were really foreign. But those who infer that because Irenaeus uses arguments such as this in regard to the Four Gospels, he is therefore a puerile and contemptible writer, probably in most cases have not read Irenaeus at all, or, if they have read him, have done so without eyes to see, or imagination to enter into, a phase of civilization in any way different from their own.

Irenaeus no doubt uses arguments which are sometimes good and sometimes bad; and so did others who were concerned with the forming of the Canon. But it is an often-told story that conclusions may be better than the reasons that are given for them. The process by which the Early Church defined the limits of its Scriptures was like the process by which opinion has ripened on many another subject before and since. There entered into it a number of varied elements; reasoning partly conscious and partly unconscious, authority, usage, the sense of affinity to things spiritual and of harmony between spiritual things already realized and appropriated, and others lying beyond, where the realization and appropriation was still to come. And may not the Christian think that there was something even more than this? May he not think that there is truth in the promise of Him who said, 'Lo, I am with you always, even unto the end of the world'? It would not even then follow that all was perfection. It does not seem to be the Will of God that either the World or the Church should leap into perfection all at once, or even make way towards perfection except by gradual and slow degrees. In all ages it has been His Will to give His servants light enough to walk by; and that light has gone on broadening down the centuries till it has reached ourselves, in measures fuller perhaps than have been vouchsafed to any generation before. Such privileges bring at once difficulties and responsibilities. The very fact that the light given to us now is penetrating into the more hidden recesses may well make it seem at times garish and disturbing. Let us wait awhile patiently and our eyes will get used to it. And, if we are tempted to elation at our superior knowledge, let us remember St. Paul's warning, 'Be not high-minded, but fear'; and again, let us remember that 'To whom much is given, of him shall much be required.'

## *Notes to Lecture I.*

### NOTE A.

*The Canons of the Quinisextine Council, of Carthage, and of Laodicea.*

IT may be convenient for the reader to have before him the text of the only synodical decisions of the Early Church relating to the Canon.

CONCILIUM QUINISEXTUM (an. 692), *Can.* ii. ... ἐπισφραγίζομεν δὲ καὶ τοὺς λοιποὺς πάντας ἱεροὺς κανόνας τοὺς ὑπὸ τῶν ἁγίων καὶ μακαρίων πατέρων ἡμῶν ἐκτεθέντας, τοῦτ' ἐστι τῶν τε ἐν Νικαίᾳ συναθροισθέντων τριακοσίων δεκαοκτὼ θεοφόρων ἁγίων πατέρων καὶ τῶν ἐν 'Αγκύρᾳ ... ἀλλὰ μὴν καὶ τῶν ἐν Λαοδικείᾳ τῆς Φρυγίας ... ὡσαύτως καὶ τῶν ἐν Σαρδικῇ, ἔτι μὴν καὶ τῶν ἐν Καρθαγένῃ [the only Western Councils mentioned] ... 'Αθανασίου ἀρχιεπισκόπου 'Αλεξανδρείας ... Γρηγορίου τοῦ θεολόγου, 'Αμφιλοχίου 'Ικονίου ... καὶ μηδενὶ ἐξεῖναι τοὺς προδηλωθέντας παραχαράττειν κανόνας ἢ ἀθετεῖν ἢ ἑτέρους παρὰ τοὺς προκειμένους παραδέχεσθαι κανόνας ψευδεπιγράφως ὑπό τινων συντεθέντας τῶν τὴν ἀλήθειαν καπηλεύειν ἐπιχειρησάντων ...

(From Bruns, *Canones Apost. et Concil. Vet. Selecti*, Berolini, 1839, p. 36 f.)

It will be observed here that κανών = any formulated and authoritative rule or set of rules, whether laid down by a Council or by some individual Churchman. Only some of those which were thus sanctioned contained lists of the Sacred Books.

Conc. Carthag. iv. (an. 419), *Can.* xxiv. ratifies Conc. Carthag. iii. (an. 397), *Can.* xlvii, which is given thus by Bruns, a few various readings from English MSS. being contributed by Dr. Westcott.

CONCILIUM CARTHAGINIENSE III. (an. 397), *Can.* xlvii. 'Item placuit, ut praeter scripturas canonicas nihil in ecclesia legatur sub nomine divinarum scripturarum. Sunt autem canonicae scripturae [+hae *W.*]: Genesis, Exodus, Leviticus, Numeri, Deuteronomium, Jesus Nave, Judicum, Ruth, Regnorum libri quatuor, Paralipomenon libri duo, Job, Psalterium Davidicum, Salomonis libri quinque, libri duodecim Prophetarum, Jesaias, Jeremias, Ezechiel, Daniel, Tobias, Judith, Esther, Esdrae libri duo, Machabaeorum libri duo. Novi autem Testamenti, Evangeliorum libri quatuor, Actuum Apostolorum liber unus, Pauli apostoli epistolae tredecim, eiusdem ad Hebraeos una, Petri apostoli duae, Joannis ap. [*om. W.*] tres, Judae ap. una et Jacobi una [Jacobi i., Judae i., *W.*], Apocalypsis Joannis liber unus. Hoc etiam fratri et consacerdoti nostro Bonifacio vel aliis earum partium episcopis pro confirmando isto canone innotescat, quia a patribus ista accepimus in ecclesia legenda. Liceat etiam [autem *W.*] legi passiones martyrum, cum anniversarii dies eorum celebrantur.'

The presence of the clause providing for the sending of the list to Pope Boniface (418-422 A.D.) shows that this form of the Canon really belongs to the Council of 419. With it should be compared Brev. Statut. Hippon. xxxvi. as given by Zahn (*Gesch. d. K.* ii. 251 f.), the text of which is however clearly in an uncertain condition.

It is generally agreed that the list appended as *Can.* lx. to the Council of Laodicea is not original, but as it may be included in the sanction of the Quinisextine Council, it seems best to give it with the variants of Westcott and Zahn.

CONCILIUM LAODICENUM (an. circ. 363), *Can.* lix. Ὅτι οὐ δεῖ ἰδιωτικοὺς ψαλμοὺς λέγεσθαι ἐν τῇ ἐκκλησίᾳ οὐδὲ ἀκανόνιστα βιβλία, ἀλλὰ μόνα τὰ κανονικὰ τῆς καινῆς καὶ παλαιᾶς διαθήκης.

[lx. Ὅσα δεῖ βιβλία ἀναγινώσκεσθαι τῆς παλαιᾶς διαθήκης· αʹ Γένεσις κόσμου. βʹ Ἔξοδος ἐξ [*om. Z.*] Αἰγύπτου. γʹ Λευιτικόν. δʹ Ἀριθμοί. εʹ Δευτερονόμιον. ϛʹ Ἰησοῦς Ναυῆ. ζʹ Κριταί, Ῥούθ. ηʹ Ἐσθήρ. θʹ Βασιλειῶν πρώτη καὶ δευτέρα. ιʹ Βασιλειῶν τρίτη καὶ τετάρτη. ιαʹ Παραλειπόμενα πρῶτον καὶ δεύτερον. ιβʹ

## Note B. 61

Ἔσδρας πρῶτον καὶ δεύτερον. ιγ´ Βίβλος Ψαλμῶν ἑκατὸν πεντήκοντα. ιδ´ Παροιμίαι Σολομῶντος. ιε´ Ἐκκλησιαστής. ις´ Ἆσμα ᾀσμάτων. ιζ´ Ἰώβ. ιη´ Δώδεκα προφῆται. ιθ´ Ἡσαΐας. κ´ Ἰερεμίας καὶ Βαρούχ, Θρηνοὶ καὶ Ἐπιστολαί. κα´ Ἰεζεκιήλ. κβ´ Δανιήλ.

Τὰ δὲ τῆς [*unc. incl.* Z.] καινῆς διαθήκης ταῦτα [*om.* IV., *unc. incl.* Z.]. Εὐαγγέλια τέσσαρα, κατὰ Ματθαῖον, κατὰ Μάρκον, κατὰ Λουκᾶν, κατὰ Ἰωάννην. Πράξεις ἀποστόλων. Ἐπιστολαὶ καθολικαὶ ἑπτά· οὕτως [*om.* Z.]. Ἰακώβου μία, Πέτρου δύο, Ἰωάννου τρεῖς, Ἰούδα μία. Ἐπιστολαὶ Παύλου δεκατέσσαρες· πρὸς Ῥωμαίους μία, πρὸς Κορινθίους δύο, πρὸς Γαλάτας μία, πρὸς Ἐφεσίους μία, πρὸς Φιλιππησίους μία, πρὸς Κολοσσαεῖς μία, πρὸς Θεσσαλονικεῖς δύο, πρὸς Ἑβραίους μία, πρὸς Τιμόθεον δύο, πρὸς Τίτον μία, πρὸς Φιλήμονα μία.

## NOTE B.

### *Harnack's Theory of the Growth of the New Testament Canon.*

HARNACK'S theory of the growth of the New Testament Canon can be stated, and is sometimes stated by himself, in a way to which exception need not be taken. But it is no less difficult to reconcile the language which he uses on some occasions with that which is used on others than to bring these latter passages into harmony with the facts. Perhaps the best summary of his views with which I am acquainted is that which is given at the end of the tract *Das Neue Testament von das Jahr* 200 ; but it is just here that the opposition between the two sides of his theory comes out most clearly. I proceed to quote what seems to be the central part of this summary, numbering the sentences for convenience of reference.

(1) 'The New Testament in the strict sense of the word is everywhere, wherever it emerges, something sudden; that is, the complete equation of the written word of the Apostles with the written word of

the Lord, the incorporation of the Acts in the Canon, and the conception of the whole collection as the tradition of the Apostolic teaching deposited in written books, forming a complete whole, and placed beyond competition (die in Schriften niedergelegte, abgeschlossene unerreichbare apostolische Lehrtradition) had no previous history in the strict sense of the word, but must be described as a change of interest in the Holy Scriptures, brought about by controversy with Gnosticism and Montanism. (2) But Holy Christian Writings or Scriptures the Church had long possessed (hatte man längst); indeed there was a time when it believed to a large extent that among the Christian writings which it possessed there was nothing which was not holy; because the Church knew that it was holy itself, and it knew also that every word was holy which was spoken or written in the name and to the praise of Christ (Acts xv. 28; 1 Cor. xii. 3; 1 Clem. 63). (3) Besides this there were holy Apostles, prophets and teachers; for the degrees and kinds of holiness were very various, as were the gifts of the Holy Ghost. (4) In the first age there was not much writing; but such writings as there were, were early collected and diffused. (5) So there came to be similar collections in the different district churches, in the greater churches no doubt several of these collections. (6) The dignity of the writings contained in them was, according as one likes to take it, either very great or very small. (7) Very great; because all was holy which preached the name of Christ, especially if it proceeded from Apostles, prophets and teachers: very small; because they did not yet attain to the position either of the Old Testament, the Sacred Volume of highest antiquity, or the Word of the Lord, and every new utterance of the Spirit might interpret or supersede that which had gone before.'

In this passage the sentences numbered 2-5 seem to me to describe very well the real state of the case. Those numbered 6 and 7 (in the second alternative) are an exaggeration; because the prophets of the New Covenant were on precisely the same footing with those of the Old, and the Apostles represented something still higher and more authoritative than the prophets. But the first sentence of all is diametrically opposed to those which follow. It makes a gulf between the spoken word and the written word which certainly did not exist. It assumes a breach of continuity where there is no breach but simply the direct and inevitable

## Note B.

development of conditions present from the first. As the following sentences show, the potentiality of the New Testament was there from the first moment when the Lord and His Apostles began to open their lips in public teaching. There was never any change in the estimate of the value and authority of that teaching. It is true that there were descending grades: but these practically do not affect the question, because (as Harnack says) there was not at first much writing of any sort, and by the Providence of God it is mainly the best which has been preserved to us. When the Church began to reflect and define, it merely gave conscious and deliberate expression to feelings which had been present inarticulately throughout. Of course there was a little oscillation at first, as there could not but be in ascertaining the true sense of a body so widely scattered and so imperfectly organized for such a purpose; but the oscillation did not take long to subside, and the result once obtained remained undisturbed.

The 'sudden change' of which Harnack speaks, and which assumes in his eyes such magnified proportions, is merely the reflexion—I had almost said, mirage—cast by the fact that the date at which it is supposed to take place is practically that at which the bulk of the evidence begins. It seems as if he could not shake himself free from the legal formula, *De non existentibus et non apparentibus eadem est ratio*. But that is not a maxim for history. The historian's duty is to look hard at the facts as soon as they do appear. They will seldom refuse to reveal something of the process which has brought them to the point at which they are, and which connects them with other facts on the further side of the chasm.

## NOTE C.

### *Debateable Points relating to the Alogi.*

I HAVE tried to hold the scales between Harnack and Zahn and to do justice to the elements of truth in the conceptions of both writers.

(1) I think that Harnack is inclined slightly to exaggerate the importance of the party, though he does not see an allusion to it in the Muratorian Fragment. On this point I go rather with Zahn. The Alogi no doubt did make a certain stir in literary circles; but it was only a side eddy in the great movement of opinion.

(2) I agree with Harnack in thinking that it is quite possible that the Alogi had a double front against Gnosticism as well as Montanism: we might add also against Chiliasm. They seem to have been just a few rationalizing Christians who cut away all that seemed to them mystical or extravagant. It was inevitable that this tendency should go further; and therefore I go with Harnack in accepting the statement of Epiphanius that Theodotus of Byzantium sprang out of this circle (*Haer.* liv. 1: ἀπόσπασμα ὑπάρχων ἐκ τῆς προειρημένης ἀλόγου αἱρέσεως).

(3) At the same time I cannot assent to Harnack's conclusion that the attitude of the Alogi is 'sehr verhängnissvoll' for the Fourth Gospel. It is worth just so much as the critical grounds by which it is supported are worth, and no more. It is clear that this handful of primitive rationalists had nothing to trust to but their own arguments. They were not in possession of any real historical tradition adverse to the Johannean authorship of the Gospel. Their attribution of it to Cerinthus was a random guess, thrown out in the heat of personal dislike: it goes so far to confirm the Catholic tradition that it agrees with it both as to time and place.

The views of Zahn respecting the Alogi will be found in *Gesch. d. K.* i. 223-227, 237-262 ; ii. 967-973, 1021 f. Those of Harnack are sharply expressed in *N. T. um* 200, pp. 58-70 ; compare *Dogmengesch.* i. 307, and index.

## NOTE D.

### *The use of the New Testament by Clement of Alexandria.*

As Clement of Alexandria is the writer to whom appeal is usually made by those who maintain the unequal authority of different parts of the New Testament, and of the New Testament as a whole compared with the Old, it may be worth while to test his evidence on the following points: (1) the equality of the two Testaments ; (2) the authority of the Acts; (3) the authority of the Epistles.

(1) It is true, as stated in the text, that there is some ambiguity in the juxtaposition of ἡ παλαιά and ἡ καινή (νέα) διαθήκη : it need not necessarily mean the writings of the two Dispensations. But with Clement of Alexandria this sense seems to lie near at hand. The double phrase seems to mean the body of laws or teaching belonging to the two Dispensations, but usually with the further implication that this body of laws and teaching is accessible in written documents. Sometimes the stress may be on the dispensation in the abstract, sometimes on its written expression.

The following seem to be fairly clear cases: *Strom.* i. 5. § 28, πάντων μὲν γὰρ αἴτιος τῶν καλῶν ὁ Θεός, ἀλλὰ τῶν μὲν κατὰ προηγούμενον ὡς τῆς τε διαθήκης τῆς παλαιᾶς καὶ τῆς νέας, τῶν δὲ κατ' ἐπακολούθημα ὡς τῆς φιλοσοφίας. Here the 'divine library' of the Old and New Testaments is opposed to the philosophical library as an instrument of education.

In *Strom.* iii. 11. § 71 the eighth commandment is ratified in Matt. v. 27 κατὰ τὴν νέαν διαθήκην.

In like manner we have in *Strom.* iii. 18. § 108, written

enactments of the New Testament (ἡ διαθ. ἡ καινή) opposed to written enactments of the Law.

Similarly in *Strom.* v. 1. § 3 we have mention of αἱ ἐντολαὶ αἵ τε κατὰ τὴν παλαιὰν αἵ τε κατὰ τὴν νέαν διαθήκην. And in *Strom.* v. 13. § 85 precepts of the New Testament are placed side by side with those of the Old.

Does this juxtaposition imply equality? Yes, because in several places Clement insists upon the common origin of both dispensations. Thus *Strom.* ii. 6. §§ 28, 29, εἰς ἀμφοῖν ταῖν διαθήκαιν δείκνυται ὁ Θεός ... ἐπειδὴ δύο αὗται ὀνόματι καὶ χρόνῳ καθ' ἡλικίαν καὶ προκοπὴν οἰκονομικῶς δεδομέναι δυνάμει μία οὖσαι, ἡ μὲν παλαιά, ἡ δὲ καινή, διὰ υἱοῦ παρ' ἑνὸς Θεοῦ χορηγοῦνται ... τὴν μίαν τὴν ἐκ προφητείας εἰς εὐαγγέλιον τετελειωμένην δι' ἑνὸς καὶ τοῦ αὐτοῦ κυρίου διδάσκων σωτηρίαν. Compare especially *Strom.* vi. 13. § 106, μία μὲν γὰρ τῷ ὄντι διαθήκη ἡ σωτήριος ἀπὸ καταβολῆς κόσμου εἰς ἡμᾶς διήκουσα κατὰ διαφόρους γενεάς τε καὶ χρόνους διάφορος εἶναι τὴν δόσιν ὑποληφθεῖσα: and *ibid.* 15. § 125, κανὼν δὲ ἐκκλησιαστικὸς ἡ συνῳδία καὶ ἡ συμφωνία νόμου τε καὶ προφητῶν τῇ κατὰ τὴν τοῦ κυρίου παρουσίαν παραδιδομένῃ διαθήκῃ.

If there is any superiority it is on the side of the New Testament and not of the Old. Thus in the extract from *Strom.* ii. 6. § 29 it is implied that the Law was 'perfected' in the Gospel; an idea which is further developed in iv. 21. § 130, ἀλλὰ νομικοῦ μὲν τελείωσις γνωστικὴ εὐαγγελίου πρόσληψις ... ἐν εὐαγγελίῳ δὲ ἤδη προκόπτει ὁ γνωστικὸς οὐ βαθμῷ χρησάμενος τῷ νόμῳ μόνον, συνιεὶς δὲ αὐτὸν καὶ νοήσας ὡς παρέδωκε τοῖς ἀποστόλοις ὁ τὰς διαθήκας δεδωκὼς κύριος. Compare v. 6. § 38, ἄλλως τε ἐχρῆν τῇ κεφαλῇ τῇ κυριακῇ νόμον μὲν καὶ προφήτας ὑποκεῖσθαι κ.τ.λ. Stress is laid upon the fact that while both Testaments proceed from the same Lord, in the Gospels He spoke 'in His own person' (αὐτοπροσώπως *Strom.* iii. 11. § 71).

(2) The fact that Clement insists so strongly as he does on the identical origin of the two Testaments is fatal to Harnack's contention that any part of the New Testament is inferior to the Old. With him the book of the Acts goes along with the Epistles. Both alike give expression to that revelation of which Christ Himself was the author through

## Note D.

the Apostles. The Old Testament and the New make up one single harmony in which the Apostles play a prominent part; λάβοις δ' ἂν καὶ ἄλλως μουσικὴν συμφωνίαν τὴν ἐκκλησιαστικὴν νόμου καὶ προφητῶν ὁμοῦ καὶ ἀποστόλων σὺν καὶ τῷ εὐαγγελίῳ (*Strom.* vi. 11. § 88).

The Acts are as a rule appealed to for plain historical facts, and their authority is as absolutely unquestioned as that of any of the other Historical Books. The book is expressly ascribed to St. Luke (*Strom.* v. 13. § 82). But in one place it is clearly placed on the same footing with the Epistles; and from the way in which it is quoted in this passage the reader may conclude what kind of estimate Clement formed of it: ὁ γὰρ ἀπόστολος ' πάντα ' φησὶ ' τὰ ἄλλα ὠνεῖσθε ἐκ μακέλλου μηδὲν ἀνακρίνοντες,' καθ' ὑπεξαίρεσιν τῶν δηλουμένων κατὰ τὴν ἐπιστολὴν τὴν καθολικὴν· τῶν ἀποστόλων ἁπάντων, ' σὺν τῇ εὐδοκίᾳ τοῦ ἁγίου πνεύματος ' τῇ γεγραμμένῃ μὲν ἐν ταῖς Πράξεσι τῶν ἀποστόλων, διακομισθείσῃ δὲ εἰς τοὺς πιστοὺς δι' αὐτοῦ διακονοῦντος τοῦ Παύλου. ἐμήνυσαν γὰρ ' ἐπάναγκες ἀπέχεσθαι δεῖν εἰδωλοθύτων ' κ.τ.λ. (*Strom.* iv. 15. § 97).

(3) Both the Acts and Epistles are quoted with the ordinary formulae for the citation of Scripture (γέγραπται, ἡ γραφή). Christ as the Divine *Paedagogus* or Tutor speaks through different organs, at one time through Moses, at another through the Apostles (*Paedag.* iii. 12. § 94). Accordingly Clement uses the highest language of reverence of the Apostles. They are more many-sided in their gifts than the Prophets: ἀλλ' ἕκαστος ἴδιον ἔχει χάρισμα ἀπὸ Θεοῦ, ὁ μὲν οὕτως, ὁ δὲ οὕτως, οἱ ἀπόστολοι δὲ ἐν πᾶσι πεπληρωμένοι (*Strom.* iv. 21. § 133). St. Paul is ὁ ἅγιος ἀπόστολος τοῦ κυρίου (*Protrept.* 8. § 81); ὁ θεῖος ἀπόστολος (*Strom.* iv. 16. § 101; 21. § 132); ὁ μακάριος ἀπόστολος (*Protrept.* 9. § 83; *Paedag.* ii. 10. § 98; *Strom.* i. 10. § 49) or ὁ μακάριος Παῦλος (*Paedag.* i. 5. § 19; 6. § 23). In like manner St. Peter is ὁ μακάριος Πέτρος (*Paedag.* ii. 12. § 127); ὁ θαυμάσιος Πέτρος (*Strom.* iii. 11. § 75); in both cases with quotations from his Epistle. St. James, St. Peter, St. John and St. Paul, are grouped together as possessed of the true γνῶσις (*Strom.* vi. 8. § 68).

We seldom read many pages of Clement without coming across quotations from the Epistles, often in thick clusters, and with such formulae as φησὶν ὁ ἀπόστολος, ὁ ἀπόστολος λέγει, παραγγέλλει, βοᾷ, ἀξιοῖ κ.τ.λ. There is really no difference whatever in the way in which the Epistles are appealed to and that in which appeal is made to other parts of the Bible. In a number of places they are expressly equated with other books. Thus with the Gospel and the Prophets, *Strom.* v. 5. § 31, δύο ὁδοὺς ὑποτιθεμένου τοῦ εὐαγγελίου καὶ τῶν ἀποστόλων ὁμοίως τοῖς προφήταις ἅπασι (cf. *Strom.* vi. 11. § 88, quoted above); with the Prophets, προφήτας γὰρ ἅμα καὶ δικαίους εἶναι τοὺς ἀποστόλους λέγοντες εὖ ἂν εἴποιμεν ' ἑνὸς καὶ τοῦ αὐτοῦ ἐνεργοῦντος' διὰ πάντων ἁγίου πνεύματος (*Strom.* v. 6. § 38); with the Gospels, τὸν Χριστὸν σοφίαν φαμέν ... ὡς αὐτὸς κατὰ τὴν παρουσίαν τοὺς ἁγίους ἐδίδαξεν ἀποστόλους (*Strom.* vi. 7. § 61).

Harnack makes two strange statements respecting Clement, one in the text and the other in a note of his *Dogmengeschichte* (i. 321 ed. 2), 'bereits die paulinischen Briefe sind ihm nicht in derselben Weise Instanz wie die Evv., obschon er sie gelegentlich als γραφαί bezeichnet'; and, 'sehr interessant ist auch, dass Clemens den parabolischen Charakter der h. Schriften fast nirgendwo an der Briefliteratur darthut, sondern an dem A. T. und dem Ev., wie er auch Stellen aus anderen Schriften fast niemals allegorisirt hat.'

We have seen in what sense Clement does assign a certain superiority to the Gospels, as any of us moderns might do, because the Lord there speaks in person. But he quotes, and not only quotes but expounds, the Epistles with all the full authority of Scripture, not once or twice but *hundreds* of times. And he in principle evidently feels himself just as free to allegorize the Epistles as any other part either of the New Testament or of the Old.

If we are to take Harnack's words quite literally, it is true that the allegorizing of the Epistles does not occur frequently; for the simple reason that the Epistles lend themselves more naturally to direct application, both on points of doctrine and of practice, than to allegorizing. But there are instances

## Note D.

enough to show that Clement had not the slightest hesitation to apply them allegorically in principle. Clear examples may be seen in *Paedag.* i. 6. §§ 33-47 (a long and very characteristic passage on ὅτε ἤμην νήπιος and γάλα ὑμᾶς ἐπότισα); *Strom.* i. 11. § 53; iii. 12. §§ 80, 84; iv. 16. § 100: v. 4. §§ 26, 61, 62; 12. § 80. In several of these places he says expressly that St. Paul is allegorizing: ὅτε ἤμην νήπιος ... τὴν κατὰ νόμον ἀγωγὴν αἰνίττεται—ὁ λόγος ἀλληγορούμενος γάλα—ἀλλὰ καὶ τὸ 'ἐπότισα' ῥῆμα τελείας μεταλήψεως σύμβολόν ἐστι—ὦ θαύματος μυστικοῦ—εἰκότως ἀλληγορῶν ὁ Παῦλος καὶ γάλα αὐτὸν ὀνομάζων 'ἐπότισα' ἐπιφέρει — πάλιν τε αὖ περὶ τοῦ νόμου διαλεγόμενος ἀλληγορίᾳ χρώμενος 'ἡ γὰρ ὕπανδρος γυνὴ' φησὶ 'τῷ ζῶντι ἀνδρὶ δέδεται νόμῳ' καὶ τὰ ἑξῆς—'ἁγίου δὲ ὄντος τοῦ νόμου' ἅγιος ὁ γάμος· τὸ μυστήριον τοίνυν τοῦτο εἰς τὸν Χριστὸν καὶ τὴν ἐκκλησίαν ἄγει ὁ ἀπόστολος—τὴν γνωστικὴν οἰκοδομὴν ... αἰνισσόμενός φησιν. Not only does Clement interpret the Epistles allegorically, but he bases upon them the practice of allegorical interpretation (*Strom.* v. 4. §§ 25, 26).

So entirely without foundation is Harnack's statement, and so conclusive is the proof that Clement ascribed to the Epistles (he treats St. Peter in the same way as St. Paul) the highest property of a Sacred Book, that of being interpreted as allegory. It is in vain to attempt to draw any real distinction between the use of the New Testament by Clement of Alexandria and the great writers who were his contemporaries and successors. He is distinguished from them only (i) in the higher value which he assigns to the wisdom of the Greeks, drawn, as he maintained, from Hebrew sources; and (ii) by the uncritical way in which he accepted as Apostolic whatever came to him with the name of an Apostle.

# LECTURE II.

### THE HISTORIC CANON.
### ESTIMATE OF THE OLD TESTAMENT IN THE FIRST CENTURY OF THE CHRISTIAN ERA.

'What advantage then hath the Jew? Or what is the profit of circumcision? Much every way: first of all, that they were entrusted with the oracles of God.'—*Rom.* iii. 1, 2.

WE are engaged in the attempt to form a constructive view of the growth of the Bible as an Inspired or Sacred Book; and as a preliminary to this, before we venture upon the more difficult problem of origins, we are seeking to map out in broad lines the conception which results when the process is more or less complete, or at least when it emerges from its passage as it were underground into the fuller light of history. In pursuance of this object we have already taken a section, so to speak, of the history of the New Testament at two of its stages. We have now to take, if we can succeed in doing so, a corresponding section of the Old Testament. This part of our subject is really, as has been said, the more critical of the two: because the conception of a Canon, of an inspired volume, was first formed for the Old Testament, and only extended

## The Old Testament in the First Century.

from it to the New. The Books of the New Testament acquired canonical value when they came to be placed on the same footing with those of the Old. It was not that any new attributes were ascribed to them, or that any new idea of Canonicity had to be constructed. The idea was already there, complete in all its parts. The only step required was that the Books of the New Testament—at first some, then all—should be brought under it. And they were so brought under it the moment that the literature of the New Covenant came to be treated as on an equality with that of the Elder Covenant, when the writings of the Apostles and their followers took rank beside the Law and the Prophets and the Psalms.

We approach then to-day this most important question: What was the estimate formed by the Jews and by the early Christians of the Old Testament? How far had they our present idea of Canonicity? What particular connotation did they attach to that idea?

In dealing with the New Testament we selected the two periods 200 and 400 A.D. In dealing with the Old Testament we cannot draw so definite a line. We shall do well to take not a year but a century. About the end of the first century after Christ a sort of formal decision seems to have been given by the Jewish doctors assembled at Jamnia on the Canonicity of certain books; and the same century saw three important groups of writings in all of which this idea is to a greater or less extent presupposed—

## II. The Old Testament in the First Century.

the works of Philo, the New Testament, and the works of Josephus[1]. From these three groups it is not difficult to understand how the Scriptures of the Old Testament were regarded in three typical sections of the Jewish people.

It should be premised that in collecting data from the New Testament I reserve for the present the deeper teaching of our Lord and the Apostles, and rather aim at giving those particulars in which the writers share the beliefs of their countrymen.

I. We may resolve the complex idea of Canonicity into the same sort of elements as those which we followed in the last lecture. In the first place we note that the special sacredness attaching to the Scriptures was expressed in their titles. It is characteristic of Philo that while he accumulates expressions which denote inspiration, he lays stress rather on the inspired person than on the inspired book. He uses the phrase 'sacred scriptures' (ἱεραὶ γραφαί), 'sacred books' (ἱεραὶ βίβλοι), 'the sacred word' (ὁ ἱερὸς λόγος), 'oracle' (λόγιον, χρησμοί)[2], &c.; but far more often he

[1] It may be convenient to remember that the works of Philo were probably nearly all composed before his embassy to Rome in 40 A.D.; that the earliest extant New Testament writing (1 Thess.) dates from about 52 A.D., and the *Antiquities* and *Cont. Apion.* of Josephus (which alone are important for our purpose) about or soon after 93–94 A.D.

[2] A number of these expressions are collected by Eichhorn, *Einleitung in d. A. T.* i. 129. It is important to note that a Historical Book, 1 Sam. i. 11, is quoted as ὁ ἱερὸς λόγος (*De Ebriet.* 36, Mangey, i. 379; cf. *De Conf. Ling.* 28, Mang. i. 427, τῶν ἐν βασιλικαῖς βίβλοις ἱεροφαντηθέντων, of the Book of Ezra).

refers directly to the writer, and that frequently with some qualifying phrase which brings out the fact that his words are inspired, that he is speaking in a rapt or ecstatic condition as the mouthpiece of God.

Philo rarely uses the particular name with which we are so familiar in the New Testament, 'scripture,' 'the scriptures,' 'holy scriptures' (ἡ γραφή, often in the sense of a particular passage of Scripture, αἱ γραφαί, ἅγιαι γραφαί [1]). Besides these we have in the New Testament ἱερὰ γράμματα [2], 'sacred writings,' and twice the word λόγια [3], 'oracles of God,' and 'living oracles' (i. e. almost 'life-giving,' animated by the Spirit). In Josephus we get 'sacred books' (ἱεραὶ βίβλοι [4], ἱερὰ βιβλία [5]), 'sacred writings' (ἱερὰ γράμματα [6]), 'books of sacred scriptures' (ἱερῶν γραφῶν βίβλοι [7]). Similar designations are found in the Talmud [8].

It is common to all these titles that they indicate a Divine origin. And this is a point which may be illustrated with overwhelming abundance. There can be no doubt that it was a rooted idea among the Jews of the first century, both Hellenistic and Palestinian,

[1] Rom. i. 2.     [2] 2 Tim. iii. 15.
[3] Rom. iii. 2; Acts vii. 38.
[4] *Ant. prooem.* 4; ii. 16. 5; iii. 5. 2; iv. 8. 48; ix. 2. 2; x. 4. 2, &c.; *B. J.* ii. 8. 12; iii. 8. 3, &c.
[5] *Vit.* 75.     [6] *Ant.* x. 10. 4; *B. J.* vi. 5. 4; *c. Ap.* i. 10.
[7] *c. Ap.* ii. 4. The references to Josephus are given by Gerlach, *Die Weissagungen d. A. T. in d. Schrift. d. Flav. Joseph.*, Berlin, 1863. The views both of Philo and Josephus are also fully discussed in a recent monograph by M. Dienstfertig, *Die Prophetologie in d. Religionsphilosophie d. ersten nachchristlichen Jahrhunderts*, Breslau, 1892.
[8] They are collected by Ryle, *Canon*, p. 292.

that the Scriptures of the Old Testament came from God. Philo expresses this in the most uncompromising manner. In quoting a verse from Jeremiah he says in so many words that it was uttered by 'the Father of All through the mouth of the prophet[1].' In Philo's conception of it the recipient of inspiration is passive, and the Divine Spirit speaks through him. 'For a prophet,' he says, 'gives forth nothing at all of his own but acts as interpreter at the prompting of another in all his utterances, and as long as he is under inspiration he is in ignorance, his reason departing from its place and yielding up the citadel of his soul, when the Divine Spirit enters into it and dwells in it and strikes at the mechanism of his voice sounding through it to the clear declaration of that which He prophesieth[2].' The saying in Gen. xv. 12, that 'about the setting of the sun a trance came' upon Abraham, is typical of this process. The sun is the light of human reason, which sets and gives place to the Spirit of God. 'So long then as our mind shines and stirs about us, pouring as it were noontide brightness into every corner of the soul, we are masters of ourselves and are not possessed; but when it draws to its setting, then it is natural that the trance of inspiration should fall upon us, seizing upon us with a sort of frenzy. For when the divine light begins to shine, the human sets; and when it sets below the horizon, the other appears above it and rises. This is what constantly happens to the prophet. The mind in us

---

[1] *De Profug.* 36 (Mangey, i. 575).
[2] *De Special. Legg.* iv. 8 (Mangey, ii. 343).

## Properties ascribed to the Old Testament. 75

is expelled at the arrival of the Divine Spirit and returns again to its home at His removal. For it may not be that mortal dwell with immortal. So the setting of the reason and the darkness that gathers round it generates an ecstasy and heaven-caused madness¹.' In another well-known passage an elaborate distinction is drawn between the different modes of inspiration. The highest is that in which the prophet simply acts as the 'interpreter' of God and in which there is the most complete identification of human and divine. Then comes the method of question and answer, in which the one alternates with the other. And lastly there are the cases in which the prophet speaks in his own person, though still as it seems possessed by the Divine Spirit².

We may observe in regard to Philo that his language bears traces of the syncretism of his whole system. The words of which he is fondest, χρησμός, λόγιον, μανία, ἱεροφάντης, ἱεροφαντεῖν, θεοφόρητος, ἐπιθειάζω, ἐνθουσιᾶν, are characteristic of Greek 'mantic,' and especially of the application of it to philosophy by Plato.

It is through this philosophical use that the terms in question come to him, as he has no respect for the ordinary methods of soothsaying³. In like manner it is from Neopythagoreanism that Philo gets the idea of the mystical vision of God⁴. As com-

---
[1] *Quis rer. div. her.* 53 (Mangey, i. 511).
[2] *Vit. Mos.* iii. 23 (Mangey, ii. 163).
[3] *De Monarch.* i. 9 (Mang. ii. 221).
[4] *De Migr. Abr.* 8, 34, 35 (Mang. i. 442, 466); *De Somn.* i. 19, 26, 32 (i. 638, 645, 649); ii. 38 (i. 692), &c.

pared with Josephus he lays greater stress on the ecstatic state in the recipient of revelation; the soul is wholly possessed and loses self-consciousness. It is also characteristic of Philo to introduce the Logos as the medium of revelation [1]. Josephus is simpler, and keeps closer to the Biblical accounts; he writes as a historian, and not as a speculative philosopher or theologian; but the underlying conception in both writers can hardly be said to differ.

We shall have more to say about the range of Philo's doctrine of inspiration presently.

The Divine origin of the prophetic word comes out especially in the New Testament in the formula 'that which was spoken by the Lord through the prophet' (ὑπὸ τοῦ Κυρίου διὰ τοῦ προφήτου) [2]. The prophet is only the channel for the Divine utterance. There is a certain ambiguity in the places in which λέγει, εἶπεν, φησίν, are used without any subject expressed. It may be God Himself who is speaking; or it may be the Scripture personified; or it may be the writer of the book that is being quoted. But there are not a few places in which this ambiguity is removed by the insertion (expressed or clearly implied) of ὁ Θεός [3].

---

[1] Dienstfertig, *ut sup.* p. 15; Siegfried, *Philo*, p. 228. I may remark that Dienstfertig seems to me to press the difference between Philo and Josephus beyond what it will really bear.

[2] So Matt. i. 22; ii. 15 (*cf.* ii. 5; iii. 3); Acts iv. 25; xxviii. 25 (cp. ii. 16).

[3] So Matt. xv. 4; Acts iii. 25; vii. 2, 3, 6, 7; xiii. 47 (cp. 22); 2 Cor. vi. 16, 17, 18; Heb. i. 5, 6, 7, 8, 13; iii. 7; v. 5, 6; vi. 13, 14; vii. 21; viii. 8; x. 5 (here the Messiah is regarded as speaking), 30; xii. 26; James ii. 11.

## Properties ascribed to the Old Testament. 77

There are other passages where the words of Scripture are directly referred to the Holy Spirit [1].

Josephus uses a number of expressions which imply Divine inspiration. He speaks of 'the Deity (τὸ θεῖον) being present with' a writer; of 'holding converse with God'; of 'being possessed or inspired by God'; of 'being filled with Deity'; of 'being in a state of Divine inspiration'; of 'the Spirit of God taking hold of' the prophet; of 'the Divine gift passing over' from one person to another. Josephus is almost as explicit as Philo in regard to the manner of inspiration. He describes Balaam as prophesying 'not as master of himself but moved to say what he did by the Divine Spirit.' And he makes him say to Balak, 'Thinkest thou that it is in our power to speak or be silent about such things when the Spirit of God takes possession of us? For He causes us to utter words such as He wills and speeches without our knowledge... I prayed that I might not disappoint thy desire. But God is stronger than my resolve to serve thee. For those who fancy (ὑπολαμβάνοντες, Niese) that of themselves they can foretell the fortunes of men are all too weak to help saying what God suggests to them or to resist His Will; for when He has entered into us nothing that is in us is any longer our own [2].'

---

[1] Matt. xxii. 43 (=Mark xii. 36); Acts xxviii. 25; Heb. x. 15.

[2] *Ant.* iv. 6. 5. Dienstfertig (*ut sup.* p. 25), after Lewinski, *Beiträge z. Kenntnis d. religionsphilos. Anschauungen d. Flav. Joseph.*, p. 35, denies that this description applies to the prophet, because Balaam is called μάντις ἄριστος and not προφήτης; but this seems to me to be pressing the particular word used too far. There is the same want of strict consistency in Josephus as in the Bible.

It is clear that in this Josephus is only paraphrasing and expanding the Biblical account[1]. But the same idea runs through his whole conception of prophecy. At the head of all the prophets is Moses, who had none like him, 'so that in whatever he said one might imagine that one heard God Himself speaking[2].' Even historical narratives, such as those at the beginning of the Pentateuch (τὰ ἀνωτάτω καὶ παλαιότατα), which were not written down by contemporary prophets, were obtained by direct inspiration from God (κατὰ τὴν ἐπίπνοιαν τὴν ἀπὸ τοῦ Θεοῦ)[3]. The predictions of the prophets were absolute truth to which the subsequent history of the nation would be found to correspond[4].

The Jewish doctors had precisely the same view as to the Divine origin of the Scriptures. They expressed it by a decision at which we are told that the schools of Hillel and Shammai arrived in concert during the decade before the destruction of Jerusalem, that the Sacred Books 'defile the hands,' i. e. that any one touching them incurred ceremonial uncleanness and had to undergo the rites of purification; the object being to prevent profane or irreverent use of the rolls on which they were written. It was equally forbidden to quote verses of Scripture lightly or profanely. And the superstitious employment of sentences from the

[1] The same sort of comment is found in Philo, *Vit. Mos.* i. 49 (Mang. ii. 124). The angel which met Balaam on the way will supply the words which he is to speak. The prophet is wholly passive, a mere channel through which they pass.

[2] *Ant.* iv. 8. 49.

[3] *Contra Apion.* i. 8.

[4] *Ant.* x. 2. 2 (cp. 5. 1, 11. 7).

## Properties ascribed to the Old Testament. 79

Bible as charms and amulets points to a similar estimate of them [1].

It followed from all this, and indeed it is a fact that needs no proof, that by the first century of our era the normative value of the Old Testament was thoroughly established. That is the ground of the appeals 'it is said,' 'it is written,' which are so frequent in the New Testament and the Talmud [2]. Josephus says that the Jews from their very birth regard their Scriptures as the 'decrees of God' (Θεοῦ δόγματα), which they strictly observe, and for which if need be they are ready to die [3]. But the most decisive proof of the authoritative character which the Jewish writers of this century attached to the Old Testament is to be seen in the use of it for purposes of allegory. The use of allegory implies a sacred text. Philo regards the scriptural text as sacred. He tells a story of one who was punished with an ignominious death for scoffing at what might seem to be trivial details in Scripture [4]. He himself held fast to the literal meaning of the text, though allowing that the literal sense was often only given out of condescension to human weakness [5]. But behind this literal sense he thinks himself justified in looking for another deeper sense, which with him usually took the form

[1] Weber, *Altsynagogale Theologie*, p. 82; also *inf.* p. 111.
[2] The use of these expressions in the New Testament is elaborately analysed by McCalman Turpie, *The New Testament View of the Old*, London, 1872. For the Talmud see especially Surenhusius, Βίβλος Καταλλαγῆς, Amsterdam, 1713.
[3] *Contra Apion.* i. 8.     [4] *De Mutat. Nom.* 8.
[5] *De Somn.* i. 40.

of philosophical abstractions. These of course are derived from his study of the Greeks. But the results are one thing, the method is another. And although Philo had a fully developed allegorical method ready to his hand, it would be a mistake to regard this as wholly Greek. He used the Stoic rules, but he was also very largely influenced by that Haggadic exegesis which had its origin in Palestine[1]. Of the same exegesis we have traces in the New Testament, as (*e.g.*) where St. Paul argues from the use of the singular 'seed' instead of the plural 'seeds.' It is a moot point how far the parallels which are found in the New Testament to the teaching of Philo are due to like influences acting upon both, and how far to the direct use of his writings. But the rarefied intellectualism by which they are characterized is so alien from the whole spirit of the New Testament, that if the former hypothesis is not to be adopted entirely, the exceptions are far more probably indirect than direct. It is hard to think that any of the Apostles had read Philo; it is more possible that words and phrases or even particular applications of the Old Testament due to Philo may have reached them through such agencies as that of Apollos.

The Rabbinical exegesis is older than both Philo and the New Testament. Scanty as are the materials for the century before our era, the beginnings of it

---

[1] Siegfried, *Philo v. Alexandria*, p. 165. Philo's acquaintance with the Palestinian Halachah is also amply proved by Ritter, *Philo u. die Halacha*, Leipzig, 1879.

## Properties ascribed to the Old Testament.

can be traced far back within its limits. Hillel was made president of the Sanhedrin by Herod about 30 B.C.[1] He belonged by birth to the Dispersion in Babylonia; but according to a well-authenticated tradition, he was moved to leave his home and journey to Palestine in order to ascertain if his interpretation of certain passages in the Law agreed with that which obtained there. On his arrival he found the study of the Scriptures actively prosecuted by Shemaiah and Abtalion; and he attached himself to them as a pupil. His own great rival at a later date was Shammai; but the points which they debated seem to us so small and so much matter of detail as to show that on all the larger and more fundamental questions which precede the application of exegesis there was substantial agreement between them. Hillel put forth seven rules for interpretation, which acquired great celebrity[2]; but these rules contained little that was new in principle or that did more than formulate the practice existing at the time[3]. But all this proves not only that the authority of Scripture was absolute, but that it was the subject of an elaborate exegetical tradition quite by the middle of

---

[1] So Edersheim, *Life and Times*, &c., i. 129; Hamburger (*Real-Encycl. f. Bibel u. Talmud, s. v.*) makes Hillel's residence in Palestine extend from B.C. 70 to A.D. 10; but the chronology of his life seems somewhat vague and untrustworthy. Bacher, *Die Agada der Tannaiten*, i. 5.

[2] These rules are given by Schürer, *Neutest. Zeitgesch.* ii. 275; they were afterwards expanded to thirteen by Ishmael ben Elisha at the end of the first century A.D. (Bacher, *ut sup.*, i. 240 ff.).

[3] Strack in Herzog's *Real-Encyklopädie*, vi. 115.

G

the first century B.C., or at least a century before St. Paul wrote his first extant Epistle.

Nor must it be supposed that this tradition related only to the Law. It can be abundantly illustrated for the other books from the time of Hillel onwards. And, what might be thought somewhat strange, the disputed books seem to be used quite as freely as the rest. The sayings of Hillel which have been preserved are not numerous, but in one of them he appeals to, and in another he expounds, passages of Ecclesiastes [1]. Johanan ben Zakkai, who saw the destruction of the Temple and founded the School at Jamnia, interprets the same book allegorically [2]. It is quoted as authoritative by his somewhat younger contemporary, Joshua ben Hananiah, who interprets it differently from his opponent Eliezer ben Hyrkanos [3]. Ishmael ben Elisha seems to have applied his rules to it [4]. A still longer list may be made for the Song of Songs, both as quoted authoritatively and interpreted allegorically, before the end of the first century [5]. And there are several instances of a like use of Esther [6].

One common feature which runs through all the first century writers is their uncompromising view of Prophecy. Between prophecy and its fulfilment there is a necessary connexion. The correspondence between them is exact. Together they form part of

---

[1] Bacher, *ut sup.*, i. 8, 10.  [2] *Ibid.* i. 39 (cf. 45).
[3] *Ibid.* i. 139, 156.  [4] *Ibid.* i. 249 (cf. 258, 263).
[5] *Ibid.* i. 46, 51, 57, 99, 115, 156, 201, 263, 318.
[6] *Ibid.* i. 95, 157, 201, 318.

that predetermined order in which the one being given the other inevitably follows. The classical expression for this is the New Testament phrase, especially characteristic of St. Matthew but found also twice in St. John, '[such and such a thing came to pass, or is come to pass], in order that the word spoken by the Lord through the prophet might be fulfilled[1]' (ἵνα ... πληρωθῇ, ὅπως πληρωθῇ). As if the prophecy cried out for its fulfilment and demanded it at the hand of God[2]. In one place in the Epistle to the Galatians (iii. 8) the Scripture itself is regarded as endowed with foresight, so that the promise made to Abraham is a 'Gospel' by anticipation (προϊδοῦσα ἡ γραφὴ ... προευηγγελίσατο)[3]. This is parallel to the saying in St. John, 'Your father Abraham rejoiced to see My day, and he saw it and was glad' (John viii. 56). The simple indication of the fulfilment of prophecy is of course extremely common.

[1] Matt. i. 22, ii. 15, 23, viii. 17, xiii. 35, xxi. 4, xxvii. 35; John xii. 38, xix. 36. Compare Surenhusius, p. 2 ff.

[2] A notable passage for the correspondence between prophecy and its fulfilment as seen by Christian eyes is an extract from the *Predicatio Petri* quoted by Clement of Alexandria, *Strom.* 6. 15. § 128: ἡμεῖς δὲ ἀναπτύξαντες τὰς βίβλους ἃς εἴχομεν τῶν προφητῶν, ἃ μὲν διὰ παραβολῶν, ἃ δὲ δι' αἰνιγμάτων, ἃ δὲ αὐθεντικῶς καὶ αὐτολεξεὶ τὸν Χριστὸν Ἰησοῦν ὀνομαζόντων, εὕρομεν καὶ τὴν παρουσίαν αὐτοῦ καὶ τὸν θάνατον καὶ τὸν σταυρὸν καὶ τὰς λοιπὰς κολάσεις πάσας ὅσας ἐποίησαν αὐτῷ οἱ Ἰουδαῖοι, καὶ τὴν ἔγερσιν καὶ τὴν εἰς οὐρανοὺς ἀνάληψιν πρὸ τοῦ Ἱεροσόλυμα κτισθῆναι, καθὼς ἐγέγραπτο. ταῦτα πάντα ἃ ἔδει αὐτὸν παθεῖν καὶ μετ' αὐτὸν ἃ ἔσται. For other passages expressing the early Christian views of the inspiration of the Old Testament, see especially Westcott, *Introduction to the Study of the Gospels*, Appendix B.

[3] It is clearly this which suggested the passages in Irenaeus and Tertullian quoted in the last lecture, p. 34 f. *Cf.* Surenhus. p. 6.

The nature of Philo's system and the object of his writings do not so much lead him to call attention to the literal fulfilment of prophecy, but his words doubtless imply such fulfilment. He uses, as we have seen, the strongest language in regard to inspiration. He makes Jeremiah speak 'in the person of God Himself[1]' (ἐκ προσώπου τοῦ Θεοῦ). And he paints the Messianic time in terms which show that he is drawing upon the prophetic descriptions (*e.g.* in Isa. vi. 13; Dan. vii. 13, 14)[2].

The purpose of Josephus is more historical, and accordingly we find him often pointing out the fulfilment of prophecy. It is the special business of the prophet to foretell the future[3]. The prophets of Israel discharged this duty, and their predictions were verified by the event. Thus Nahum foretold the destruction of Nineveh, which came to pass after a hundred and fifteen years[4]. Hezekiah learnt all that was about to happen accurately from Isaiah[5]. So marvellously true were the prophecies of Isaiah and so confident was he that he had said nothing false that he wrote them all down in a book in order that posterity might compare them with the event. Nor did he stand alone in this, but twelve other prophets did the same. And everything bad or good that happened to the Jews was all in accordance with their prophecies[6]. Jeremiah foretold

---

[1] *De Cherub.* 14 (Mang. i. 148).
[2] Edersheim in *Dict. Chr. Biog.* iv. 385.
[3] See the passages collected by Gerlach, *Weissagungen*, &c., p. 26.
[4] *Ant.* ix. 11. 3.   [5] *Ibid.* 13. 3.   [6] *Ibid.* x. 2. 2.

alike the Babylonian captivity and the catastrophe under Titus[1]. There is a lengthy panegyric upon Daniel, whose books show that he held converse with God, and who had this distinction among his fellow-prophets, that whereas they foretold what would happen in the future, he gave the exact time when they would happen; and whereas they foretold evil and so drew upon themselves the hatred of kings and people, he was a prophet of good things, and with his cheering predictions not only won credence by their accomplishment, but was held by the people to be truly divine. His writings stand to this day as proof of 'the undeviating accuracy of his prophecy[2]' (τὸ τῆς προφητείας αὐτοῦ ἀκριβὲς καὶ ἀπαράλλακτον).

Some of the reasoning and expressions used by these writers are noticeable as signifying in different ways the minute perfection of the Scriptures. Philo's whole method of exegesis involves a conception of inspiration which is nothing short of verbal. He lays down broadly that there is 'nothing superfluous' (περιττὸν ὄνομα οὐδὲν τίθησιν) in the Law[3]. Little words that are seemingly unnecessary, and indeed just because they seem unnecessary, all have their deeper meaning; the repetition of the name when God calls to Abraham (Gen. xxii. 11), such Hebraisms as 'let him die the death,' 'blessing I will bless.' A profound philosophy lies hid in such phrases as 'brought him out' (ἐξήγαγεν αὐτὸν ἔξω) applied to Abraham. The ἔξω denotes the

---

[1] *Ant.* x. 5. 1.      [2] *Ibid.* 11. 7.
[3] *De Prof.* 10 (Mang. i. 554).

outermost place of all, *i. e.* freedom from the trammels of the body; 'parted down the middle' (μέσα διεῖλεν) of the victims of Abraham's sacrifice has reference to the two halves into which the λόγος τομεύς divides all things; when it is said 'thou shalt not plant thyself a vineyard,' 'thyself,' just because it seems superfluous, contains a special warning against pride—it is God who plants and not man. The smallest and most subsidiary parts of speech, particles, adverbs, prepositions, acquire on this method exaggerated importance and receive elaborately expanded meanings [1].

What makes Philo's treatment of the text which lay before him the more remarkable is that his interpretations are based not upon the Hebrew original but upon the Septuagint version. He lays down that while most men know little of the true nature of things and therefore give them faulty and defective names, Moses made use of words which are the most exact and expressive possible[2]. Philo is constantly enlarging upon this perfection of language, and deducing the most elaborate inferences from it: but the strange thing is that he bases these inferences on the properties of the Greek and not of the Hebrew. The fact was that he regarded the Greek translation as itself a product of divine inspiration as much as the original. He is the first to add to the story of Aristeas—which made the Seventy translators produce a harmonious text by comparing their versions together—

---

[1] Philo's methods are abundantly illustrated in Siegfried, *Philo v. Alexandria*, pp. 168–196.

[2] *De Agricult.* 1 (Mang. i. 300).

the further touch that this harmony was obtained, not by comparison of results, but by supernatural aid: the translators, according to him, were inspired prophets who 'did not produce one one rendering and another another, but all the same words and expressions as though some invisible prompter were at the ear of each of them[1].'

The Rabbis do not interpret the Old Testament quite in the same manner as Philo, but their interpretations are just as minute and verbal. They too seem to attach an equal importance to every word in a sentence, even the smallest particles. And their whole exegesis is based on the assumption that the text must be taken strictly as it stands. It would be wrong to say that there was no attempt to get at the spirit beneath the letter, but there can be no doubt that what we should think a narrow and unhappy literalism greatly preponderated.

It is just here that the New Testament is so superior alike to Philo and to the Talmud. The New Testament does not indeed escape Rabbinical methods[2], but even where these are most prominent they seem to affect the form far more than the substance. And through the temporary and local form the writer constantly penetrates to the very heart of the Old Testament teaching[3]. I hope to return to

[1] *Vit. Mos.* ii. 7 (Mang. ii. 140).
[2] For an excellent discussion of three of the most conspicuous instances of this, see an article by Dr. Driver in the *Expositor* for 1889, i. 15 ff.
[3] Conspicuous examples would be St. Paul's treatment of the subject of faith, and the call of the Gentiles.

this subject at a later stage in our inquiry; for the present it will be enough to note that, although in a broader and deeper sense than any which we have met with hitherto, there are yet a few expressions scattered over the New Testament which do seem to attribute to the Scriptures of the Older Covenant, not only authority in matters of faith and life, but a kind of ultimate and inviolable perfection.

Such would be the great saying in St. Matthew's Gospel, 'Verily I say unto you, Till heaven and earth pass away, one jot or one tittle (an iota or a letter-tip) shall in no wise pass away from the Law till all things be accomplished' (St. Matt. v. 18). And again (St. John x. 35), 'The scripture cannot be broken' (λυθῆναι, 'undone,' 'treated as if it were invalid'), where we must note also even in passing the further ambiguity whether 'the scripture' means the whole body of Scripture collectively or whether it means the particular passage of Scripture: a distinction however which may seem more important than it is. For even if we take the narrower view and restrict the saying to the particular passage, it would hardly be applied to that unless it represented a general principle which might be applied to other passages as well. Something similar may be said of a like ambiguity in the famous passage which is the only one in which a direct equivalent for our word 'inspired' occurs in the Bible. Even if we do not say 'Every scripture is inspired of God,' but 'Every scripture inspired of God is also profitable, for teaching, for reproof,' &c. (2 Tim. iii. 16), we should be obliged to interpret the words

## Properties ascribed to the Old Testament.

by the current conception of what Scriptures were so inspired, and we should find that it included all, or very nearly all, those which form our present Old Testament.

Lastly, when the Second Epistle which bears the name of St. Peter affirms that 'no prophecy of Scripture is of private interpretation,' and adds that 'no prophecy ever came by the will of man, but holy men spake from God, being moved by the Holy Ghost' (2 Pet. i. 20, 21), the judgment in question certainly covers the prophetic writings, and perhaps others not strictly prophetic into which a prophetic element enters; but it would hardly go beyond these.

The language of Josephus is more explicit. He expressly denies that there is any discord or discrepancy in the Hebrew Scriptures, and he claims for them in this an advantage over all other books[1]. He also appeals to it as proof of the attachment of the Jews to their Bible that in all the long lapse of time 'no one has ever dared to add or subtract or alter anything in it[2].' And in the Preface to his *Antiquities* the same writer (after contrasting the lawgiver of Israel with those of other nations who refer to the gods the sins of men, whereas he conceives of God as pure and unmixed goodness in which men must use all their efforts to share) goes on to assert that those who inquire into it will find that in His law 'there is

---

[1] *Contra Apion.* i. 8 : μήτε τινὸς ἐν τοῖς γραφομένοις ἐνούσης διαφωνίας . . . οὐ μυριάδες βιβλίων εἰσὶ παρ' ἡμῖν ἀσυμφώνων καὶ μαχομένων.

[2] *Ibid.* : τοσούτου γὰρ αἰῶνος ἤδη παρῳχηκότος οὔτε προσθεῖναί τις οὐδὲν οὔτε ἀφελεῖν αὐτῶν οὔτε μεταθεῖναι τετόλμηκεν.

nothing whatever that is unreasonable (ἄλογον) or unbecoming the majesty and goodness of God[1].'

We may conclude these quotations with a sort of chorus of the leading Rabbis of the end of the first and beginning of the second centuries in praise of the inexhaustible riches of the Law. 'R. Elieser said: "If all the seas were ink, and all the reeds were pens, and heaven and earth were rolls, and all men were scribes, they would not suffice to write the Torah which I have taught (*i.e.* what I have taught out of the Torah) and have made it no smaller, as little as a man makes the sea poorer who dips the tip of his brush in it." R. Joshua said: "If all the seas were ink, and all the reeds pens, and heaven and earth were cloth (tent-cloth which was sometimes used for writing), they would not suffice to write the words of Torah which I have taught (*i.e.* the knowledge which I have drawn from the Torah), and I have made it no poorer." R. Akiba said: "I cannot tell how much my teachers have said, but they have made the Torah no poorer, neither have I myself; as little as a man makes the apple of Paradise poorer by smelling at it; he has the enjoyment thereof and the apple is no poorer; as little as one makes less the stream from which he fills his pitcher, or the lamp at which he lights his own[2]."'

[1] *Ant. prooem.* 4.
[2] Weber, *Altsynagogale Theologie*, p. 84 f. The particular kind of hyperbole which runs through this passage seems to have been frequently applied in other connexions: see examples in Bacher, *Agada d. Tann.* i. 28 n.

## Canon of the Old Testament.

II. But now the question arises—and it is a question to which the answer is not quite so simple as those of which we have hitherto been treating—What are the Scriptures to which all this high inspiration and authority are attributed? Was there a fixed and determinate number of books which possessed these properties to the exclusion of all others?

The Canonical Books of the Old Testament were of course by no means the only religious books which were in circulation among the Jews of Palestine and of the Dispersion in the first century. Besides them there were the books which are now classed together in our larger Bibles as the Apocrypha. And besides the books which are more commonly printed under this title, there were others, like the Psalms of Solomon, the Book of Enoch, the Book of Jubilees or Little Genesis, the Assumption of Moses, composed in part before the Christian era and in part before the Fall of Jerusalem in 70 A.D., or composed soon after that event, like the Fourth Book of Ezra and the Apocalypse of Baruch. All these books—not to speak of others which were more probably of Christian origin—were more or less on the lines of corresponding works in the Canonical collection. To what extent were they separated from these? And if separated, on what principle was the separation made, and how was it maintained?

It is often said that two Canons were current, a larger Canon especially at Alexandria and among the Jews of the Dispersion, and a smaller Canon in

Palestine. And there is thus much truth in the statement that many of these Apocryphal Books were included in the Alexandrian translation, and so gained currency, especially in Christian circles; that the early Christian writers of Alexandria were much given to the use of Apocryphal Books, and that the greatest of them, Origen, deliberately defended that use in his famous controversy with Julius Africanus about the additions to Daniel. It is true also, on the other hand, that the restricted Canon was in the first instance the work of the Jewish doctors [1], and that so far as it maintained itself in the Christian Church it did so through the disposition which was shown by some of the most learned and influential of the Fathers to go back to the Jewish tradition, the *Hebraica veritas*, which the Reformed Churches afterwards took as their standard [2].

And yet there are considerable qualifications to be made on both sides. The great majority of these

---

[1] Lagarde (*Mittheil.* iv. 345) has the curious and I believe quite untenable idea, that the Jewish Canon arose among the *Diaspora* out of the desire to demonstrate the antiquity of the Jewish literature (as in Joseph. *c. Apion.*). He thinks that the Palestinian Canon may be a correction or modification of the Hellenistic. See on the other side König, *Einleitung*, p. 449.

[2] The chain of writers who maintain what is substantially the Jewish as distinct from the Alexandrian Canon includes Melito of Sardis, Origen (in theory if not in practice), Athanasius, Cyril of Jerusalem, Amphilochius and Gregory Nazianzen, Rufinus of Aquileia, and most emphatically and clearly, Jerome. On this branch of the history, see especially Westcott, *The Bible in the Church*; Buhl, *Kanon*, p. 49 ff.; Wildeboer, *Het Ontstaan*, &c., p. 66 ff.

## Contents of the Old Testament. 93

Apocryphal Books were composed not in Egypt but in Palestine; and the extent of their circulation both amongst Jews and Christians seems to have been determined not by any geographical boundaries so much as by the difference between popular and learned opinion. With the Jews learning was more exclusively concentrated upon the Scriptures; and with the Jews also the deference paid to the opinions of the learned was more complete; so that when we add to this the greater centralization and more effective authority of the schools of Jamnia and Tiberias, we are not surprised that the Rabbinical tradition presents greater unity and continuity than the corresponding tradition amongst Christians.

The two writers from whom we have been especially quoting both illustrate the real nature of the opposition. Philo's ideas of inspiration are very wide. The centre and type of all inspiration with him is the Law of Moses. He does indeed, as we have seen, use exceedingly strong expressions in regard to the prophets, but he is fond of describing both prophets and psalmists as 'followers or disciples of Moses' (Μωϋσέως γνώριμοι, φοιτηταί, θιασῶται), as if their inspiration was referred to their connexion with him. We have seen that Philo extended his theory of inspiration to the Septuagint translators. Nor does he stop there. He speaks in terms of the utmost reverence of the Greek philosophers. Plato is the 'most sacred' (ἱερώτατος), Heraclitus the 'great and renowned,' Parmenides, Empedocles, Zeno, and Cleanthes, 'godlike men, and as it were a true and in the strict sense sacred band[1].' But with Philo all good men are inspired[2]. Indeed, he claims to have had moments of inspiration himself[3]. And yet in spite of this very comprehensive theory Philo never quotes as authoritative any but the Canonical Books; it is clear that he attributes to them an authority which is really unique in its kind[4].

Josephus in like manner makes some use of Apocryphal materials in the course of his history, but he is quite explicit in laying down a list of twenty-two Books, five of the Law, thirteen Prophets, and four containing hymns to God and patterns of life for men, which really correspond to our own Canon. He assigns a reason for this of which we shall have more to say presently.

In regard to the New Testament the case stands thus. The great mass of authoritative teaching is all derived from the Canonical Books. But there are some instances in which it is clear that the writer has been influenced by Apocryphal texts[5]. There are also a few quotations which cannot be exactly identified in the Books of our present Canon,

---

[1] Passages in Schürer, *Gesch. d. Jüd. Volkes*, ii. 868.

[2] *Quis rer. div. her.* 52 (Mang. i. 510).

[3] *De Cherub.* 9 (Mang. i. 143); *De Migr. Abraami*, 7 (Mang. i. 441); also Dienstfertig, *ut sup.*, p. 17.

[4] *Cf.* Drummond, *Philo Judaeus*, i. 15.

[5] The books of which most use has been made in this way are Wisdom and Ecclesiasticus: see especially, for St. Paul an essay by Grafe in *Theol. Abhandlungen Carl von Weizsäcker gewidmet* (Freiburg i. B., 1892), p. 253 ff.; and for St. James, Dr. J. B. Mayor's commentary, p. lxxiii. ff.

## Contents of the Old Testament.

and in regard to which there are ancient statements referring them to lost Apocrypha or Pseudepigrapha. Lastly, in the Epistle of St. Jude there is an express quotation from the Book of Enoch, which is treated as if it were the genuine work of the patriarch. The first group of facts is of no more importance than that St. Paul should quote as he does from Aratus or Epimenides[1]. The instances which come under the second have all some element of doubt about them[2]. But the quotation from the Book of Enoch is quite unequivocal and it definitely prevents us from saying that no Apocryphal Book is recognised by a Canonical writer. In this, as in so many other things, it is impossible to draw a hard and fast line, though in any case the use of the Apocrypha bears a very small proportion to that of the Old Testament, and in respect to spiritual authority enters into no sort of competition with it.

What we see in the first century is thus a considerable body of literature of a quasi-prophetic character, or at least written with a view to edification, springing up most thickly in Palestine, but circulating also in the principal centres of Hellenistic Judaism, everywhere treated with a certain respect, and most of it enjoying an extended popularity, which no doubt in many cases encroached upon the authority of the Canon. But we see also at the same time, that in proportion as we rise in the

---
[1] Acts xvii. 28; Tit. i. 12.
[2] These instances are discussed by Ryle, *Canon*, p. 154 f., and in a different sense by Wildeboer, *Het Ontstaan*, &c., pp. 44-47.

scale of spiritual intelligence and insight, and in proportion as there is a deliberate intention to decide what is authoritative and what is not, there is an increasing tendency to draw a line round the books of our present Canon and to mark them off from all others.

It must have been really before the latter half of the first century that this Canon was formed. We have seen that the twenty-two Books of Josephus were neither more nor less than the Old Testament of our own Bible. We count there thirty-nine books; but the difference is due to the fact that Books which we count separately were combined together in a single volume. The Twelve Minor Prophets were so combined; also what are with us the two Books of Samuel, Kings, and Chronicles, form each one volume, as do Ezra and Nehemiah, Judges and Ruth, Jeremiah and Lamentations. The way in which Josephus speaks of this collection shows that it was not any new thing, but already well established in his day. And the discussions which seem to have gone on in the Rabbinical School at Jamnia about the end of the century also imply a completed Canon. Or rather we ought perhaps to say a Canon completed provisionally but not as yet definitively. For the discussions turn not so much on the question whether certain books ought to be admitted into a collection then being formed, as whether they had been rightly admitted into a collection already existing[1]. After the beginning of the second century

---

[1] Ryle, p. 171 f.; Buhl, *Kan. u. Text*, p. 25 f. That the disputed books were treated by the leading Rabbis of the first century as

## Contents of the Old Testament. 97

a few sporadic doubts appear here and there, but they never made serious impression. There was just a small section of books the position of which was less secure than the rest, but that was all. The different books were on a rather different footing [1]. The doubts about the Book of Jonah only find expression in late works. Those as to Ezekiel came to a head at a particular date, and were solved by an individual doctor, Hananiah the son of Hezekiah, a contemporary of St. Paul. Those in regard to the Book of Proverbs were probably dismissed quite early. The hesitation as to Ecclesiastes and the Song of Songs was more persistent: these books evidently formed the subject of continued discussion in the school at Jamnia. On the Song of Songs, R. Akiba seems to have pronounced the decisive word. 'God forbid,' he said, 'that any man of Israel should deny that the Song of Songs defileth the hands (*i.e.* is canonical [2]); for the whole world is not equal to the day on which the Song of Songs was given to Israel. For all the Scriptures are holy, but the Song of Songs is the holiest of the holy; and if there is dispute, it is groundless except in the case of Koheleth [3].' The dispute as to Koheleth and Esther lasted longest. That as to Esther went on into Christian times and

---

Canonical will have been seen from the references given above, p. 82. It is said however that while the School of Hillel affirmed, that of Shammai denied, the Canonicity of Ecclesiastes (Buhl, p. 23). See also below, p. 107.

[1] For the following see Ryle, p. 192 f.; Buhl, pp. 28-31.
[2] See p. 111 below.     [3] Ryle, p. 199.

extended to a number of Christian writers. It is not surprising that Christian theologians should have hesitated to incorporate this book into their Bible, but they finally acquiesced in its presence through the deference paid to Jewish tradition.

We have confined ourselves so far to the evidence of the first century A.D. And we are not concerned at present to speculate as to origins. The whole question of origins we leave for investigation in subsequent lectures. We may however ask whether there are no finger-posts to point the way back behind the Christian era. There are such finger-posts, of which recent works on the Canon have made ample use. The starting-point here is the Jewish tradition as to the divisions of the Canon and the order of the Books. The main outlines of this tradition can be traced back as far as the first notice which has come down to us of anything like a Canon, viz. the prologue to Ecclesiasticus, written after, but probably not very long after, the year 132 B.C. That prologue contains repeated reference to a collection of writings consisting of 'the Law, the Prophets,' and certain 'other books,' which the language used implies lay, not only before the author of the prologue, but also before his grandfather, the author of the Hebrew original, now known to us in its Greek form and under its Greek title Ecclesiasticus. Its translator, the younger Jesus son of Sirach, says of the elder that 'when he had much given himself to the reading of the Law and the Prophets and the other books of their fathers, and had gotten therein good judgment, he was drawn on also

## The Jewish Tradition.

himself to write something pertaining to learning and wisdom.' The inference is a little less clear that the books so closely studied by the grandfather were already known to him under the same three divisions [1]. But, the fact that the books are described under these divisions three times over in the compass of a small page, and without anything to suggest that the idea of the three divisions is a novelty, would seem to show that it had been sometime established, and therefore would go back to a time hardly short of that of the grandfather, or in other words we may say to a date not later than the decade 170–160 B.C.

A piece of evidence, disputed but on the whole probable, is supplied by the treatise *De Vita Contemplativa* which passes for Philo's. Here in § 3 (Mangey, ii. 475) there is a reference to 'laws, oracles delivered by prophets, and hymns.' Of recent years the genuineness of this treatise has been much questioned, but since the monograph of Massebieau the tide of opinion seems to have turned in its favour [2].

The next trace of the threefold division would be in St. Luke's narrative of the Walk to Emmaus (St. Luke xxiv. 44), where reference is made to 'the Law, the Prophets and the Psalms' as prophesying

[1] Dr. Cheyne thinks that this was the case. 'Sirach ... had "the Law and the Prophets, and the rest of the books," the latter collection being a kind of appendix, still open to additions' (*Job and Solomon*, p. 185).

[2] Differently Wildeboer, p. 32 f. Massebieau's treatise is entitled, *Le traité de la Vie Contemplative et la question des Thérapeutes*, Paris, 1888.

of Christ. Then would come Josephus, who gives the number of the books—five of the Law, thirteen of the Prophets (including the Historical Books), and four of Hymns and practical teaching, making a total of twenty-two.

This assignment does not exactly agree with that of the Hebrew tradition[1], which we have in full in the Talmudic treatise *Baba Bathra*, confirmed substantially by Jerome's *Prologus Galeatus*[2]. Josephus mixes the Jewish with the Greek tradition, borrowing the three-fold division from the one, the number of the books and the order (or absence of order) from the other. In the Alexandrian Version there was no really traditional order, but the books were usually classed together roughly according to subject.

In the Hebrew tradition too there is what at first sight appears to be a rough classification of subjects. This however is not systematically carried out; and the deviations from it are significant.

The three divisions are called the Law, the Prophets, and the *Kethubim* (*i.e.* 'Writings') or *Hagiographa*. The Law is homogeneous. The Prophets are also homogeneous; the Historical Books coming first under the name of the Former Prophets, and then the Prophets strictly so called, or the Latter Prophets. But why is it that Daniel is not classed among the Prophets? and why is not Chronicles classed as history?

---

[1] This gives five books of Law, eight Prophets, and eleven *Kethubim* or *Hagiographa*; in all 24.

[2] The preface to his version of the Books of Kings: cp. also the preface to Daniel.

## The Jewish Tradition.

For some time it has been seen what is the answer to these questions. The truth undoubtedly is that the threefold division represents three successive layers or stages in the history of the Collection. The Books of the Law were collected first; the Prophets and Histories second; and the reason why the Book of Daniel was not included among the one and the Books of Chronicles among the other was simply that at the date when the second collection was made they had not been composed, or at least were not currently accepted in the same sense as the other books [1].

Here there is clearly a gleam of light thrown over the history of the Canon. The results obtained through it have recently been called in question, but only in support of an arbitrary theory which sacrifices good reasons to bad ones [2]. The phenomena really fit in well together. And there is now a large amount of consent among scholars that the Canon of the Law was practically [3] complete at the time of the promulgation of the Pentateuch by Ezra and Nehemiah in the year 444 B.C., and that of the Prophets in the course of the third century B.C.[4] As to the closing of the

---

[1] The Books of Chronicles were probably composed but not accepted.

[2] Duhm, *Jesaia* (Göttingen, 1892), p. vi. Lagarde, who casts some doubts upon the integrity of the Book of Daniel, yet treats Dan. ix. 2 as written under Antiochus Epiphanes and as implying a collection of Prophetic Writings (*Mittheil.* iv. 344).

[3] Cornill, Kuenen, and others assume a certain limited amount of redaction after this date. Cornill would make the process complete by about 400 B.C.

[4] Cornill places the completion of this portion of the Canon about

## II. The Old Testament in the First Century.

Canon of the third group, the *Kethubim*, there is perhaps more room for difference of opinion. A common view is that the distinct recognition of these books as Scripture would be not later than 100 B.C. Many data seem to make this at least a *terminus ad quem*. The Book of Daniel is presupposed in a part of the *Sibylline Oracles* (iii. 396–400) which there seem to be good grounds for dating about the year 140[1], and in the First Book of Maccabees (i. 54, ii. 59, 60) which falls in the early years of the next century. Ecclesiastes is quoted with the formula 'it is written' in a Talmudic story of a conversation between Simon ben Shetach and Alexander Jannaeus[2] (B.C. 105–79). The Psalms, Proverbs, Job, and Chronicles were current in the Greek version, which had already a long history behind it in the time of Philo and the New Testament[3]. And all these books are quoted as authoritative in recorded sayings of the

250 B.C. (p. 102), Wildeboer about 200, which however is characterized by Buhl (p. 12) as 'entschieden zu spat.'

[1] Schürer, *Gesch. d. Jüd. Volk.* ii. 794–799.

[2] Ryle, *Canon*, p. 138 f.

[3] Perhaps at once the most conspicuous and the most interesting example of this is the rendering of Ps. xl. 6. The Hebrew has here literally 'ears hast thou digged' (i.e. probably 'opened,' though some understand 'pierced') 'for me': the LXX followed by Heb. x. 5 has σῶμα δὲ κατηρτίσω μοι. The most probable explanation of this is that the original rendering was ὠτία, which became corrupted into σῶμα through the duplication of the final ς of the preceding word ἠθέλησας (ΗΘΕΛΗϹΑϹΩΤΙΑ—ΗΘΕΛΗϹΑϹϹΩΜΑ). As this change must have taken place before the archetype of all the extant MSS. of the LXX (the four minuscules in which ὠτία is found probably derive it from Aquila or Symmachus) as well as Ep. to Hebrews, it is thrown back to a very remote antiquity.

## The Jewish Tradition. 103

Rabbis from Hillel onwards, with some traces of a difference of opinion as to Ecclesiastes [1].

The significant part in the Jewish tradition is the assignment of books to the three groups, not their arrangement within the groups. The internal order appears to be due to reflexion partly critical and partly suggested by the subject-matter. We must of course beware of assuming that the reasons assigned by the later Rabbis were those which determined the original authors of the collection. Thus it is hardly likely that the true reason is given for the sequence of the Major Prophets, among whom Jeremiah and Ezekiel are placed before Isaiah. The Talmudic tract accounts for this by saying that the Books of Kings end with desolation, that Jeremiah is all desolation, that Ezekiel begins with desolation and ends with consolation, and that Isaiah is all consolation, so that desolation is fitly joined to desolation and consolation to consolation; an idea which is not without its pathos and beauty, but which belongs rather to the time when the harps were hung up and the Rabbis were occupied with the wistful retrospect of their past history, than to the simpler motives at work when the books were first collected. That the place assigned to Isaiah has been affected by the incorporation of the last twenty-seven chapters, which are really later than Jeremiah and Ezekiel, would be a welcome supposition if it were probable, but it appears more likely that Jeremiah was placed next to the later chapters of

[1] *Supra*, p. 97.

2 Kings, with which his book is so closely connected, and Isaiah ' immediately before his contemporary Hosea[1]. The order of the Minor Prophets probably does aim at being chronological. But here too the chronology is rather such as might be arrived at by a not very recondite criticism than handed down from the time when the books were composed.

It is however a fact of real importance that the Jews should have preserved the memory of the steps by which the Canon was formed. It was not preserved everywhere. The Alexandrian translators and those who followed them seem to have arranged the books simply by their subject-matter. And the varied classifications proposed at a later date by Christian Fathers[2] (such for instance as the four Pentateuchs with two supernumerary books in one of the lists of Epiphanius) are all of the nature of learned afterthoughts. But the central line of Jewish tradition as handed down by the Palestinian Rabbis does seem to retain a slender thread of genuine historical reminiscence. It is true that the oldest Rabbinical treatise which touches upon the subject of the Canon, the *Baba Bathra*, contains a number of statements about the authorship of the books which are absurd enough. But these it is clear are no traditions in the strict sense, but only guesses which have grown up round the tradition, and which have no better warrant than

---

[1] So Buhl, p. 38; cf. Ryle, p. 227 f.; Kirkpatrick, *Theol. of Proph.* p. 360, n.

[2] See the tables in *Studia Biblica*, iii. 227–232, and in Ryle, *Canon*, Excursus C.

## Separation of Apocryphal and Canonical.

that which belongs to Rabbinical criticism of the second or third centuries.

III. We have spoken so far freely of Apocryphal and Canonical Books, using the words in their later sense to denote a certain class of writings; but in approaching the third section of our subject, the means by which these two classes were discriminated from each other, we have first to ask what was meant by the word 'Apocryphal,' not as we might conceive it used by the first framers of the Canon whose motives we can only reach by conjecture, with which we have not as yet to do, but in the first century of our era when the Canon begins to have a sufficient history. The Greek ἀπόκρυφος is a translation of a late Hebrew or Aramaic word meaning 'hidden,' 'withdrawn from publicity.' It had at first a much milder signification than that which we attach to it. In a literal sense it was used of the rolls which were put away because they were worn out or because of faults in the writing. In a more metaphorical sense it meant that a book was not suitable for public reading. It implied in itself nothing more than this, no suspicion as to authorship, no doubts as to doctrine. There could not well be a better commentary upon this use than is contained in the famous letter of Origen to Africanus in defence of the story of Susanna. Africanus had criticized this as not contained in the Hebrew Canon. Origen replies that the Jews had done all in their power to withdraw from the knowledge of the laity facts which seemed to cast an imputation on their elders and rulers, 'some of which,' he adds, 'are preserved in apocryphal books.' In like manner the sawing asunder of the prophet Isaiah alluded to in the Epistle to the Hebrews was not to be found in any of 'the public books' (τῶν φανερῶν βιβλίων) but occurred in one of the Apocrypha, and the account referred to by our Lord of the murder of Zacharias the son of Barachias was not in any of the books of the Old Testament, having been excluded from them because it too cast a stain upon the judges of Israel. The Apocryphal Books thus spoken of might clearly have every other claim to respect although they were not accounted fit for public reading[1].

There was however another sense of the word 'apocryphal,' branching off from that just mentioned. The ramification is well marked in the familiar passage (xiv. 44–46) at the end of the Fourth Book of Ezra. After the destruction of the ancient Scriptures Ezra and his five companions by means of a special inspiration write out ninety-four books in forty days. Of these ninety-four, twenty-four are the Canonical Books which he is bidden to publish openly that worthy and unworthy alike may read in them, but the remaining seventy are to be kept secret and put into the hands only of the wise. This is a fiction intended to explain the reservation till so late a date

---

[1] See especially Zahn, *Gesch. d. Neutestl. Kanons*, i. 123 ff.; Wildeboer, p. 79 f. König argues against the equivalence of the Greek and Hebrew terms (*Einleitung*, p. 467 f.); he would make Origen's use more nearly in accord with that of other Fathers.

## Separation of Apocryphal and Canonical. 107

of the Fourth Book of Ezra itself, but the larger number is evidently chosen to cover other works of a like nature which had been or might be published. There were in circulation not a few such Apocalypses put forward under ancient names (Enoch, Moses, Baruch) and needing the same excuse. But these were not the only works to claim an esoteric character. The Apocalypses in question do not seem to have been treated as esoteric; they were in fact popular among the early Christians. But the Gnostic leaders put forth similar claims for their own productions. These were really formidable enemies. And so the idea of 'esoteric' became almost synonymous with 'heretical.' It was thus that 'apocryphal' acquired the bad connotation with which it is found from Irenaeus and Tertullian onwards [1].

The double sense of the word is imprinted strongly upon the history of the Old Testament Canon. The discussions of which records have come down to us from the Jewish schools have for the most part to do with the question what works were to be considered 'apocryphal' in the milder sense of 'withdrawn from public use in the synagogue.' They deal with books which had already obtained a certain amount of recognition and which it was not sought to deprive of that recognition entirely [2]. The criticisms directed against them

---

[1] *Cf.* Holtzmann, *Einleitung in d. N. T.* p. 146, ed. 3.

[2] This seems to be a truer description of the question at issue than that which is given either by Buhl or Wildeboer. According to Buhl (p. 25 f.) the controversies in the Jewish schools imply the existence of a Canon, and arose out of attempts to eject ('excanonisiren')

are not of that root and branch character. If the Book of Ezekiel was questioned it was because it presented certain difficulties when compared with the Law. A famous doctor of the first half of the first century, Hananiah the son of Hezekiah, set himself to solve these difficulties, and with that all opposition to the Book was removed. If there was for a brief moment some hesitation about the Book of Proverbs, it seems to have been because it was thought to give too seductive a picture of vice[1], and so to be unsuited to the young. If there was a longer and better grounded objection to the Book of Ecclesiastes, it was (1) because it was thought to be inconsistent with itself, (2) because it was thought to be inconsistent with the Psalter, and (3) because it contained doubtful doctrine—all natural criticisms, and criticisms which are made on a larger scale to this day. The Song of Songs was probably rescued by the introduction of the Haggadah or Jewish method of allegorizing [2]. It was this which probably led R. Akiba to assign to it

certain books from it. According to Wildeboer (pp. 63–65) they are proof that the Canon itself was not yet formed. Of the two, Buhl seems to be nearer the mark: it is true that the controversies presuppose the existence of a Canon, and true also that in a strict sense the disputed books were in danger of being ejected from it, but only to be placed on the lower grade of books regarded with all respect but not considered to be suitable for public reading: it would by no means follow that they were reduced at once to the level of profane literature. See however Additional Note A: *On the Date of the Formation of the Jewish Canon*.

[1] The principal passage objected to was Prov. vii. 7–20.

[2] Instances of such allegorical interpretation from the earliest period are given by Bacher, *Agad. d. Tann.* i. 57, 115, 201, 263, 318.

## Separation of Apocryphal and Canonical.

so high a value. The same method was applied to the Book of Esther [1], which also made good its place because it was thought to show signs of inspiration, as involving knowledge of things which only inspiration could have revealed (Esth. ii. 22; ix. 10, 15, 16)[2].

It will be observed that all these arguments turn upon the internal evidence of the book itself. That which turns upon the comparison of doubtful with acknowledged books presents the closest analogy to the criteria applied to the case of the New Testament; but the doubts raised were less serious.

Where Christian writers spoke of books as 'apocryphal' in the stronger sense, the Jews spoke of them as being simply 'outside' the Canon. This term is applied to the First Book of Maccabees, the two Wisdoms, and to the writings of Christian and other heretics [3]. There is however this difference; that whereas the latter may not be read at all, a book like Ecclesiasticus may be read as one would read a letter [4].

The only traces of an attempt of any 'outside' books to gain admission to the Jewish Canon are in the case of Ecclesiasticus and 1 Maccabees. The former is twice quoted in the Talmud with the formula usually reserved for the citation of Scripture;

---

[1] Bacher, i. 318.
[2] *Ibid.* i. 397; ii. 49. For further details in regard to these discussions see Ryle, *Canon*, pp. 192–201; Buhl, pp. 28–30; Wildeboer, pp. 55–60.
[3] Ryle, p. 188; *cf.* König, *Einleitung*, p. 466.
[4] R. Akiba, quoted by Buhl, p. 8; Ryle, *ut sup.*

## II. The Old Testament in the First Century.

and there is other evidence that it stood high in honour[1]. But it never attained to Canonical rank; and there is still less proof of such a dignity being assigned to 1 Maccabees. In matters of religion the Jews were a docile people; and the decisions of the scribes and doctors, once definitely given, were not questioned.

When we ask on what positive principle the Old Testament had its lines of demarcation drawn so clearly, direct evidence from the time of the real formation of the Canon fails us. But if we look for the ideas current in the first century of our era, one principle at least stands out prominently. Alike in Philo, Josephus, and the Talmud the central conception appears to be that of Prophecy. We have seen how Philo and Josephus differ in what they understand by this; how Philo's idea is derived largely from the Greek 'mantic,' while that of Josephus is more strictly Jewish and Biblical. But both writers agree in taking a very high view of the degree of Divine possession or inspiration which Prophecy implies. To both Moses is the greatest of the prophets, 'the prophet' of whom the rest are but copies. And both writers regard the gift of prophecy as extending beyond the Canon[2]. Josephus thought that the prophetic gift was imparted to individuals like John Hyrcanus; and Philo, as we have seen, claimed a share of it for himself. Still, Philo makes a tacit distinction, as he appeals only to the Canonical Books as

---

[1] Ryle, p. 184.
[2] Gerlach, *Weissagungen*, &c., p. 36.

## Separation of Apocryphal and Canonical. 111

primary authorities. And Josephus lays down quite explicitly that there was an unbroken line of prophets from Moses to the time of Artaxerxes Longimanus[1] (465-425 B.C.), and that the books written after that date are not deserving of equal credence because the prophetic gift had ceased. The Canon is with him coextensive with the active exercise of prophecy, and it is the prophetic inspiration which gives the books their value. Josephus was doubtless mistaken in supposing that all the books of the Canon could be got within those limits, and that the Historical Books were all composed by contemporary prophets. But his leading idea is an intelligible and a sound one. And the same idea is distinctly enunciated in several Talmudic passages. R. Akiba excludes Ecclesiasticus as having been written 'since the days of the prophets.' The tractate *Seder Olam* lays down that till the time of Alexander the Great the people prophesied through the Holy Spirit, but from that time onwards there were only the 'wise men.' Another tractate says that no book written since the cessation of prophecy 'defiles the hands'[2] —another Talmudical expression reserved for the Canonical Books. And it is in agreement with this view of the nature of inspiration that even the authors of the Hagiographa are called 'prophets[3].' It is

---

[1] *I.e.* to Esther (Buhl, p. 35).

[2] On 'defiling the hands,' see above, p. 78, and for fuller details, Buhl, p. 7; Wildeboer, p. 77 ff.; Ryle, p. 186 f.; Robertson Smith, *O. T. J. C.*, p. 185, ed. 2; Weber, *Altsynagog. Theol.* p. 82; König, *Einleitung*, p. 450 ff., &c.

[3] See the several passages in Buhl, pp. 8, 35, 37.

a satisfaction to find such ample evidence that the Jewish Church in discharging this perhaps the most important of all its functions, should have had consciously in view a principle which is so real and so fruitful.

In Christian times one incidental attempt was made to give an altogether wider scope to the Canon of the Old Testament. Tertullian in arguing for the admission of the Book of Enoch, which he assumes to be the genuine work of the patriarch, urges that it contains prophecies of our Lord, and that Christians ought not to reject whatever really belonged to them. He adds an appeal to the well-known text on inspiration (2 Tim. iii. 16) in the form that 'all scripture which is suitable for edification is divinely inspired[1].' Such a principle as this would have thrown open the doors very wide. But, like so much in Tertullian, it was only an idea struck out in the heat of the moment, and was not pressed further either by himself or by any one else.

The Canon of the Old Testament, like that of the New, was very early associated with the mystical significance of numbers. There were several different ways of reckoning the total of the Books, of which two were older and more important than the rest. The Talmudic tradition gives the number as twenty-four (counting Ruth and Lamentations separately).

---

[1] *De Cult. Fem.* i. 3: *Sed cum Enoch eadem scriptura etiam de Domino praedicarit, a nobis quidem nihil omnino reiciendum est, quod pertineat ad nos. Et legimus omnem scripturam aedificationi habilem divinitus inspirari.*

## Symbolism of Numbers. 113

This is the total in one place mentioned, and in one place adopted, by Jerome[1]. It is mentioned in like manner by Hilary of Poitiers[2] (who makes up the number differently by adding Tobit and Judith), and is adopted by Victorinus of Pettau[3] and in Mommsen's list[4]. There is yet earlier authority for it in 4 Ezra xiv. 45, where the twenty-four books 'first written' are clearly those of the Jewish Canon. Jerome, Victorinus, and the list connect the twenty-four Books with the 'twenty-four elders' of the Apocalypse; Hilary with the twenty-four letters of the Greek alphabet; the Rabbis connect them with the 'twenty-four watches' in the Temple[5].

But there is another numeration, equally or even more ancient, which by combining Ruth with Judges and Lamentations with Jeremiah, makes the total twenty-two. This is found inferentially in Melito of Sardis and Rufinus, expressly in Josephus, Cyril of Jerusalem, Leontius and Nicephorus, and expressly also with the further equation of the twenty-two Books with the twenty-two letters of the Hebrew alphabet in Origen, Athanasius, Gregory Nazianzen, Epiphanius (in one of his lists), Jerome, and Hilary of Poitiers[6]. There can be no doubt that this calculation also is of

---

[1] *Prol. Galeat.* and *Prol. in Ezr.*
[2] *Prol. in Psalm.* 15.
[3] On Apoc. iv. 7–10 (Migne, *Patr. Lat.* v. 324).
[4] *Stud. Bibl.*, iii. 223. As the MS. in which this list is contained has now left this country, it is best to call it after the scholar who first called attention to it.
[5] Fürst, *Kan. d. A. T.* p. 3.
[6] See the tables in *Stud. Bibl.*, iii. 227–232.

I

Jewish origin, as it is not only found in Palestine where Josephus learnt it and Melito went to seek it, but it is clearly adapted to the Jewish Canon and to the Hebrew alphabet. There is reason to think that the reckoning 'twenty-four' came not from Palestine but from Babylonia[1]; and besides the imposing list of authorities for the lower number, its equation with the Hebrew alphabet has every appearance of being older and more original than that with the Temple-watches.

I do not think it has been noticed that behind this number 'twenty-two' there lay in the minds of those who first called attention to it a profound significance. The number 'twenty-two,' more particularly as representing the Hebrew alphabet, played a prominent part in Jewish cosmological speculation. Dr. Edersheim gives the following account of this, based mainly upon the Book *Yetsirah*: 'We distinguish the substance and the form of creation; that which is, and the mode in which it is. . . . In the *Sepher Yetsirah* these Divine realities (the substance) are represented by the ten numerals, and their form by the twenty-two letters which constitute the Hebrew alphabet—language being viewed as the medium of connexion between the spiritual and the material; as the form in which the spiritual appears. At the same time number and language indicate also the arrangement and the mode of creation, and, in general, its boundaries. . . . If the ten *Sephiroth* (i.e. the numbers) give the substance, the twenty-two letters are the form of creation and of revelation. "By giving them form and shape,

[1] Fürst, *Kan. d. A. T.*, p. 4.

and by interchanging them, God has made the soul of everything that has been made, or shall be made." "Upon those letters, also, has the Holy One, Whose Name be praised, founded His holy and glorious Name." These letters are next subdivided, and their application in all the departments of nature is shown. In the unit, creation: [in] the triad, world, time and man are found. Above all these is the Lord[1]." Is it not obvious to see in these speculations as to the alphabet the middle link between cosmological theory and the Canon? And are we not at once reminded of Origen comparing the Four Gospels to the four elements and Irenaeus to the four winds and four quarters of the globe, if not of anticipations of both in the *Shepherd* of Hermas?

One more preliminary question remains to be answered before we embark on our larger inquiry. It is necessary for the inquirer to take up a definite attitude towards the criticism of the Old Testament. What is that attitude to be? What is the attitude which should be taken up by one who is not a specialist and can only claim to have studied the subject from without as conscientiously and as disinterestedly as he can? Such an one, I cannot help thinking, will feel that the case for what is called the critical view of the Old Testament comes to him with great force. In England until quite lately, although we have had critical commentaries and

[1] *Life and Times of Jesus the Messiah*, ii. 692. I venture to correct an evident misprint of punctuation in the last sentence but one.

monographs on portions of the Old Testament, we have not had any complete and connected presentation of the critical theory as a whole. This we now have for the literature in Dr. Driver's well-known *Introduction*[1], and for history and literature combined in the *Hibbert Lectures* for last year—a book which, though quite uncompromising in its criticism, wins upon us, not only by the charm of an attractive style, but by its evident candour and enthusiasm[2]. When we turn from these to the leaders of Continental opinion, Kuenen and Wellhausen, and compare their writings with those which maintain either the traditional view or a view but slightly modified from the traditional, it is impossible to resist the impression that the critical argument is in the stronger hands, and that it is accompanied by a far greater command of the materials. The cause of criticism, if we take the word in a wide sense and do not identify it too closely with any particular theory, is, it is difficult to doubt, the winning cause. Indeed criticism is only the process by which theological knowledge is brought into line with other knowledge; and as such it is inevitable.

[1] It is right to add that besides a long list of works dealing with portions of the Old Testament, Dr. Cheyne also contributed to the *Expositor* for 1892 a brief but connected review of most of the points now in debate (now reprinted in *Founders of Old Testament Criticism*, London, 1893). No divergence of opinion in connexion with this or any other recent work of his can obscure the debt which I owe to my old friend.

[2] My one complaint against the author would be that he follows some of his authorities rather too faithfully; but he is receptive of influences from a standpoint other than his own, and I question whether he will remain quite where he is.

## Critical Presuppositions. 117

And yet I cannot but think that the open-minded inquirer who retains his balance and is not simply carried off his feet by the set of the current, will not be able to avoid a suspicion that there is after all, especially in the way in which the critical case is presented on the Continent, something essentially one-sided. Kuenen wrote in the interest of almost avowed Naturalism [1], and much the same may be said of Wellhausen. But to do so is to come to the Bible with a prejudice, just as much as in the case of those who come to it with the determination to find in it nothing but Supernaturalism. Both alike are apt to force their views upon the Bible instead of being

---

[1] I observe that Mr. Montefiore (*Jewish Quart. Rev.*, Jan. 1893, p. 305) demurs to a similar description of Kuenen's view by Prof. Robertson (*cf.* also Driver, *Introd.* p. 194), on the strength of the opening sentences of the *Religion of Israel*, which do assert the rule of God in the world. It is true that the reservation is made, but it is kept very much indeed in the background. For instance, in regard to the subject before us, Dr. Kuenen expended a whole volume of 593 large octavo pages (*Prophets and Prophecy in Israel*, London, 1877) in proving that the prophets were *not* moved to speak by God, but that their utterances were all their own. The following extract will, I think, do justice to the position which Dr. Kuenen really held: 'We do not allow ourselves to be deprived of God's presence in history. In the fortunes and development of nations, and not least clearly in those of Israel, we see Him, the holy and all-wise Instructor of His human children. But the old *contrasts* must be altogether set aside. So long as we derive a separate part of Israel's religious life directly from God, and allow the supernatural or immediate revelation to intervene in even one single point, so long also our view of the whole continues to be incorrect, and we see ourselves here and there necessitated to do violence to the well-authenticated contents of the historical documents. It is the supposition of a natural development alone which accounts for all the phenomena' (*Prophets and Prophecy*, &c., p. 585).

content to take them from it. And to one fallacy in particular I think we may say that both writers are exposed. It was natural that in pursuing a perfectly unfettered inquiry and correcting one by one the traditional dates of documents and institutions, there should be a tendency to lay too much stress on the first mention of either; with the result of either confusing that first mention with the real origin of the document or institution, or at least allowing far too little for growth and not sufficiently considering what the process of growth involves. This is a direction in which it would seem that the researches of the critical school will bear to be supplemented.

Kuenen and Wellhausen have mapped out, on the whole I believe rightly, the main stages of development in the history of Hebrew literature. The next thing to be done was to determine the corresponding steps in the history of the people and of the religion. But at each step there is an argument backwards as well as forwards. The question at each successive stage is, What does that stage imply? What are its antecedents? How must it have been reached? What an amount of religious preparation is implied (*e.g.*) in the writings of Amos and Hosea! Our own scholars have paid and are paying especial attention to this line of investigation. Foremost among them in this respect is one of the ablest and most independent of our theologians, Dr. A. B. Davidson of Edinburgh. In his steps has followed, perhaps rather more one-sidedly, Professor James Robertson of Glasgow, in

## Critical Presuppositions.

the *Baird Lectures* for 1889[1]; our own Professor of Hebrew in his *Introduction*, and Dr. Robertson Smith, so long a leader in the vanguard of criticism, have shown themselves quite alive to this point of view; and it is significant that just in this point the Hibbert Lecturer is distinguished—and distinguished to his advantage—from the Continental critics who would otherwise be nearest to him. But it can hardly as yet be said either that the balance of critical inquiry has been fully redressed or that the resources of a really scientific method for the study of the Old Testament have been exhausted. The true cure for a one-sided presentation of the facts is not to be sought in less of science but in more, not in laxer methods but in stricter. It remains to be seen how much of the current theories will be endorsed twenty years hence. Some of them I feel sure will have been pronounced impossible.

In such a position of things it has seemed best to start from the critical theories, not as something fixed and absolute, but provisionally and hypothetically. In any case, whether they are true or not, it concerns

---

[1] I have experienced the same difficulty as Mr. Montefiore (*ut sup.* p. 304) in ascertaining what exactly is Prof. Robertson's own critical position. He uses a number of arguments which seem to me good and sound in restriction of current critical theories, but they fall far short of restoring the traditional view in its integrity or with only such slight modifications as are proposed (*e.g.*) by Bp. Ellicott. I gather that Prof. Robertson would go some way further than this, but he does not make it clear how much further. If this represents a real suspense of judgment, I would be the last to find fault with him.

us to know how far a full belief in Divine revelation is compatible with them. We may reasonably say that what they offer to us is a *minimum* which under no circumstances is capable of being reduced much further, and that the future is likely to yield data which are more and not less favourable to conclusions such as those adopted in these lectures. But if or in so far as that expectation should be realized, the argument which we are about to follow would be strengthened, and any confirmation of faith which it may bring would be more assured.

In speaking of critical theories of the Old Testament the layman may wish to be reminded what the crucial points in these are. Two may be described as general and two as particular. The *general* points are (i) the untrustworthy character of Jewish traditions as to authorship unless confirmed by internal evidence; they are not in fact traditions in the strict sense at all, but only inferences and conjectures without historical basis: (ii) the composite character of very many of the books—the Historical Books consisting for the most part of materials more or less ancient set in a frame-work of later editing; some of the Prophetical Books containing as we now have them the work of several distinct authors bound up in a single volume; and books like the Psalms and Proverbs also not being all of a piece but made up of a number of minor collections only brought together by slow degrees. Two *particular* conclusions are of special importance: (i) the presence in the Pentateuch of a considerable element which in its

## Critical Presuppositions.

present shape is held by many to be not earlier than the Captivity[1]; and (ii) the composition of the Book of Deuteronomy not long, or at least not very long, before its promulgation by King Josiah in the year 621, which thus becomes a pivot-date in the history of Hebrew literature[2]. To these positions, thus broadly stated, I must, so far as my present judgment goes, confess my own adhesion[3]. But the working

[1] As to the extent of the document or group of documents there is very general agreement, but the agreement is less complete as to its date. Some writers of weight, Dillmann, Baudissin, Kittel (to whom may be added Buhl, *Kanon u. Text*, p. 8), still incline to place the main portion before the Exile. The substantial difference between the two views is however not very great. Reasonable supporters of the exilic or post-exilic date allow that many of the institutions of the so-called Priest's Code are far older than the Code itself; and on the other hand, those who hold that the document is in the main pre-exilic, regard it as possessing a private and 'ideal' character, confined to a limited circle among the priests and not put into general circulation (see Driver, *Introduction*, p. 134 f.).

[2] It is quite possible to hold this view as to the date of Deuteronomy and yet to give a natural sense to the word 'found' in 2 Kings xxii. 8, and to acquit Hilkiah and those who acted with him of a direct share in the composition of the book as well as in its publication. It is no doubt right to make allowance for the different conceptions of what is honourable current in different ages, but we ought not to widen the gap without a clear necessity and substantial evidence. These seem to me to be wanting for the view which has been put forward by Mr. Montefiore in the *Hibbert Lectures*, pp. 179-181, and Dr. Cheyne in the *Expositor*, 1892, i. 95-99 (*Founders of O. T. Criticism*, pp. 267-272).

[3] With the view of the critical position given above may be compared another formulated with far more trenchant force by a Roman Catholic writer in the *Contemporary Review* for April 1893, p. 473 f. I doubt much whether some of the conclusions adopted by this writer will stand the test of time, but it cannot be denied that they have strong advocates at the present moment.

out of them has not deprived the Old Testament of any of its value. On the contrary, stumbling-blocks have been removed; a far more vivid and more real apprehension of the Old Testament both as history and religion has been obtained; and, as I also hope to be able to show, the old conviction that we have in it a revelation from God to men is not only unimpaired but placed upon firmer foundations.

## NOTE A.

*On the Date of the Formation of the Jewish Canon.*

THE controversies as to the date of the formation of the Jewish Canon seem really to turn upon the ambiguity in the meaning of the word 'Canon' itself. If by 'Canon' we mean the estimate of certain books as sacred and inspired, then we have proof that the Canon of the Old Testament existed from the time of Hillel, Philo and the New Testament, if not from the time of the books of Maccabees and Ecclesiasticus. But if by the Canon we mean that this estimate was formally and authoritatively recognised and that a list of books was drawn up to which the estimate applied, then we cannot say that the Canon of the Old Testament was formed before the transactions at Jamnia at the end of the first and beginning of the second centuries. It is just as in the case of the New Testament; we may say that the Canon begins with the Muratorian Fragment or with the decree of the Council of Laodicea; and even then, whichever view we took, it would be rather arbitrary. The really essential thing both for the Old Testament and the New, is the authority with which the several books were invested. In the many cases where the authorship of the book is known, this authority can be traced up beyond the book itself to the person of the writer; and in other cases where the authorship is not known it came to be attached to the book by analogy. Whenever a book is regarded as sacred, it is so in some sense and degree from the first. As it is the object of these lectures to trace especially this part of the process in question, it will not be necessary to dilate further upon it here.

# LECTURE III.

### THE GENESIS OF THE OLD TESTAMENT.
### THE PROPHETIC AND HISTORICAL BOOKS.

'If I say, I will not make mention of Him, nor speak any more in His name, then there is in mine heart as it were a burning fire shut up in my bones, and I am weary with forbearing, and I cannot contain.'—*Jeremiah* xx. 9.

'The purpose of God according to election.'—*Romans* ix. 11.

AT the back of all belief in Revelation or Inspiration there lies the still larger belief in an active Providence, to which the Hebrews gave a more significant and moving name, 'the living God.' If we think of nature as an aggregate of blind forces, then there is clearly no room for communication of any kind between God and man. But the moment we assume that 'this universal frame is not without a Mind,' the moment we assume a real personal Will at the centre of all the infinite network of causation, the further assumption of some such thing as Revelation and its correlative Inspiration becomes easy, natural, and probable [1].

---

[1] I may quote here the words of one who is more of a philosopher than I am, and I do so the more gladly as they repair an omission of mine by defining the relation of Inspiration to Revelation. 'The idea of a written revelation may be said to be logically involved in the notion of a living God. Speech is natural to spirit; and if God is by

We may treat it, if we will, in the first instance as a hypothesis, but it is one of those hypotheses which group together and explain such large tracts of phenomena that with most of us it holds a place among the established axioms of thought. Believing that there is a God, a Supreme Mind, a Personal Being, endowed in the highest perfection with attributes which we are compelled to conceive of as like our own, we find no difficulty in believing that this great all-ruling central Personality seeks to draw to Itself the multitude of puny personalities which Its Will has called into existence—personalities as it might seem of infinitesimal moment when judged by their place in the material universe, but every one of which acquires a far higher value when we remember that it is made in the image of its Creator, that it is spirit face to face with Spirit, conscious of its affinity and earnestly desiring to realize that affinity so far as it may. There is an upward movement in the mind of man which takes away any surprise that we might feel at an answering condescension on the part of God.

We are prepared then to think that the Epicurean

nature spirit, it will be to Him a matter of nature to reveal Himself. But if He speaks to man, it will be through men; and those who hear best will be those most possessed of God. This possession is termed "inspiration." God inspires, man reveals: inspiration is the process by which God gives; revelation is the mode or form—word, character, or institution—in which man embodies what he has received. The terms, though not equivalent, are co-extensive, the one denoting the process on its inner side, the other on its outer' (Dr. Fairbairn, *Christ in Modern Theology*, p. 496). The context shows that it is as correct to say, 'God reveals'; but it is through man that the revelation takes concrete shape.

notion of gods holding aloof from men is inadequate; we are prepared to find the finger of God traceable in human affairs; and we ask, if so, what is the method of its working?  One feature in that method seems to stand out very clearly.  It is what St. Paul calls 'a purpose or design, according to election (or selection).' That vast Divine plan of which we see 'huge cloudy symbols' as it were projected into the universe takes a more definite shape as our gaze lingers upon it.  We observe in it a progression.  The light broadens as we descend down the ages.  But this broadening light has not been diffused uniformly over all mankind.  It has been concentrated or focussed in particular races, families, and individuals.  Where it has spread in the world at large it has spread as a rule from these smaller centres.  There is an apportionment of parts in the mighty drama.  On the great world-stage different races have different functions.  Functions which are rudimentary or only slightly developed in the one are highly developed in another.  It was not given to the Semitic race to lay the foundations of science.  Its achievements were not great in art or law and political organization.  The branch of it which has left the most enduring monuments of itself in these departments is the Assyrian, not the Hebrew.  But for the Hebrew it was reserved beyond all other peoples to teach the world what it knows of Religion. From that point of view which we have seemed justified in taking we shall say that it was the instrument specially chosen of God for that purpose.  We do not deny a Divine guiding in other races.  Not wholly in the dark did men of other nationality grope after an object of worship and of praise. But it is from the Hebrew stock that we have the Bible, and the Bible is by general consent the highest expression, the most perfect document, of Religion.

Our survey of the ways of God predisposes us to think of the Bible as something more than a purely human product, a collection of idle fancies thrown out towards an irresponsive heaven. But if it is more than this, if it is the record of a real communication from God to man, by what processes has that communication been made? How has the necessary contact between the Spirit of God and the spirit of man been established? What are its extent and limits? These are the questions which we are to set ourselves, so far as our analysis will carry us, to answer. And the first part of our answer will be that at which I have already hinted, that here too there is 'a purpose or design of God according to selection.' Just as one particular branch of one particular stock was chosen to be in a general sense the recipient of a clearer revelation than was vouchsafed to others, so within that branch certain individuals were chosen to have their hearts and minds moved in a manner more penetrating and more effective than their fellows, with the result that their written words convey to us truths about the nature of God and His dealings with man which other writings do not convey with equal fulness, power, and purity. We say that this special moving is due to the action upon those hearts and minds of the Holy Spirit. And we call that action Inspiration.

## III. The Prophetic and Historical Books.

In claiming for the Bible Inspiration we do not exclude the possibility of other lower or more partial degrees of inspiration in other literatures[1]. The Spirit of God has doubtless touched other hearts and other minds (I use the double phrase because in these matters thought and emotion are in close union) in such a way as to give insight into truth, besides those which could claim descent from Abraham. But there is a difference. And perhaps our language would be most safely guarded if we were to say that when and in so far as we speak of the Bible as inspired in a sense in which we do not speak of other books as inspired, we mean precisely so much as is covered by that difference. It may be hard to sum up our definition in a single formula, but we mean it to include all those concrete points in which as a matter of fact the Bible does differ from and does excel all other Sacred Books.

I. I am to speak to-day of a class of Biblical writers in which this difference stands out as prominently as in any, the Prophets. Perhaps I may go a step further. For in truth the prophetic inspiration seems to be a type of all inspiration. It is perhaps the one mode in which the most distinctive features of Biblical Inspiration can be most clearly recognised.

---

[1] I had intended to throw into an Additional Note a summary view of the Sacred Books of non-Christian Religions, but this has been so excellently done by Bp. Westcott in *The Cambridge Companion to the Bible*, pp. 15–21, that I content myself with referring to what he has written.

Not that even the Prophets are a class absolutely by themselves. On the contrary, they are a class to which there was a large amount of external analogy. And we need to consider the analogies before we can properly appreciate the difference. Once again we have to look for the 'purpose of God according to selection.'

Let us begin by taking a section of the history of Israel, for which as it happens our documents are specially clear and vivid, and evidently animated by a fresh and faithful recollection of the events described. The Books of Samuel present us with the picture of an early stage in the development of Prophecy. Let us take it in three of its characteristic manifestations. Let us take first the Prophet under that name; then the Seer; then a side on which Priest and Prophet are rather closely associated. On each of these sides we shall find a state of things which reminds us of the institutions of ethnic religions [1].

We remember the scene in which Saul, seeking for his father's asses, meets the company of prophets coming down from the high place of Gibeah with psaltery and tabret and pipe and harp before them [2]; and how on another occasion—if indeed it is another and tradition has not made two separate incidents out of one [3]—the same Saul, pursuing a nobler prey,

---

[1] Professor Huxley has devoted a large part of a long essay (*Ess. on Controverted Questions*, pp. 132–198) to the discussion of these analogies.

[2] 1 Sam. x. 5, 6, 10–13.

[3] Both stories are told as explaining the origin of the proverb 'Is Saul also among the prophets?'

penetrated into the midst of the school of the prophets at Ramah, and was caught by their enthusiasm and cast off his clothes and prophesied before Samuel, and lay down naked all one day and night [1]. Clearly the exercise of the prophetic gift was often accompanied by strong physical excitement. Music appears to have been sometimes used to produce this excitement. For when Elisha is called in by the allied kings of Israel, Judah and Edom, to save them from the straits of their war with Mesha, he must needs have a minstrel to play before him and so stir up the prophetic inspiration [2].

It is true that these instances mark the furthest limit which is reached in this direction by Hebrew prophecy; and the contrast is far more striking than the resemblance when we pass to the priests of Baal on Mount Carmel cutting themselves with knives and lancets in order to force the god to answer their appeal [3]. Still we must recognise the fact that other races and religions have a prophetic order besides

---

[1] 1 Sam. xix. 23, 24. It does not however appear that such a condition was in any sense characteristic of the prophets. We know that Saul was liable to attacks of madness.

[2] 2 Kings iii. 15.

[3] It is a debated question how far (the lower kinds of) prophecy in Israel can rightly be compared with the fakirs and dervishes of the East: see on the affirmative side Schultz, *Theol. d. A. T.* p. 219 f., 249; Ryle, *Canon*, p. 39; Wellhausen and Stade as quoted by Robertson; and on the negative, Robertson, *Baird Lectures*, p. 87 ff.; König, *Offenbarungsbegriff*, pp. 60–64. König strongly opposes the view of Kuenen and Wellhausen, accepted in part by Montefiore (*Hibbert Lectures*, p. 76 f.), that Hebrew prophecy was of Canaanite origin.

## The Earlier Prophets.

the Hebrew, and that the external phenomena of prophecy, though more violent and undisciplined, were not wholly dissimilar in kind.

If we were to inquire into the mental condition of the prophet in receiving his revelations we should find much the same thing. Dreams are characteristic of the early narratives in the Book of Genesis [1] : their significance is assumed in the Book of Judges (Gideon, and the soldier's dream prognosticating the success of his attack on the Midianites) [2]; and it is in the form of a dream that Samuel receives the warning of the calamities which are to befall the house of Eli [3].

Again, it is assumed that the prophetic revelation is sometimes made through the medium of trance or ecstasy. The typical example of this is Balaam, falling down prostrate [4] with the inrush of the Divine *afflatus*, though having his eyes open [5].

In all these respects we seem to be at the level of the ideas current among ancient peoples generally. This too would be true of the description, so graphic in its details, of Samuel as a Seer—the kind of subject about which he is consulted, the fee or present which

[1] Gen. xx. 3 ff.; xxviii. 12 ff.; xxxvii. 5 ff.; xli. 1 ff.
[2] Judges vii. 13 f.
[3] 1 Sam. iii. 3 ff. At a later date however dreams are regarded as characteristic of false prophets: *cf.* Jer. xxiii. 25; König, *Offenbarungsbegriff*, ii. 10.
[4] Num. xxiv. 4 (*Q. P. B.*). Although Balaam is not strictly a prophet of Jehovah he is in this instance regarded as inspired by Jehovah.
[5] This again is a condition by no means characteristic of the higher prophecy: see König, *Offenbarungsbegriff*, i. 114 f., ii. 48 f.; Montefiore, *Hibbert Lectures*, p. 121.

is usually brought by those who consult him, his answers, and the signs which his questioner is to meet with [1]. In all this we seem to have a still more homely version of the Teiresias or Phineus of Greek legend.

Lastly, we have at the same period a still more elaborate consulting of the oracle associated with the priesthood. The full apparatus of such an oracle appears in the archaic narrative at the end of the Book of Judges of the household of Micah, with his shrine or chapel, his image, his 'ephod'[2] and teraphim, and the Levite to serve them. These things seem to be all taken as matters of course, and the Danites set great store by the possession of them, although it is obtained by theft[3]. In like manner David welcomes Abiathar the priest when he comes to him 'with an ephod in his hand' and makes use of him to inquire as to the dangers which threaten him and the success of his designs[4]. Again, we do not feel that we are on the exalted platform of spiritual religion, but that we are rather moving amongst the naive ideas and usages of a primitive age. The religion of that age is of course not ex-

---

[1] 1 Sam. ix. 6-8, x. 2 ff.

[2] The exact nature of the 'Ephod' is a point still much disputed. Not only Köhler, König and Oehler, but Riehm and Nowack (Oehler, *Theol. d. A. T.* p. 578, ed. 3), take it to be everywhere a part of the priestly dress (as in Ex. xxviii. 6 ff.): on the other hand, Wellhausen (*Gesch. Isr.* pp. 249, 297), Schultz (*Alttest. Theol.* p. 135 n., 'keineswegs unwahrscheinlich'), and Montefiore (*Hibb. Lect.* p. 43) take it to be an image.

[3] Judges xviii. 5, 10-13, xviii. 14-26.

[4] 1 Sam. xxiii. 1-12.

hausted by such ideas and usages. It had its deeper side, of which we shall come to speak later, but for the present we observe that they do exist, and that they form a real link of connexion between the people of revelation and its neighbours and contemporary peoples over a wide extent of the ancient world.

When we follow out the fortunes of the prophets we find them under Samuel, perhaps for the first time [1], congregating in settlements, in which their enthusiasm is fanned by companionship and sympathy. The next occasion where attention is called to these coenobitic communities is some two centuries later, in the time of Elijah and Elisha. It may be true that there are differences in the description of them at the two periods, but it seems wrong to press those differences to the extent of denying their identity. They are sufficiently accounted for by the changes which would come simply with lapse of time. Such an institution would naturally have fluctuations in its history. The communities would die down and revive again. In the time of David and his successors we hear more of individual prophets than of schools of the prophets. Still there are traces even then of prophets as a class and of the fellow-feeling existing between its members [2].

Prophecy was really a profession; and not only through but beyond the days of the Monarchy it was

---

[1] On the probability of this see Schultz, p. 217 f.

[2] 1 Kings xx. 35, 'a certain man of the sons of the prophets' (in the reign of Ahab); cp. the story of the old prophet of Bethel under Jeroboam (1 Kings xiv. 30, 31, &c.).

a profession strongly manned. In the persecution begun by Ahab and Jezebel Obadiah hides no less than 400 prophets in a cave. It is clearly a numerous body whom Ahab consults before he goes out to death. Jeremiah implies a number of prophets both in Jerusalem and among the exiles; and Ezekiel also evidently speaks of them as forming a considerable body [1].

But where there is a professional class there are sure to be professional failings. All members of the order would not be equally sincere. There would be small natures among them as well as large. They would be apt to fall into conventional and unreal ways of speaking. They would be under a great temptation to adapt their prophecies to their own interests and to the wishes of their hearers. Thus the half-hearted prophet sinks a step lower still and becomes the false prophet. He will 'speak smooth things and prophesy deceits,' 'saying, Peace, peace, when there is no peace [2].' Such are 'blind watchmen,' 'dumb dogs,' 'greedy dogs,' 'shepherds that cannot understand [3]'; they have 'seen vanity and lying divination'; they 'daub with untempered mortar [4].'

Will it be thought that in collecting all these particulars I hold a brief against the Prophets and desire to say all I can in their disparagement? God forbid. I only wish to look the facts full in the face, to blink nothing of all that can rightly be said against them, so

---

[1] Ezek. xiii. 2 ff., xxii. 25, 28, &c.
[2] Is. xxx. 10; Jer. vi. 14, &c.
[3] Is. lvi. 10, 11.
[4] Ezek. xiii. 6, 10, &c.

## The Religions of Moab and Israel. 135

that with a clear conscience we may go on to speak of their great and imperishable services, and of the ample proof that they really spake as they were moved by the Holy Ghost. Once more let us think of the 'purpose of God according to selection.' Not all who wore the prophet's mantle were true prophets; not all even of the true prophets always had the fullest insight vouchsafed to them.

But before we finally turn down the page and pass over to the more positive side of our inquiry, let us first take an unique opportunity that is put in our way for forming a comparative estimate of the prophetic religion. One of the most notable discoveries of recent years was that of the so-called 'Moabite stone.' Now this discovery gives us a most unexpected glimpse through an absolutely contemporary document of the religion of a people closely allied to Israel both in its origin and in its civilization. Perhaps the first thing that strikes us about it will be the superficial resemblance of the Moabite religion to that with which we are more familiar. We might almost imagine that we were reading, *mutatis mutandis*, a passage from the Old Testament. It will be remembered that 'Chemosh' is the national god of the Moabites. The inscription runs thus :—

'I am Mesha' son of Chemoshmelek (or Chemoshshillek), King of Moab, the Daibonite. My father reigned over Moab for thirty years, and I reigned after my father. And I made this high place for Chemosh in QRHH, a high place of salvation, because he had saved me from all the kings (?), and because he let me see my pleasure on all them that hated me. Omri was King of Israel, and he afflicted Moab for many days, because Chemosh was angry with his land. And his son succeeded him; and he also said, I will afflict Moab. In my days said he thus; but I saw my pleasure on him, and on his house, and Israel perished with an everlasting destruction. And Omri took possession of the land of Mehedeba, and it (i. e. Israel) dwelt therein, during his days, and half his son's days, forty years; but Chemosh restored it in my days ... And the men of Gad had dwelt in the land of 'Ataroth from of old; and the King of Israel built for himself 'Ataroth. And I fought against the city, and took it. And I slew all the people of the city, a gazingstock unto Chemosh, and unto Moab. And I brought back thence the altar-hearth of Davdoh(?), and I dragged it before Chemosh in Qeriyyoth. ... And Chemosh said unto me, Go, take Nebo against Israel. And I went by night, and fought against it from the break of dawn until noon. And I took it, and slew the whole of it, 7,000 men ... and women and [men-servants?], and maid-servants: for I had devoted it to 'Ashtor-Chemosh. And I took thence the vessels of YAHWEH, and I dragged them before Chemosh,' &c.[1]

There is real piety in this. The king is not strictly monolatrous, for he mentions a compound deity, 'Ashtor-Chemosh,' as well as 'Chemosh.' But his worship is practically concentrated on Chemosh,

---

[1] The translation is taken from Dr. Driver's *Notes on the Hebrew Text of the Books of Samuel*, p. lxxxvii.

## The Religions of Moab and Israel. 137

quite as much we may believe as his opponent Ahab's would be concentrated upon Jehovah. To Chemosh he refers all his own successes and those of his people. It is the anger of Chemosh which caused their subjugation and his favour which gives them victory. The destruction of their enemies is pleasant to him. Chemosh, or the oracle of Chemosh, directs their attack; and the king shows his gratitude by the dedication of offerings which are specially acceptable when they are taken from the sanctuaries of rival gods.

In all this there is at least the foundation of a religious character. We cannot exactly say that the name makes no difference, because the name Jehovah (YAHWEH) had for the Israelite a rich significance of its own. But if we look upon it as merely the symbol for God, the Supreme Power, that is what Chemosh stood for to the Moabite. And even one of the better sort of Israel's kings could not speak in terms of greater loyalty and devotion. It is true that there runs through the inscription a vein of vindictiveness and cruelty; but to that parallels might be found westwards of the Jordan. The doctrine 'Love your enemies' belongs to the New Testament, and only to a few of the most enlightened spirits, like the author of the Book of Jonah and of Isaiah xix. 18-25, in the Old.

When however we come to take in other authorities the curtain is lifted from other sides of Moabite religion which shows what a gulf there was between it and the religion of Israel. We remember a fact recorded in the Book of Kings of this very same Mesha which either falls after the date of the inscription or else is glossed over in it. We remember how when Mesha was hard pressed by the Western Powers he offered up his own son, who should have reigned in his stead, for a burnt-offering upon the wall[1]. It was no doubt a desperate case and the last tremendous sacrifice of a brave man struggling for liberty. But even so it would not have been possible at this time to a worshipper of Jehovah. It is perhaps probable that the blank which is mercifully left in the story of Jephthah's daughter is to be filled up in a similar sense[2]. But Jephthah was a wild bandit chief in a backward region and a lawless age[3]; and in any case all suspicion of human sacrifices in the name of Jehovah had long been left behind. The emphatic prohibitions of the Law and the horror expressed at the act of Ahaz and Manasseh, who made their

---

[1] 2 Kings iii. 27.
[2] This is still contested by Köhler (*Lehrbuch d. Bibl. Gesch. A. T.* ii. 100 ff.) and König (Oehler, *Theol. d. A. T.* p. 576, ed. 3). The main point is that she bewails her virginity (Jud. xi. 37) and not her life: it is argued that if dedicated to the service of Jehovah she could not marry, and that her life might be commuted for a money-payment (Lev. xxvii. 4). But there is an ominous correspondence between Jud. xi. 39 and 34.
[3] The case in regard to human sacrifices is tersely summed up by Baudissin (*Jahve et Moloch*, p. 60 f.): *populus Israelitarum Jehovam colens semper immolationem hominum aversatus est. Solus Jephtha filiam immolavit; sed is trans Jordanem inter idololatras vivens Jehovae cultum cum cultu gentili commiscuit.* Among those who think that there are traces of human sacrifice in the Old Testament is Mr. Montefiore (*Hibb. Lect.* p. 40).

## The Religions of Moab and Israel.

sons to pass through the fire to Molech[1], show in what estimation they were held. Then we turn to the story of Balaam and the scenes in the plains of Moab (Num. xxv. 1–9). The best modern opinion dissociates these from the worship of Baal-Peor[2]. They seem rather to lead on to the idolatry than to be occasioned by it. But there is abundant evidence that like abominations were practised in the name of religion[3].

It is part of the mystery of things that He who made of one blood all the nations of the earth and has nowhere left Himself without witness, more or less clear, should yet permit evil so to blend itself with good even in that which is most sacred. The great problem for the student of religions is why the religion of Israel alone should be so remarkably free from this baser mixture. Why was not the worship of Jehovah like the worship of Baal, or Tammuz, or Cybele, or Astarte, or Mylitta? Why was it not like the worship of a race so nearly akin to Israel as the Moabite? The Christian has a simple answer ready. He seeks it in that which is the subject of these lectures. He believes that there has been a special Divine influence at work, not making out of Israel an altogether new creation under wholly new conditions, but taking the conditions as they were, sifting and straining out of them something purer

---

[1] Lev. xviii. 21, xx. 2; 2 Kings xvi. 3, xxi. 6.
[2] See Baudissin in Herzog, *Real-Encykl.*, ii. 33; Dillmann on Num. xxv. (p. 169).
[3] Hos. iv. 14; Jer. ii. 20; 1 Kings xiv. 24, xv. 12; 2 Kings xxiii. 7.

and higher than they could produce of themselves, guarding the precious growth from contamination, guiding its upward progress, filling it with a vital and expansive power which none can give but God. And if we are asked to define the measure of this special influence, we can see it reflected in that wide margin which remains when the common elements of the Biblical religion and other religions have been subtracted and that which is peculiar to the Bible is left.

There is a 'purpose of God according to selection'; there is an 'election' or 'selection of grace'; and the object of that selection was Israel and those who take their name from Israel's Messiah. If a tower is built in ascending tiers, those who stand upon the lower tiers are yet raised above the ground, and some may be raised higher than others, but the full and unimpeded view is reserved for those who mount upwards to the top. And that is the place destined for us if we will but take it.

We have spoken of the lower levels attained by the seers and professional prophets. From the fact that these classes are upon a lower level, we may be apt to do injustice to them. Samuel told Saul how he might find his asses; but he had a higher vocation in the world than that. A part of his vocation—no small part of it—was to find Saul himself, and so take the first step towards welding the loose collection of tribes into a nation. Another and even more important part lay in the organizing of those 'schools of the prophets' which contained in themselves the germs of such great things to come. Partly through them and partly in his own person Samuel wrought a reformation in the land, the fruit of which was seen under Saul's successor.

In the case of the prophets it is only natural that certain conspicuous figures should stand out and overshadow the rest. We do not know how much of the solid basis of Israel's religion may have been due to unnamed and unknown workers. The great advances no doubt came from the great men, and it was they who really deepened the roots of religious conviction. But at all times there must be disciples to mediate between the leaders and the crowd. It is not enough to propound a great truth: it must be spread abroad, and carried home, and hardened by iteration.

Accordingly we can see that even the lower order of prophets must have had a very useful function. They were a sort of clergy, among whom would be found good members and bad; but yet if the average of Israel's religion was better than the average of their neighbours', it was largely their doing. They interpreted the great prophets to the multitude, and brought them into contact indirectly with many whom they could never have reached directly.

Hence we are not surprised to find that those who are called relatively 'false prophets' are so not because their fundamental ideas are wrong in themselves but because they are wrongly applied[1]. Their

---

[1] I cannot go with König who in the work referred to below (i. 33, &c.) insists upon an absolute opposition between the false prophets and the true. It is surely far nearer the mark to say with Montefiore

fundamental ideas are really right but they are applied in a conventional mechanical way, and it is not seen how they are overruled by some deeper and larger principle newly enunciated. Thus, for instance, when Jeremiah bids the people not to trust 'in lying words, saying, The temple of the Lord, The temple of the Lord, The temple of the Lord, are these[1]' buildings, the splendid pile which Solomon had raised, it was perfectly true that the temple *was* the Lord's and that it was under His protection. And when Micah complains that the prophets divine for money while they profess to 'lean upon the Lord, and say, Is not the Lord among us? no evil can come upon us[2],' it was not to be gainsaid that the Lord was really among them: so far, good: but the inference was a wrong one, that His hand contained no chastisements. Nowhere does the antithesis between the lower and the higher prophecy come out more clearly than on this very point. All this vain confidence is scattered to the winds by that magnificent paradox which is the

(*Hibbert Lectures*, p. 205 f.): 'These prophets were not all of them either vicious or deceitful. Perhaps now-a-days the tendency is to rehabilitate these so-called " false prophets " too easily, for the evidence of Ezekiel and Jeremiah cannot be lightly set aside. But there were clearly wide gradations of character among them, from the hypocritical charlatan to the honest if deluded enthusiast.' God does not act *per saltum* in revelation any more than in nature; lower forms lead up to higher, mixed forms to pure; the special influences at work in these latter do not involve any breach of continuity. This may also be taken as a reply to Kuenen (*Prophets and Prophecy in Israel*), who goes to the opposite extreme of reducing true prophets and false to the same level.

[1] Jer. vii. 4.     [2] Micah iii. 11.

main theme of the prophet Amos: 'You only have I known of all the families of the earth: *therefore* I will punish you for all your iniquities[1].'

The lower prophecy had its function and its place; but by the Providence of God and by the guidance of His Spirit, only the products of the higher prophecy have come down to us in the shape of authoritative writings. Here again there is a 'selection.' If we put aside the Book of Daniel, which is not exactly a prophetic work in the same sense as the rest and which had a different place assigned to it in the Jewish Canon, there can be no mistake as to the remainder of the Books which fill this section of our Bibles. The three so-called Major Prophets and twelve Minor are the central representatives of Israel's religion, the culmination of all religion before the coming of Christ.

It is noteworthy how as we rise in the scale of prophecy one by one the concomitants of the older and lower stages fall away. Ephod and teraphim are consigned to the owls and to the bats. The links which connected prophecy with mantic disappear. Every kind of physical stimulus is discarded. The prophet no longer seeks to work himself up into a state of physical excitement in order to court revelation. The revelation comes to him whether he will or no. We may almost say of these higher prophets,

> 'Through no disturbance of the soul
> Or strong compunction in [them] wrought,
> But in the quietness of thought'

[1] Amos iii. 2.

they receive the motions of the Spirit. The hand of God may be heavy upon them, but yet they do not lose their full personality. Instead of being mere passive instruments their intelligence is active[1]. They are not a mere flute or lyre for the Spirit to blow through; or, if they are, there is a fine quality of tone which belongs to the reed or to the strings. The impulse is given, and all the faculties and powers of the man are stirred to unwonted energy, in which however, as if to give it the stamp of nature and reality, there mingles something of his weakness as well as of his strength.

The prophets are before all things impassioned seers of spiritual truth and preachers of religion. They are often described as statesmen and as social reformers. Some of them were statesmen, but not all—the figures of Isaiah and Jeremiah bulk so large that we are apt to take them as a type of the rest, even where their circumstances were exceptional. More were social reformers[2]. But in either case it was only as it were incidentally in the discharge of a higher mission[3]. The fields of statesmanship and of social

---

[1] 'The lower the grade of prophecy, the more does the ecstatic condition become the normal one for inspiration; whereas in the higher and riper stages it occurs but seldom—principally in the initial revelation which constitutes the prophet's call' (Riehm, *Messianic Prophecy*, p. 25 E. T.; comp. Duhm, *Theol. d. Proph.* p. 86.)

[2] The function of the prophets as social reformers has been recognised by others besides theologians: see J. S. Mill, *Representative Government*, p. 40 ff. (p. 17 popular edition).

[3] The pages (*H. L.* pp. 150–153) in which this point is brought out by Mr. Montefiore form a striking passage in a striking chapter.

reform were but departments in that economy of life which took its shape from a true insight into the nature and attributes of God and the duty of man. This insight was granted to the prophet, and he followed it out into all its consequences. Especially in the crises of the national history he came forward to warn, to threaten, and to reassure—not because the nation as such was the first thing in his mind, though doubtless his kinsmen according to the flesh had a strong hold upon him, but because at such times a deeper view was obtained into the methods of God's working and a stronger incentive was given to the performance of human duty.

Upon what grounds then are we to rest the authority with which the prophets spoke—an authority which still breathes in their writings? We remember that they too were not 'like the scribes.' They do not reason, but command. They do not conjecture, but announce. The moods which they use are the categorical imperative and future. Their insight takes the form of intuition and not of inference. Whence did they come to have these characteristics? What is it that lies in the background of their teaching? If we listen to them they will tell us. With one consent they would say that the thoughts which arose in their hearts and the words which arose to their lips were put there by God.

But this only throws us back upon the further question, which forms the gist of the problem at the present day, What guarantees have we that they were not mistaken? How do we know that they are not projecting their own thoughts outside themselves and ascribing them to an external cause? This is the heart of the matter. And the one point on which we must firmly take our stand is the belief that in this contention of theirs the prophets were not mistaken, that their utterances had a cause outside themselves, a real objective cause, not to be confused with any mental process of their own.

This I think is enough. We are not called upon to formulate a theory, for which the data are perhaps insufficient, as to the exact mode in which God conveyed His Will to them. In the most important work on the subject before us, a work of much learning and ability and starting from critical premises though perhaps applying them somewhat wilfully, it is contended that when the prophets say 'God spake' to them, what is meant is a literal and actual voice audible to the bodily ear, and when they say 'They saw,' what is meant is an actual literal sight presented to the waking eye[1]. I do not think that we are compelled to go so far as this. There is a great tendency in an age and in a state of civilization like that to which the prophets belonged to express the higher and more abstract processes of the human mind in terms of the lower and more concrete. The prophets chose the simplest expressions they could find, expressions which would convey the desired meaning so far as it could be apprehended to their contemporaries, but expres-

---

[1] König, *Offenbarungsbegriff d. A. T.* ii. 9 ff., 142 ff. In criticism of this view see especially Riehm, *Messianic Prophecy*, p. 29 ff. E. T.

## The Prophetic Inspiration.

sions which are not intended to be judged from the standpoint of an advanced psychology, and which if they are so judged would certainly be pronounced inadequate. But the essence of them consists in this, that the words which they repeat and the visions of revelation which they describe are not merely their own inventions, but are suggested and brought home to them from without in such a way that they were irresistibly attributed to God and given out as coming from Him. We believe that they were right, and we do so on a number of grounds which seem to us exceedingly strong.

We believe it on the strength (1) of the glimpses which the prophets give us into their own consciousness on the subject; (2) of the universal belief of their contemporaries; (3) of the extraordinary unanimity of their testimony; (4) of the difficulty of accounting for it in any other way; (5) of the character of the teaching in which this Divine prompting and suggestion results—a character which is not only not unworthy but most worthy of its source.

(1) We may premise, in speaking of *the witness which the prophets bear to themselves*, that they are persons whose word may well be believed. They are persons as little likely to deceive as to be deceived. Their writings bear the stamp of singleminded veracity, and in the way in which they grapple with the evils around them they come before us as the wisest and sanest of their generation. But the case is one where considerations of this kind hardly need to be introduced; because we have not to do with a claim

which is denied and has to be made good, but with one which is generally acquiesced in and the references to which come in quite incidentally as if it were taken for granted. The sincerity of the prophets' own belief cannot be called in question; and it will be allowed that in common matters they are competent witnesses; the only question possible is whether they have analysed their consciousness correctly.

But in regard to this we must observe that they have at least analysed it very strictly. It is remarkable what a clear and firm distinction they draw throughout between what comes from God and what comes from themselves [1]. There are in their minds two trains of thought running parallel to each other, and they never seem to have the slightest hesitation as to which facts shall be referred to the one and which to the other. It is the characteristic of the false prophets to confuse the deceits of their own heart with the word of the Lord [2]. The true prophet is never in any doubt. He may have to wait some time before a revelation comes to him—Jeremiah on one occasion waits ten days—but he does not antici-

---

[1] Note (*e.g.*) in this connexion the dialogues which the prophets are represented as holding with the Almighty and the way in which they describe their own feelings: Amos vii. 2–9, 15, viii. 1, 2; Micah vii. 1–10, 18–20; Isaiah vi. 5–12, xvi. 9–11, xxi. 2–10, xxii. 4–14, xxv. 1–5, xxvi. 8–18, xxix. 11, 12, xl. 6, xlix. 3–6, l. 4–9, lxiv. 6–12; Jeremiah i. 6–14, iv. 10, 19–21, v. 3–6, x. 19–25, xii. 1–6, xiv. 7–9, 13–14, 18–22, xv. 10–21, xvii. 15–18, xviii. 18–23, xx. 7–18, xxxii. 16–25, &c. It is probable that some of the chapters referred to are not by the authors whose names they bear (see below, p. 240 f.); but that would only enlarge the range of testimony.

[2] Jer. xiv. 14.

pate the desired moment[1]. The prophets always know and very frequently set down the precise time when the word of the Lord 'came to them.' They are not endowed with any standing and permanent inspiration, but a special access of the Divine gift is vouchsafed to them for special purposes.

(2) Nor is it as if they were conscious of this gift only within themselves; its presence is *universally recognised by their contemporaries*. Observe for instance the position which Isaiah holds both before court and people. The message of the prophet may be unwelcome; and in bad times he may meet with opposition from false prophets or from worldly counsellors who are determined to go their own way, and who think by suppressing the messenger to evade the message[2]; but his mission from God is not questioned. And just as men were aware when they had a prophet among them, so also they were aware when there was no prophet: 'We see not our signs: there is no more any prophet; neither is there among us any that knoweth how long[3].' And we have already seen how the Jews looked upon the cessation of prophecy as having taken place at a certain time, which the later writers regarded as regulating the limits of the Canon[4].

(3) Another proof that the prophets were not the victims of hallucination is supplied by *the extraordinary consistency of their language* in regard to them-

---

[1] Jer. xlii. 7.  [2] Amos vii. 10-13; Jer. xxxviii. 6.
[3] Psalm lxxiv. 9.
[4] 1 Macc. ix. 27; Joseph. *c. Apion.* i. 8; *sup.* p. 111.

selves and their mission. If one prophet here and another there had supposed themselves to be sent by God and to have words put in their mouths by Him, it would not have been so surprising. But as it is we find the whole line of prophets, stretching over a succession of centuries, from Amos, from Nathan, from Samuel, from Moses, to Malachi, all make the same assumption. The formulae which they use are the same: 'Thus saith the Lord,' 'The word of the Lord came,' 'Hear ye the word of the Lord.' Such an identity of language implies an identity of psychological fact behind it; but, if an individual may be subject to delusions, it is another thing to say that a class so long extended could be subject to them—and to delusions with so much of method about them.

From this group of arguments which turn ultimately upon the consciousness of the prophets we pass (4) to another group which arise from *the difficulty of accounting for that consciousness on any other hypothesis* than its truth. First there are the circumstances of the call of the prophets. We never hear of a prophet *volunteering* for his mission. It is laid upon them as a necessity from which they struggle to escape in vain. Moses pleads that he is 'slow of speech and of a slow tongue.' Isaiah tells us how he thought himself undone because he was a man of unclean lips and he dwelt among a people of unclean lips. Jeremiah shrinks back like a child when the call comes to him. He curses the day on which he was born. Ezekiel has full warning of the kind of reception he will meet with: it will be as though briers and thorns were with him and he dwelt among scorpions. Amos had had no preparation for his mission: he was neither a prophet nor a member of any prophetic guild, but 'a herdman and a dresser of sycomore trees[1].' So far from circumstances leading up to the call of the prophets it was just the opposite. And when the prophet came forward to speak, in most cases it was with some paradox which seemed rather to traverse than to follow from the teaching of his predecessors[2].

Again, if we take a wider range and ask, Whence did the prophets of Israel get this doctrine of theirs? we cannot answer, as some have attempted to do, that it was from any special aptitude either of the Semitic race in general or of the Hebrew race in particular. It is sufficient refutation of this to point to the kindred nations Moab and Ammon. Here we see the picture of what Israel and Israel's leaders and teachers would have been without any Divine intervention. Or if we look at Israel itself, we observe with what constant struggle and effort, how fitfully and uncertainly, the people were kept up even to the lower level of their own Monotheism. It is plain enough that their creed was no natural product, but rather one which went against nature; bestowed from without, and not generated from within.

[1] Exod. iv. 10; Isa. vi. 5, xx. 14; Jer. i. 6; Ezek. ii. 6; Amos vii. 14.
[2] Amos iii. 2, v. 18 ff., 21 ff.; Isa. i. 12 ff.; Jer. vii. 4, &c.

## III. The Prophetic and Historical Books.

And yet once more, if we open out our horizon wider still, if we weigh the prophets' work by the standard not of any special aptitudes of race but of the common aptitudes of men, we are obliged to confess that their teaching is not such as could have been arrived at by any of the ordinary methods current then or even by any of those which are current now. A perfectly just and holy and good God is not the result of any induction. The presence of evil in the world, of pain and sorrow and sin, prevents us from arguing directly from the character of the creation to the character of the Creator. It is a bold and masterful solution to say that there is evil in the world, and yet that God is good—perfectly good, and that if we hold fast to the belief in His goodness, it will verify itself to us in spite of all appearances to the contrary. But such a belief could not be given by any of the methods of science, ancient or modern. It is a splendid venture of faith, a far-darting gleam of intuition, shot through the gloom and tangle of existence, we may most surely believe at His instance and motion, Whom by His own help alone we can at all adequately search out and know.

(5) This is what makes the teaching of the prophets so infinitely precious to us and *stamps it with undying authority*. We want it as much to-day as ever it has been wanted in the past[1]. It is often assumed that

---

[1] M. James Darmesteter has recently published an enthusiastic essay on the value of Hebrew Prophecy in the immediate present and future (*Les Prophètes d'Israël*, Paris, 1892). Its burden may be summed up in few words. 'Le rôle et la mission du prophétisme . . .

Christianity has superseded the teaching of the Old Testament; but we really need the Old Testament to correct, I do not say Christianity itself, but the very imperfect conceptions which we are apt to form of it. It was an inevitable consequence of the Incarnation and of the contact of the Gospel with the Greek mind that recourse should be had to metaphysics. The Church of the early centuries employed the best metaphysics to which it had access; and it employed them upon the whole wisely and well. But in order to moralize our metaphysics, to fill them with warmth and emotion, we need to go back to the Old Testament and to that part of the New which is not Greek but Hebrew[1]. Again, how much richer and deeper is the old prophetic idea of the 'living God' than our modern terminology, the Absolute, the Infinite, the Unconditioned, the First Cause, or than the eighteenth-century notion of the Moral Governor, which has indeed a certain gravity when it is used as Bishop Butler was wont to use it, but is bare and arid and comprehends but little of the attributes of the Father of spirits. 'Jehovah, Jehovah, a God full of compassion and gracious, slow

c'est de vivifier les deux religions de fait qui aujourd'hui se disputent la France et demain se la partageront en paix, celle de la science et celle du Christ. . . . Seul il peut rendre à l'Église le souffle d'avenir, en lui rendant le sens des formules d'où elle est sortie : et seul il peut donner à la science la puissance d'expression morale qui lui manque ' (pp. xiii. f.).

[1] This may, I hope, be taken to represent the measure of truth in the antithesis, which Matthew Arnold was so fond of drawing between Hellenism and Hebraism.

to anger, and plenteous in mercy and truth; keeping mercy for thousands, forgiving iniquity and transgression and sin; and that will by no means clear the guilty.' 'Thus saith the high and lofty One that inhabiteth eternity, whose name is Holy: I dwell in the high and holy place, with him also that is of a contrite and humble spirit, to revive the spirit of the humble, and to revive the heart of the contrite one.' 'For Thou art our Father, though Abraham knoweth us not, and Israel doth not acknowledge us: Thou, O Jehovah, art our Father; our Redeemer from everlasting is Thy name.' 'Surely He hath borne our griefs, and carried our sorrows: yet we did esteem Him stricken, smitten of God, and afflicted. But He was wounded for our transgressions, He was bruised for our iniquities: the chastisement of our peace was upon Him; and with His stripes we are healed[1].' Forgive me for reminding you by one or two such familiar examples what wonderful things there are in the writings of the prophets[2]. The last passage recalls to us the part which they played in drawing πολυμερῶς καὶ πολυτρόπως, 'by divers portions and in divers manners,' that unimaginable portrait which we have seen transferred from heaven to earth and realized in Christ.

Let us stand back for a moment and without losing ourselves in details or remembering more than the salient features which their names bring back to us, let

---

[1] Exod. xxxiv. 6, 7 (a prophetical passage); Isa. lvii. 15; lxiii. 16; liii. 4, 5.

[2] See Additional Note A: *Modern Prophets*.

us think what such names as Amos, Hosea, Isaiah, Jeremiah mean. Looking at them so, and thinking also of the place which they have held in history and the spiritual nutriment which their writings have afforded to generation upon generation of the best of earth's children, can we be doing wrong if we endorse the claim which they make, in no spirit of boastfulness or self-seeking, to be chosen vessels for receiving and transmitting the revealed Will of God?

II. It is well known that the Jews classed the Historical Books of the Old Testament among 'the Prophets.' The Books as they stand in our Bibles (with the exception of Ruth) from Joshua to the end of Kings are called by them the Former Prophets, in contradistinction from the Latter Prophets, to whom we as a rule confine the name. The idea was that the history of each successive generation was written by a contemporary prophet; and as the prophetic literature in the narrower sense does not begin until the reign of Jeroboam II in Israel and Uzziah in Judah, the narratives of whose reigns fall in the second half of the Second Book of Kings, it was natural that the great bulk of the historical writings (Joshua—2 Kings xiv.) should be roughly described as the work of the older prophets.

There was a large element of truth in this Jewish tradition. The older historical writing was all of it the work of prophets. We may even go back beyond the Book of Joshua. The historical portions of the Pentateuch were also as we shall see very largely

## III. The Historical Books.

composed by prophets. And it is true that much of this historical activity was contemporary. I do not mean that the Historical Books as we now have them were written *pari passu* with the events, or were even in all cases based directly upon works so written. The character of these books in their different parts varies greatly: sometimes the narratives of which they are made up are nearer to the events, and sometimes they are more remote from them. But at least from the time of David onwards there must have been a very fairly continuous historical literature upon which our present histories are based, though in varying proportions, and in different degrees of directness.

A wrong impression is apt to be conveyed in regard to these Hebrew histories from the associations with which we come to them derived from modern historical writing or from the classical historians of Greece and Rome.

In the first place, it must be remembered that Hebrew history was as a rule, and especially for the earlier periods, anonymous. The writers had not a literary object in the sense of seeking any fame or reputation for themselves. Their object was either simply to record the facts, or else more often to draw a religious lesson from the facts. They might at times wish to advance the interests of a particular class or order; but all personal interests, and in particular interests connected with literary composition, were not only in the background, but were absolutely non-existent. No Hebrew historian thought either of himself or of his predecessors as possessing a right of property in their work.

## Characteristics of Hebrew Historians. 157

He was just as ready to have the products of his pen used by others as he was to use himself the stores which had come down to him.

Secondly, we must remember that the Hebrew historians were very numerous. The writing of history was one of the functions of the prophetic order, and that order was recruited by a constant succession from Samuel to Malachi. It would of course be utterly misleading in speaking of the prophets to think only of the Four Prophets the Greater, and Twelve Prophets the Less, in our Bibles. As I have already said, the prophets were the clergy of their time, and although of course only a small proportion of them took up the writing of history, still the number who did so from time to time cannot have been inconsiderable. At a later date the priests also took up the work of history-writing. But they too wrote under precisely the same conditions: the work is carried on not so much by single individuals as by successions of individuals partly going over old ground and partly entering upon new.

Lastly, we have to remember that their writings did not take the form of printed books. They were not produced in wholesale editions, but by single copies at a time. And the writer of each new copy would not consider himself slavishly bound to the text of his predecessor. He would be something between a scribe and an author or editor. He was bound by no rules; and he would either simply transcribe or add and subtract as he felt moved to do at the moment. Both his additions and subtractions would be due to different motives—sometimes to the use of other authorities, and sometimes to the particular religious interest which was dominant with him in writing.

The best analogy for Hebrew historical writing would be not our modern literary histories or the works of ancients like Tacitus or Thucydides, but the monkish chroniclers of the Middle Ages. What we have to think of is works existing in few copies, and those copies exposed to many mischances from the violent and turbulent character of the times; passing often from hand to hand and enriched on the way by insertions and annotations; so that it would be the exception for any of them exactly to reproduce the original from which it was copied. This would all be done in perfectly good faith; and although the result as it has come down to us may seem rather complicated, it is really simple in the way in which it has come about, and indeed natural and inevitable.

Here it is that we have to dismiss our modern associations, which are not at all relevant to the circumstances. A prejudice may easily be created which ought not to exist. The prolonged attention which has been given to the Historical Books of the Old Testament and the skill of a series of investigators have succeeded to a very great extent in separating the layers of gradual accretion which have gone to make the books which we now possess what they are. But it must be confessed that the nomenclature which they have been compelled to use has about it something rather repellent—'first Jehovist,' 'second Jehovist,' ' third Jehovist,' 'first Elohist,' 'second Elohist,' ' first

## Characteristics of Hebrew Historians. 159

redactor,' 'second redactor,' 'Deuteronomistic redactor,' 'priestly redactor,' 'interpolator' here and 'interpolator' there [1]. All this has a formidable sound; and with us it would convey the idea of something not quite honest as well. We naturally think of a writer partly passing off his predecessors' work as his own and partly tampering with it not very ingenuously. Any such idea must be dismissed. What it really means is only that as one hand laid down the pen, another— and in most cases a kindred and friendly hand—took

[1] The following is the critical apparatus to the Pentateuch extracted from Cornill's *Einleitung*, which however, it should be said, goes perhaps to the furthest limits which have as yet been reached in this direction:—

| | |
|---|---|
| $J^1 J^2 J^3$ | successive contributors to the Jehovistic document. |
| $E^1 E^2$ | successive contributors to the Elohistic document. |
| J E | combination of J group with E group. |
| D $D^h$ $D^p$ | the author of 'Urdeuteronomium,' with two later redactors. |
| J E D | combination of JE with Deuteronomy. |
| P $P^1$ $P^2$ $P^x$ | the author of the Priestly Code with its later additions ($P^x = P^3 P^4 P^5$, &c.). |
| R j | the editor who combines J and E. |
| Rd, $Rd^2$ | two authors or editors, the first of whom combines JE with P, contributes to Joshua and Judges, and writes most of Kings, while the second is a later redactor of that work. |
| Rp. | the editor who combines JED with P. |

It will be understood that the discrimination of so many different hands represents an enormous amount of labour, which will be apt to seem wasted. It may perhaps be wasted; it may perhaps carry refinement beyond the point which the evidence justifies; it may apply an unreal standard. But the antecedent improbability seems to be a good deal lessened by the considerations in the text. In the end the specialists must decide; and our own scholars may be trusted to decide judiciously.

it up, each working after a manner which had become traditional.

But another question will be asked, and it is my duty to attempt to answer it. Granting that no blame attaches to these successive narrators, can we claim for them any special inspiration? And if so, where does it reside? It is important to bear in mind the double function which belongs to every historian. He has not only to narrate events but to interpret them. In the histories of the Bible the first of these functions was as a rule subordinate to the second, and a different measure has to be applied to it at different periods, and according as it is regarded from different aspects.

In the art of narrative as such the Hebrew historian has no superior. Nothing can exceed the simple dignity of his style or the sureness of touch with which he lays his finger on the springs of human emotion. Stories like those of Joseph or the revolt of Absalom are unsurpassed for beauty and pathos; the scenes of Elijah on Carmel and in the wilderness are solemn and moving in the highest degree. Among the ancients Herodotus probably comes nearest. Among the moderns those are best who, like our own Bunyan, conform most closely to the Biblical model.

It is otherwise when we turn from the form of the narrative to its substance. Here there is a great variety, corresponding to the different degrees of nearness in which the historian stands to the events.

# Inspiration of the Hebrew Historians.

Here too we may say that the Hebrew historian at his best is very good indeed. In a story like that of Absalom we feel that we are being told the simple naked truth with the utmost clearness and impressiveness. The familiar tale awakes in us at this day the very same emotions which the scenes themselves awoke among those who witnessed them. The reason is that the document on which this part of the narrative is based is an excellent one, a pure transcript of nature, drawn from fresh and vivid recollection. We cannot say as much for the story of Joseph, although that is equally lifelike, because there is not the same guarantee that the writer is near his subject. The beauty and delicacy of characterization may be due to the moulding influence of imagination, acting gradually upon traditional material.

On all this side of history-writing it is difficult to claim for the Biblical historians inspiration in the sense of praeternatural exemption from error. The Historical Books of the Old Testament have now for some time been examined with complete candour and very closely. A final result may not have been obtained in all cases, but still the broad outlines may be regarded as fairly well ascertained. The different sources have been discriminated, at least with an approximate degree of accuracy, and it is possible to tell within rough limits in what sort of relation the record stands to the facts, where the interval is great and where it is small, and what sort of disturbing influences are likely to have intervened.

If we take the results as we find them without any

straining, it cannot be said that there is evidence in the case of the Biblical Histories of the suspension of ordinary psychological laws. An oral tradition which has travelled over several centuries cannot be trusted in the same way as the testimony of eyewitnesses and contemporaries. And it would be hard to deny that there are portions of the history of Israel which have no better foundation. Then again although we may acquit the Hebrew historian of many of the distorting influences to which his modern successors are liable, still it must in strict justice be allowed that he has some distorting influences of his own. If he is free from literary ambitions and egotisms, he is not wholly free from the tendency to idealize and glorify institutions of which he is proud, or to read back into the past the conditions with which he is familiar in the present. To escape such tendencies would at the date and under the circumstances under which some of the Hebrew historians wrote have been something more than human, and however willing we may be to admit supernatural interference where the proof is sufficient the proof on this side of the facts is wanting. Rather, when candidly considered, the facts really tell the other way. It is not in this direction that we are to look for the signs of inspiration.

For these we must turn to another quarter. We have said that the duty of the historian is not only to narrate but to interpret. It was this further duty of which the Hebrew historians were most keenly conscious and which brought them in contact with the spirit of Revelation. History was not with them a series of disconnected annals of wars and dynasties. It was rather a gradual unfolding of the kingdom of God upon earth, or in other words of 'the purpose of God according to selection.' At two periods in particular this conception was very dominant. One was under the influence of the Book of Deuteronomy in the years which followed the publication of that book and among the schools by which it was most closely studied. The other was at the end of the Exile and immediately after the Restoration[1]. These were the periods during which the Historical Books of the Old Testament received their present shape. But it would be a mistake to regard the fundamental conception as present in those periods alone. It really stretches over the whole of the ground which Hebrew history-writing covers. Already as far back as the Jehovist we find a fully developed consciousness that the people to which he belonged and the beginning of which he was describing was one in which all the nations of the earth were to be blessed. Think for a moment of the significance of that single fact. It contains in itself implicitly if not explicitly the germs of Christianity. What other nation ever had so high a sense of its vocation? What other nation ever retained such a sense on so slender a thread of national greatness and prosperity? How did it survive fire and water, the extinction not only of national liberties but as it seemed of national existence?

[1] For some instructive remarks on the characteristics of these two periods see Montefiore, *Hibbert Lectures*, pp. 231-234, 315 ff., and on the conception of history in the Books of Chronicles, pp. 445-449.

## III. The Historical Books.

We can see now why it was that the prophets of Israel were also its historians. It was in them that this consciousness of the true vocation of Israel burned most brightly. It was they who were commissioned to cherish and educate it and to fill it with contents of ever-increasing richness and fulness.

Hence we must not be surprised if we do not always find the prophetic historians upon the same or upon the highest level. In this as in other things Revelation proceeds by way of growth, by development, by a gradual opening of the eyes to higher ranges of truth. To reach the highest summits of all we must go not to the Former Prophets but to the Latter, not to Genesis and Exodus or to the Books of Samuel and Kings, or even to those of Ezra and Nehemiah, but to Jeremiah and Second Isaiah, to the prophecy of the New Covenant and to the doctrine of the Suffering Servant.

And yet, as in the body those members 'which seem to be more feeble are necessary, and our uncomely parts have more abundant comeliness,' so also in Revelation: that also is an organism, a connected and coherent structure, fitly joined and compacted together. A continuity runs through it all, and even that which seems to be lower is necessary as a stepping-stone to the higher. Therefore it is wrong to speak in terms of disparagement even of that which seems to be humblest. The moral which holds good for the life of the individual holds good also on the grandest scale of the fulfilment of the Divine purpose.

## Inspiration of the Hebrew Historians.

> 'Our times are in His hand
> Who saith, " A whole I planned,
> Youth shows but half; trust God: see all, nor be afraid." '

There are vessels of greater honour and vessels of lesser honour; there are riper products and products less ripe; but all alike have their place in the economy of Revelation.

## NOTE A.

*Modern Prophets.*

ONE sometimes sees an estimate of certain modern writers which is so appreciative and indulgent as to place them practically on a level with the Hebrew prophets. The chief names which would be mentioned in such a connexion in this country are those of Carlyle, Ruskin, Browning, and Tennyson. It would seem however in regard to these writers as if one of two things were true. Either what they say is based fundamentally on the Christian Revelation, and their contribution to literature consists in restating portions of that revelation, clearing them from misunderstanding and objections, and applying them to modern life; or else it embodies individual views of the writer. This second element is of very doubtful value. It would be most conspicuous in the writings of Carlyle and Ruskin. As to the former I would not deny that some of the truths of Christian morals—hardly the most recondite—are urged by him with real force and passion; but even these are wrapped up in an amount of rhetorical declamation which has already begun to pall upon the public taste, and by the side of them is much that is positively false and misleading. The Gospel of the Strong Man is for instance a strange kind of revelation. And in regard to the other there is so much that is either overstrained or simply eccentric and erratic that a special gift of discernment is necessary to separate the wheat from the chaff. Ruskin probably approaches most nearly to the prophet when he least supposes himself to do so.

All the four writers who have been named possess real *charismata* in different degrees of purity and strength, but to compare them with the prophets and apostles shows only defective criticism on the one hand and imperfect apprehension on the other. On the greatest points of all, those which relate to the character and attributes of God, the Bible is not only supreme but unique. The believer in the Bible has no need to exaggerate: he has but to state the facts as they really are.

# LECTURE IV.

### THE GENESIS OF THE OLD TESTAMENT.
### THE LAW AND THE HAGIOGRAPHA.

'What great nation is there that hath a god so nigh unto them as the Lord our God is whensoever we call upon Him? And what great nation is there, that hath statutes and judgements so righteous as all this law, which I set before you this day?'—*Deuteronomy* iv. 7, 8.

'Would God that all the Lord's people were prophets, and that the Lord would put His Spirit upon them!'—*Numbers* xi. 29.

I. To the Jews the one primary revelation was the Law; all else was secondary. Even as far back as the Book of Ecclesiasticus, the Law as given by Moses was identified with Wisdom itself[1]. This idea was developed by the Rabbis, who regarded the Law as existing before the Creation, and saw in it the plan on which God had made the worlds[2]. No second revelation like it was possible. It had exhausted all the revelation which God could give to man. The passage in Deuteronomy (xxx. 12), 'It is not in heaven, that thou shouldest say, Who shall go up for us to heaven and bring it unto us, that we may hear it and do it?' which St. Paul used to illustrate

---

[1] Ecclus. xxiv. 23; *cf.* ver. 1 ff.
[2] Weber, *System d. altsynagog. Theologie*, p. 14.

## Estimate of the Law.

the nearness of the Gospel, was interpreted by the Jews to mean that the Law had been given once for all, and that there was no other revelation left in heaven like it[1]. If Israel had only kept the Law there would have been no need for Prophets or *Hagiographa*[2]. None of the other books could compare in sanctity with the Law. It was not permitted to sell a copy of the Law and buy the other books with the price[3]. The usage of the Rabbis is not constant: although the other books are often quoted as Scripture, they are also frequently treated as on the same footing with the Kabbala or traditions of the scribes[4].

The same estimate prevailed at Alexandria as in Palestine. More than two-thirds of the extant writings of Philo are occupied with themes taken from the Pentateuch. According to him, Moses combined in his own person the four most perfect gifts possible to man, those of king, lawgiver, priest, and prophet. He is the greatest of all lawgivers, whose laws, unlike those of others which are being constantly overturned, will last as long as the sun and moon endure, as they have lasted unshaken through all the vicissitudes of Jewish history[5].

We have seen that the Law was the first of the

[1] Wildeboer, *Het Ontstaan*, &c., p. 83.
[2] *Ibid.*
[3] Robertson Smith, *O. T. J. C.* p. 161, ed. 2.
[4] Wildeboer, p. 83 f.; Zunz, *Die gottesdienstl. Vorträge d. Juden*, p. 46 n., ed. 2.
[5] *Vit. Mos.* iii. 23, ii. 3 (Mang. ii. 163, 136); *cf.* Drummond, *Philo Judaeus*, i. 15.

## IV. The Law and the Hagiographa.

three divisions of the Old Testament to attain to what we should call canonical authority; and it so overshadowed the other divisions that even in the New Testament the one name 'Law' is used to cover the rest[1]. Even our Lord, as reported to us, so far accepts the current formulas as to apply the term 'Law' both to Prophetical Books and Psalms.

And yet Christianity was soon to work a change in this estimate of the Law. To the Christian the Old Testament was of value in proportion as it testified to Christ. Hence we find that the books most largely quoted were Genesis, Deuteronomy, Isaiah, and Psalms. And the Book of Genesis was quoted, not as part of the Law, but as the record of an older and in some ways higher dispensation, inasmuch as it linked on more immediately and naturally to the age of the Messiah[2]; while from Deuteronomy just those parts were quoted which were least legal[3]. Our Lord did not in set terms repeal the Law, though He showed that it was to be superseded by principles of greater simplicity and efficacy. And what He taught implicitly, St. Stephen and St. Paul taught explicitly. That Christ is the end of the Law as a means of making men righteous, that other and more powerful influences must be brought to bear if the world is to be regenerated, is the burden of the great Apostle. He succeeded beyond all expec-

---

[1] The clear cases are St. John x. 34; xii. 34; xv. 25; 1 Cor. xiv. 21.

[2] Rom. iv. 13, 14; Gal. iii. 17, 18.

[3] *E.g.* Deut. vi. 4, 5; xviii. 15, 18; xxx. 12-14.

## Estimate of the Law.

tation in effecting the change, less perhaps through any theoretic teaching, which was but imperfectly apprehended, than through the force of circumstances. The Gentile converts far outnumbered the Jewish, and it was natural that the Law should have but a slight hold upon them. The different parts of the Old Testament were treated as more upon an equality: or rather, by a silent process, Prophecy virtually took the place of Law, and it was just the prophetic element in the Pentateuch and the other books that came to be of most importance.

Now in these latter days a like tendency is discernible. The Prophets are once more placed before the Law, but in a different sense and on different grounds. It is no longer the predictive side of prophecy which is prominent. And the reasons which have brought the Prophetical Books once more to the front are in the first instance critical rather than doctrinal. The world does right to insist on having documents of unquestioned genuineness and authenticity. And such the Prophetical Books undoubtedly are. It is probable that in some cases, from causes which are little more than accidental, the works of two or more prophets may have come down to us under a single name, but that hardly detracts at all from their value. They are no less authentic as an expression of the prophetic spirit, and the name is but a small matter.

It is otherwise with a book which is either directly historical or has a historical background. There everything depends upon the date and the relation in which the record stands to the facts. From this point of view the Pentateuch has been far more nearly affected by critical investigation than the Prophets. However much we may believe that there is a genuine Mosaic foundation in the Pentateuch, it is very difficult to lay the finger upon it and say with confidence here Moses himself is speaking.

Perhaps it is as yet rather too soon to speak of the 'results' of modern criticism, but if not its 'results,' at least its strongly pronounced tendency is to spread the composition of the actual Pentateuch as we have it over the period covered by the Monarchy and the Exile. If we ignore minor subdivisions, which are numerous, and look only at the broad distribution of the masses, the component parts of the Pentateuch may be said to be three: (1) a double stream of narrative, the work of prophets, variously dated between 900 and 750 B.C., which forms the greater part of the Book of Genesis, but also runs through Exodus and Numbers; (2) the Book of Deuteronomy, the greater part of which belongs to a date not very long before 621 B.C.; and lastly (3) the Priest's Code, which either falls at the end of the Exile or else had a latent existence somewhat before it.

The mere statement of these facts will explain why modern criticism in seeking to get at the heart of Israel's religion takes its starting-point from the Prophets and not from the Law. It cannot however do so without qualification: partly for a critical reason, but still more for a theological. Critically it is certain that the oldest parts of the Pentateuch, the

## Mosaic Element in the Law.

double stream of prophetical narrative just spoken of, the so-called Jehovist and Elohist, are older than the oldest of the writing prophets. And theologically those prophets imply a large inheritance of belief and practice, much of which is no doubt ultimately traceable to Moses and the Mosaic age. It is satisfactory to find this Mosaic substratum so distinctly recognised even by the most critical of the critics, although we may question whether some of them refer to it quite so much as they ought[1].

Assuming then, provisionally and until future inquiries confirm or refute it, that the critical theory of the composition and origin of the Pentateuch is in the main right, we have to ask, What is its bearing on the question of Inspiration? From this point of view we are reminded that there are three strains, so to speak, in the Pentateuch—a Mosaic strain, a prophetic strain, and a priestly. Each of these has the measure of inspiration proper to it.

(1) At the head stands that which belongs to Moses. We have said that the strictly Mosaic element

---

[1] 'The time of Moses is invariably regarded as the properly creative period in Israel's history, and on that account also as giving the pattern and norm for the ages which followed. . . . The prophets who came after gave, it is true, greater distinctness to the peculiar character of the nation, but they did not make it; on the contrary, it made them.' 'But within the Pentateuch itself also the *historical* tradition about Moses (which admits of being distinguished, and must carefully be separated from the *legislative*, although the latter often clothes itself in narrative form) is in its main features manifestly trustworthy, and can only be explained as resting on actual facts' (Wellhausen, *Sketch of the History of Israel and Judah*, pp. 7, 18). *Cf.* Montefiore, *Hib. Lect.* p. 15 f.

in the Pentateuch must be indeterminate, because the nature of the documents does not permit us to define it exactly. We can only argue backwards from the character of Israel's religion when the light of history falls more fully and clearly upon it. The working out of this appertains to the Theology of the Old Testament, and is not germane to the present inquiry. It might however perhaps be said that all that is most fundamental in the teaching of Moses was summed up in two correlated pairs of propositions[1]: (i) 'Jehovah (Yahweh) is the God of Israel, and Israel is the people of Jehovah'; (ii) 'Jehovah is a righteous God, and requires righteousness in those who worship Him.' Of course it did not follow that these propositions had at first that high and spiritual interpretation put upon them which they received later at the hands of the prophets. 'Jehovah Israel's God' implies monolatry, but not at first and in the strict sense monotheism. And in like manner the idea 'Jehovah a righteous God' would expand as the idea of righteousness expanded. But it is just this expansive property which is most characteristic of the Mosaic religion. It contains the germ of all the after-development, the promise of yet greater things to come.

The further question may be asked whether the Mosaic religion in its turn must not have had its antecedents, not merely such general antecedents as underlay all primitive religion, but certain special antecedents which not only suggested the form which it took itself, but also enabled it to take a hold of the

[1] *Cf.* Wellhausen, *Sketch*, p. 8 ff.; Montefiore, *Hib. Lect.* 31 ff., 44 ff.

people to whom it was addressed. I think we may answer this question in the affirmative, though to discuss it would also lie outside the limits of our subject [1].

We are concerned not so much with the contents of the Mosaic or pre-Mosaic theology as with the source from which it was derived. In the prophetic age Moses himself was universally regarded as a prophet. 'By a prophet the Lord brought Israel up out of Egypt, and by a prophet was he preserved,' writes Hosea (xii. 13); and the same thing is implied by Micah (vi. 4). The famous passage in Deuteronomy (xviii. 15, 18), twice quoted in the New Testament (Acts iii. 22, vii. 37), speaks of Moses as a prophet typical of the whole order. There was however a certain consciousness that his inspiration was higher, his intercourse with God closer, than that of other prophets. 'If there be a prophet among you, I the Lord will make Myself known unto him in a vision, I will speak with him in a dream. My servant Moses is not so; he is faithful in all Mine house [2]: with him will I speak mouth to mouth, even manifestly, and not in dark speeches; and the form of the Lord shall he behold' (Num. xii. 6-8 [3]). This passage is assigned to the prophetical narrative, and so would be older than the middle of the eighth century B.C.

---

[1] See Additional Note A: *The Pre-Mosaic History in the Pentateuch.*

[2] 'Er ist betraut mit [der Leitung von] meinem ganzen Hauswesen ' is the expressive translation of Socin (in *Die Heil. Schrift. d. A. T.* ed. Kautzsch).

[3] *Cf.* also Deut. xxxiv. 10.

## IV. The Law and the Hagiographa.

The same document (not discriminating between its parts) contains the account of the vision of the Burning Bush [1], and that wonderful description of the vision on Sinai [2] which marks a very exalted form of revelation. These visions are essentially on the same lines with those in Isaiah and Ezekiel, but more fundamental, inasmuch as they imply a new or strongly enforced view of the Divine nature. We ought not perhaps to use them without reserve for Moses himself, but there can be little doubt that they describe truly, if symbolically, the way in which revelations were made to him. The distinction, we may be sure, was impressed upon his consciousness when he had a mandate to speak and when he had not, when he was speaking his own words and when he was speaking the words of the Lord, as sharply and as strongly as it was upon the consciousness of Isaiah or Jeremiah. 'Thus saith the Lord' has no weaker meaning in the Pentateuch than it has with them. The inspiration of Moses was like that of the prophets, but differs from theirs by its greater originality. The prophets introduced no new principle into religion. They developed with great freshness and force principles already existing. They drew them out to their logical consequences and applied them under new circumstances; but except perhaps in connexion with the Messianic hope, glimpses of which, if very partial

---

[1] Exod. iii. 1–12, but not vi. 2–11, which is assigned to P.
[2] *Ibid.* xxxiii. 12–xxxiv. 9. The only question appears to be whether this passage belongs as a whole to the Jehovist or to the compiler who unites JE.

glimpses, came to one after another of the prophetic succession, they taught nothing which gave so decisive a bent to the religion not only of a single nation but of the whole world.

We should then perhaps be justified in placing the inspiration of Moses by itself, as that not only of a continuator but a Founder. Out of the common ground of the prophetic inspiration it rises in a manner above it, because it was granted to Moses to head the line of prophets and to give that first impulse which they kept alive.

(2) It is just this relation which is apparent in the Pentateuch itself. We have spoken of a triple strain of inspiration in the Pentateuch—of Moses himself, of prophets, and of priests. But that of Moses alone is primary; that of prophets and priests is derivative and secondary. Unfortunately if we take our present documents, the Pentateuch as it has come down to us, the part which is due in it to Moses—great as it really must be—is dim and inferential, while that which is due to prophet and priest can be marked out with considerable clearness. The literary analysis has shown that the oldest portion, the twofold narrative, running sometimes side by side and sometimes combined, is prophetical; the latest portions are the work of priests. The Book of Deuteronomy presents a double character[1]: we may see in it the hand at once of prophet and priest: it falls at a time when the instances of Jeremiah and Ezekiel show how both might be united. It would not however be wrong to

[1] Montefiore, *Hibbert Lectures*, p. 175 ff.

say that the prophetic spirit predominated; and it is just that which made it of all parts of the Law the most evangelical [1].

But between these great literary works and the time of Moses there was a continuous chain both of prophetic and of priestly activity. And it is the fruits of this activity which are embodied in the Pentateuch. Wellhausen is probably right in singling out as the most faithful picture of the work of Moses as lawgiver that which is given in Exodus xviii, where he is described as sitting to judge the people from morning till evening, hearing their cases and giving them answers [2]. Here we may see the beginning of the Torah, which consisted in the first instance of decisions given in response to direct inquiry and in the name of Jehovah. The Law grew up out of the collecting and generalizing of such decisions. We can trace this practice of Moses downwards through the period of the Judges, though we must not argue from the name that it was characteristic of all of them. We hear of Deborah, the prophetess, the wife of Lapidoth, dwelling under the palm-tree between Ramah and Bethel, where the children of Israel came to her for judgment (Judges iv. 4, 5). And again we hear of Samuel going in circuit to Ramah and Gilgal and Bethel (1 Sam. vii. 16, 17).

But these functions of judgment were not confined to the higher prophets, nor were they always exercised under conditions of the higher inspiration. There

---

[1] See especially St. Mark xii. 29–31.
[2] *Sketch of Hist. of Israel and Judah*, p. 19.

is the same shading-off of higher into lower, of what we call natural into what we call supernatural, here as elsewhere. Moses is represented as at the advice of Jethro appointing a number of inferior judges who are to relieve him of the lighter cases. All we are told concerning them is that they are to be 'able men, such as fear God, men of truth, hating unjust gain' (Exod. xviii. 21). These are fit qualifications for the application of known principles. The harder cases, involving new and untried principles, were reserved for the ear of Moses himself, and we may suppose for those who succeeded to the authority of Moses. But it was just these harder cases which gave their distinctive stamp to the codes preserved for us in the Pentateuch.

(3) Parallel to this prophetic judging, and perhaps not always to be accurately distinguished from it, was another kind more closely connected with the sanctuary and the special prerogative of the priests. There too the people came to 'inquire of the Lord.' Certain ceremonies were prescribed for the purpose— in particular the use of the Urim and Thummim, which appears to have been a sort of lot, which gave the answer 'yes' or 'no[1].' Not a very elevated form of religious activity, it may be thought; rather upon much the same level as that heathen oracle of which king Ahaziah sent to inquire at Ekron (2 Kings i. 2). In the last lecture we saw that Prophecy also had its humble side; but just as an Isaiah grew out of the

[1] Robertson Smith, *O. T. J. C.* p. 292, n. i; Schultz, *Theol. d. A. T.* p. 257 f., ed. 4.

one, so also a Hilkiah or a Jeremiah grew out of the other. The same 'purpose of God according to selection' worked both through the prophetic order and through the priestly order[1]. And the result of its operation, in part upon each separately and in part upon both combined, may be seen in the actual codes, forming a progressive series, which are collected for us in the Pentateuch.

Let us take as a specimen the oldest and simplest of these codes, the so-called 'Book of the Covenant' (Exod. xx. 23–xxiii. 33). This book is older than the prophetical narrative in which it was incorporated, and according to Cornill[2] embodied 'the customary law of the early Monarchy'; that is to say, it not only contains the formulated decisions of that age, but the formulated decisions which had accumulated gradually up to that age. Looking at this code, there are two things which strike us about it. One is its essentially religious character. The provisions of it are expressed as coming from God Himself. They carry with them Divine sanction, and are based upon the Divine attributes. 'Ye shall not afflict any widow, or fatherless child. If thou afflict them in any wise, and they cry at all unto Me, I will surely hear their cry, and My wrath shall wax hot, and I will kill you with

---

[1] The difference between the prophetic and priestly elements in the Law is well marked by Wellhausen, who compares the Torah of the priests to a spring which is constantly running, and that of the prophet to one 'which is intermittent, but which when it is in action, wells up all the more powerfully' (*Gesch. Israels*, p. 413).

[2] *Einleitung*, p. 75.

## The Oldest Code.

the sword; and your wives shall be widows, and your children fatherless' (Exod. xxii. 22-24). If a neighbour's garment is taken in pledge, it is to be restored to him before sundown. 'For it is his only covering ... wherein shall he sleep? And it shall come to pass, when he crieth unto Me, that I will hear; for I am gracious' (ibid. ver. 27). When we consider this characteristic, which is not peculiar to the Book of the Covenant but runs through the whole legislation from first to last, we see clearly how an element of inspiration enters into it. The lawgiver, whoever he is, the succession of lawgivers, have really 'stood in the council'[1] of the Almighty. They speak, and are authorized to speak, in His name. The consulting of the Lord was not a mere delusion. It was an expression of the fact that Israel was really the people of His choice, that He had promised to dwell with them and walk with them, and that He should be their God and they would be His people.

The second characteristic is the anxious sense of justice which breathes through all the clauses, especially towards the weak and defenceless—the stranger, the widow, the fatherless, the poor, the slave[2]. It is

---

[1] Jer. xxiii. 18, 22.
[2] Comp. Huxley, *Essays on Controverted Questions*, p. 52 : 'The Bible has been the *Magna Charta* of the poor and of the oppressed; down to modern times, no State has had a constitution in which the interests of the people are so largely taken into account, in which the duties, so much more than the privileges, of rulers are insisted upon, as that drawn up for Israel in Deuteronomy and Leviticus; nowhere is the fundamental truth that the welfare of the State, in the long run, depends on the uprightness of the citizen so strongly laid down.'

in this early code that we find that little touch of humane sentiment even towards dumb animals, 'Thou shalt not seethe a kid in its mother's milk.' No doubt the particular form which the sense of justice takes is conditioned by the age to which it belongs. It is in some respects of a rudimentary kind. For instance, we find here that very law of retaliation, the eye for an eye and tooth for a tooth, which was to be repealed under the Christian dispensation. Even this provision was probably in the first instance a mitigation of existing practice; it seems to have meant not 'an eye shall be exacted' but 'only an eye shall be exacted.' But side by side with this principle we have the germs of another which was destined ultimately to supersede it. The Christian precept is, 'Love your enemies.' But a distinct step has been taken towards loving one's enemy when it is laid down that his ox or his ass are not to suffer, that they are to be restored to him when they go astray, and that, enemy though he is, if his ass should fall down under its burden it is to be relieved. The consideration which is extended to an enemy's chattels may soon come to be extended to himself.

But there is another side to the Pentateuchal legislation of which so far little has been said, the cultus or regulations for worship. Some simple regulations of this kind enter into the Book of the Covenant of which we have just been speaking. These of course expand and multiply until they take up a large part of the completed Pentateuch. The laws as we now have them probably date from every period in the history of Israel, some of them, like the institution of sacrifice, circumcision, the sabbath, going back some way beyond Moses, very possibly to the time before the Hebrew nation had separated from its Semitic kindred. On the other hand, some of the latest provisions appear to fall between Ezekiel and Ezra, and some it may be even later than Ezra. It would be out of place for me to attempt to particularize. The more exact determination of dates must be left to those whose business it is to make a special study of the Old Testament. Only by the way I would venture to suggest that special caution should be used in applying the argument from silence.

The ceremonial law is the chief monument of the work of the priests, and brings home to us more than anything else their share in the development of Israel's religion. Can we claim for them inspiration in this? Of the two main tests which we applied to the work of the prophets—their own consciousness and the character of the result of their work—in the case of the priests we have access only to the latter. But we can stand back, as it were, from this work of theirs as it has come down to us, so as to see it as a whole and let the leading principles disengage themselves from the mass of details; and so looking upon it we can ask ourselves whether it is such a product as is worthy to have come from God—to have come from Him, that is, in the way in which other forms of revelation have come from Him, through avowedly human channels and by human and natural processes, yet with an impulse and guidance communicated to those processes by the Holy Spirit.

A natural prejudice is excited against the work of the priests by two things: on the one hand by the attitude of opposition to it taken up at certain times by the Prophets, and on the other hand by its complete abrogation on the coming of Christ.

Although it may be true that the ceremonial system was not perfected until after the Exile, there must have been at least an elaborate cultus long before this. Some of the grandest passages in the Prophets are aimed directly against superstitious devotion to the externals of worship while the moral law was neglected[1]. The burning zeal of the Prophets for spiritual religion frequently takes this negative form of denouncing a worship which was clearly not spiritual.

There lies the gist of the whole matter. The cultus doubtless might be unspiritual, but if it was, the fault lay not in the cultus, but in the worshipper. The system so laboriously built up by the priests was expressive of some of the profoundest truths of Israel's religion. On two sides more especially. It provided a definite sensible outlet of which many a worshipper gladly availed himself for feelings of thankfulness; and it also expressed, and by expressing deepened, the sense of guilt and reconciliation with God. We are apt to think of the Law as a mere burden. We have only to turn to the Psalms to see that it was very far from being that. 'How amiable

[1] Amos v. 21-24; Micah vi. 6-8; Isa. i. 11 ff.; Jer. vii. 21 ff., &c.

## The Ceremonial Law.

are Thy tabernacles, O Lord of hosts! My soul longeth, yea, even fainteth for the courts of the Lord: my heart and my flesh crieth out for the living God¹.' The writer of this did not find the Temple-worship burdensome. The very sparrows seemed to him happy because they made their nests in the sacred courts. It was a kindred spirit who wrote Psalms xlii and xliii. He too is athirst for God, that is for the house of God, where he once went with the multitude with the 'voice of praise and thanksgiving among such as keep holyday².' It is the same joy of pilgrimage to Jerusalem which animates the Psalms so-called 'of Ascents' or 'Degrees³.' Or if again we think of the Law not so much as a system of worship but as a collection of multitudinous precepts, we have but to look at the latter half of Ps. xix or Ps. cxix to see that these too might form a delightful study. Not the Psalmists alone but many a Rabbi in after-ages speaks with the ring of sincerity in his words of the pleasure which he took in the study of the Law⁴, though his methods may seem to us arid and mistaken.

The same experience is repeated from age to age. It makes all the difference whether we look at these

¹ Ps. lxxxiv. 1, 2.
² Ps. xlii. 1–5.
³ Pss. cxx–cxxxiv.
⁴ I may be allowed to express my sympathy with Mr. Montefiore in his generous defence of this side of later Judaism. I have long thought that Christian writers have done it much injustice. But Mr. Montefiore himself seems to me somewhat to undervalue the ceremonial side of the Law.

things from without or from within. A hard mechanical external worship, performed unwillingly as a mere routine and divorced from spiritual religion and morality, is at once joyless and valueless. The Prophets, speaking in Jehovah's name, rejected that. But it does not follow that they would equally reject the warm and heartfelt service of souls which dwelt lovingly on the significance of all that wealth of details which a piety like their own had constructed, not without the Spirit of God.

Still less can a Christian undervalue the Levitical system. True, it has been done away. But why? Because its function had been discharged, its work was done. The sacrifices of the Old Covenant were types and shadows of a yet greater and more efficacious Sacrifice. Do not, my brothers in Christ, do not let us surrender this belief which has been precious to so many generations of those who are gone. Many things concur to shake it; and this present age is apt to be impatient of that the full bearings of which it does not understand. By the very nature of the case it cannot understand them. We cannot understand how God feels towards sin. It seems to us easy to forgive largely because we are indifferent to it. Forgiveness implies a change—or what we are obliged to call a change, though our words are random words and we are speaking of things that lie far beyond our ken—in the relation of God to sin. And if anything could bring about such a change, if anything could appeal to the Father's heart, if anything could possess an infinite value,

## The Ceremonial Law.

surely it was the Death so undertaken out of boundless love and compassion for suffering humanity of the Incarnate Son. Do not let us use hard and in truth irreverent language about a penalty exacted and a debt paid. Some kind of necessity there was, but such a necessity as we cannot gauge. We know that it was there, not from any abstract reasoning for which we have not sufficient premises, but only from the facts in which it issued. *A priori* arguments the cautious Christian, who does not seek to be wise beyond what is written, will avoid. But at the same time he will feel that to reject the idea of a true sacrifice is to evacuate of its meaning much of the language of the New Testament which speaks of the Death of Christ not only as a sacrifice but as 'propitiatory,' and speaks of it thus not only in one place but in many. Moreover, besides the language of Scripture, he will see that the assumption which he is making at once fills with meaning the old Levitical sacrifices. It gives them a point in which they culminate and are fulfilled, so that they are no longer needed. The keystone, as it were, is dropped into the arch; and instead of coming to a mutilated and abrupt conclusion, the ancient system ceases only because it has passed by a natural and foreordained transition into something higher. So the counsels of God are rounded off and consummated.

But besides the direct value of the cultus as a cultus and for the profound religious ideas which it expresses, it had also another function which although indirect was hardly less important. The institutions embodied in the Law were for Israel the great bond of cohesion. They were the outward and visible sign of national unity. And as spirit is too volatile a thing to be preserved unless it is expressed in forms, it was the formal and ceremonial side of the Law which kept the nation together, and so protected and safeguarded the spiritual treasures of which it had the stewardship. Without the iron framework supplied by the Law, without the exclusiveness which was only another side of the cohesiveness which the Law generated, in the age of trial which followed the Captivity Israel must have gone to pieces. It could hardly have failed to be absorbed and submerged as other nations were. But with it would have perished the stores of Divine teaching which its previous history had accumulated. Fragments might have survived here and there; but they would have been fragments from a wreck: the few scattered planks and spars which were all that remained of a noble vessel that would never more carry its living freight to their destination. The unity and cohesion which were the marks of a Divine purpose would have been lost. We might still have had a few stray books or portions of books, but we should have had no Bible[1].

II. I would fain linger over these themes, but the exigencies of my subject compel me to pass on to another of its main divisions, the so-called *Hagiographa*, a somewhat miscellaneous collection of Sacred Writings

[1] I owe this point, which seems to me very good and true, to Mr. Headlam.

which make up the third section of the Jewish Canon. It will only be possible here to touch upon some of its salient features—the Psalms, the Wisdom Books (Proverbs, Job, and Ecclesiastes), the Song of Songs, Daniel, and Esther.

But before entering upon questions of detail, some preliminary remarks of a more general character may be made upon the inspiration of this section.

Revelation, as it is presented to us in the Old Testament, is like an inland lake which receives indeed a certain amount of surface drainage, but is fed mainly by springs which penetrate deep down into the earth. The water which wells up from these hidden sources spreads out to meet the rills which come down from the surrounding slopes and absorbs them. Dropping metaphor, we may say that there were at the heart of Israel's religion certain great formative or generative principles which increasingly as time went on permeated the nation and infused themselves into others besides those with whom they arose. The authors of these principles which I have described as formative and generative are the law-makers and prophets, not speaking or acting in their own name or by any initiative of their own, but by what they claimed to be a commission direct from God. The persistent work of these men had its effect. In spite of the difficulties with which they had to contend and the opposition with which they were met they were not mere voices crying in the wilderness. They did succeed in leavening the people with something of their own spirit. Even at the worst times there was a 'remnant' who had not bowed the knee to Baal; and after the discipline of the Exile the influence of the written and spoken word together became more and more dominant. To adopt a phrase which has been recently used, Israel became 'a Church-nation.' 'Before the Exile,' we are told, 'it was only the prophets and their disciples who had a sense of their divine mission to proclaim the true God; after the Exile, it was the entire nation in its corporate capacity[1].' I suspect that this is put somewhat too absolutely. There were 7,000 of the faithful in the Northern Kingdom alone of whom Elijah was ignorant, and there is evidence enough that the teaching of the other prophets fell at least upon some fruitful soil besides their own more immediate disciples. But an exaggeration may mark a tendency; and the tendency was no doubt in the direction indicated. So it came about that there were many in Israel, more at some periods than at others, and especially more in the later periods than the earlier, who without being either law-makers or prophets themselves had yet deeply imbibed the teaching of law-makers and prophets. So deeply did they imbibe this teaching, it took so powerful a hold upon them, that they in turn were able to give true and adequate expression to principles which they did not originate and which they helped to develope only in a minor degree. It was not for nothing that the Word of God had come to them so directly; it was not for nothing that they had lived in such close contact with men who were

---

[1] Cheyne, *Aids to the Devout Study of Criticism*, p. 171.

the immediate channels and organs of revelation; it was not for nothing that they were themselves members of a nation which had a prophetic and even, as it has been said, a 'Messianic' function[1]. It was through them that the nation discharged this function. In a certain sense and degree the devout wish of Moses, that all the Lord's people might be prophets, came true. The Spirit of the Lord was really upon them, and they too became organs and channels of its working—if not exactly main arteries, yet those smaller channels by which it is dispersed and distributed and brought to bear upon the life of men.

The books known as the *Hagiographa* were the work of these men, and are the expression of the part which they played in the economy of revelation. At the head of them stand *the Psalms*—a book endeared alike to Jew and Christian, a book which carries with it the *testimonium Spiritus Sancti* as few besides.

Here again we are confronted at the outset with a critical problem. The Psalter has been called the 'key to the Old Testament[2]'; and it is true that neither the criticism nor the history of the Old Testament can be regarded as complete until the place of the Psalter in relation to them has been determined. Its importance will be seen at once when we consider how much it contains of the spirituality of the Old Testament. Our whole conception of the history of Israel's

---

[1] Bp. Westcott, quoted by Cheyne, *Aids to the Devout Study*, &c., pp. 139, 151.

[2] By Dr. C. A. Briggs, in *North American Review*, Jan. 1892, p 104.

## IV. *The Law and the Hagiographa.*

religion is affected according to the stages in it to which this mass of spiritual song is assigned. Already it would seem as if a revolution were being wrought in the older view which regarded the age from Ezra onwards as an expanse of dry and barren legalism. If the Psalter is really, as it is contended, in the main the 'hymn-book of the Second Temple,' that alone is enough to redeem the period to which it belongs from any such charge. And this might well be thought sufficient compensation for the denuding of earlier periods, that the later should be enriched out of their abundance. We must not however allow ourselves to be influenced by considerations of this kind. The object of history and criticism is to give to every period its due.

The question as to the date of the different parts of the Psalter is still *sub judice*[1]. Much attention has been called to it of late, and very divergent views are current[2]; but the whole position is a hopeful one. If in some directions the data are scanty and liable to be strained

---

[1] See Additional Note, p. 270 : *The inferior Limit for the Date of the Psalter.*

[2] It is characteristic of this divergence that of two of the most recent monographs on the date of portions of the Psalter, both by able and competent men and going closely into their respective subjects, one maintains that all the psalms of Book I (i–xli), with the exception of Pss. i and xxxiii, were written before the Babylonian Exile (E. Sellin, *Disputatio de Origine Carminum quae primus Psalterii liber continet*, Erlangen and Leipzig, 1892), while the other, taking a group of eleven psalms, eight of which belong to Book I, contends that all are the work of the same author writing at the end of or soon after the Exile, whose name even is elicited through a hint of Lagarde's as 'Phadaias' or 'Phadael' (Rahlfs, *Ani und Anaw in den Psalmen*, Göttingen, 1892).

# The Psalms.

beyond what they will legitimately bear, in other directions they are plentiful; and the patient labour which is being devoted to them cannot long be without fruit.

Thus much is clear. The Psalter as we have it is made up of a number of smaller collections, which once had a separate existence. The best analogy for the history and structure of the Psalter would be that which is supplied by our own hymn-books. Just as the hymns of Watts and Wesley, of Newton and Cowper, of Lyte and Keble have been to a greater or less extent incorporated into succeeding collections, so also a number of minor collections have contributed to make our present Psalter. Fortunately the Jewish editors kept their materials together more than ours do, so that it is possible even now to distinguish some of these smaller collections. Two of them seem to have borne originally the name of David [1]; and it is of course ultimately from them that the whole volume came to be regarded as David's. A similar process seems to have been at work in the smaller collections and in the larger. A group of Psalms would be brought together, some with headings attached to them; and the heading which stood first would be taken to cover the whole group. When the group was broken up or inserted in a larger book, this first heading would be

---

[1] It has been rendered highly probable that in the original order of Book II the Davidic psalms (li–lxxii) came first, then the Korah psalms (xlii–xlix), and then a group of Asaph psalms consisting of Pss. l, lxxiii–lxxxiii (Driver, *Introd.* p. 350; Robertson Smith, *O. T. J. C.* p. 199, &c.).

repeated with each of the psalms which it was thought to cover. It has been acutely pointed out that there is one instance in which this can be proved to have been the case. There is a little group, Pss. cxxi-cxxxiv, each of which is headed in our Bible, 'a Song of Degrees' (A. V.) or 'Ascents' (R. V.), *i.e.* in all probability a psalm sung on pilgrimage by those who went up to attend the great feasts at Jerusalem. But although each of these Psalms is now headed 'a song of degrees, or ascents,' the Hebrew is strictly not 'a song,' but 'the songs,' which is clearly the general heading of the group repeated by inadvertence without alteration before each Psalm [1]. In like manner we can easily understand how as an appendix came to be added to a group which bore a name, that name was soon taken to cover the appendix as well. And we can also understand how because the whole Psalter was headed by a Davidic collection it too came to be regarded as throughout Davidic.

It is now generally agreed that the headings which have come down to us are of very little direct value. But indirectly their value may be considerable. In conjunction with other data they may enable us to determine the succession of the different parts of the Psalter [2]. They may give us a clue to the date of the editorial processes to which both whole and parts have been subject.

For besides this external editing, if we may so call it, which brought the groups of Psalms together and

[1] Robertson Smith, *O. T. J. C.* p. 203.
[2] See the quotation from Budde in Additional Note, p. 270 *inf.*

provided them with headings, there was no doubt a good deal of internal editing as well. The fact that the Psalter was used in the Temple services would naturally lead to a certain amount of adaptation. Many of the Psalms we may be sure were not originally written with this object. Some modification would be needed in order to fit the expression of private feeling for public worship; and we can also well believe that ideas and allusions which sounded archaic and out of date would be modernized. Just as in our own hymn-books the form in which the hymn is actually sung often differs considerably from the original, so also in the Jewish Church the same thing would take place, but probably on a larger scale, because, as we have already said, all idea of literary property and of the obligations entailed by it was absent.

We shall have to return to this side of the subject when we come to consider the history of the Psalter along with the other books as a collection itself and part of a collection. But for the present the main question before us is that of Inspiration. In what sense can we say that the Psalms are inspired?

In the first place we have to note that there are a number of instances [1] in which the Psalmist adopts forms of language which we are accustomed to associate specially with prophecy. These are for the most part cases in which Jehovah Himself is introduced as speaking. In Ps. xii. 5 we have an asseveration

---

[1] These are collected by Dr. Cheyne, *Aids to Devout Study*, &c., p. 152 n. Compare the same writer's commentary on Pss. lxii. 11. lxxxv. 9.

quite after the manner of the prophets: 'I will arise, saith the Lord : I will set him (*i.e.* the poor and needy) in safety,' &c. In Ps. xlvi. 10, as a climax to the song of triumph which is commonly referred to the destruction of the army of Sennacherib, a short emphatic sentence is referred to Jehovah Himself: 'Be still, and know that I am God : I will be exalted among the nations, I will be exalted in the earth.' In three other psalms (Pss. l. 4–23, lxxv. 2–6 [1], lxxxi. 6–16) longer passages are put in the mouth of Jehovah; the psalmist becomes His spokesman, just like the prophets. And again in no less than three places (Pss. xlix. 4, lxii. 11, lxxxv. 8 [2]) we seem to have glimpses of the process by which the psalmist received some special revelation, in every case as coming from without, from God, and clearly distinguished from any imagination of his own.

Now it is somewhat remarkable that when we come to look into the authorship of the psalms which contain these references, two (Pss. xii, lxii) are ascribed to David, three (xlvi, xlix, lxxxv) to the 'sons of Korah,' and three more (l, lxxv, lxxxi) to Asaph. In other words, six out of eight are Levitical. They are the work not of prophets but of priests. Again, in this connexion we observe that Miriam is called a 'prophetess' (Exod. xv. 20, E) on the occasion of her song of triumph over Pharaoh ; that in Chronicles the Levitical singers are several times called 'seers' (1 Chron. xxv. 5 Heman, 2 Chron. xxix. 30 Asaph,

---

[1] Or, according to some, vv. 2–5, or 2–4.
[2] See Cheyne and Baethgen, *ad loc.*

xxxv. 15 Jeduthun); and that in the same books the service of music and song is described as 'prophesying' (1 Chron. xxv. 1–3 *ter*). And we remember how, in the earlier period at least, the prophets made use of music as a stimulus to inspiration (1 Sam. x. 5 f.; 2 Kings iii. 15)[1].

It would be wrong to argue at once from these data that the psalmists possessed the full measure of prophetic inspiration. It is rather by an extension of its use that the word 'prophesy' comes to be applied to them. And the comparative rarity of prophetic passages in the Psalms leaves us free to suppose that even in these there may be a certain literary element. The alternative must be open that they are not directly the work of prophets speaking prophetically, but rather modelled upon prophetic utterances. We may however rightly infer that a hard and fast line is not to be drawn round the prophetic inspiration, as if the prophets had it in its fulness and none beside them. Here, as elsewhere, we cannot doubt that there was the same gradual shading off of higher into lower forms and *vice versa*. In the Church of the Old Covenant as in that of the New every man had his proper *charisma*; and the self-same Spirit expressed Itself in many degrees and ways.

We must needs trace the influence of that Holy Spirit through the whole Psalter—through the whole generally, though not alike in every part, for it must be admitted that sometimes we are conscious not only of human limitations, but of the violence of human passion.

[1] See Riehm, *Einleitung in d. A. T.* ii. 199.

## IV. The Law and the Hagiographa.

The organ-music of the Psalms is of wonderful compass and range. It has its low notes as well as its high. But taken altogether, and when due allowance has been made for the imperfection of the human medium, it remains the classic to all time of prayer and praise!

Let us think for a moment what that means. When we have mentally put aside every verse which bears upon itself the mark of a lower stage of religious attainment, how many hundreds, nay how many thousands, remain which even to this day, and even translated out of their original tongue into foreign and alien modes of speech, are the most perfect expression we can find of religious emotion[1]! This little nation, the shuttlecock of its powerful neighbours, so devoid of greatness in arts or sciences, after all these centuries of religious and social advance, puts into our mouths words which for penetrating truth and beauty we could never approach ourselves!

If we were to take away from our hymn-books all they contained which was the mere echo and shadow of the Psalter, how much of value would be left? This insignificant book of a hundred and fifty sacred poems—truly the product of a nation because every one of them is to all intents and purposes anonymous—has been teaching the world, dictating to the world

---

[1] The Psalms as expressive of religious emotion have been the theme of much eloquent writing. Among recent examples may be mentioned, Church, *Gifts of Civilisation*, pp. 391–441, *Advent Sermons*, pp. 13 ff., 39 ff.; Fairbairn, *Christ in the Centuries*, p. 72 f.; Cheyne, *Aids to Devout Study*, p. 154 f.

## The Wisdom-Literature.

its prayers and its praises, ever since it was first composed! Shall we not say—*must* we not say—that the book which has done that bears the outward stamp and sign of the Spirit of God? Does it not enter, so conspicuously as to compel us to recognise its importance, into the working out of that vast design by which God has first formed and then kept alive the knowledge of Himself amongst men?

The Psalms are not all hymns. Some take a philosophical or didactic turn (notably Pss. xxxvii, xlix, and lxxiii); and in this they touch another branch of Hebrew literature which is represented within the Canon by the group of books, Proverbs, Job, and Ecclesiastes[1]. These books are the work of a class who stand out clearly in the history of Israel by the side of prophets and priests, though the allusions to them are naturally fewer, as they did not play so prominent a part in the public life of the nation. This is the class of the 'Wise Men.' They did not exactly constitute an order in the same sense as the prophets. We hear nothing of 'schools of the wise' like the schools of the prophets. And yet their activity is in any case spread over many centuries; they conform to the same models, and keep up a continuous literary tradition.

[1] There is much very valuable literature on the Wisdom-Books, notably in English the sections in Dr. Driver's *Introduction*, and Dr. Cheyne's *Job and Solomon*; but I must discharge a debt of gratitude by saying that for my particular purpose I have found nothing so helpful as the popular studies by Dr. A. B. Davidson in *Book by Book*. Dr. Davidson has a singular power of getting at the heart of a religious conception.

## IV. The Law and the Hagiographa.

It is remarkable that there should have been such a definite assignment of subjects as there is between the 'wise men' on the one hand and prophets and priests on the other. The wise men do not deal with the larger political issues, with the national aspirations, with the Messianic hope; they have little to say as to law or cultus; but they confine themselves to problems of individual life and conduct. The strong religious background is common to this with the other leading forms of Hebrew literature; but it is concerned in the first instance with practice and morals rather than with theology proper, though we shall see in a moment how it might rise from the one to the other.

The most characteristic product of the Wise Men is the *Book of Proverbs*. From this alone we might judge what an extended history the class must have had, though it has not found any chronicler. The historians of Israel were concerned with the ways and dealings of God, and not with the achievements— literary or otherwise—of men. Like the Psalms, the Book of Proverbs is highly composite, and consists of a number of smaller collections brought together in one larger collection. These smaller collections in turn we can hardly doubt represent the gradual accretions of gnomic material contributed by many minds, and much of it handed down orally from mouth to mouth before it was committed to writing. This seems a fair inference from the fact that the same proverb is so often repeated with but slight variation. The tradition which connects Solomon with this gnomic Wisdom is good and early[1]; and it is quite possible that some of the proverbs which have come down to us may be ultimately derivable from Solomon himself, though we cannot determine which—the titles, in this respect, not really helping us. I hope in the next lecture to say a little more about the chronology of the book. It must suffice for the present to express the opinion that relatively the small collection xxv–xxix is probably the earliest, and that while the Appendix (xxx, xxxi) is no doubt the latest of all, there seem to be good reasons for regarding i. 7–ix as the latest of the larger divisions. This view[2] is not only probable on literary grounds, but also gives the best sequence in connexion with our present subject, which leads us to consider the Book of Proverbs primarily in its bearing upon the history of Inspiration and Revelation.

Here we must start from the fact that the Wisdom which finds its expression in the Book of Proverbs is, in its genus at least, no monopoly of Israel. When the document just referred to in the Book of Kings speaks of the wisdom of Solomon, its standards of comparison

---

[1] 1 Kings iv. 29–34 (in our English Bibles, =v. 9–14 in Heb.), referred by Kamphausen (in Kautzsch's Bible) and by Kittel to that 'Book of the Acts of Solomon' (1 Kings xi. 41) which Kittel describes as the oldest piece of historical writing in Hebrew (*Gesch. d. Heb.* ii. 50); otherwise Cornill, *Einl.* p. 121.

[2] It was first put forward in the form here adopted by Dr. A. B. Davidson, and is mentioned with approval by Dr. Driver (*Introd.* p. 381), but in regard to the position of cc. i–ix is accepted by many other scholars (*e.g.* Cornill, *Einl.* p. 262; Cheyne, *Expos.* 1892, i. 245).

are taken outside Israel. 'Solomon's wisdom,' it says, 'excelled the wisdom of all the children of the East, and all the wisdom of Egypt. For he was wiser than all men; than Ethan the Ezrahite, and Heman, and Calcol, and Darda, the sons of Mahol: and his fame was in all the nations round about[1].' And elsewhere we gather that Edom in like manner was famous for its wisdom[2]. Such wisdom naturally took the form of shrewd observations on life. We find such observations in the Book of Proverbs, but we find there something more. It is not likely that the proverbs of Edom or of the East if they had been preserved to us would have had for their keynote that which runs through not only the Book of Proverbs but the whole Wisdom-literature, 'Behold the fear of the Lord, that is wisdom; and to depart from evil is understanding[3].' We cannot doubt that the wisdom of Israel differed from that of the neighbouring nations by the way in which it ran up into religion; nor can we doubt that it was as much superior to theirs as the religion of Israel was superior to their religion. But there is this further characteristic of the Book of Proverbs, that its teaching rises upwards in an ascending scale which seems roughly to correspond with the chronological succession of its different portions. The lower stratum begins with the observations on life and manners, on man in society, on the effect of good and evil fortune upon character. We

---

[1] 1 Kings iv. 30 f. (v. 10 f. Heb.).
[2] Jer. xlix. 7; Obad. 8.
[3] Job xxviii. 28 (cf. Prov. i. 7, ix. 10; Eccles. xii. 13). I quote the maxim in the form in which it is most familiar.

## Proverbs.

can imagine that here there would be much in common with the gnomic literature of the East generally. But with the Hebrews these observations would take a more religious cast and colour, until there is gradually formed that identification of Wisdom with Religion, as it were the 'grave and beautiful damsel named Discretion' who discourses with Christian the pilgrim on his way to Mount Zion. And then the teacher-poet, having reached this high conception and looking out upon the world in the light which it gives, begins to see the scattered indications of wise appointment in nature, in man, in the social order and moral constitution of things, converge inwards until they meet in that Divine attribute by virtue of which God made the world.

> 'The Lord possessed me in the beginning of His way,
> Before His works of old.
> I was set up from everlasting, from the beginning,
> Or ever the earth was.
> When there were no depths, I was brought forth,
> When there were no fountains abounding with water.
> . . . . . . . . . .
> There was I by Him, as a master workman:
> And I was daily His delight,
> Rejoicing always before Him;
> Rejoicing in His habitable earth;
> And my delight was with the sons of men[1].'

This sublime picture of Creative Wisdom was not suffered to remain a mere poetical ornament of the book in which it occurs. It gave the first suggestion of the idea which is taken up in the prologue of St. John's Gospel: 'In the beginning was the Word,

---
[1] Prov. viii. 22-24, 30, 31.

and the Word was with God, and the Word was God. ... All things were made by Him; and without Him was not anything made that hath been made. In Him was life; and the Life was the light of men[1].' It is needless to say what a momentous influence this idea has had on the whole after-course of Christian theology. If we believe that that theology expresses, however roughly and approximately, what God designed that man should think about Himself, then in the carrying out of that design the eighth chapter of Proverbs has played an important part, and it is only the natural and fitting climax and culmination of the rest of the book.

The *Book of Job* contains a personification of Wisdom not less sublime, though introduced with a different purpose and not so directly on the line of development of fundamental theological ideas. At least it does not point forward in like manner to the future, but emphasizes—nobly and most effectively emphasizes—an idea already obtained, that of the unsearchable transcendence of God.

Taking the Book of Job as a whole, it might be urged that it struggles with a problem to which it does not furnish a completely satisfactory or final solution. The prosperity of the wicked and unmerited suffering of the righteous was a stone of stumbling to the Hebrew mind. It is repeatedly coming up, as in the didactic Psalms to which reference has been made, but nowhere is there such a sustained attempt to grapple

[1] St. John i. 1, 3.

with it as here in the Book of Job. And even here only once, and that obscurely and almost doubtfully, does the argument pierce through to that belief in a future life which gives the best answer to Job's perplexities.

To say this however means but little, if it is said in disparagement of the book as inspired or as a vehicle of revelation. God has willed that the different steps in the progress of revelation should be closely linked each to each, and the time for belief in a future state was not yet. It has been no less truly than finely observed that for the Hebrew 'it was not defect but excess of religion that postponed so long the doctrine of immortality[1].' It was because within the sphere of revelation the sense of the presence of God was so full and so intense, that this life only seemed to suffice and it did not seem necessary to fall back upon a further life to come. But it has evidently been a part of the order of revelation that one lesson should be learnt thoroughly before passing on to another. The very form of the Book of Job, a dialogue in which the speakers take different sides, ensures the thoroughness of the lesson. A more earnest wrestling with a deep and difficult problem, a stricter testing of all the side lights thrown upon it by current beliefs, a stronger effort to get nearer to the central truth, was not possible at that stage of revelation. And all this searching of heart was the best guarantee that the step in advance with which it ends should be no unstable footing, but firmly and well taken.

[1] Dr. A. B. Davidson in *Book by Book*, p. 180.

## IV. The Law and the Hagiographa.

The Book of Job is of course splendid poetry; and the poetry enhances its effectiveness and value; but it does not constitute its inspiration. The inspiration lies deeper down in that strong religious sense, that active energy of religion, which determines the course at once of thought and of imagination. If we believe, as the Christian does believe, that our life is surrounded as if by a circumambient ether of spiritual influence in which all alike live and move and have their being, but which becomes stronger in the individual in proportion as he is fitted to receive it; if we believe, as we may fairly do from the products which lie before us at this day, that there have been ages and regions in which for the accomplishment of some larger purpose God has willed that this spiritual influence should be as it were focussed and concentrated; then we shall not hesitate to say that the age and the region in which were composed these books of the *Hagiographa*, Psalms, Proverbs, and Job, certainly came under that description. It is not merely that an individual here and there is touched by a stronger prompting, but we feel that there is a sympathetic movement behind the individual. Of course then, as at all times, Israel, the nation, was like a drag-net which gathered in of every kind both bad and good; but there was so large a nucleus of religious minds deeply impressed by certain fundamental truths that they acted and reacted upon each other. Their work seems to come with a mass and volume which is not merely that of single units. In this respect there is a decided gain now that it has come to be understood how much of the religious history of Israel is anonymous, so that especially in books like the Psalter and Proverbs we find ourselves compassed about by a very 'cloud of witnesses.' And even within the narrower limits of the Book of Job, the almost general agreement that the speeches of Elihu are to be separated from the rest of the poem, and the fact that (as we have seen) there are several psalms which treat of the same subject, remind us that we are in the presence not of isolated speculations and aspirations, but of a connected movement of thought setting in one direction.

Here no less than in the case of the Prophets it is right to insist on an external objective cause for the phenomena we are considering. It is not that holy men of old took upon themselves to speak, but they spake as they were moved by the Holy Ghost. The reasons why we insist on this may be reduced in brief to three: (1) the very gradual way in which the prophetic inspiration, the nature of which is clear, shades off into that of the other books, the nature of which is more obscure; (2) the difficulty of otherwise accounting for the wide interval which separates the religious products of Israel from those of the nations round, allied as many of them were by blood and civilization; and (3) the fact that the character of these products, as they have come down to us, by no means gives the lie to but rather tends decidedly to confirm the view, which early became established and has kept its hold ever since, that they owe their origin to the Spirit of God.

## IV. The Law and the Hagiographa.

Still there are no doubt well-marked grades of inspiration in the Canon; and there are some books which have their place quite upon the outskirts of it, and one or two in which inspiration is hardly perceptible at all. I do not include in this number the *Book of Ecclesiastes*, for which I am under no temptation to apologize, as it has become almost the custom to do. Of course it is not to be contended that Ecclesiastes is on the highest plane of Old Testament revelation, still less on that of the New; but it has a plane of its own. Just as there was room and more than room for a St. Thomas among the Apostles, so also there is a fitting place for this grave and austere thinker among the wise men of Israel. Two things are conspicuous about him. First his absolute sincerity. He looks out into the world, and he sets down unflinchingly what he sees. He will not prophesy smooth things. His experience must have been really narrow and unfortunate: he had fallen upon evil days: but he will not gloss over unpalatable truth, or paint it otherwise than it is presented to him. Nor is his gloomy view of things due to morbid self-consciousness, as with so many of the moderns who might claim kinship with him. He does not taste 'with the distempered appetite' of self-love. His natural bent was towards melancholy. But he deals with it honestly; and so it was that his eyes were opened to see something of the hidden meaning in the darker side of life. 'It is better to go to the house of mourning than to go to the house of feasting: for that is the end of all men; and the living will lay it to his heart. Sorrow is better than laughter; for by the sadness of the countenance the heart is made better' (or 'glad'). 'The heart of the wise is in the house of mourning; but the heart of fools is in the house of mirth. It is better to hear the rebuke of the wise, than for a man to hear the song of fools' (Eccles. vii. 2-5). The author of this book was no shallow or feeble soul; and his book is bracing as well as moving. It contains other noble sayings which have not I think always had justice done to them [1].

For the second striking fact seems to be this, that in spite of all his perplexities the author still comes back to the simple faith of Israel. The end of the matter is with him still, 'to fear God and keep His commandments; for this is the whole duty of man' (Eccles. xii. 13). I am aware that this and other expressions of the like kind have been rejected as interpolations, but I have little doubt that they are genuine. For these reasons. (1) If the book had been originally without the saving clauses, it is more probable that it would have been left out of the Canon altogether

---

[1] Among these is Eccles. v. 2, so magnificently applied by Hooker, *Eccl. Pol.* i. 2. 2. It may be true that the God of Ecclesiastes is a severe and distant God, and not 'our Father which is in heaven.' But the lesson of religious awe needs to be learnt first; and it greatly deepens the sense of Fatherhood to remember that He who condescends to be called by that name is none other than the 'High and Lofty One, that inhabiteth eternity.' Nor does it detract from the value of the principle which the Preacher enunciates that it is concerned in the context with a minor matter of vows. We are I fear in danger of giving way to a sentiment which shrinks from the austere side of religion.

P

than fitted for inclusion in it by their insertion. A pious scribe would have passed it by. (2) It seems to me to be psychologically more probable, especially in a son of Israel, that he should have this reserve in the bottom of his soul than that he should give way to blank and unredeemed pessimism. And (3), as Cornill truly says, the thought is not confined to the suspected passages but runs through the whole book[1]. The same writer well remarks that this feature in the book, its fidelity to the leading principles of Israel's religion, is the greatest triumph of which that religion can boast[2]. To probe to the bottom the misery of the world, to find nothing but chaos and unsolved enigmas, to follow the logic of thought wherever it leads, and yet suddenly to stop short of the obvious conclusion, that there is no God and no moral government of the world at all, but instead to fall back on the simple plain practical duties of religion, shows how strong was the hold which those duties had and how hard it was to shake an Israelite's faith.

And for this reason we may be glad to have Ecclesiastes included in our Canon, because of the assurance which it gives that even a pessimist may have a place in the kingdom of heaven. It is possible to go down to the grave without a smile; it is possible not to shake off the burden of the mystery in all its oppressive weight to the end, and yet provided there is no tampering with conscience or with primary truth, to be held worthy to help and teach even from the pages

---

[1] *Einl.* p. 250.   [2] *Ibid.* p. 248.

## The Song of Songs.

of Holy Writ those who have a like experience and like difficulties.

Almost in many ways at the opposite pole to Ecclesiastes is the *Song of Songs*. The author is no pessimist, 'sicklied o'er with the pale cast of thought.' He is one who enters keenly into life and whose blood courses warmly in his veins. The Song of Songs, as it is now understood, is just an idyll of faithful human love, and nothing more. It is never quoted in the New Testament, and contributes nothing to the sum of revelation. Its place in our Bibles is due to a method of interpretation which is now very generally abandoned. What are we to say to such a book? There can be no question of inspiration, as we have so far understood it, even in the case of Ecclesiastes. The question rather is whether we can see any Providential purpose which has been served by the inclusion, and which is still served by the retention, of the book in the Canon. I think we may discern such a purpose. If we were forming a Canon ourselves for the first time and the book were presented to us, we should probably say, with all admiration for its beauty, that it was not beauty of such a kind as we should associate with Sacred Scripture. But now that it has been in the Canon so many centuries the position is different. In the first place, we may welcome it as a proof of the catholicity of Scripture. *Nihil humani a se alienum putat.* As now understood the book does teach a moral lesson. When it is seen that the persons in the drama besides the chorus are three and not two, and that the heroine of the story resists the advances of a powerful monarch in order to be true to her shepherd-lover, the picture which results is simple and beautiful and worthy of its poetical setting. The poem, as it stands in the Canon, is not only a consecration of human love, but also a consecration of the love of nature. It sets its seal upon that open receptive sympathetic spirit to which all the works of the Lord are good and made for man to take his delight in.

A further consequence of the inclusion of the book in the Canon is that the ideas which it expresses have been shielded from profanation, and as it were set apart for holy uses. I do not think that we need deprecate the allegorical use of the Song of Songs, so long as it is quite understood that this is not its original meaning. We often apply the great sayings of poets and imaginative writers in senses which were not originally intended, but which are not the less apt and beautiful. And there is a special reason why we should do so here, because the Church has for so many centuries specially singled out the Song for this mode of interpretation. There is pertinence in the criticism 'that the Song is only allegorical in so far as all true marriage to a religious mind is allegorical[1].' But not 'all true marriage' has been fitted for such a use by having the same veil of sanctity thrown over it.

If the Canon of the Old Testament is anywhere

[1] *Expositor*, 1892, i. 253. Compare Driver, *Introd.* p. 423 f.

# Esther.

at fault it is in regard to the *Book of Esther*. It is not probable that the book is strictly historical, though it is also not a pure romance like Judith and Tobit. The writer has a good knowledge of Persian manners and customs; in particular he seems to be familiar with the life of the Court, and the character of Ahasuerus (Xerxes) is in accordance with history. But there is reason to think that the account of the origin of the name given to the Feast of Purim is not correct[1]; and if so, the interval between the composition of the book and the events of which it treats must have been considerable. In that interval there was time for a nucleus of tradition to assume the rounded literary shape in which it is presented to us.

In spite of some opposition at first the book became very popular among the later Jews[2]. It played skilfully upon that form of patriotism the motto of which is 'Love thy friend and hate thine enemy.' According to it the Jews were not the victims but the actors in a sort of Sicilian Vespers in which no less than 75,000 of the population hostile to them fell. The numbers are sufficient to relieve the national conscience of this stain.

But whatever attraction the book may have had for the Jews, it could have but little for the Christian. Accordingly we find that it was the last of all the

---

[1] This inference is based upon a treatise by Lagarde, referred to by Driver, *Introd.* p. 455; Cheyne, *Expos.* 1892, i. 260; Robertson Smith, *O. T. J. C.* p. 184 n.

[2] Ryle, *Canon*, p. 199 f., compared with Driver, *Introd.* p. 452.

## IV. The Law and the Hagiographa.

books in the Hebrew Canon to obtain sanction in the Church. It was omitted from the list of Melito, placed last on that of Origen, relegated to the class of ἀναγινωσκόμενα by Athanasius, omitted by Gregory Nazianzen and by Amphilochius,—who notes however that it was 'added by some,'—omitted again later by Leontius, and classed among the disputed books by Nicephorus.

It is not quite clear what was the origin of this prolonged resistance—how much of it was due to the original omission in the list of Melito, propagated through the History of Eusebius, in which case it would be a survival of the early Jewish opposition to the book; or how much is to be set down to direct objection to its character and contents. There was certainly room for such objection. The Book of Esther derives no sanction from the New Testament. It has often been pointed out that it does not even name the name of God; and it adds nothing to the sum of revelation[1]. The book, as we have seen, after a time secured its place in the Jewish Canon, and through the Jewish passed over into the Christian Canon, but more we may believe by way of tacit acquiescence than of active approval. Its reception was doubtless helped by the typical interpretation according to which the deliverance of the Jews stood for a deliverance of the Church[2].

---

[1] See however for a different estimate of this book Additional Note B: *The Religious Value of the Book of Esther.*

[2] Hieron. *Ep.* liii. *Ad Paulinum*, § 8 (ed. Migne, i. 547): *Esther in Ecclesiae typo populum liberat de periculo, et interfecto Aman,*

## Daniel.

The *Book of Daniel* again brings up the question of authorship. And here too it is difficult not to feel that the critical view has won the day. The human mind will in the end accept that theory which covers the greatest number of particular facts and harmonizes best with the sum total of knowledge. Now in regard to the Book of Daniel these conditions appear to be far better satisfied by the supposition that the book was written in the second century B. C. than in the sixth[1]. (1) It is found that the writer's acquaintance with the history of the earlier period is imperfect, but that it becomes more and more exact as he approaches the times of Antiochus Epiphanes (176-164 B. C.). (2) Hebrew philologists are clear in their opinion that the language of the book favours the later date. Two points in this part of the evidence can be appreciated by those who are not Hebraists. There occur in the book no less than three names of musical instruments which are Greek and not Hebrew or Aramaic. But although it is barely conceivable that these names might have become naturalized in the East as early

*qui interpretatur* iniquitas, *partes convivii et diem celebrem mittit in posteros.*

[1] On the details of the evidence which follows see the *Introductions*, especially those of Driver and Cornill, the scholarly edition by Mr. A. A. Bevan, Cambridge, 1892, and a pamphlet by Kamphausen, *Das Buch Daniel und die neuere Geschichtsforschung*, Leipzig, 1893. But even the most moderate critics now take this side—Delitzsch, Riehm, Strack, von Orelli, Schlottmann, and others (Driver, p. 483). Even those who (like Meinhold in Strack and Zöckler's *Kurzgef. Kommentar*) assign part of the book to an earlier date, place the later chapters in the time of Antiochus Epiphanes.

## IV. The Law and the Hagiographa.

as the sixth century, it is far more probable that they would be introduced by the conquests of Alexander. We have also the strange fact that in a book supposed to belong to the age of Nebuchadnezzar the name 'Chaldaean' is used not for the imperial nation itself but for a class of astrologers or soothsayers (Dan. ii. 2, 4, 5, 10, &c.). (3) There is a notable silence in regard to the existence of the book from the sixth century to the second, but from the second century onwards it exercised the greatest influence over all succeeding literature. (4) There is the place of the book in the Jewish Canon—not as in our Bibles among the Prophets next after Ezekiel, but in a place to itself, nearly at the end of the *Hagiographa*. This seems to show that the book was not written until the Canon of the Prophets was closed.

If we follow these indications we are obliged to conclude, that the name of Daniel is only assumed, and that the real author is unknown, but that he lived under Antiochus Epiphanes, and that he wrote, as some critics would say precisely, in the early part of the year 164 B.C.[1] The first question then which I must consider put to me is, How it is compatible with the character of a Sacred Book to bear a name which does not by strict right belong to it. We ought indeed to have discussed this question before, because although the Book of Job no doubt does not claim to have been written by the patriarch, the name of the author is assumed probably

---

[1] So Cornill, *Einl.* p. 258 f.; Cheyne, *Bampton Lectures*, p. xxxvi.

in the case of the Book of Jonah, and certainly in that of Ecclesiastes. The last-named book is a good example of the real significance of this assumption. The author speaks of himself under three names, as Solomon, as 'the Preacher[1],' and as one of the 'wise men' (Eccles. xii. 9, 11). The last is evidently his true designation. The first is a disguise so transparent as to be no disguise at all.

The use of assumed names marks the last stage in the formation of the Jewish Canon[2]. Once more we must remember how lightly the Hebrews thought of authorship. Their writers had absolutely no personal ambition. The 'wise man' who wrote Ecclesiastes did not in the least care to be known as the author of a striking book; he *did* care to put forward certain lessons, the fruit of much thought and ripe experience, which might be of use to others besides himself. But by this time the Jews were beginning to look with a jealous eye upon all writings which claimed to speak with authority. The Law had long been recognised as a Sacred Book. The writings of the ancient prophets and teachers were being collected and diligently and reverently studied. How was a book like Ecclesiastes to gain a hearing among them? The author had recourse to the simple device of heading his work with the name of the typical Sage or 'Wise man,' the first and greatest of his order. In spite of this it was a long time before

---

[1] On this title see especially Driver, *Introd.*, p. 437.

[2] See Additional Note C: *The Origin and Character of Pseudonymous Literature among the Jews.*

## IV. The Law and the Hagiographa.

the book obtained assured recognition. The question of authorship hardly arose. If the book was doubted it was on account of its contents, and not because it was or was not written by Solomon. The fact that it bore Solomon's name seems to have had just the effect of gaining for it a hearing, and then to have dropped entirely into the background.

So again with the Book of Daniel. The author lived at the time of the Maccabaean struggle. His whole soul went out into that struggle, and he earnestly desired to say a word of encouragement and exhortation to the little band who were rallying round the law of their fathers. First, he wished to give them examples of steadfast loyalty to that law, and an assurance that God would be with those who were true to it even under bitter persecution. To this purpose of his there were features in the traditional story of Daniel which appeared to lend themselves; and so he took that story and worked it up in the way which seemed to him most effective. He may have had written materials before him—probably he had [1]; but what he sat down to write himself was not history, but a homily addressed to the patriots to strengthen their courage and faith under the trials to which they were exposed.

---

[1] On several points the Book of Daniel receives rather striking, if partial, confirmation. Such would be, the name Belshazzar (which however really belonged, not to the king, but to the crown-prince), and in a less degree those of Shadrach, Abednego, Arioch, Nebuchadnezzar's buildings (Kamphausen, *ut sup.*, p. 10), and (also very partially) his madness (see especially Schrader, *Cuneiform Inscriptions*, ii. 125 ff. *E. T.*).

## Daniel.

But there was more in his mind than this. He was fired with the grandest of all the hopes which his nation had ever entertained. The belief in a coming Messiah had taken hold of him. To most onlookers the rising under the Maccabees must have seemed a desperate sacrifice of noble lives. To him it bore the certainty of victory. What were these mighty empires which in their pride lifted up themselves against the Lord and against His people? They were like that colossal figure, mingled of gold, silver, brass, iron, and clay. A stone 'cut without hands' should strike it and it should be broken in pieces, while the stone grew into a mountain and filled the whole earth (ch. ii). Again, they were like four strange and powerful beasts, the last armed with ten horns and a little horn, stronger and more wicked than his fellows. But another scene succeeds. The thrones of judgment are set and the Ancient of Days takes His seat. The beast is slain; and there is brought before Him 'one like unto a son of man' who receives an everlasting dominion (ch. vii). There are other visions to the same general effect. The author of the Book of Daniel looked for a solution of the troubles amongst which he lived in the coming of the Messianic Kingdom. This was not conceived exactly in the sense in which his expectation was fulfilled, but was closely identified with the nation of Israel. As in other parts of prophecy, the fulfilment surpassed the anticipation. But among all the many threads of prophetic forecast which were drawn together and brought to realization by Christ there was none which so struck the imagination of His contemporaries, and none which has left a more conspicuous, if others have left a deeper mark upon Christian theology.

The belief of the Hebrew prophets was true. There is One Whom all things in heaven and earth obey; Who makes use of instruments on which may be traced here and there the flaws of human imperfection; and Who guides the course of history by ways which not even the wisest can wholly know, to ends which not even the most inspired can wholly see, until they are suddenly displayed in all their glorious perfection.

# Notes to Lecture IV.

## NOTE A.

### The Pre-Mosaic History in the Pentateuch.

ONE of the great problems in connexion with the Book of Genesis is the question as to the origin of those portions which point to some sort of contact with Babylonia (the stories of the Creation and the Flood, and the Kings of the East in Gen. xiv). The dominant tendency in the critical school—at least among the more advanced critics—is to regard this contact as taking place in historic times, after the Exile or during the later Monarchy. But the accumulating evidence, of which the Tell-el-Amarna tablets are the last and in some ways the greatest instalment, of the spread of Babylonian culture over Western Asia as far as the shores of the Mediterranean at a period long anterior to the Israelite conquest of Canaan seems to make the other hypothesis distinctly more probable, that the stories in question really go back to this period, and that they were no mere superficial importation, but that they represent an ancient deposit long assimilated and thoroughly recast by the Hebrew mind under the influence of Revelation. The data in Gen. xiv. are of course different in character from the Cosmogony and the story of the Deluge, but in view of the picture presented by the Tell-el-Amarna tablets it seems to me quite possible that they may be derived from some archaic record, treasured up on the soil of Palestine itself. We may believe that there is a real historical kernel in the narrative without claiming that the narrative as a whole is strictly historical.

A somewhat similar question arises as to the Egyptian details in the later chapters. I confess that I have never been satisfied with the view that they are to be accounted for solely by the relations between Israel and Egypt in the early period of the Monarchy. It may be seen by any of the critical analyses (in that of Addis's *Documents of the Hexateuch*, i. 70 ff., the facts are brought out very clearly) that the narrative rests on two fundamental documents which are at once distinct and independent of each other, the one belonging to the Northern Kingdom and the other to the Southern, and yet present a large amount of substantial resemblance. This resemblance points back to a ground stock of tradition, which must be older—and considerably older—than its two divergent branches. And the genuine Egyptian element is found in this as well as in the later ramifications.

But even upon these assumptions it is a delicate and difficult matter to decide how far the Book of Genesis is historically verifiable. I doubt whether even the specialists are as yet quite in a position to do so. But I fear that I could not for myself go the whole way with Mr. Watson in his little book, *The Book Genesis a true History*, London, 1892.

## NOTE B.

### *The Religious Value of the Book of Esther.*

I AM anxious to correct as far as possible whatever may be subjective and due to imperfect appreciation in these lectures; and therefore I gladly avail myself of permission to print a criticism of the remarks in the text by Mr. Lock. He writes as follows :—

'Esther was the first book of the Bible I learnt to care for as a child; so I feel inclined to resent any undervaluing of it, and should like to ask these questions about your paragraph :—

'(*a*) Is there *any* evidence for direct (Christian) objection to its character and contents?

'(*b*) If not, is it well to suggest that there may *have* been, when the survival of Jewish opposition would quite adequately explain the facts?—[It is rarely that the arguments for or against a book are definitely formulated. But I doubt if the omission of the book from Christian lists is adequately accounted for by the survival of Jewish opposition, because by the time of these lists its position in the Jewish Canon was assured, and it was read regularly at the feast of Purim. And the objections from a Christian point of view lay so near at hand that it is difficult to think of them as not operating consciously or unconsciously.]

'(*c*) Is it not true that "without adding to the sense of revelation," yet it furnishes one of the most striking illustrations of God's over-ruling Providence in History? and may it not be taken as a great example to Christians whose lot has fallen among those who are not Christians? For though there is no naming of the name of God, yet there is a deep sense of personal vocation to do His work; there is a faith in self-sacrificing intercession; and a type of courage, loyalty, and patriotism such as is scarcely found elsewhere in the Bible.—[It will I think be agreed that the main lesson of the book, which culminates in ch. iv. 10–16, is here very happily described. And this lesson may perhaps reconcile us to the position of the book within the Canon. If deductions have to be made for the sequel in ch. ix. 5–19, similar deductions have to be made in other books (*e.g.* for Ps. cix).]

'(*d*) Could it not then be put on the same level with Ruth, with Philemon? Can they be said to add to the sum of revelation?'

# Notes to Lecture IV.

## NOTE C.

### *The origin and character of Pseudonymous Literature among the Jews.*

IT would seem that among the Jews the composition of pseudonymous books had its rise on the one hand in the very subordinate position of the idea of literary property, and on the other hand in the strong sense of the continuity and solidarity which pervaded the order of prophets and of priests, and the class of the 'Wise men.' Priest and prophet were alike so conscious of deriving their own legitimation from Moses, they had such a firm belief in the Mosaic origin of the institutions which had come down to them, the authority of those institutions seemed so directly traceable to the Word of the Lord spoken to Moses, that when it came to them to amplify and expand the code as they found it so as to bring it into further agreement with the traditional practice of their own day, it seemed to them natural to treat the whole of this customary law as homogeneous and delivered through the same channel at the same time.

A similar mode of feeling led to the attribution of later religious poetry to David and of later Wisdom-literature to Solomon. Judged by our standard this attribution was not justified. It is also true that the ancients were not themselves so indifferent to the moral character of literary impersonation as is sometimes supposed (see on this point especially the first of two articles by Prof. J. S. Candlish in *The Expositor*, 1891, ii. 91 ff., 262 ff.). Still it must be remembered that truthfulness has been a virtue of slow growth. Some forms of intellectual sincerity have hardly had full recognition before our own day. And there are many steps and stages as we make our way backwards. There is no greater difficulty in regard to this than there is in regard to other limitations and qualifications which mark the pro-

## Note C.

gress of Revelation. The case is somewhat similar to that of the patriarchs and others, who though in the main represented as good and holy men, and though not unaware of the duty of truthfulness, do not strictly observe it. So, although it cannot be said that the authors of books like Ecclesiastes and Daniel had no intention of obtaining, and did not as a matter of fact obtain, greater authority for their works by giving them names which did not belong to them, and although it would also have been admitted that such action was not strictly right, still it was also not greatly condemned, at least not so much condemned that otherwise good men might not fall into it.

But the fact of pseudonymous attribution, even within the circle of books now included in the Canon, seems to be so clearly proved and to be in the stronger cases (*e.g.* Ecclesiastes) so generally acknowledged that no antecedent objection can be taken to it as a hypothesis where the grounds for it, though less absolutely conclusive, are yet distinctly preponderating.

# LECTURE V.

## THE GROWTH OF THE OLD TESTAMENT AS A COLLECTION OF SACRED BOOKS.

'Now go, write it before them on a tablet, and inscribe it in a book, that it may be for the time to come for ever and ever.'—*Isaiah* xxx. 8.
'The Law of Moses, and the Prophets, and the Psalms.'
*St. Luke* xxiv. 44.

I. THE first stone of the Bible may be said to have been laid when the religious teachers of Israel, men endowed as we have seen with special gifts for the discharge of a special mission, began to commit the substance of what they taught to writing; when the authority of the spoken word passed over to the written word; and when there began to be not only inspired men but inspired books, the constituent parts —at first scattered but by degrees brought together— of an inspired volume or Bible.

The change from speech to writing was in its consequences most momentous. It is due to it that the teachers of Israel have been enabled to give the law to far-off generations and to races of men dispersed throughout the whole world. But in essence and idea the change was a very small one. It was in fact no change at all. The authority of the word written was precisely the same as that of the word spoken, neither less nor more. It was inherent in the person who wrote or spoke, and was derived from the special action upon that person of the Spirit of God. Whether he wrote or whether he spoke made no difference to those who were first addressed, though the fixing of authoritative speech in authoritative writing established a permanent centre of vast and ever-widening influence in after-time.

We ask therefore, When did this change, at once so small and so stupendous, take place? The Critical School would assign it to two great moments in the history of Israel: (1) the moment at which the prophets of action made way for the writing prophets, *i. e.* according to the current view, when Amos and Hosea succeeded to Elijah and Elisha in the middle of the eighth century; and (2) at the promulgation of the Deuteronomic Law by Josiah in the year 621 B.C.

'The Question,' says Wellhausen, 'why it was that Elijah and Elisha committed nothing to writing while Amos a hundred years later is an author, hardly admits of any other answer than that in the interval a non-literary had developed into a literary age[1].' And Professor Ryle, speaking of Deuteronomy, writes: 'It is not till the year 621 B.C., the eighteenth year of the reign of King Josiah, that the history of Israel

---

[1] *Sketch of Hist. of Isr. and Jud.* p. 71. As Elisha lived till the reign of Joash (797-782 B.C.) and Amos prophesied under Jeroboam II, the successor of Joash (781-741 B.C.), the interval between the two must have been less than fifty years; but that is a detail.

presents us with the first instance of "a book," which was regarded by all, king, priests, prophets, and people alike, as invested not only with sanctity, but also with supreme authority in all matters of religion and conduct [1].'

In any case these are epoch-making events, landmarks of great importance in the history of the Bible. But just as the ceremonial laying of the first stone is as a rule not the actual beginning of the building to which it belongs, so here we may well ask ourselves whether these two events which stand out conspicuously above the surface are the true beginnings of the Bible, the one of the Canon of the Prophets, the other of the Canon of the Law.

Perhaps we ought to acquiesce in the former of the two dates, though with a less trenchant distinctness than is ascribed to it by Wellhausen. Whatever it may really mark, the interval between Elisha and Amos does not mark the first beginnings of a literary age. Writing we know to have been much older. The Tell-el-Amarna [2] tablets date from the fifteenth century B. C.; and although they are in another script, it is not likely that a fully developed writing-hand should be current in Palestine without having any effect upon the native character. The Moabite stone shows that this was not the case; or at least that Hebrew writing too was fully developed quite a

---

[1] *Canon of O. T.* p. 47.

[2] A writer in *The Academy*, March 4, 1893, p. 204, proposes to substitute Tel-beni-Amran; but Professor Sayce defends the older name, in the vernacular form which he adopts, Tel-el-Amarna (*ibid.,* April 8, p. 310).

century—we know not how much more—before Amos.[1] Nor can it be assumed that writing was only used upon a hard material like stone. For there was in any case a mass of literature in existence long before Amos and Hosea: not only scattered songs like those incorporated in the Book of Numbers[1], or the Song of Deborah, which might have been handed down for some time orally, but collections of such songs, the Book of Jasher and the Book of the Wars of the Lord; and not only these, but a quantity of historical writing, the early narratives embodied in the Books of Judges, Samuel and Kings, and the two great historical documents of the Pentateuch. We have not, it is true, any extant prophetical book older than Amos. Some scholars assign an earlier date to the prophecies of Joel and Obadiah[2]; but I cannot avail myself of this opinion, because to the best of my judgment the arguments against the earlier date seem to preponderate[3]. Nothing of any real importance turns upon the question whether Amos and Hosea had writing predecessors, and there is no direct evidence that they had; still it would in some respects be strange if it were not so. We know that St. Paul, the first of New Testament authors, wrote letters which were lost before any which have survived[4]; and that is what we should have expected in the case of the prophets. There is nothing in the

---

[1] Num. xxi. 14, 15; 17, 18; 27–30.
[2] Including Prof. Kirkpatrick (*Doctrine of the Prophets*, pp. 34 ff., 57 ff.).
[3] As stated (*e.g.*) by Dr. Driver.    [4] See below, p. 335.

least tentative about the prophecy of Amos and Hosea. Neither as literature nor as religious teaching does it bear the marks of an age of beginnings. Jerome's criticism of Amos as *rusticus sermone* seems to have been wholly *à priori*, based upon his rustic origin and calling. We are assured that, on the contrary, his style is pure and classical[1]. We can in fact see for ourselves even in the English version that he is no unpractised writer. His literary dress sits easily upon him; he is not like one wearing armour which had not been proved. The formulae which are characteristic of the prophetic writing are all there, without any hint that they are newly coined[2]. The religious ideas are such as must have had a long history behind them. The fusion of morality and religion is complete. And not only does the prophet himself teach very exalted doctrine, but he assumes that it will be understood by those to whom it is addressed; the nation itself must have had a long discipline[3].

But although we may conjecture that there were writing prophets before Amos, we cannot prove it.

[1] Driver, *Introd.* p. 297.
[2] Such for instance as the opening words, 'The words of Amos ... which he saw concerning Israel,' &c. (*cf.* Is. i. 1, 'The vision of Isaiah ... which he saw'; Hab. i. 1, 'The burden which Habakkuk the prophet did see,' &c.); 'Thus saith the Lord' (Amos i. 3, 6, 9, 11, 13, &c.); 'Hear this word that the Lord hath spoken' (Amos iii. 1; cf. iv. 1, v. 1), &c.
[3] Stress is very justly laid on these points by Dr. A. B. Davidson in two articles in *The Expositor*, 1887, i. 161 ff., ii. 161 ff. The whole argument as to the *presuppositions* of the early prophets is fully worked out by Professor James Robertson, *Baird Lectures*, pp. 50–166.

We must therefore content ourselves with pointing out that, so far as the authority with which he speaks is concerned, Amos had many predecessors. In this, acting prophets and writing prophets are as one. The history of the prophetic order does but repeat itself. Amos before Amaziah priest of Bethel (Amos vii. 10-17); Elijah before Ahab; Nathan before David; Samuel before Saul; the picture is in all its essential features the same. The embryonic germ of the Canon of Prophetic Scriptures is as old as Prophecy itself. Development of course there was in the teaching of the prophets; but all through their long line, the conception of Prophecy, as the Word of God, had nothing added to it. It is as complete in Moses as in Malachi. As seen at the time, the change from speech to writing was little more than an accident, though it was made to serve a mighty purpose.

The existence of writing prophets before Amos must be regarded as uncertain. Perhaps it is probable that if there had been such we should have heard more of them. But however that may be, there can be no question about the Law. Traces of law committed to writing and accepted by the people as authoritative go back far beyond Josiah. No doubt the promulgation of the Deuteronomic Code by that king was a very striking event. When we look at it we soon see that the promulgation of what is now believed to be the full (or nearly the full) Pentateuchal legislation by Ezra and Nehemiah in the year 444 B.C. is really modelled upon it. The later scene is an amplified counterpart of the earlier. But again we have to ask whether that in its turn does not bear the same sort of relation to an earlier event still. In order quite to appreciate the state of the case we need to have the scene under Josiah set before us. 'And the king sent, and they gathered unto him all the elders of Judah and of Jerusalem. And the king went up to the house of the Lord, and all the men of Judah and all the inhabitants of Jerusalem with him, and the priests and the prophets and all the people, both small and great: and he read in their ears all the words of the book of the covenant which was found in the house of the Lord. And the king stood by the pillar (*or* on the platform, R.V. marg.), and made a covenant before the Lord, to walk after the Lord, and to keep His commandments, and His testimonies, and His statutes, with all his heart and all his soul, to confirm the words of this covenant that were written in this book : and all the people stood to the covenant[1].' It is one of those ideal moments sometimes reached in history when a thrill of high·resolve has passed through king or leaders and people, and all alike have risen to the full consciousness of their vocation.

But now let us see if there is nothing like it. And first let us fix our attention upon the ceremonial of the promulgation. Rather more than two centuries before, in the *coup d'état* which overthrew the usurping queen Athaliah, another graphic scene is presented to us. The young king Joash is brought out of his

[1] 2 Kings xxiii. 1–3.

## Beginnings of Written Law.

hiding, and the guards collected together by a stratagem for that purpose are ranged round him; and the high-priest Jehoiada puts upon him 'the crown and the testimony'; and he is anointed, amid shouts and clapping of hands. Then we read that 'when Athaliah heard the noise of the guard and of the people, she came to the people into the house of the Lord: and she looked, and, behold, the king stood by the pillar (*or* on the platform, R.V. marg.), as the manner was, and the captains and the trumpets by the king; and all the people of the land rejoiced, and blew with trumpets.' And then a little later: 'And Jehoiada made a covenant between the Lord and the king and the people, that they should be the Lord's people; between the king also and the people [1].'

The one thing which is wanting here is the 'Book of the Law.' For its place is hardly taken by the 'testimony' (ver. 12), both the reading and meaning of which is disputed [2]. Otherwise the ceremonial is extremely like that which accompanies the promulgation of Deuteronomy; the king standing 'by the pillar' (or 'on the platform'—the same word with the same ambiguity), and the solemn covenant of king and people with Jehovah.

But a parallel for the 'Book of the Law' is not far to seek. We have already had occasion to speak of the Book of the Covenant, the oldest of all the Pentateuchal Codes. This book is incorporated in one

---

[1] 2 Kings xi. 12-14, 17.
[2] Several critics substitute 'bracelets,' as an emblem of royalty (*Q. P. B., ad loc.*).

of the two primitive documents, the Elohistic or the Jehovistic [1], it is not certain which ; and one or other of them contains an account of its solemn acceptance by the people. First sacrifices are offered, and the altar is sprinkled with a part of the blood; and then the book is read in the audience of the people. 'And they said, All that the Lord hath spoken will we do, and be obedient. And Moses took the blood, and sprinkled it on the people, and said, Behold the blood of the covenant which the Lord hath made with you [2].' We do not take this as evidence for the time of Moses; we take it as evidence for the age to which the documents belong, *i.e.* in any case for a date earlier—we cannot say positively how much earlier—than 750 B.C. But at that date what element in the fundamental idea of Canonicity is missing? We have a book, a law-book, solemnly read and accepted by the people as binding; and binding, because it comes from God.

This is as far as we can go in the way of written documents, but the next step carries us back to Sinai itself. The narrative of the events which happened at Sinai is some centuries later than those events, and therefore cannot be guaranteed to represent them with literal accuracy. It is however, as we have seen, when we first meet with it a double narrative, woven together from two separate documents. One of these

---

[1] Addis confidently claims the Book of the Covenant, with the whole of Ex. xxiv. 1-14, for the Elohist (*Documents of the Hexateuch*, i. 137 ff.); Driver refers it, with Ex. xxiv. 3-8, to the Jehovist; Socin does not discriminate.

[2] Exod. xxiv. 5-8.

probably comes from the Northern Kingdom, the other from the Southern. They were composed independently of each other. Yet in their general tenor they agree. Both alike describe the giving of the Law as associated with an awe-inspiring theophany. The event clearly had a strong hold upon the popular imagination. Perhaps there are traces of a similar belief as early as the Song of Deborah[1], which would be a long stepping-stone towards the age of the Exodus and the Wanderings. But what is a theophany but the highest conception which the men of those days could form of a sanction investing that to which it was applied with inviolable sanctity? I cannot undertake to say exactly what it was that God was pleased to reveal through Moses; but whatever it was, it contained the germ and potentiality of all that was to follow, and we may be sure that from the very first it was accepted as coming from God Himself.

There are then four stages in the history of the Law: (1) the actual beginnings, limited in extent and indeterminate in outline, which Moses was inspired to lay, of the Pentateuchal legislation, with its acceptance by the people; (2) the committal to writing of the Book of the Covenant, already regarded as heaven-given and binding upon the conscience; (3) the promulgation of the Deuteronomic Code by Josiah in 621 B.C.; and (4) the final promulgation of the complete, or all but complete, body of Pentateuchal laws by Ezra and Nehemiah in 444 B.C. There is a common likeness

[1] Compare the Rev. G. A. Cooke's excellent monograph, *The History and Song of Deborah*, Oxford, 1892, p. 31.

running through each of these stages. They are all constructed on the same pattern. The body of laws is added to from time to time, and there is an increase in bulk in the later as compared with the earlier Codes. The committal to writing begins, so far as a critical analysis of the existing documents will carry us, with the Book of the Covenant. But the fundamental idea which lies at the root of the Canon of the Law, the idea of a legislation given and received as coming from God and therefore absolutely binding upon the conscience, was present from the very first.

II. In the case of the Law there was a more or less regular machinery, in the first place for the preservation, and afterwards for the multiplication, of the sacred writings. Their sacredness is implied in the fact that some of them at least were deposited with the ark in the Holy of Holies. For instance in regard to the Book of Deuteronomy, the Levites are commanded to take it and put it by the side of the ark of the covenant, that it might be there 'for a witness against Israel[1].' The priests were the proper custodians of the Law, and they were expected in certain cases to furnish copies of it. Thus the king for the time being is enjoined as soon as he succeeds to the throne to have a copy made of the law of the Monarchy from the standard exemplar which is in the charge of the priests, and he is to keep it by him and read in it as a perpetual reminder of his duties [2].

---

[1] Deut. xxxi. 26. Compare 1 Sam. x. 25.
[2] Deut. xvii. 18-20.

In the case of the prophets there was less security both for the safe-keeping of the original writings and for their regular transmission. The Book of Jeremiah in particular supplies us with more than one incidental glimpse of the history of a prophetic writing—the circumstances under which it was composed and published, the authority with which it was received, and the risks it ran of mutilation or destruction. For twenty-three years after his call Jeremiah had confined himself to oral prophecy [1]. His prophecies had been delivered usually in some conspicuous public place, now just outside one of the gates of Jerusalem, now in the court of the temple [2]; but he had committed nothing to writing. It was not until the fourth year of Jehoiakim (605-4 B.C.) that he received an express command, conveyed to him like other Divine commands, to write down what he had spoken. We may note in passing that this long delay shows that written prophecy had by no means entirely superseded oral. It shows also that the prophets themselves were far from being aware of the full significance of the change. Nor could we have a better example of the action of that great overruling Providence of which the prophets were but instruments. There was a Power at work behind the Bible, the full designs of which were beyond the ken even of those who had the deepest insight into them.

Jeremiah did not write himself, but dictated to his disciple Baruch, who wrote we may suppose on a

[1] Compare Jer. xxv. 1, 3, with xxxvi. 1 ff.
[2] Jer. xix. 2; xxvi. 2.

roll of roughly prepared leather[1]. Jeremiah is in hiding, but a year (or according to another reading, four years[2]) later Baruch is told to take the roll into the temple and read it to the assembled people. It is a special fast day, so that the temple is crowded, and Baruch takes his stand on the steps leading into the upper court, where his words will be well heard. The reading makes a profound impression. The princes hear of it, and the roll must go to the king. Jehoiakim reads in it a little way, but his anger gets the better of him. He takes up a scribe's knife which lay near, cuts the roll into shreds, and throws them into the brazier which warmed the apartment in which he was sitting. The result is only that a second amplified copy is written in which the impending fate of Jehoiakim himself is described more plainly[3].

There is much to be learnt from this narrative. We infer not only from the long delay in writing down the earlier prophecies, but still more distinctly from the enlarged edition which tells us that there were added 'many like words,' that the prophets did not feel themselves strictly bound to a literal reproduction of their spoken addresses. We gather that the publication of a book of prophecies might be very similar to that of a book of laws. We see that the written words of a prophet, read by the mouth of another, were received with the same deference as the spoken words. They may of course be defied, as they were defied by Jehoiakim, but such defiance is an act of

---

[1] Jer. xxxvi. 1–4.   [2] Jer. xxxvi. 9 (*Q. P. B.*).
[3] Jer. xxxvi. 9–32.

impiety which brings down swift punishment. We learn also that the natural scribe and custodian of a prophet's writings is a trusted disciple.

This last inference might have been drawn from a much earlier passage. More than a hundred years before Isaiah had received a command, ' Bind thou up the testimony, seal the law (*or* the instruction) among My disciples[1].' It is Jehovah who is speaking, but commentators are agreed that the disciples in question are personal adherents of Isaiah to whose care the prophetic oracle is emphatically committed. Once more we observe that the charge to take steps for the permanent preservation of a prophetic writing comes by direct inspiration. The ' binding and sealing' are expressive of the authority which the writing in question is to carry.

But now, when we remember how these prophetic rolls were to be preserved, we see at once to what dangers they must have been exposed. The number of a prophet's disciples would often be small. It would seem as if Baruch was the only one in immediate personal attendance upon Jeremiah. But if so, when the prophet was gone and he was gone, who was to take their place? When the life of a book depended upon a single copy and a single guardian its continued existence was a precarious matter. The men of those days lived in times quite as troublous as that 'present distress' of which St. Paul wrote to the Corinthians[2]. Their country wasted by successive invasions; Jerusalem twice taken

---
[1] Is. viii. 16.   [2] 1 Cor. vii. 26.

and once sacked and destroyed; hurried flights, like that of Zedekiah's men of war 'by the way of the gate between the two walls, which was by the king's garden[1];' long marches into the interior, with all the chances of flood and field; the few precious scraps of roll hastily stowed away in the first receptacle that offered, and then perhaps committed as a last bequest by one dying exile to another. Can we wonder if, when the attempt was made to collect what remained from the wreck, it was attended by serious difficulties? At first there was no central body to make the attempt. Little by little there grew up, and from Ezra onwards we may believe that there flourished, a class of scribes specially devoted to the collecting, transcription, and study of the ancient writings. But in many cases the mischief was done before these came into their hands. Ownerless fragments of MS. were straying about. Portions of the work of one prophet would be mixed up with the work of another. And the editors into whose hands they came had no clue to discriminate between them. Sometimes mere juxtaposition in place, the fact that two or three rolls or portions of rolls were found together in the same case, might be held to prove identity of authorship. And so nothing would be easier than that intrusive matter should sometimes make its way into the later collections, or that the order of a prophet's writings should not be preserved. In fact the ancient editors would often have no real advantage over us moderns, while they were without many of our methods and appliances.

[1] 2 Kings xxv. 4.

Hence they have left, and it was natural that they should leave, something still to be done both in the rearrangement of the order of the prophecies and in the assignment of the authorship of particular portions. The longest and the most important of the Prophetic Books have perhaps suffered most; both Jeremiah and Isaiah from dislocation of order, and Isaiah also from the mixing up of anonymous fragments of prophecy with his own. We must leave it to specialists to decide how far the process has gone. Some of them are perhaps inclined to run into extremes; but we cannot dispute the major premiss from which they start, and a sober judgment is likely to prevail in the end.

As we descend in time the need for collected and multiplied editions became greater. It is important to trace this growing need, because we are apt to forget that the production of books depends quite as much upon the readers as on the writers. Before there can be a demand for books there must be a reading public. But it must have taken some time before such a public was formed. In Greece the signs of a reading public hardly begin much before the Peloponnesian War[1]. In Palestine they are no doubt older than this, though at first they do not extend very far. The chief students of the prophetic writings were probably for some time the prophets themselves. We see traces of this when we find in Isaiah and Micah, for instance, or in Jeremiah and Obadiah, passages which resemble each other so

[1] F. B. Jevons, *History of Greek Literature*, p. 45.

closely that as the one does not seem in either case to be directly dependent upon the other, the alternative hypothesis becomes probable, that both are dependent upon some older writing now lost [1].

Next would come the activity of Schools. We have seen that Isaiah had disciples to whom we doubtless owe not the final collecting and arrangement of the Book of Isaiah as we have it, but that of some of the minor groups of prophecies included in it. It is not however clear that they continued the literary work of their master. It is otherwise when we come to Deuteronomy. The point at which this book—or rather the nucleus of the present book—enters the stream of Hebrew literature is very strongly marked. 'As it fixed for long the standard by which men and actions were to be judged, so it provided the formulae in which these judgments were expressed; in other words it provided a religious terminology which readily lent itself to adoption by subsequent writers [2].' In two directions this influence is apparent: partly upon succeeding prophets, Zephaniah, Jeremiah, Ezekiel, and the Second Part of Isaiah—Jeremiah in particular showing constant signs of it; and still more upon succeeding historians. Even Deuteronomy itself is probably not the work of a single writer, but of a school or succession of writers, who have left their impress deeply traced upon the Books of Joshua, Judges, Kings, and in some-

---

[1] Driver, *Introd.*, pp. 203, 208 f. Cornill (*Einl.* p. 137 f.) disputes the genuineness of Is. ii. 2–4, which is however defended by Duhm.

[2] Driver, *Introd.*, p. 95.

## Influence of Schools.

what less degree upon the Books of Samuel. The editors who brought together the historical materials contained in these books worked in the Deuteronomic spirit and carried on the Deuteronomic tradition. Jeremiah himself has left his mark upon a group of psalms—possibly upon a group of psalmists— as well as upon other later writers[1]. Ezekiel was evidently a close student not only of his predecessors among the prophets but of the older collections of laws. The Book of Job is the centre of a number of affinities which may be due not so much to literary dependence as to the fact that the writers move in a similar circle of ideas[2]. When we descend to Zechariah we find direct references to the 'former prophets[3].' The literature of the later period generally,

---

[1] Hitzig went further than any other critic has done in claiming a number of Psalms as the actual composition of Jeremiah: viz. Pss. v, vi, xxii, xxviii–xxxi, xxxv, xl, lv, lxix, lxxi; more doubtfully, Pss. xiv, xxiii–xxvii, xxxii–xxxiv, xxxvii, xxxix, xli. This list has been recently examined by W. Campe (*Das Verhältniss Jeremias zu den Psalmen*, Halle, 1891), who finds real affinities in Pss. i, vi, xxxi, xxxv, lxxix, cxxxv; in all these cases the priority is on the side of Jeremiah, and the coincidences proceed from the study of his writings —in some of the instances at least much later than the time of the prophet. It is not however denied that the influence of Jeremiah may be traceable in other parts of the Psalter. Dr. Driver finds the most marked resemblance to Jeremiah in Pss. xxxi, xxxv, lxix, and lxxix. Dr. Cheyne also pronounces against Jeremiah's authorship, but in favour of Jeremiah's influence not only in the Psalter but in the Books of Kings, Job, Second Isaiah, and Lamentations (*B. L.* p. 135; cf. Driver, *Introd.*, pp. 189, 408, 435).

[2] Cp. Driver, p. 408.

[3] Zech. i. 4, 6, vii. 7; compare the references in Driver, *Introd.* p. 323 n., and for Zech. xi–xiv those on p. 331 n.

the post-exilic prophets, the later psalms and Chronicles all show a close and systematic study of the older writings.

There can be no doubt that by this time these writings were not confined to the use of prophets or priests, but that they were somewhat widely diffused among the people generally. We have had an instance from the Book of Deuteronomy in which a portion at least of the Law was to be in lay hands: the king was to have a copy made of the portion relating to him. But the strong injunctions several times repeated in this book that the precepts of the Law are to be taught diligently by the fathers to the children and that they are to be 'for a sign' upon the hand and 'for frontlets' between the eyes[1], although no doubt in the first instance referring to oral teaching, would soon give rise to written teaching as well.

The Exile must have given a great impulse to the study of the former Scriptures. They were the chief consolation which the people had now that they had lost the temple and its services. The reading of the Law seems to have been the primary object of the synagogues, the date of the institution of which is uncertain, but probably goes back nearly if not quite to the time of Ezra[2]. Already in the pre-exilic period provision had been made for the public reading of portions of the Law. Every seven years at the

---

[1] Deut. vi. 7–9; cp. iv. 9, xi. 19, 20.
[2] Similarly Schürer, *Neutest. Zeitgesch.* ii. 358.

feast of tabernacles the Book of Deuteronomy is to be read before the assembled people[1]. By means of the synagogues this public reading was organized, so that it took place regularly every sabbath[2]. By the time of our Lord readings from the Prophets were added to those from the Law[3]. An historical origin for this practice has been found in the Maccabaean persecution, but the evidence is insufficient[4]. There can be no doubt that these readings would tend to confirm and deepen the reverence paid to the Law and the Prophets, or in other words, the idea of their Canonicity; while the fact that they were not confined to the officials of the synagogue, but that readers were invited from among the congregation, would extend their influence through all classes of the nation.

It is easy to see how a number of causes combined to enhance the authority both of the Law and of the Prophets. For the Prophets, there was first the inherent force of the prophetic word and the commanding utterance of the prophets themselves, and then the signal confirmation of their predictions by the Exile and the Return. For the Law, there was the long series of solemn promulgations of different portions

---

[1] Deut. xxxi. 10–13.
[2] Acts xv. 21; Joseph. *Contr. Apion.* ii. 17. § 175: ἀλλὰ καὶ κάλλιστον καὶ ἀναγκαιότατον ἀπέδειξε παίδευμα τὸν νόμον οὐκ εἰσάπαξ ἀκροασομένοις οὐδὲ δὶς ἢ πολλάκις, ἀλλ' ἑκάστης ἑβδομάδος, κ.τ.λ. See also a learned article by Dr. A. Büchler in the *Jewish Quarterly Review*, April, 1893, pp. 420–468.
[3] Luke iv. 16 ff.; Acts xiii. 15.
[4] Zunz, *Gottesdienst. Vorträge*, p. 6.

at different periods of the history. The Law too gained in strength from the calamities of the Exile. The national conscience was thoroughly aroused, and it was felt that the sufferings which the people had to undergo were the just punishment for their disobedience. They came back from the Exile a changed nation, as determined to observe strict fidelity to the Law as their fathers had been ready to break it. The leaders, Ezra and Nehemiah, took full advantage of this temper. The Pentateuchal Law was read on two successive days with every circumstance of solemnity; then the feast of tabernacles was duly kept; and then a national fast and confession of sins formed the fitting preliminary to the conclusion of a covenant, to which Nehemiah and a number of priests, Levites, and heads of the people religiously set their seals[1]. Nor was the Law when thus ratified, or the Prophets, suffered again to pass into oblivion, for the founding of the order of the scribes and the institution of the synagogues with their lessons helped to keep them in continual remembrance.

This is what we mean when we say that the Canon of the Law and of the Prophets was formed. The complete Canon of the Law may be said to date from the year 444 B.C. It formed the first body of Jewish Scripture in the strict sense. That it stood for a time alone appears amongst other things from the fact that the schismatic community founded by the renegade priest Manasseh and the Samaritans on Mount Gerizim

---

[1] Neh. viii-x.

## The Canon of the Prophets.

soon after 432 B.C.[1], took over from the Jews only the Pentateuch and acknowledged no other sacred book.

Although there was at this time all the potentiality of the Canon of the Prophets, such a Canon did not exist actually until by degrees the conviction grew and became established that the line of prophets had come to an end. It is very commonly held that the Canon of the Prophets was formed in the course of the third century B.C. In the 'praise of famous men' at the end of the Book of Ecclesiasticus, written probably about 190–180 B.C., there is mention in their order of Isaiah, Jeremiah, and Ezekiel, and of the Twelve Minor Prophets, who even then seem to have been combined in a single volume[2]. And in the Book of Daniel (ix. 2) there is express reference to Jeremiah as one of a collection of Sacred Books.

But what in the meantime of the *Hagiographa*? There too the foundations of the Canon were being laid. First for the Wisdom-Books. There is a little notice in the Book of Proverbs from which I cannot but think that all criticism of that book ought to start. The collection of proverbs which begins with chap. xxv has this heading, 'These also are proverbs of Solomon, which the men of Hezekiah king of Judah copied out.' Some critics ignore this; others argue against its

---

[1] This date seems probable, at least for the beginnings of the schism, though Josephus puts the events in question later; see Montefiore, *Hibb. Lect.*, p. 352, and Stade, *Gesch.* ii. 188–191, there referred to.

[2] Ecclus. xlviii. 20, xlix. 6–10.

authenticity. No doubt it is true that 'also' ('These also') points to the previous portions of the book, and therefore was probably inserted when the book assumed its present shape; but it by no means follows that the rest of the note is of the same date. Nor does it follow either that because all the proverbs are not Solomon's, none of them are his, or that even if the attribution to Solomon were wholly invalid, the mention of the 'men of Hezekiah' must necessarily break down with it. A little unpretending notice of this kind, directly concerned with the business of the scribe, has all the ring of genuineness—all the ring of truth to fact and of having been inserted while the facts were still fresh in remembrance. But if that is so, we get a most valuable clue in more directions than one. In the first place, we learn that the reign of Hezekiah was an age of collecting and copying[1]. We learn that Hezekiah had a staff of men who were employed in this work; and we learn that they turned their attention more particularly to proverbs. Here then we have a stage—and I am inclined to believe the first stage—in the formation of the book which we know as the Book of Proverbs. Other like stages would come in due time. I am myself disposed to strike a balance between the conflicting views of critics, some of whom maintain that the Book of Proverbs is post- and others that it is

[1] We may observe in passing that the very casual allusion to the scribe's penknife in the scene with Jehoiakim (Jer. xxxvi. 23) about a hundred years later goes to show that such activity was not improbable.

pre-exilic, by putting some parts of it before and others after the Exile[1]. I do not think it likely that it took the complete form in which it has come down to us before the period of the scribes in the special and narrower sense who followed after Ezra.

But from the first, just as the Prophetic Books, even when they only existed singly, had all the authority of the prophets, so also the collections of proverbs even before they were combined into a substantial volume had all the authority of the 'wise men.' There can be no doubt that these *viri pietate graves* were prominent figures in Jewish society. They must have been deferred to quite as much as the leading Rabbis in the period of the Talmud; and they deserved it more, because they were creative minds—and minds creative within the sphere of Revelation, and under those influences which are characteristic of Revelation. In other words, they too were not uninspired by the Holy Ghost. We saw in the last lecture what heights this inspiration reached in the Books of Proverbs and Job; and although the Book of Ecclesiastes may be on a somewhat lower level, it has a special value as being based on an exceptional kind of experience.

Corresponding to the note from which we started in the Book of Proverbs is another not quite so distinct,

[1] The question as to the date of the Book of Proverbs was ably argued by Mr. Montefiore in the *Jewish Quarterly*, July, 1890, p. 430 ff. The summing up was in favour of the later date, for which Kuenen declared in the posthumous issue of his *Onderzoek*; but it must be admitted that some solid arguments were left on the other side. I should not like to speak dogmatically, but I believe that there is truth in both views.

but leading to a similar inference in the Psalms. You will remember how at the end of Ps. lxxii comes in that strange little comment, 'The prayers of David, the son of Jesse, are ended.' It is not really the end of the Psalms attributed to David, for others in the later portions of the Psalter bear his name. And it is probable that the Davidic Psalms of the First Book (Pss. i–xli) formed originally an entirely distinct collection from those of the Second Book to which the note in question is appended. What the note means is that a particular collection containing all the so-called Davidic Psalms to which the editor had access was finished.

Our reason for thinking that the two Davidic collections in the First and Second Books of our present Psalter were originally distinct is that the same psalm appears with but slight variation in each (Ps. xiv = Ps. liii [1]). If the editor of the second collection had been acquainted with the first collection he would hardly have thought it necessary to repeat just one psalm out of it. At the same time the fact that only one psalm, with a portion of a second, is repeated, would go to show that the authors of the two collections had access to wholly different tracts of material. The circles in which they moved in their search for psalms intersected each other only at this single point. The inference is that the earlier psalms were widely scattered and were brought together from divers quarters. Of course that would not be the case with the psalms which were in the possession of

[1] Compare also Ps. xl. 14–17 with Ps. lxx.

*The Canon of the Hagiographa.*

the Levitical guilds, the sons of Asaph and the sons of Korah. These would be naturally kept together from the first. But the observation just made would strengthen the conclusion, in itself probable enough, that many of the older psalms were not in the first instance composed with a view to the temple-worship, but were afterwards adapted to this—just as in our own hymn-books many of the hymns had their origin as the expression of private devotion and were not intended for congregational use.

If then we admit, as we may certainly admit, that the Psalter as we have it was the 'song-book of the second temple,' it by no means follows that the individual psalms were all composed in the period of the second temple. I cannot think that it has been at all proved that there was no psalmody in the first temple. The simple fact that a body of singers (Ezra ii. 41) returned from captivity is strong presumption to the contrary. Still less can we believe that the art which had reached such high perfection in the Song of Deborah and in David's elegy was never employed for purposes of devotion until after the Exile. Here again the plain inference that the psalms addressed to a 'king' belong to the times of the Monarchy should not I think be resisted [1].

But the question of pre-exilic psalms, interesting as it is, is too large for me to enter upon here; nor has

---

[1] So, to name only a few of the most recent authorities, Driver, *Introd.* p. 360; Kautzsch in *Stud. u. Krit.* 1892, p. 588; Baethgen, *Psalmen*, p. xxv; Sellin, *De Orig. Carm.* &c. p. 44 ff.; König, *Einleitung*, p. 401.

## V. The Old Testament as a Collection.

it a very essential bearing upon our present subject. In the canonization of the Psalms two steps are important. One is the forming of the collections; the other is continued liturgical use. The collecting of psalms was more akin to the collecting of proverbs than of prophecies. As soon as prophecies began to be written down at all it was natural to bring together and to preserve the works of the same author. But when the scattered works of different authors are thus combined, it is proof that attention is being drawn to that particular branch of literature and that a special value is set upon it. At this point the Psalms and the Proverbs or Wisdom-Books diverge. The latter receive their stamp from the authority of the 'wise men,' the former from their use in public worship. If the gold of the temple was sanctified by the temple[1], how much more inevitably would the prayers and praises offered up in the courts of the Lord's house acquire a sanctity of their own! In this respect the Psalms had an advantage over the Prophets. The date at which readings from the Prophets took their place in the synagogues beside the readings from the Law was in any case much later than that at which the Psalms were systematically used in the central worship at Jerusalem. And as each new hymn or collection of hymns was taken up by the temple-choirs, its place was assured in the sacred volume.

The two most important divisions of the *Hagiographa* are thus accounted for. There remain the five *Megilloth* or 'Rolls' (Song of Songs, Ruth,

---

[1] Matt. xxiii. 17.

Lamentations, Ecclesiastes, Esther), Daniel, Ezra and Nehemiah, Chronicles. The Rolls were read in the synagogues at certain specified seasons—the Song at the Passover, Ruth at Pentecost, &c. But the fact that the day assigned to Lamentations is the 9th of Ab, the anniversary of the destruction of Jerusalem, would show that this was a late arrangement. It also appears that when the Jews reckoned the Books of the Old Testament as twenty-two, Ruth went with Samuel and Lamentations with Jeremiah. The reason for the canonizing of these books was therefore not liturgical. We must rather see in it the work of the scribes during the second century before our era, and especially during the fifty years of subsidence and prosperity which followed the Maccabaean rising. The determination of this last division of the Jewish Canon, and with it of the Canon of the Old Testament generally, must have proceeded from above downwards. The agency through which it was brought about cannot have been popular usage, which was lax and indiscriminate, but must have been an authority of some kind. And the authority in question can only have been that which had already framed the Canon of the Law and of the Prophets, the only court of appeal before which the claims of the later books ever seem to have been argued, the authority of the scribes[1].

[1] There is I believe thus much foundation for the tradition respecting the 'Men of the Great Synagogue.' On this see Ryle, *Canon*, pp. 250-272; Driver, *Introd.* p. xxxiii ff.; König, *Einl.* p. 445 ff.

## V. The Old Testament as a Collection.

III. But when we have realized this, we are still not at the end of the problem propounded to us; we still have to ask what principle they followed in deciding what was Sacred Scripture and what was not. Why for instance, to take concrete examples, were the Books of Chronicles included in the Canon and the Books of Maccabees excluded from it? Why were Esther, Ecclesiastes, and Daniel placed on one side of the line, and Judith, Ecclesiasticus, and Wisdom on the other? There are indeed two questions, which ought to be kept distinct. First, the historical question, What were the motives which influenced those who framed the Canon as a matter of fact? and secondly the dogmatic question, What are the considerations which weigh with us in accepting their decision now?

We have seen that the central idea with the Jews was that of Prophecy (*sup.* p. 110). Their rough conception seems to have been that books composed during the prevalence of Prophecy were inspired in the strict and true sense, and that those composed after the cessation of Prophecy were not. I am only saying what their idea was, not that it was carried out with perfect accuracy. A margin, and a somewhat broad margin, has to be allowed. There needed to be not only the fact that Prophecy should cease, but also the conscious recognition that it had ceased, which would naturally take some time longer. The idea was probably a vague and general idea, not precise and definite. Equally wanting in precision would be also the dating of the later books which were candidates for admission to the Canon. A book like Chronicles or Ecclesiastes, for instance, would glide quietly into circulation, and no one would know to fifty or a hundred years when it had been composed. There is one book which bears its date upon its front, the Wisdom of the Son of Sirach. In that case the author gives his name and makes it clear (at least his grandson makes it clear) to within ten or twenty years when he lived. And the consequence was that it was excluded from the Canon. The book was read and treated with respect but not regarded as Canonical [1].

The Books of Daniel and Ecclesiastes probably gained their place in the first instance under cover of the names which they bore. In both cases there would be a predisposition to receive them—Ecclesiastes because it continued the line of the works of the Wise Men, for the analogy of works of established authority would always carry great weight; and Daniel because it struck the patriotic and prophetic note at the time of the Maccabaean rising. Perhaps if Ecclesiasticus had been anonymous and had not revealed its true date and character so plainly it might have had the same fortune as Ecclesiastes.

That the scribes acted *bonâ fide* in their decisions appears from the fact that some of the books which they excluded were just those which fell in most entirely with the spirit of the later Judaism. The strong particularism of Judith, the many popular beliefs which find their way into Tobit, and the whole tone and tenor of Ecclesiasticus, would commend them. It

[1] *Cf.* König, *Einleitung*, p. 469.

is difficult to see what can have told against these books except the knowledge of their later date and perhaps an undefined sense of difference between them and the elder Scriptures. The Book of Wisdom, which would otherwise have had the strongest claims, would be excluded because it was written in Greek. That fact alone would be sufficient to decide against it. Hebrew was the 'holy language[1].' And the highly centralized 'scribism' of Palestine would require as a first condition in any book which claimed to be regarded as 'Scripture' that it should be written in it. But at the time when the Canon was practically formed the Book of Wisdom was probably not written, or if written it was unknown[2].

Some difficulty is raised in connexion with the view now largely held that there are in our Psalter psalms of Maccabaean origin. For my own part I very much doubt whether there are any such psalms. It seems to me, as well as I can judge at present, that the difficulties caused by the assumption that there are outweigh the arguments for them[3]. One of the psalms most confidently set down as Maccabaean is already quoted as prophetic Scripture fulfilled during the Maccabaean insurrection in the First Book of Mac-

[1] Dr. Neubauer in *Stud. Bibl.* i. 50.
[2] The Book of Wisdom cannot be dated with any precision, but König is probably right in regarding it as giving expression to a 'pre-Philonian Alexandrianism,' and as written somewhere between Ecclus. and Philo (*Einl.* p. 489).
[3] Even writers so conservative as Driver (p. 363 'as it seems') and Baethgen (*Psalmen*, p. xxxi) allow the existence of Maccabaean Psalms. But this is still questioned by Robertson Smith (*O. T. J. C.* pp. 207 f., 437 ff.), and König (*Einl.* p. 403).

## Maximum and Minimum Canon. 257

cabees. And if we believe, as many do believe, that the Greek version of the Psalter is not later than c. 100 B.C., the number of steps implied between it and the original composition of the Hebrew psalms is so great as to make it difficult to get them all into the interval[1]. If there are Maccabaean psalms, they slipped in as part of a collection which already had a high degree of sanction. As entirely new compositions they could hardly have done so.

Such seems to be the account, so far as it can be given, of the historical formation of the Canon. And for all practical purposes the Canon of history and the Canon of doctrine are the same[2]. The Canon is one of the possessions of the Church Universal, inherited from the days when the Church was still undivided. The *minimum* Canon at least is common to East and West, to Catholic and Protestant, to every branch and sect into which Christendom has ramified. Clearly it could not be touched without adding one more to those causes of disunion which good men all the world over are bent upon diminishing.

The English Churchman in particular is in a happy position. He can mediate here, as his Lutheran brother can also in this respect mediate, between the

[1] See Additional Note A: *The inferior Limit for the Date of the Psalter.*

[2] Cardinal Bellarmin regards the determination of the Canon as simply the expression of historical facts: *Ecclesiam nullo modo posse facere librum canonicum de non canonico nec contra, sed tantum declarare quis habendus canonicus, et hoc non temere nec pro arbitratu, sed ex veterum testimoniis* (ap. Poertner, *Die Autorität d. deuterocanon. Bücher d. A. T.*, Münster i. W. 1893, p. 1 n ).

severed branches of the Church of Christ. He has most of the advantages, without the drawbacks, at once of the *maximum* Canon and of the *minimum*. Our Sixth Article begins by endorsing the Jewish Canon, and then goes on to add certain other books which it commends 'for example of life and instruction of manners.' In other words, it gives to the Apocrypha an amount of deference which its best members fully deserve. For this there is excellent historical foundation. The Article does but follow the precedent of the choicest spirits in the Ancient Church, both Jewish and Christian. It connects the Church of our own day directly with them. And besides, it does, at least roughly and approximately, correspond to the facts.

Any definition in a matter of this kind which is to cover a wide extent of time and space and is to unite divers races and conditions of men, must be rough and approximate. It may not meet all the refinements of the critical conscience. But a reasonable man who is not anxious to erect his own judgment into a law and who would distrust his own judgment if it could be so erected, may well be content with what is given him.

At the same time it must be remembered—and the conclusion is pressed upon us by the whole of this part of our inquiry—that the boundaries of the Canon, though fixed for us historically, are not fixed in the sense of a hard and fast impassable barrier. It is out of the question to say that the Book of Esther is wholly filled with the Spirit of God and the Book of Wisdom wholly devoid of it. There are books of the

## Deuterocanonical Inspiration. 259

Old Testament which stand out clearly and indisputably with a difference which really amounts to a difference of kind from all other books which could possibly be compared with them, those of the New Testament alone excepted. But there are others in which this difference fines down gradually till it is hardly a difference in kind at all. And just as there is a descending scale within the Canon, there is an ascending scale outside it. Some of the books in our Apocrypha might well lay claim to a measure of inspiration.

This will appear when we examine them as we have examined the Canonical Books, to see what ideas they themselves express upon the subject. The son of Sirach believed himself to be inspired. He compares himself by a graphic image to one of the channels used for irrigation. In the common version his words run thus: 'I also came out as a brook from a river, and as a conduit into a garden. I said, I will water my best garden, and will water abundantly my garden-bed: and lo, my brook became a river, and my river became a sea. I will yet make doctrine to shine as the morning, and will send forth her light afar off. I will yet pour out doctrine as prophecy, and leave it to all ages for ever. Behold that I have not laboured for myself only, but for all them that seek wisdom [1].' There are other passages which make the same implication, which is also found in the Book of Wisdom [2].

[1] Ecclus. xxiv. 30–34. The last verse is omitted by the Syriac and Dr. Edersheim.
[2] Wisd. viii. 2, 9–21.

It is somewhat differently expressed by the younger son of Sirach in the prologue to his grandfather's work. There he says that his grandfather, 'when he had much given himself to the reading of the law and the prophets and other books of our fathers, and had gotten therein good judgment, was drawn on also himself to write something pertaining to learning, to the intent that those which are desirous to learn, and are addicted to these things, might profit much more in living according to the law.'

We may observe in passing, as a point of real distinction between the Canonical and Non-Canonical Books, that the writers of the latter, especially the son of Sirach, display an amount of self-consciousness on the subject of authorship which is wanting in those of the former. The passage first quoted from Ecclesiasticus is not free from boastfulness—a quality wholly absent from the Canonical Scriptures, and in that respect a speaking witness to their inspiration. The writers of these Scriptures knew that their words were not (in any sense of which they could boast) their own words at all.

The younger son of Sirach uses language adapted to his Greek readers. He has already a Canon. And yet it is clear that he puts no impassable gulf between the work of his grandfather and the Canonical Books. He regards his grandfather as taking his start from these, but almost in a manner continuing them as literature. He also will write 'something pertaining to learning (παιδείαν, culture, religious culture or discipline) and wisdom.' The idea is

## Deuterocanonical Inspiration.

probably that which the Jews attached to their 'wise men,' a class to which the elder son of Sirach really belonged. The way in which he characterizes his own work is indeed a fair description of it. 'And I,' he says, 'was the last to watch, as one that gleaneth after the grape-gatherers: by the blessing of the Lord I attained (ἔφθασα), and filled my winepress like a gatherer of grapes[1].' This is just what the son of Sirach was—a gleaner after the vintage. His grapes are real grapes, and the wine pressed from them is real wine; but the main vintage was over before he entered upon it. We may note here too by the way an interesting expression of the consciousness that Israel's Bible is being closed. The writer seems to hope that there may be room for his own book, though he does not venture to put it quite on a level with those which have gone before. The metaphor from irrigation in the passage first quoted is to the same effect. The Canonical Books, the writings of acknowledged inspiration, are the river; his own book is a trench cut from it to water his garden. He cannot lay claim to the creative gift, but he can convey what others have created to the soil which thirsts for it.

The term 'Deuterocanonical' (if we may put our own sense upon it [2]) would describe well such books as

---

[1] Ecclus. xxxiii. 16. This is somewhat altered from the common version: the opening phrase is borrowed from Mr. Ball's excellent *Variorum* edition. Some of the expressions are important (*e.g.* ἔφθασα, which I believe means 'attained my object,' not 'I outstripped others,' as Fritzsche).

[2] See Additional Note B: *The use of the term Deuterocanonical in the Roman Church.*

Ecclesiasticus and Wisdom. It is sufficiently clear that at the time when these books were written there was already a conception of Inspiration in the Proto-Canonical Books. The writers of the later books are conscious of this, but they seem to claim something similar for themselves and to hope that their own words would not be let die. There is some ground for their claim. Behind them too we can see the great principles of the revelation made to Israel, though there are flaws in their way of applying them.

IV. And yet it would not have been possible to make such claims if the conception of Inspiration had been as fixed and as strict as it afterwards became. One conspicuous fact proves that it did not attain to this position all at once. That fact is the state of the text of the Septuagint Version. It is well known that many of the Apocryphal Books in our larger Bibles were originally incorporated in the text of Canonical Books. For instance, the Song of the Three Children, the Story of Susanna, and Bel and the Dragon are all episodes inserted in or added to the Greek version of the Book of Daniel; the Prayer of Manasseh is a like episode in the Second Book of Chronicles; there are a number of additions to the Book of Esther, while the Book of Ezra has been curiously turned about and appears in two different forms, in one of which the original has been treated with great freedom[1]. But such liberties could not

[1] The Book which is sometimes called the First (LXX and A. V.) and sometimes the Third (Vulg. and Art. vi.) Book of Esdras is a

have been taken after the strict view of the sacred character of the Canonical Books was fully established. There was clearly a period, especially for the Third Division of the Canon, when a laxer view prevailed.

The drawing of the cordon more tightly round the Canonical Books and the gradual stereotyping of the Canonical Text were processes which went on side by side. There was the same sort of gradation in each. Just as the Books of the Law were the first to be formed into a Canon, so also they were the first to attain comparative fixity. We see this from the much smaller amount of variation in the Septuagint. The Prophetical Books come next to them; and the *Hagiographa* are last, both in the demarcation of their limits and in the reducing to some sort of restraint and order of the licence of their transcribers. By degrees there took place an equalizing of the three divisions of the Canon. Even with the Jews all were Scripture, and all shared in the properties of Scripture. And with Christians the old pre-eminence of the Law was done away, and the other books were brought up to the same level with it in sacredness and authority.

It was natural that there should be an analogous process in regard to the doctrine of Inspiration. There too it is easy to trace a gradual levelling up

patchwork mainly from 2 Chron., Ezra, and Nehemiah. [But a new view of this book which assigns it a somewhat higher character is being put forward by Sir H. H. Howorth in a series of letters to *The Academy.*] The Second Book of Esdras (LXX) is our Ezra and Nehemiah. In the Vulgate, 1 Esdras = our Ezra, 2 Esdras = our Nehemiah.

of the conception. The principle at work is one of the commonest to which the operations of the human mind are subject—the *Principle of Extensions*. I do not think that there is one of the points which go to make up the strictest form of the traditional doctrine which has not some warrant in the books themselves. But that which originally had reference to some particular mode or organ of revelation was extended so as to cover the whole. Limitations were forgotten. Propositions which were true within a defined area became so elastic that they ceased to be true.

We have seen how emphatic are the precepts of the Law. The imperatives are as strong in the earliest code as in the latest. The Book of the Covenant ends with the same sanction of threats and promises[1] as Deuteronomy. Those in the later book are somewhat expanded and accentuated, but in principle they are the same. We saw too that the binding force of this primitive code was recognised no less than that of the complete Pentateuchal legislation. 'All that the Lord hath said will we do and be obedient.' It was impossible to add anything essential to this. Human words could not express the obligation of the Law more strongly.

Again, the prophetic 'Thus saith the Lord' knows no degrees. Whether it is command, or whether it is doctrine, or whether it is prediction, it is alike unhesitating. The prophets were as convinced of the authority of their utterances as they were of their own existence.

[1] Ex. xxiii. 20–33.

## The Conception of Inspiration.

Here we have a twofold standard to which it was natural that everything should be referred. And we can see what an easy step it would be to the doctrine of plenary or verbal inspiration. By precisely the same process by which the one term, 'the Law' (ὁ νόμος), or the double term, 'the Law and the Prophets,' came to be used for the whole of the Old Testament Scriptures, the attributes of the Law and the attributes of the Prophets were extended to all the books, and to all the parts of all the books, included in the Canon.

The Law was as binding as law could be. The inspiration of the prophets for its particular purpose was plenary. But even here there is something further to be considered. Because the Law was binding in all its parts upon the generation or succession of generations to which it was given, it did not follow that all the parts were of equal importance, or that it could not be first corrected and ultimately repealed by the same authority by which it was given.

And for the Prophets, although it is true that the strongest sayings in the New Testament may be paralleled from the Old, even they do not exhaust the whole matter. The formula which is common to the Gospels of St. Matthew and St. John and the Acts is found already in the First Book of Kings. We read there that Solomon thrust out Abiathar from being priest, 'that he might fulfil the word of the Lord which He spake concerning the house of Eli in Shiloh' (1 Kings ii. 27); and again in the beginning of the Book of Ezra, the raising up of Cyrus is ascribed to the same cause, 'that the word of the Lord by the mouth of Jeremiah might be fulfilled' (Ezra i. 1). This apparently mechanical pre-determination of history is a corollary from two doctrines—on the one hand the doctrine of the absolute sovereignty of God, and on the other hand the identification of the prophet's word with the Divine counsel. Both are true. But then there is also here, as indeed in all places where the sovereignty of God is appealed to, the complementary truth of the free-will of man which in some way inscrutable to us is taken up into the Divine foreknowledge, so that predictions which are positive so far as the principles on which they turn are concerned, may yet be conditional so far as they depend on human action[1]. The essential thing in predictive prophecy is the insight which it gives into the Mind and Will of God, and into the laws and tendencies in which that Will finds expression. But it will not always be possible for us to lay the finger upon exact and literal fulfilments. We see the surface of things; but the Divine working does not lie upon but only *comes to* the surface, and is carried on largely out of our sight in a course deflected from the direction at which we see it.

Yet one more item in the later conception is based

---

[1] Compare Kirkpatrick, *Doctrine of the Prophets*, p. 137: 'How have Hosea's prophecies been fulfilled? Does it seem that they reach far beyond any fulfilment to which we can point, and have failed of accomplishment? It must be remembered that all prophecy is conditional. It expresses God's purpose, which is so mysteriously conditioned and limited by man's folly and obstinacy. Yet in spirit, if not in the letter, it has been and is being fulfilled.'

directly upon precedents which are found in the Scriptures to which they are applied. When Josephus says that in all the ages which have elapsed since the Jews received their Sacred Books no one had dared to add anything to them or to take away from them or to alter anything in them [1], he clearly has in his mind Deut. xii. 32 : 'What thing soever I command you, that shall ye observe to do : thou shalt not add thereto nor diminish from it.' This is from the oldest portion of the book: substantially the same words are repeated in the Preface (Deut. iv. 2); and they are adapted with a wider reference in the Book of Proverbs, 'Every word of God is pure. . . . Add not thou to His words, lest He reprove thee and thou be found a liar' (Prov. xxx. 5, 6).

It is obvious however that these passages are only applicable by inference to the Bible or to the Old Testament as a whole, because at the time when they were written there was still much to be added and there were some things to be altered. What they seem to mean in the first instance is that the prophetic word or word spoken prophetically as coming from God must be given in full; there must be no tampering with it by addition or subtraction, so as to make it mean something different from what was intended [2].

---

[1] *Contr. Apion.* i. 8.
[2] A good example of this is supplied by a criticism of Origen's upon Heracleon (Brooke, *Fragments of Heracleon*, p. 51, from Orig. *Comm. in Ev. Joan.* ii. 8): ἀναιδέστερον δὲ ἱστάμενος πρὸς τὸ ' Καὶ χωρὶς αὐτοῦ ἐγένετο οὐδὲ ἕν' μηδὲ εὐλαβούμενος τὸ 'Μὴ προσθῇς τοῖς λόγοις αὐτοῦ ἵνα μὴ ἐλέγξῃ καὶ ψευδὴς γένῃ,' προστίθησι τῷ 'οὐδὲ ἕν' τῶν ἐν τῷ κόσμῳ καὶ τῇ κτίσει, κ.τ.λ.

It is like Balaam's reply to the messengers of Balak : 'If Balak would give me his house full of silver and gold, I cannot go beyond the word of the Lord, to do either good or bad of mine own mind: what the Lord speaketh, that will I speak[1].'

We are constantly being brought back to prophecy and the prophetic inspiration, which I have already described as 'typical of all inspiration.' But it will be seen that it is not strictly safe to transfer what is said of this to all other kinds of inspiration. The psalmists and wise men had an inspiration of their own, which may be in part prophetical, but in any case is not so entirely. Still less is it safe to transfer what is said of the prophet speaking or writing as a prophet, to another function of the same man writing as a historian. The inspiration of the prophet was a special gift bestowed upon him at particular times and for particular purposes. It did not inhere in his person absolutely; nor was it present with him at all times. We can usually tell by the mode of speech when it was present. But the inspiration of the prophet was remote from the writing of history. To this extent only the two things might be connected, that the knowledge of the ways of God acquired in inspired moments might, when applied without the *afflatus*, give an insight into the meaning of the history. There is evidence that it did give such an insight. But there is no evidence to show that it in any way superseded the ordinary use of historical materials, or that it inter-

[1] Num. xxiv. 13.

fered with that use in such a way as to prevent possibilities of error.

One of the chief instruments in the advance of knowledge is the *distinguendum*. And it is this method of ' distinctions ' which needs to be applied if we are to form an exact idea of Inspiration. It was most natural, and in a manner most right, that the wonderful insight obtained from such countless places in the Old Testament should cast a halo round the whole. For many a devout soul that halo has been enough. But new ages bring new needs. The progress which the present age is making is largely an intellectual progress, and its special need is for more precise definitions. These it is our duty to attempt to offer. But the Scriptures themselves remain what they are. No definition can affect their essential nature. If they have had power in the past, they will have power also in the future. The great moving forces of the moral world come from them. The best that we know of God is derived from their pages. And the forces which they set in motion are permanent forces; and the light which shines from them is also permanent; it shines, and will shine, as long as the sun and moon endure.

## NOTE A.

*The inferior Limit for the Date of the Psalter.*

I MAY perhaps be allowed to express the opinion that for a methodical determination of the date of the Psalter the last argument to be applied in order of time should be that from the identification of historical allusions. These allusions are for the most part so vague and our knowledge of the history of the period into which they are to be fitted is so imperfect that no satisfactory conclusion can be drawn from them until the more external data have been fully estimated.

All the study which I have myself been able to give to the subject goes to endorse the view recently put forward by one of the most judicious of Old Testament scholars.

'If I am not mistaken, the conclusions of the Books [into which the Psalter is divided], the parallel texts [of Psalms repeated in these Books or elsewhere], the Elohistic redaction of the Middle Books, and the separate collections indicated by the superscriptions, may furnish a most valuable basis for ascertaining the history of the Psalter' (Budde in *Theol. Literaturzeitung*, 1892, col. 250).

It would be obviously out of place for one who is not an Old Testament scholar to attempt to work out these problems in detail, but he may perhaps without intrusion give a specimen of the kind of considerations on which he thinks that stress may well be laid.

We may take as an instance Ps. lxxix, which is one of those which are most confidently set down to the Maccabaean period. Between the composition of this Psalm and its inclusion in the Septuagint Version the following steps must have intervened.

(1) The adding to the Psalm of the superscription 'a Psalm of Asaph' in the Hebrew. It is hardly likely that this would be done immediately after the composition of the Psalm. We should naturally suppose that some time would elapse.

(2) The inclusion of the Hebrew Psalm in the little collection of Asaphic Psalms (Pss. l, lxxiii–lxxxiii). It is possible that this might take place at the same time as the adding of the title.

(3) The grouping of the little collection of Asaphic Psalms with another little collection of Korahite Psalms (Pss. xlii–xlix), and of both with a collection of Davidic Psalms (Pss. li–lxxii). The whole of this process need not have taken place at once.

(4) The redaction of the collection thus formed by the substitution of the name 'Elohim' for 'Jehovah.' It is, I conceive, really improbable that this redaction occurred after the time of the Maccabees.

(5) The disturbance of the order of the last-formed collection, so that the Davidic Psalms came to be interposed between the Asaphic Psalms l and lxxiii. All this implies a considerable history for the collection. At some time or other the miscellaneous titled Psalms lxxxiv–lxxxix are added to it.

(6) We now have a complete collection; but that collection has to be embodied in the full Psalter of 150 Psalms. That is another great and important step.

(7) When the whole Psalter is complete the idea after a time arises of dividing it into Five Books, like the Pentateuch. It is agreed that these divisions are, in part at least, artificial; and therefore it is not probable that they were made at the same moment as the first gathering together of the 150 Psalms.

(8) At some time or other, possibly but by no means

certainly, at the time of the collecting of the 150 Psalms, these have attached to them a continuous numeration. But between this first numeration and the making of the Septuagint Version certain variations of numbering had been introduced. The numeration in fact itself has a history. This appears both from the artificial combination of certain Psalms (*e.g.* Ps. cxliv. 1–11, 12–15) and separation of certain others (*e.g.* Pss. ix, x; xlii, xliii), and also from the differences between the numeration of the Hebrew and the Septuagint. The separation of Pss. ix, x, may have taken place after the making of the Septuagint Version, but not that of xlii, xliii, or the combination of Ps. cxliv. In the archetype of our leading MSS. of the LXX a supplementary Psalm is added (Ps. cli) which is expressly described as ἔξωθεν τοῦ ἀριθμοῦ.

(9) Also the headings to the Psalms must have had a considerable history, as may be seen from the variants in the LXX headings. It would probably not be difficult for a Hebraist to say how far it is likely that the additional headings in the LXX were introduced as new Greek headings in that Version, and how far they had already found their way into the Hebrew copy from which it was translated. Antecedently it would seem that the making of new headings would be more likely to be carried on by the scribes of Jerusalem than by those of Alexandria. We note that the additions to the titles of Pss. xxiv, xlviii, xcii, xciii, xciv (Heb.), all have reference to the services of the Temple.

It is possible that the number of these different stages might be slightly reduced by supposing that some of them were coincident. But on the other hand there are several of them for which it seems natural to assume a considerable lapse of time.

Taking them altogether I find it extremely difficult to get them all into the interval between the Maccabaean Revolt and the date (which many of the critics who accept Maccabaean Psalms place about the year 100 B.C.) of the Septuagint Psalter. I do not say that the difficulty is insuperable; but

I do think that the critic who ignores or makes light of it is like an army with a strong force of the enemy in its rear.


NOTE B.

## *The use of the term Deuterocanonical in the Roman Church.*

THE term 'Deuterocanonical' does not appear to be older than the sixteenth century. Its use is sanctioned by Roman Catholic theologians, but with the proviso that it does not imply a lower degree of authority.

Thus Poertner, *Die Autorität d. deuterocanon. Bücher d. A. T.* (Münster i. W. 1893), p. 1 *n.*: 'Obwohl die Kirche diesen Ausdruck "deuterocanonisch" für anerkannt kanonische Schriften nicht zurückweist, so ist es doch nicht ihre Absicht, damit eine geringere Meinung von den deuteroc. Büchern hinsichtlich ihrer dogmatischen und ethischen Geltung documentieren zu wollen, wie dies mit Unrecht von Zoeckler (*Die Apokryphen d. A. T.*, München. 1891, S. 22), Keerl (*Die Apokryphen d. A. T. Ein Zeugniss wider dieselben*, Leipzig, 1852, S. 164) und anderen behauptet worden ist.

'Die im 16. Jahrhundert aufgekommene Benennung "deuterocanonisch" bezeichnet nur Bücher, welche zu einem anderen als dem von den Juden aufgestellten Kanon d. A. T., nämlich zum Kanon der christl. Kirche, gehören. Die zum jüdischen Kanon gehörigen Schriften wurden missverständlich "protocanonisch genannt."'

Compare Loisy, *Histoire du Canon de l'Ancien Testament*, Paris, 1890, p. 6: 'Dans l'Église catholique on désigne ordinairement ces mêmes écrits, ainsi que les parties du Nouveau Testament dont la canonicité a été jadis contestée, sous le nom de deutérocanoniques. On appelle protocanoniques les livres dont la canonicité n'a jamais été l'objet d'un doute. L'emploi de ces termes ne remonte pas à l'antiquité : on n'a

T

commencé à s'en servir qu'après la définition du canon par le concile de Trente (*vid.* Sixte de Sienne, *Biblioth. Sancta*, lib. I. § 1). Ils n'impliquent aucune différence entre les Livres saints au point de vue de la canonicité entendue dans le sens qui a été indiqué plus haut, car tous les livres reconnus par l'Église comme inspirés sont également canoniques : le témoignage rendu par l'Église à la divinité de leur origine est le même pour tous et n'admet pas de degrés. La distinction des protocanoniques et des deutérocanoniques n'a de valeur qu'au point de vue de l'histoire : elle retient le souvenir des anciens doutes, en même temps qu'elle affirme la canonicité des écrits touchant lesquels ces doutes se sont produits.'

This teaching is based ultimately upon the decrees of the Tridentine and Vatican Councils.

CONC. TRIDENT. Sess. iv, *Decret. de Canon. Script.*: ' Sacrosancta oecumenica et generalis Tridentina synodus ... omnes libros tam veteris quam novi testamenti ... pari pietatis affectu ac reverentia suscipit et veneratur.' [*Sequitur Index LL. SS.* ' Genesis ... Esdrae primus et secundus, qui dicitur Nehemias, Tobias, Judith, Esther ... Sapientia, Ecclesiasticus ... Jeremias cum Baruch ... Daniel ... duo Machabaeorum primus et secundus' ...] ' Si quis autem libros ipsos integros cum omnibus suis partibus, prout in ecclesia catholica legi consueverunt, et in veteri vulgata latina editione habentur, pro sacris et canonicis non susceperit ... anathema sit.'

CONC. VATIC. Sess. iii. cap. 2, *De Revelatione*: ' Haec porro supernaturalis revelatio secundum universalis Ecclesiae fidem, a sancta Tridentina Synodo declaratam, continetur in libris sanctis. ... Qui quidem veteris et novi Testamenti libri integri cum omnibus suis partibus, prout in ejusdem Concilii decreto recensentur, et in veteri vulgata latina editione habentur, pro sacris et canonicis suscipiendi sunt. Eos vero Ecclesia pro sacris et canonicis habet, non ideo, quod sola humana industria concinnati, sua deinde autoritate sint approbati ; nec ideo dumtaxat, quod revelationem sine errore contineant ; sed propterea, quod Spiritu Sancto inspirante conscripti Deum habent auctorem, atque ut tales ipsi Ecclesiae traditi sunt.'

## Note B.

Now, while I think that we may prefer the terms of our own Article, at the same time I confess that the Roman definitions on this head do not seem to be irreconcilable with fact and history, or to be such as need divide Churches. All that is asserted is that the longer list of the Books of Holy Scripture has been received in the Church as Canonical (*i.e.* as Divinely inspired). As a matter of history this is true : the longer list was so received by the main body of Christians down to the Reformation. And as this statement is not accompanied by any definition of Inspiration or of what is implied in Canonicity, it seems to leave room for the attribution to the different books of different degrees of value and authority. It may be the case that this is not implied in the term Deuterocanonical; but it is also not excluded by it. If 'Canonical' means regarded by the Church as possessing inspiration, then it may be correct to say that Canonicity does not admit of degrees: a book either possesses inspiration or it does not: but it is another question whether there may not be degrees of authority and value in the products of inspiration. And I understand that this is left an open question. Compare especially what is said by M. Loisy on p. 212 as to the evidence furnished by the Acts of the Council of Trent to the intentions of the Council :—

'En déclarant tous les Livres saints également canoniques, le concile n'a pas prétendu supprimer entre eux toute distinction, et il n'a ni pensé ni voulu condamner d'une manière générale les anciens auteurs qui ne recevaient pas dans leur canon les deutérocanoniques. Les Actes sont formels à cet égard. Dans la congrégation générale du 12 février, la majorité décide, au sujet de la distinction à faire entre les livres "qu'on laissera cette question comme les saints Pères nous l'ont laissée"; dans la congrégation générale du 27 mars, on rappelle cette résolution et on l'explique par "la difficulté du sujet"; et la congrégation générale du 1er avril sanctionne les déclarations en s'opposant à ce qu'on remette en question ce qui a été antérieurement approuvé dans les réunions plénières. Il suit de là que, dans la pensée du concile, l'égalité de tous les livres au point de vue de la canonicité n'entraîne pas leur égalité absolue à tous égards ; qu'il peut exister entre eux des différences notables qui ne portent pas atteinte à leur caractère de livres canoniques ; mais la détermination de ces différences est, pour le moment, une question d'importance secondaire, assez embrouillée d'ailleurs, et plus propre à défrayer les disputes de l'école qu'à fournir matière aux délibérations d'un synode.'

M. Loisy goes on to illustrate the nature of the differences in question from the discussions of the Council. His whole book is written with conspicuous lucidity and moderation, and well deserves to be studied.

# LECTURE VI.

## THE GENESIS OF THE NEW TESTAMENT.
### GOSPELS AND ACTS.

'Forasmuch as many have taken in hand to draw up a narrative concerning those things which have been fulfilled (*or* fully established) among us, even as they delivered them unto us, which from the beginning were eyewitnesses and ministers of the word, it seemed good to me also, having traced the course of all things accurately from the first, to write unto thee in order, most excellent Theophilus; that thou mightest know the certainty concerning the things wherein thou wast instructed.'—*St. Luke* i. 1–4.

I. LET us place ourselves by the side of the Evangelist, and from this elevated point let us take as it were a bird's-eye view of the process which he describes as having preceded and led up to the composition of his own Gospel.

But first we must define the point in question chronologically; in other words, we must have some approximate idea when the preface which has just been read and the Gospel which it introduces were written.

Roughly speaking, there are three opinions which may be said to be at present held: (1) that of the Left wing in criticism, that the Gospel dates from

## VI. The Gospels and Acts.

about the year 100 A.D. or from the early years of the second century; (2) that of the extreme Right, that it was written about the year 63 A.D.; (3) the middle view, which would place it together with the Acts about the year 80 A.D.

The only tangible argument in favour of the first of these views is the assumption that the author of the Gospel and Acts, which are now admitted to be by the same hand, had read the *Antiquities* of Josephus, which were written and published about the year 93-94. But this assumption I am not alone in believing to be wholly erroneous. It rests on little more than the fact that both writers relate or allude to the same events, though the differences between them are really more marked than the resemblances[1].

For the date 63 A.D. there is in like manner only one substantial argument, that the Acts was probably written about the time at which the narrative contained in it ends, and of course the Gospel a little before. But to this there are two objections: (i) that the process described in the preface implies a longer period than would fall within the year A.D. 63; it is probable that the common basis of our three Synoptic

---

[1] Schürer sums up the controversy by saying that either St. Luke has taken no notice of Josephus at all, which he thinks the simpler and more probable supposition, or at once forgot everything that he had read (*ap.* Keim, *Aus dem Urchristenthum*, 1878, p. 2; Keim himself argues at length on the affirmative side: see also the authorities enumerated by Holtzmann, *Einleitung*, p. 374, ed. 3, and Lightfoot, art. 'Acts of the Apostles' in *Dict. of Bib.* i. 1. 39, ed. 2). A very full *résumé* of the question is given by Clemen, *Chronologie d. Paulin. Briefe*, Halle, 1893, p. 66 ff.

## Date of St. Luke. 279

Gospels was itself not committed to writing so early; and (ii) that there is a rather strong presumption that the Gospel was written after and not before the Fall of Jerusalem in A.D. 70.

These considerations, which appear to me to be sound, turn the scale in favour of the third view; which would be more precisely that the Acts was written about 80 A.D. and the Gospel some time in the five years preceding.

We look back then across that great catastrophe, the ruin of the Jewish state and nation ; and we see that among Christians there has been considerable activity on the lines which the Evangelist himself is following. He evidently knows of a number of attempts to narrate the Life of Christ, or what we should call 'Gospels.' They need not all have been as extensive as our Gospels, but the words used (ἀνατάξασθαι διήγησιν) imply connected written narratives, something more formal than mere notes, and something more fixed than oral tradition. Among these written narratives there would naturally be some which the Evangelist—whom I will venture hereafter to call, as I believe that he is rightly called, St. Luke—took as his authorities in the composition of his own Gospel. When he speaks of recording the events as they had been 'delivered' or 'handed down' by those who 'from the beginning were eyewitnesses and ministers of the word,' there is nothing to prevent this 'handing down' from being partially at least in writing. The tradition might be oral, or might be written ; but as it had been made clear just before that there were in circulation a number of written documents, we may be sure that some of these would be made use of, even though they may not have been to St. Luke's mind wholly satisfactory—at least not such as to deter him from making a new attempt. We cannot be surprised at this, because we find on looking at our present Gospels that, although St. Luke covers to a considerable extent the same ground as St. Matthew and St. Mark, he yet adds to both of them sections of great interest, which alone would be amply sufficient justification for him in writing.

Had St. Luke those two other Gospels before him? Is there any proof that documents bearing those names were in circulation before he wrote? We look about for side lights; and we find among the scanty remains of literature which have come down to us from the age succeeding the Apostles, two remarkable statements by the Bishop of Hierapolis in Phrygia, writing about or not later than the year 125 A.D. One of these statements is expressly referred to an informant who must have been a person of note belonging to an elder generation than his own. The second statement may and perhaps probably does come from the same source as the first[1], but need not do so necessarily. This writer tells us that St. Mark 'having become interpreter of St. Peter' (*i.e.* probably what the words would strictly mean, the helper of the Apostle in putting what he wished to say into more finished Greek or into Latin) 'wrote down as far as he remembered accurately, though not in order, the

---

[1] Weiffenbach, *Die Papias-Fragmente* (Berlin, n. d.), p. 12.

## The Synoptic Problem. 281

things said or done by Christ[1].' And he goes on to explain that these notes were made from the occasional preaching of St. Peter. He further proceeds to tell us that St. Matthew 'composed the oracles of the Lord in Hebrew (*or* Aramaic), and that every one interpreted them as he was able[2].'

These statements are of course very familiar ground to students of the Synoptic problem. They at once raise a number of questions as to the relation of the documents so described to the Gospels which bear the names of St. Mark and St. Matthew. And as a necessary preliminary to answering these we are thrown back upon a close literary analysis of the relation of all three Gospels to each other. That analysis has been going on more or less upon its present lines for quite thirty years, and yet I cannot take upon myself to say that any completely acceptable result has been arrived at. The latest researches have in fact had rather the effect of opening up new questions than of closing old ones. The problem is indeed one of extraordinary difficulty and complexity. I do not of course mean that there are not some conclusions which seem to disengage themselves, but even these to one who tries to look at the whole subject impartially are so crossed by conflicting indications, that I should not in my present responsible position and with my present degree of knowledge and insight like to propound them for your acceptance[3].

---

[1] Eus. *H. E.* iii. 39. 15.       [2] *Ibid.* § 16.
[3] A survey of the present position of the question, as I conceive it, is given in the supplemental art. 'Gospels' in *Dict. of Bib.* i. 2.

It must not be thought that I despair of a solution. I greatly hope that before very long a sustained and combined effort, for which the circumstances are now particularly favourable, may be made to grapple at close quarters with the difficulties and wring from them a better result than has been obtained hitherto. If we do not do it, others will, because attention is being very much directed to the subject. I would however lay stress on the hopes which I entertain from combination. I feel sure that more could be done in this way than by individual efforts however skilful.

So far I have spoken of the scientific problem of the origin and composition of the Synoptic Gospels. But no doubt the more pressing question, and the question which will have the deeper interest for those who hear me, is not as to the origin of any of the Gospels but as to their historical character. Ultimately there is sure to be some connexion between the two questions. And for myself, I deprecate positive pronouncements about the miracles or any other part of the Gospel narrative, which must be devoid of a strict scientific basis until the analysis of the sources is completed. At the same time, for those whose faith cannot wait for the results of scientific analysis I would venture to say a word of reassurance. I could not at this moment undertake to pronounce upon the relation of the statements of Papias to our first two

---

1217–1243; also in a briefer and more popular form in the Introductions to the Synoptic Gospels in *Book by Book*, and in a series of articles in *The Expositor*, 1891, i. 81 ff., 179 ff., 302 ff., 345 ff., 411 ff.

Gospels. I could not undertake to pronounce upon the origin and structure of the three Synoptics. Composite I believe they are; the First and Third certainly, the Second probably. But how composed is a question which I should be obliged to reserve. On this point however I can speak with great confidence, though I cannot claim to have collected the materials for the argument as fully as I hope some day to do— that the great mass of the narrative in the First Three Gospels took its shape before the Destruction of Jerusalem, *i.e.* within less than forty years of the events.

We possess for historical criticism a singular advantage. In the middle of the period during which the Gospels must have been composed there took place this tremendous, world-shaking catastrophe, which stretches like a chasm across the history, with a wholly different state of things on each side of it. On one side the splendid temple of Herod, with its magnificent services regularly attended by streams of pilgrims from far and near; a system of feasts of which the temple was the centre; the Sanhedrin in full power; an elaborate hierarchy of priests, jealously watched by the party of the Scribes and Pharisees; traces of a number of other parties; the patriots, excited, turbulent, sanguine; another party 'die Stillen im Lande,' quiet, patient, God-fearing people, scattered in ones and twos about the country, eagerly cherishing the Messianic expectation, but with no temptation to political excitement and disorder; yet another party of Hellenizers, adherents of the dynasty of the Herods, a party of some strength during the early years of the century and elated, as we may believe, by the brief reign of Herod Agrippa I (41-44 A.D.), but after that date dwindling, and by the Fall of Jerusalem abolished off the face of the earth. This on the one side; and on the other side, the temple an utter ruin; its sacrifices and services stopped; Jerusalem no longer the centre of pilgrimages, except to forlorn souls like the author of the Apocalypse of Baruch, whom we might imagine coming to weep over its ashes; the whole order of priests, such as survived, deprived of their occupation; the party of fanatical patriots stamped out in blood; the Messianic hope not wholly crushed, but in part still cherished with increased but now anxious longing, and in part passed over to the rapidly rising sect of Christians, which no longer has its centre of gravity at Palestine, but has already struck deep roots far away, in Antioch, Ephesus, Corinth, Rome; the one spiritual rallying-point of the nation now identified with the Rabbinical school at Jamnia and its teachers.

Was there ever an easier problem for the critic to decide whether the sayings and narratives which lie before him come from the one side of this chasm or the other? 'If therefore thou art offering thy gift at the altar, and there rememberest that thy brother hath aught against thee, leave there thy gift before the altar, and go thy way, first be reconciled to thy brother, and then come and offer thy gift [1].' 'Woe unto you, ye blind guides, which say, Whosoever shall swear by

[1] Matt. v. 23, 24.

the temple, it is nothing; but whosoever shall swear by the gold of the temple, he is a debtor. Ye fools and blind: for whether is greater, the gold, or the temple that hath sanctified the gold¹?' A leper is cleansed: 'And Jesus saith unto him, See thou tell no man; but go thy way, show thyself to the priest, and offer the gift that Moses commanded, for a testimony unto them².' 'And when the days of their purification according to the law of Moses were fulfilled, they brought Him up to Jerusalem, to present Him to the Lord . . . and to offer a sacrifice according to that which is said in the law of the Lord, A pair of turtle-doves, or two young pigeons³.' 'And there was one Anna, a prophetess . . . which departed not from the temple, worshipping with fastings and supplications night and day. And coming up at that very hour she gave thanks unto God, and spake of Him to all them that were looking for the redemption of Jerusalem⁴.' 'And they send unto Him certain of the Pharisees and of the Herodians, that they might catch Him in talk. And when they were come, they say unto Him . . . Is it lawful to give tribute unto Caesar, or not⁵?' 'Verily I say unto you, Ye shall not have gone through the cities of Israel, till the Son of Man be come⁶.'

I might spend a great part of the morning quoting sentences of this kind the significance of which lies quite upon the surface. But really it is an elementary exercise in criticism which any one may practise for

¹ Matt. xxiii. 16, 17.
² *Ibid.* viii. 4.
³ Luke ii. 22, 24.
⁴ Luke ii. 36–38.
⁵ Mark xii. 13, 14.
⁶ Matt. x. 23.

himself. All it needs is a New Testament and a pencil, backed by some realization of the conditions which I have described and some hesitation to assume among the peasants of Palestine unlimited historical knowledge and dramatic imagination.

It will be observed that the passages quoted are taken from all three Gospels and are of all kinds— some belonging to the common matter of all three Gospels, some to the double narrative, and some to a portion peculiar to a single Evangelist. These last are the more interesting because they are taken from the first two chapters of St. Luke, chapters which stand quite alone and the history of which is uncorroborated. Yet the instances I have given—and they might be easily and largely added to—show that they represent truly, and indeed with minute truth, the situation as it was at the Birth of Christ, a situation of which after the year 70 A.D. the very elements must soon have been forgotten.

What I contend for is not at once and necessarily that the sayings and acts in question took place exactly as they are recorded, nor yet that they may not have passed from one document to another, or that the documents in which we now have them may not be later than the year 70, but that the moment at which they took their substantial shape either through being committed to writing or by becoming stereotyped in the mind of a person who afterwards committed them to writing, was a moment at which the surrounding and formative conditions were those of the period before and not after the Fall of Jerusalem. I have not quoted from the Fourth Gospel, though I might just as easily have done so; and the inference would have been the same, that the narrative in that Gospel, whenever it was set down upon paper, assumed substantially the shape in which we have it under conditions similar to those which lie behind the Synoptic Gospels, and bearing even stronger marks of originality and nearness to the facts [1].

Another phenomenon in the Gospels, which is I confess to me very wonderful and a striking proof of the early date and authentic character of their contents, is the way in which they preserve a terminology of their own quite distinct from that which is current in the Church all around them. In the period during which the Gospel-tradition was being gradually committed to writing the Church possessed teachers of commanding power who were framing theological systems and impressing them upon their disciples. We have only to think of St. Paul and St. John and the author of the Epistle to the Hebrews, and in a somewhat less degree of St. Peter and St. James. Each of these writers has his characteristic vocabulary. And I do not think that we could have been at all surprised if traces of these several vocabularies had been found in the Gospels. To a certain extent such traces are found in the Gospel of St. John, and in a less and I think not at all suspicious degree in the Gospel of St. Luke compared with the Epistles of St. Paul. But looking at the Gospels as a whole,

[1] Instances are given in *The Expositor*, 1892, i. 293-296.

how small is the impression which has been thus made upon them! And how distinct and easily recognisable is their own characteristic vocabulary[1]!

Take for instance a term, like 'the Son of Man.' We know how constantly it occurs in the Gospels. In the Epistles, Pauline and Catholic together, it never occurs at all, unless perhaps it is obliquely hinted at in the Epistle to the Hebrews (ii. 6). In the Acts it occurs once in the exclamation of St. Stephen (vii. 56), and it is found twice in the Apocalypse (i. 13, xiv. 14) in places where the reference is almost as much to the Book of Daniel as to the Gospel tradition. Another phrase, 'the kingdom of God' or 'of heaven,' occurs it is true more frequently in the Epistles, but by no means so frequently in proportion as in the Gospels. The relation here is just what we might expect. The 'doctrine of the kingdom' is taken for granted in the Epistles, as something fundamental which does not need to be repeated. It has been pointed out by Weizsäcker[2] that the regular word for disciples, $\mu\alpha\theta\eta\tau\alpha\acute{\iota}$, though constantly used in the Gospels and Acts, disappears

---

[1] Since this was written I see that von Soden in an essay contributed to the volume in honour of Weizsäcker (*Theol. Abhandl. &c.*, p. 113 ff.) has instituted a detailed comparison of the terminology of the Gospels and the Epistles. The result is on the whole confirmatory of what is said above. The main body of the Gospels shows remarkably little contact with the Epistles. This becomes somewhat greater in certain outlying portions; but here I suspect that von Soden presses the contact too far. For some further remarks on this essay see below, p. 317 f.

[2] *Apost. Zeitalt.* p. 36.

## Criticism of the Gospels. 289

entirely from the rest of the New Testament, where the substitutes are ἀδελφοί and ἅγιοι[1].

Then again take another of the commonest of all terms. We know how in the Epistles 'Christ' has become almost a proper name. It may perhaps retain rather more of its true meaning than we are apt to realize; but if not exactly a proper name it is rapidly becoming one. In the Gospels, on the other hand, it nearly always means, as in the mouth of our Lord and His strict contemporaries it must have meant, 'the Messiah.' The point of the Gospels is that up to the very last all but the inner circle of the disciples are kept in suspense as to whether Jesus were 'the Christ' or no. The compound phrase 'Jesus Christ' occurs a few times[2], but always with one exception (John xvii. 3), as it should do, in words of the Evangelist and not of our Lord Himself. The true phrase, the natural phrase in our Lord's lifetime, is of course that which we find three times in St. Matthew, 'Jesus *who is called Christ*' (Matt. i. 16, xxvii. 17, 22).

Corresponding to this on the negative side is a point which has been often noticed. It is a leading idea with the author of the Fourth Gospel that Jesus is the 'Logos' or 'Incarnate Word of God.' But he

[1] The statistics are striking: μαθητής occurs in the Synoptic Gospels 160 times, in St. John seventy-eight, in the Acts twenty-eight (μαθήτρια once), and in the other books not at all. The reason for the change is obvious. During the lifetime of Jesus, the disciples were called after their relation to Him; after His departure the names given to them indicated their relation to each other and to the society.

[2] Matt. i. 1, 18 (v. l.), xvi. 21 (v. l.); Mark i. 1; John i. 17, xvii. 3, xx. 31.

reserves this designation strictly for the prologue, where he is speaking in his own person, and our Lord is *nowhere* made to apply it to Himself.

If we wish to appreciate the full force of these examples we have only to turn to a Gospel that was really composed in the second century. The Apocryphal Gospel of Peter is based upon our Gospels and borrows some of its terms from them (*e. g.* μαθητής); but it is very soon apparent when the writer begins to walk by himself. In the Canonical Gospels the title Κύριος is frequently applied to our Lord by the disciples and others as a term of reverential address; on the other hand in the narrative of the Evangelists it is rare—it occurs not at all in St. Matthew or the genuine text of St. Mark, though twice in the last twelve verses, eleven times (and once doubtfully) in the later Gospel of St. Luke, and six times in St. John. In the narrative of the Gospel of Peter it is the standing title; no other is used[1]. The malefactors whose knowledge of our Lord must have been of the smallest are made to describe Him as 'the Saviour of men.' Twice over the word used for the 'first day of the week' is the Christian term, κυριακή, 'the Lord's day.' We observe also that Herod Antipas is not called 'tetrarch' but 'king' (as he is indeed sometimes in the Canonical Gospels), and, what is of more importance, that the high-priests, both Annas and Caiaphas, drop out, and that he takes their place.

In all these ways the contrast between the Apocryphal Gospel and the Canonical Gospels is marked.

[1] It occurs nine times in sixty verses.

## Criticism of the Gospels.

The latter are really like a 'garden inclosed.' Intrusive elements seem to be carefully kept out of them. They preserve the type of language, as it can be abundantly shown that they also preserve the type of idea, which was appropriate just to the short three years of our Lord's public ministry, and no more.

I have no doubt that this too is a line of argument which can be considerably extended. I have only chosen those examples which are so plain that no one can avoid noticing them or miss their significance. They also go to prove that our Gospels must have taken their substantial shape before the Destruction of Jerusalem. But there are a number of other indications which also point to that event, some as still in prospect, others as just past, and which so mark the point of time at which our Gospels were being composed or redacted. Some of these are commonplaces of criticism, but there is one to which I have alluded on a public occasion once before, but shall venture for the sake of illustration to allude to again. You will remember how in that prophecy in which the disasters of the Jewish nation and the Second Coming of the Son of Man are so closely connected, attention is called to the signs by which these events are to be preceded. Among these is one which receives a pointed application. 'When therefore ye see the abomination of desolation (spoken of by Daniel the prophet, standing in the holy place *St. Matthew*; standing where it ought not *St. Mark*)— let him that readeth understand, then let them that are in Judaea flee unto the mountains: let him that is on the housetop not go down to take out the things that are in the house,' &c.[1] Observe that remarkable insertion, 'Let him that readeth understand.' Clearly it is a sort of 'aside,' a hint to Christians who may read the book to give heed to its warnings. The time has not yet come for them to take effect, but it is near at hand. We observe further that precisely the same insertion, the same whispered warning to the readers, occurs in two out of the three Gospels, and at exactly the same place. It follows that it belongs to their common original, which must also have been in writing. I am aware that some critics speak of this apocalyptic discourse as a 'fly-leaf' circulating separately, and others adopt what is at the present moment a rather fashionable explanation, seeing in it a little Jewish apocalypse incorporated in the Gospels[2]. But there does not seem to be sufficient reason to detach it from its surroundings; in other words, it is in all probability really a part of that common narrative which gives to our first three Gospels their strong resemblance of form. And it is one among many indications that this common narrative was composed within sight of the troubles which it describes, but before they had reached their climax. Eusebius speaks of an 'oracle' which warned the Christians to flee from Jerusalem before it was beleaguered[3]. There can be little doubt that the oracle in question, if it was not this very passage,

---

[1] Matt. xxiv. 15 ff.=Mark xiii. 14 ff.; cf. Luke xxi. 20 ff.
[2] This theory I believe dates from Weiffenbach's *Wiederkunfts-gedanke Jesu*, Leipzig, 1873. With Weiffenbach it is bound up with the curious idea, which his book expounds, that the Second Coming which Christ predicted for Himself was really the Resurrection.
[3] Eus. *H. E.* iii. 5. 3.

was based upon it. It was not however obeyed quite literally, as the actual flight was 'not to the mountains,' but to Pella, a little city of Peraea[1]. A fact which again shows that the text has not been altered after the event.

But indeed all three Gospels—not only the older documents out of which they are composed, but our present Gospels as we have them—lie under the shadow of the Fall of Jerusalem. The slight alterations which have been introduced, especially in St. Luke[2], defining the allusions to that event in accordance with the history, are enough to show that the compilers of the Gospels were alive to the correspondence between prophecy and its fulfilment. But in one emphatic passage reported without variation in all three Gospels, it seems to be expressly asserted that the events, not only of the Fall of Jerusalem but of the Coming of the Son of Man, should take place within the lifetime of the generation to whom they had been predicted[3]. Can we think that these words and others like them would have been left standing if our Gospels had been composed as late as some imagine? So simple an expedient as omission, in what was confessedly a selection of materials, would have raised no scruples and would have lain close at hand.

Of this then I think we may rest assured, that the

---

[1] Holtzmann, *Die Synoptiker*, p. 22. Eusebius makes the oracle designate Pella as the place of refuge.

[2] *Cp.* Luke xxi. 20 ff., compared with Matt. xxiv. 15 ff., Mark xiii. 14 ff.; Luke xxi. 25, compared with Matt. xxiv. 29, Mark xiii. 24.

[3] Matt. xxiv. 34 = Mark xiii. 30 = Luke xxi. 32; *cf.* Matt. x. 23.

whole process of the composition of our first three Gospels, a process no doubt highly complicated and in its details obscure, must be comprised within limits of which the furthest is not later than the year 80 A.D.[1] The complexity and obscurity arise from the number of hands which have had a share in it. There were I suspect not only two hands, but two sets of hands, working under somewhat different conditions. There were the original authors of the primary documents, the 'eyewitnesses and ministers of the word' of whom St. Luke speaks, partly drawing upon the current tradition and partly putting an individual stamp of their own upon it in accordance with their own circumstances. These oldest documents would not be very lengthy, and would soon be absorbed in longer compositions. It is difficult for instance to identify the rough notes of St. Mark even with so much of our Second Gospel as lies at the base of the others. No doubt they were included in this, but they can hardly be co-extensive with it. And again, when we take the common matter of St. Matthew and St. Luke it does not seem that either Evangelist simply made a transcript of a single document lying before him. There must have been disturbing causes at work, probably involving the use of other documents, to account for the divergences both of text and order between them.

---

[1] I have not gone into the question as to the internal evidence to the Fourth Gospel partly from considerations of space and partly because I have written at some length on this subject in *The Expositor* for 1891, ii, and 1892, i.

## Criticism of the Gospels.

And then when the book leaves the hand of its author it is evident that in the early stages of transmission the functions of copyist and editor were apt to run into each other. For instance, it is not improbable that our St. Mark is descended from a copy which did not exactly reproduce its predecessor, even after the Gospel had assumed substantially its present form. It would seem that processes were going on very similar to those which have already been described in the case of the historians of the Old Testament, but more complex and difficult to unravel, because the period to which they must be referred was one of still greater movement and confusion, and because the number of individuals concerned in them was probably greater.

We can form some idea of what may be called perhaps the pre-canonical or pre-historic age of Gospel-composition, *i.e.* the period before they had attained the form in which we now have them, from the traces of their early history as soon as they had attained it. There are abundant traces in the MSS. and other authorities for the text of the Gospels that they were copied at first with great freedom. Possessors of copies did not hesitate to add little items of tradition, often oral, in some cases perhaps written, which reached them. These enriched copies would become the parents of a long line of ancestry, which usually included the texts current at the time of the invention of printing, and therefore also the texts which were translated for our Bibles. A multitude of examples will occur to every Biblical scholar. The English reader will see many of them if he will look at the margin of his Revised Version, or note the omissions in the Revised Version as compared with the Authorized. Such for instance would be the paragraph of the Woman taken in Adultery, the verse and a half which describes the moving of the waters in the pool of Bethesda or Bezetha, that which describes the Bloody Sweat in the garden of Gethsemane, the full expanded text of the incident of the sons of Zebedee and the Samaritan village, and many other minor instances. The variety of the authorities which support or omit these different passages shows that they did not all come in at one time and under the same influences, but one here and another there, though no doubt all—at least all of any importance—early, while there was still a living tradition and other Gospels were current beside the Canonical.

In addition to the instances which as I have said because they happened to have a place in the MSS. used by the early printers have also left their mark on the Authorized and Revised Versions, there are a number of others which were suppressed long before this date. Attention has of late been drawn—and very rightly drawn [1]—to a particular group of authorities, headed by the famous Codex Bezae at Cambridge, which represents a type of text which enjoyed a large circulation in the second century, though the characteristic features of it were rapidly falling out of use when we reach the fourth. The study of this text is

[1] See besides Prof. Rendel Harris' *Study of Codex Bezae*, especially Resch, *Aussercanonische Paralleltexte zu den Evangelien*, Leipzig, 1893.

calculated to throw much light on the early history of the Gospels; and we can, as I have said, argue backwards from it even beyond the point to which the extant authorities will carry us, because the tendencies which find expression in it are only the continuation of tendencies which were already at work before our Gospels became what they are.

I refer to all this to show that at first freedom was the rule, scrupulous accuracy the exception, in propagating the text of the Gospels. Much of this may be due to the fact that these early copies were probably to a large extent the works, not of professional copyists but of private individuals, whose interest was strong in the subject-matter of what they wrote, and who were glad to record any stray saying or act of Christ which came in their way, even though it were not found in the copy before them. Do not let me convey an exaggerated idea as to the result of this manifold activity. It has not affected our Bibles to any really serious extent. Scholars are able to say pretty definitely, or within narrow limits, what the Evangelists wrote. The average opinion may be found expressed in the Revised Version, which is not indeed accepted unanimously, but the *maximum* of difference would not be great or practically important. Nor does it follow that all the rejected readings are necessarily devoid of historical truth. The floating traditions and documents that were about, and from which the adventitious matter was obtained, doubtless contained many grains of truth. All that is meant by the rejection of such readings is that they were not

## VI. The Gospels and Acts.

part of what the Evangelists, those who brought the Gospels to their final shape, really wrote. Supposing it were the case, as was at one time thought, that one particular form of text was supernaturally inspired and free from error, and all other forms uninspired and fallible, then indeed it would be a difficult and precarious task to mark off this exact stratum of text from those which came before and after it. But as it is, we seek the inspiration of the Gospels elsewhere. No Christian needs to ask if the sayings of the Lord Jesus are inspired. Those sayings, and the deeds of mercy and love by which they were accompanied, have been recorded for us by honest and, as the preface to St. Luke also shows, careful and laborious historians. This praise we can claim for them; and there was doubtless also a Providence which watched over the tangled maze of collecting, adjusting, compiling, copying and multiplying copies—who that looks at the Gospels as they are can doubt that a Providence has watched over them? But the processes in question were natural processes, carried out naturally. The Life described in the Gospels was supernatural, but just as the Divine in it shone through a veil of human flesh, so also it was capable of being related, and it was related, in the 'tongue of the children of men.'

The freedom of which I have been speaking was not confined to the scribes and copyists. It appears also as soon as we cross the frontier of the Canon and observe how the Gospels are quoted in the next generation after the Apostles. The little volume, commonly known as the Apostolic Fathers, which contains all that has come down to us from this early date, presents a problem which is not yet altogether solved. Quotations from the Gospels are not numerous. Most of them are taken from the Sermon on the Mount. And although there is on the whole sufficient reason for believing that the writers were acquainted with our present Synoptic Gospels, in any case their text is in several places not adhered to very closely. There are also some peculiar phenomena connected with these quotations. For instance, Clement of Rome quotes several verses which look like a combination of the texts of St. Matthew and St. Luke in an order which does not quite agree with either. A portion of the same passage is quoted by Polycarp, and the whole by Clement of Alexandria; single phrases also occur in other writers; all with closer resemblance among themselves than with our Gospels[1]. It must be admitted too that the form which the passage assumes in these writers is even more rounded and antithetical than it is in our Bibles. What is the explanation of this? There are two competing views. One is that Clement of Rome quoted in the first instance freely from memory; that Polycarp and Clement of Alexandria were both familiar with his Epistle[2], and that the way in which they reproduced the original was influenced by it; that in fact another version obtained currency all through the one free

[1] See Resch, *Agrapha*, pp. 96 f., 136 ff.; *Expositor*, 1891, i. 417 ff.
[2] This was certainly the case with Clement of Alexandria; the Epistle of Polycarp is too short to enable us to judge.

quotation on the part of the Roman Clement. This was the only explanation given by Bishop Lightfoot [1]. The alternative is that all the succession of writers are quoting, not from our Gospels, but from another document like them. This again is the only view entertained by a recent writer who has gone most elaborately into the subject, Dr. Alfred Resch [2]. Dr. Resch does not however adopt the theory which found favour with writers like the author of *Supernatural Religion*, that the source of the quotations was an Apocryphal Gospel; but he thinks that this is one of a number of examples of the survival in use of one of the foundation-documents of our Synoptics, neither more or less than the collection of 'Oracles' which we are told was the work of the Apostle St. Matthew. These opposed but not mutually exclusive views are not perhaps as yet ripe for positive decision. Indeed, I am tempted to make a small addition to them. There is yet another element which ought perhaps to be taken into account, the element of *catechizing* [3].

The case appears to stand thus [4]. It is on the whole probable that each of the Apostolic Fathers implies the use of one or other of the Synoptic Gospels. This is so not very decisively with St. Clement,

[1] In Clem. Rom. *ad Cor.*, xiii. 2.

[2] *Agrapha, ut sup.*

[3] Reference should be made to an elaborate essay, 'Die Katechese der alten Kirche,' by Dr. H. J. Holtzmann in *Theol. Abhandlungen Carl von Weizsäcker gewidmet*, Freiburg i. B., 1892, p. 61 ff.

[4] The present writer's view of the details of the subject may be found in *The Gospels in the Second Century*, London, 1876.

who however seems to have a trace of St. Mark as well as of the two companion Gospels. It is so with the Epistle of Barnabas, which has one clear quotation, introduced by γέγραπται, and other slighter reminiscences of St. Matthew. The same holds good for the Epistles of Ignatius, which distinctly imply the First Gospel, and in a less degree for the Epistle of Polycarp. The *Didaché* has more quotations; and here the use of both the First and the Third Gospels is undoubted.

There is however a tendency apparent throughout this literature, marked in Clement, very marked in the *Didaché*, and marked also as we overstep the limits of this period in Justin, to combine together phrases from these two Gospels, St. Matthew and St. Luke. So much is this the case that the hypothesis has been more than once thrown out that the writers in question, more particularly Justin, quoted at least at times not from our separate Gospels but from a *Harmony of the Gospels*[1]. We know that Justin's disciple Tatian composed such a Harmony. That was not published until after Justin's death; but it would not be improbable that some sort of rough draft might have been used by both master and scholar before its pub-

[1] Engelhardt, *ap.* Weiss, *Einleitung*, p. 42; Schürer in *Theol. Literaturzeitung*, 1891, col. 66 (what Schürer contends for is 'eine Mischung des Matthäus- und Lucas-Textes,' which he thinks that at least in one instance Justin must have had before him in writing); Rendel Harris, *Diatessaron of Tatian*, p. 54; *Gosp. in Second Cent.*, p. 136 n. A new element is introduced into the question by the discovery of the Gospel of Peter, which uses all four Gospels and was probably used by Justin.

lication. Indeed because Tatian composed a Harmony it would not follow that his was the first of its kind. Just as there is now known to have been a Theodotion-version of the LXX before Theodotion, so also there might be a *Diatessaron* or *Diatrion* (not of course precisely under that name) before Tatian's. Besides Tatian's Harmony there was another as we know composed probably very soon after his by Theophilus of Antioch. This would show that the idea of harmonizing or combining the Gospels was in the air.

There is however another, and I think perhaps a simpler and better explanation, suggested by the *Didaché*. Converts to Christianity, especially converts from heathenism, underwent a short course of instruction, similar to that which the Jews were in the habit of imparting to their proselytes, and consisting mainly of simple moral teaching. With the Jews this moral teaching took the form of an expansion of the Ten Commandments; with Christians there was added to this or inwoven with it a like summary of teaching from the Sermon on the Mount. It was natural that this should be reproduced freely. Just as the liturgical prayers were extemporized on the same general pattern[1], so also would the catechist extemporize, but as it were within a given framework or on a given model. Teaching like this would soon become familiar, as familiar as the Church Catechism among ourselves; and a Christian writer would fall unconsciously into it, without consulting his copy of the Gospels.

[1] *Cf.* Lightfoot, *Clement*, i. 382 ff. (esp. p. 386), ed. 2.

## Early Use of the Gospels. 303

This I suspect may have had something to do with the form of the early quotations. But we must beware of laying down any hard and fast rule. Different influences would be at work in different cases: sometimes catechizing; sometimes quotation from memory; sometimes the form adopted by some previous writer; sometimes, we may believe, the parallel language of some pre-canonical or extra-canonical writing.

But one thing does come out, and is in agreement with all that we have observed hitherto, that there was certainly no bondage to the letter of the Gospels, no straining after verbal exactness. The Christians of those days knew their Gospels; or perhaps we should put it that they knew *the Gospel* through the medium of the Gospels; but their knowledge was not checked and controlled by constant reference to the MS.

The fact is that at first the Gospels were not studied or quoted for their own sake as Gospels, *i.e.* as Sacred Books, the work of inspired men. They are valued not so much for themselves as for their contents, and especially for a part of their contents. They were regarded mainly as vehicles for the 'Words of the Lord[1].' The whole stress lies upon these. It is strongly contended by a writer who has given more than five and twenty years of study to the early stages of the Gospel-tradition[2], that St. Paul himself had

---

[1] See especially Weiss, *Einleitung*, p. 24 ff., ed. 1.
[2] A full and searching examination of Dr. Resch's views on this subject will be found in Mr. Knowling's *Witness of the Epistles*, London, 1892.

before him a written collection of these sayings. And it is true that he appeals to them with some frequency and with absolute deference as the highest rule of Christian faith and conduct[1]. But he nowhere refers to the literary framework in which they are set. Although, if he had such a document in his possession, it can hardly have been any other than the collection made by the Apostle St. Matthew, he does not make the slightest allusion to its authorship. He sees nothing of the disciple; he thinks only of the Master.

Perhaps it is on the whole more probable that St. Paul had not access to such a document as Dr. Resch supposes; at least it cannot be considered proved that he had. But the same usage prevails even after the introduction of written Gospels. The favourite name for Gospels is *Logia*, 'Oracles of the Lord'; and the formula of quotation, when any is used, is not 'St. Matthew writes in his Gospel' or 'St. Mark records such an act or saying,' but only 'remembering the words of the Lord Jesus,' 'remember what the Lord said in His teaching,' 'as the Lord said[2].'

The next stage would be that which we find in the writings of Justin, who repeatedly refers to certain 'Memoirs of the Apostles,' adding in one place, 'which are called Gospels[3].' The term 'Memoirs' covers narrative as well as discourse, and as a matter of fact

---

[1] 1 Thess. iv. 15; 1 Cor. vii. 10 (*cp.* 12, 25), ix. 14, xi. 24 f.; Acts xx. 35.

[2] Acts xx. 35; Clem. *ad Cor.* xiii. 1, xlvi. 7; Polyc. vii. 2; *cf.* 2 Pet. iii. 2. Further references are given by Weiss, *Einl.* p. 25.

[3] Apol. i. 66; *cf. ibid.,* 33, 67; *Dial. c. Tryph.* 100, 103, 105, 107.

## History of the name Gospels.

Justin has made large use of evangelical narrative in forms distinctive not only of each of the four Canonical Gospels, but as it now appears also of the Gospel according to Peter, but with preference for our present Gospels of St. Matthew and St. Luke. The Gospels are now treated as wholes; we observe too that stress is laid upon their Apostolic origin. Yet the name 'Memoirs' would not seem to suggest the idea of special sacredness; and although it would be wrong to insist upon the name alone, because Justin is writing for those who are not Christians and therefore naturally chooses a term which they will understand rather than one so technical as 'Gospels,' still his manner of treating them is in agreement with his choice of a title. They are historical authorities, authorities of weight as coming from Apostles, but not more. Only a slight use is made of the Gospel of Peter, but no distinction is drawn between it and the other Gospels. Indeed it would seem to be not only included among the 'Memoirs of the Apostles,' but to have itself suggested the designation [1].

But we must not make the mistake, which is too often made, of taking a single writer as representative of the whole body of the Church. Justin was a philosopher who came over to the Church with literary

---

[1] This was pointed out by Mr. A. C. Headlam in *The Guardian* for Dec. 7, 1892, and is now widely accepted. The question is discussed with scrupulous care by Dr. Swete (*Akhmîm Fragment*, p. xxxiii ff.), who sums up in a negative sense but has to have recourse to a hypothetical version of Ps. xxii. 18 ἔβαλον λαχμόν.

habits already formed. His extant writings are addressed to persons outside the Church who would understand what was meant by a 'biography' but would not understand what was meant by a 'Gospel.' Hence we cannot be surprised if, so far as the name is concerned, he treats the Life of Christ as he would treat the Life of Socrates. But it by no means follows that Christians speaking among themselves would do so. Indeed he tells us that biographies of Christ had already received a special title—and that title was the appropriation of a word which had been originally used to denote the whole message of salvation. This was the title current in the Church generally, and Justin implies that his own name 'Memoirs' was merely a paraphrase of it adapted to his Pagan and Jewish readers. I do not think that we need any further proof than this single word 'Gospel,' narrowed down from the 'tidings of good' which the Apostles spread throughout the world, first to the general substance of the Life of Christ, and finally to particular records of that Life, to show that these were never even from the first on the same footing with profane writings. It took some time to define the exact nature of the difference. There were certainly at first no special scruples connected with the wording of the record. But there was a latent consciousness, which gradually became more and more distinct, that the authentic records of the Life of Christ were books to themselves.

This consciousness must have been already far advanced when Justin was writing. Soon after the death of Justin, between Justin and Irenaeus (*c.* 160–170 A.D.), two facts stand out which bear striking testimony to it. One is the *Diatessaron* of Tatian; the other is Heracleon's commentary on St. John.

When the author of *Supernatural Religion* wrote in 1874 it was possible to say—whether justly or not, is another question—that there was 'no evidence whatever connecting Tatian's Gospel with those in our Canon'[1]; and it was possible to fence with the theory that the *Diatessaron* was only a later name for the Apocryphal Gospel according to the Hebrews[2]. Now the substance and an approximate text of the *Diatessaron* itself lies before us; and it is found to be, as orthodox writers had maintained, a simple digest of the four Canonical Gospels with the prologue to the Gospel of St. John at its head.

Much about the same time with the *Diatessaron*, Heracleon, a disciple of Valentinus and one of the leaders of the Italian school of Valentinian Gnostics, put forth a commentary on St. John's Gospel, in which it is interpreted strictly as Holy Scripture, with all the apparatus of allegory which by this time was applied to the Old Testament. There is no distinction between the words of Christ and the parts of the Gospel which are due to the Evangelist. The latter are expounded as an authoritative text in the same manner as the former[3].

But the way in which Heracleon sits down to write

[1] *Sup. Rel.* ii. 161, ed. 6.  [2] *Ibid.* p. 160.
[3] See Mr. A. E. Brooke's *Fragments of Heracleon* in Cambridge *Texts and Studies*, vol. i. No. 4.

this commentary shows that he is not introducing any new conception, but is acting upon one which is already settled and established. Nor does Heracleon stand alone. All the other Valentinian leaders, as well Ptolemaeus his colleague in the West as those of the Anatolic or Eastern branch of the School, our knowledge of which is derived from the so-called *Excerpta Theodoti*, place the Fourth Gospel with the other Gospels on the same footing of Divine authority [1]. The large use of this Gospel which Irenaeus attributes to the Valentinians generally [2] is abundantly confirmed. But this wide-spread use among the disciples is hardly possible without some sanction on the part of the master; and what we know of the system of Valentinus lends support to the view that he too drew from the same source.

What we may suspect for Valentinus is now, I think it may be said, proved for his contemporary and rival Basilides. A most convincing paper was recently read here in Oxford by Dr. Drummond of Manchester College on the question 'Is Basilides quoted in the *Philosophumena* [3]?' The affirmative answer which Dr. Drummond gives, and I think it must be agreed rightly gives to this, carries with it also an affirmative to the question whether Basilides himself and not merely his followers quoted from the Fourth Gospel.

[1] See *Expositor*, 1891, ii. 417.
[2] *Adv. Haer.* iii. 11. 7.
[3] This paper is printed in the *Journal of Biblical Literature* (Boston, U.S.A., 1892), p. 133 ff.

## The Canon of the Gospels.

Here then we have, as I cannot but think, decisive evidence for the use of the Fourth Gospel as a sacred text a full generation earlier than some scholars would assign to it. The epithet 'decisive' would not be the most appropriate for another highly interesting inquiry recently published in this country, Dr. C. Taylor's *Hermas and the Four Gospels*. Dr. Taylor maintains that the famous passage in Irenaeus about the 'fourfold Gospel' was anticipated in a writing as early as the *Shepherd* of Hermas, about 140 A.D.[1] The *Shepherd* is from first to last an allegory, the details of which are significant though the writer himself only partially explains them; so that when the Church afterwards identified with the Son of God, under the figure of an aged woman who becomes young, is represented as sitting upon a bench or stool planted firmly upon four feet[2], there is certainly a resemblance to the place in Irenaeus where the Church Catholic spread throughout the four quarters of the earth is said to be stayed upon four pillars which are the Four Gospels, corresponding also to the Four Cherubim over whom is seated the Word[3]. And when it is further said that the stool has four feet and stands strongly because the world also is 'held together by four elements' (διὰ τεσσάρων στοιχείων κρατεῖται), we are reminded that

---

[1] Dr. Salmon, Zahn, and some others place this still earlier, c. 100 A.D. It is probable that this opinion has something to do with Zahn's summary rejection of Dr. Taylor's view, at which Dr. Resch expresses some surprise (*Parallcltexte*, p. 13).

[2] *Vis.* iii. 13. 3.

[3] Iren. *Adv. Haer.* iii. 15. 8 (ed. Stieren; ii. 11, 12 ed. Harvey); Taylor, *Hermas*, p. 13 ff.

## VI. The Gospels and Acts.

Origen compares the Four Gospels to the elements of the faith of the Church, of which elements the whole world consists[1]. Now we know that Irenaeus treats the *Shepherd* of Hermas as Scripture and that Origen treats it almost as Scripture, quoting from it repeatedly and mentioning the fact that some did so regard it. When therefore the question is asked whether the two later writers are wholly independent of the earlier or the coincidence between them is purely accidental, though I admit that the case is not so clear as to convince a gainsayer, I confess that to me there seems to be a real probability that they are not independent, and that Hermas gave the hint which Irenaeus and Origen have followed[2]. But if so, then Hermas also knew the fourfold Gospel, and even in his day the Canonical Four were detached from the rest.

We come last to the newly discovered Gospel of Peter, which has an important bearing upon the early use and authority of the Four Gospels. I take it as proved, or at all events decidedly probable, that Justin used this new Gospel, not largely but yet that he did use it along with the others. This would fix its date as hardly later than the end of the first quarter of the

---

[1] *Comm. in Ev. Joan.* i. 6 (Lomm. i. 13); Taylor, *Journ. of Philol.* xxi. 69 f.

[2] This view is accepted as at least possessing some probability by Resch, *ut sup.*, by Dr. T. K. Abbott in *Class. Rev.* 1892, p. 454, and by an anonymous reviewer in *The Academy*; it is rejected by Zahn, *Theol. Litteraturblatt*, 1892, col. 268 ff., by a careful critic in *The Guardian*, Mar. 29, 1893, and by Holtzmann in *Theol. Literaturzeitung*, 1893, col. 228 f.

second century[1]. What then is the relation of the Gospel of Peter, so far as it has been recovered, to the Canonical Gospels? The *primâ facie* view I think is decidedly that it made use of all four[2]. Characteristic features of each of the four reappear in it—features so characteristic that the coincidences cannot be the result of accident, but point unmistakably to a connexion of some kind. The only alternative to direct use (for we may put aside altogether the hypothesis that the Gospel of Peter is prior to our Gospels) would be that which is adopted by Harnack and von Soden in a full and careful discussion of the subject, viz. that the writer of the Apocryphal Gospel made use not of our present Gospels but of the separate lines of tradition which those Gospels embody. Both Harnack and von Soden are of opinion that the writer had before him our Second Gospel; but the coincidences with the First, Third, and Fourth they would explain not by literary contact but by personal contact with the circle of tradition out of which each of those Gospels arose. There is an obvious difficulty in this

---

[1] Similarly von Soden in *Zeitschr. f. Theol. u. Kirche*, 1893, p. 91. On the assumption that Harnack proves his point as to the use of the Gospel in the *Didaché* and by Ignatius and Polycarp, it would then, von Soden thinks, be about contemporary with the rescript of Trajan (112 A. D.).

[2] Most English critics who have expressed themselves so far take this view. Mr. E. N. Bennett speaks doubtfully (*Class. Rev.* 1893, p. 40). M. Lods thinks that the writer uses the First and Second Gospels, perhaps the Third, not the Fourth (*L'Evangile et L'Apocalypse de Pierre*, p. 72). But Dr. Schürer thinks it probable that he was acquainted with all four Gospels (*Theol. Literaturzeitung*, 1893, col. 35). So too Zahn in *Neue kirchl. Zeitschrift*, 1893, p. 190 ff.

view. The First Gospel was no doubt composed in Palestine; but the Fourth Gospel, even if not the work of St. John, must have been composed at or near Ephesus, and the Third Gospel in one or other of the centres of Hellenistic Christianity. We must therefore suppose either that the author of the Gospel of Peter visited in succession Palestine, Ephesus, and the unknown place of origin of the Third Gospel, or else that the different types of tradition embodied in the First, Third, and Fourth Gospels went on for a number of years existing in their distinctness apart from those Gospels; in other words, that besides such Johannean teaching as naturally circulated round the person of the Apostle during the thirty years of his lifetime at Ephesus, the tradition which St. John had left behind him also preserved its distinctive features for a still longer period in Palestine—and in like manner for St. Luke and St. Matthew. This however is a supposition which cannot be regarded as probable. In particular I doubt if such minute coincidences and resemblances as are found between the Gospel of Peter and the Canonical Gospels can be naturally explained in any other way than by direct literary dependence.

But if so, the Gospel of Peter implies the existence of our Four Gospels, and except perhaps a slight amount of collateral tradition [1], I do not see that it

---

[1] There is what seems to be a bit of good tradition in § 7 (ed. Robinson, = 26 ed. Harnack): ἐγὼ δὲ μετὰ τῶν ἑταίρων μου ἐλυπούμην, καὶ τετρωμένοι κατὰ διάνοιαν ἐκρυβόμεθα· ἐζητούμεθα γὰρ ὑπ' αὐτῶν ὡς κακοῦργοι, καὶ ὡς τὸν ναὸν θέλοντες ἐμπρῆσαι. Schürer (ut sup.) thinks that the view

implies anything else. As a literary substratum the Canonical Gospels cover very nearly the whole ground which the Apocryphal Gospel covers. No further literary antecedent seems necessary.

But if we take this view another consequence follows. If we believe that the author of the Gospel of Peter started from our Four Gospels as his main basis, it must also be allowed that he used them with very great freedom [1]. In developing the hints which they supplied he gave free rein to his own imagination; he was not bound by any scruples to adhere to them verbally.

Neither is there much force in the argument that the Petrine writer as a Docetist did not recognise the restrictions of Catholic tradition. The heretical character of the Gospel is by no means prominent [2]. It does just come out in a few slight expressions; but it is surprising to find how much of the substructure which is really inconsistent with Docetism has been retained unaltered. The Gospel circulated in orthodox

(expressed by Robinson) will not hold that the author knew no other Gospel besides those in the Canon. M. Lods accepts a few touches as coming from tradition and adds, 'L'évangile de Pierre me représenterait bien les derniers temps du règne de la tradition orale' (p. 79).

[1] To say this is not the same thing as to say with Harnack (p. 33) that the author regarded any of the Gospels as 'eine .. zum Theil unglaubwürdige Darstellung.'

[2] In this I agree with Mr. E. N. Bennett, *Class. Rev.* 1893, p. 40, and with M. Lods, *L'Evangile, &c.*, pp. 37 ff., 73 f. The resemblance in substance between the view expressed in this paragraph and that of M. Lods is so great that I ought perhaps to explain that I had not seen his treatise when it was written.

communities; and we must also remember that at the time when it was written there was a large tentative element in Christian doctrine, in regard to which, though the mind of the Church was clearing itself, it was not yet clear. We must not think of every heretical teacher as necessarily out of communion.

It would therefore be hazardous to say that the Gospel of Peter represents Docetism but not Catholic Christianity. Its tendencies may be exaggerated by its origin, but they are not wholly due to it. We do not in fact need to have recourse to such a supposition; because the phenomena which are characteristic of the Gospel of Peter are only just what we have already found to be characteristic generally of the age in which it arose. They may be rather more marked in degree; but that is all.

The whole of this first period in the history of the Gospels, up to and in some cases beyond the death of Justin, has for its leading characteristic freedom. The way in which the Gospel of Peter makes use of the Four Gospels has its analogue in the way in which Justin makes use of the Gospel of Peter. The Gospels are treated primarily as historical authorities; and historical material of any sort was welcome. A book in particular which bore the name of an Apostle would not be too closely questioned. It was really a continuation of the state of things described by Papias, when a living oral tradition, by no means without value, ran side by side and competed with the Gospels. The principal difference was that the concurrence was now not so much of oral tradition as of writings.

## The Canon of the Gospels.

It is certainly very remarkable how the Four Gospels are singled out, if our interpretation of the facts is correct, not later than the first quarter of the second century. When it is said 'singled out' there was naturally in this at first something vague. It does not seem to be more than an undefined sense that the Four Gospels which we call Canonical were superior to the rest. The use of these Gospels did not at first exclude the use of all others; but when once a line was drawn round the Four, they would become every day more and more predominant, until at last their competitors are not only degraded to a lower level but shut out altogether. The later stages in the process are graphically depicted in the story of Serapion[1]. By his time, *i.e.* by the end of the second century, the circulation of the Gospel of Peter had shrunk to a mere local usage; the bishop of a great centre like Antioch had not heard of it until it was specially brought to his notice; at first he was inclined to let it be, until it became clear that there were heretical features in it, but that fact brings about its suppression. We are clearly at the point where Clement of Alexandria speaks of the 'four Gospels handed down' to the Church [2] with a fringe of others; and we are prepared for the further step which we find in Irenaeus and Tertullian when even that fringe is cut away.

In the canonization of the Gospels there can be no doubt that public reading in the Churches bore an

---

[1] Eus. *H. E.* vi. 12; p. 16 *sup.*
[2] *Strom.* iii. 13. § 93.

important part[1]. We learn from Justin that already in his day this was practised. The Gospels were read by the side of the Old Testament Prophets. It is probable that at first this public reading was not confined strictly to the Four Gospels. Just as the Gospel of Peter was read at Rhossus, so we may believe that the Gospel according to the Hebrews would be read in the Nazarene communities of Pella and the neighbourhood. But besides the watchfulness against heresy, the usage of the great Churches would by degrees thrust out the usage of the less. There would be a process of levelling, which would become more and more rapid as communication between the different Churches increased and the bonds of discipline which held them together became more firm.

But all the time that this was going on the mere juxtaposition of Old and New Testament in the public services would lead to the assimilation of the one to the other. The attributes which were ascribed to the writings of the Prophets would come to be ascribed also to the Gospels. From the very first the Gospels contained the elements of a Sacred Book. The 'Words of the Lord Jesus' could not but be sacred. And it was but an easy step from the Words themselves to the record of the Words. Besides, the Acts recorded were equally sacred, and indeed had a still more momentous place in the scheme of Christian doctrine. The consciousness of this was evidently at work from the time that the biographies of Christ took the name of 'Gospels,' *i.e.* almost as far back as

---

[1] See especially Zahn, *Gesch. d. K.* i. 141 ff.

we can trace them[1]. It is significant that this title is shared by the Canonical Biographies with those which were not ultimately ratified as Canonical. This alone would tend to show that it was an established usage before the marking out of the fourfold Gospel. From this early date there was thus the germ, already large and strongly developed, of the full conception which we find at the end of the century, according to which the Gospels are treated in all their parts as sacred and as not admitting possibilities of mutual collision or error. We have seen that this was not the universal doctrine[2]. It was not a doctrine scientifically defined or embodied in any authoritative formula; but it was no doubt widely current, and might be said to represent the general mind of the Church.

At the same time we cannot forget the simple natural way in which St. Luke speaks in his preface. For his record, as a record, he claims no supernatural aid. He does claim those human qualities which would make such a record valuable. He does claim care and research extended over the whole of the events which his history covers. He does claim— what for us is most important—to have gone to those who were eyewitnesses of the facts or who helped in the early preaching of them[3].

[1] The earliest instances of the use of εὐαγγέλιον in the sense of a book would be, *Did.* 8, 11, 15 *bis*; Ign. *Philad.* 5, 8. Dr. Taylor (*Witn. of Herm.* p. 6) compares ἀγγελία ἀγαθή in Herm. *Vis.* iii. 13. 2.
[2] Lecture I, p. 46 *sup.*
[3] The question how far the Gospels represent a strictly historical interest is fully discussed by von Soden in the essay mentioned above

Neither can we forget that the way in which the Gospels were treated for a full half-century at the lowest estimate after they were written is in complete agreement with the account thus given of them. They are treated as histories, the best histories current, but still not such as excluded all others or repelled all possibilities of improvement for themselves. If once we give up the strict verbal accuracy of every detail, and do not multiply incidents to an incredible extent merely in order to satisfy every difference of expression in the Gospels, they will themselves reveal to us their true character. There is a rather wide margin in their narratives which is not in perfect harmony. The attempts to harmonize them in a strict sense have notoriously failed. The Gospels are what the attempts to unravel the history of their origin would lead us to expect that they would be, not infallible, but yet broadly speaking good and true records of those Words which are the highest authority for Christians, and of that Life on which they base their hopes of redemption.

II. All that applies to the third Gospel of course applies also to the Acts. Both works are certainly by the same author; they are addressed to the same

(p. 288). He reduces this quite to a *minimum*. We observe however (1) that his conception of history is very narrow and modern; the idea of history with him excludes the didactic element, which with the Biblical writers is rarely absent; (2) that he regards as products of deliberate invention many sections which most of us would consider to be simple history; (3) that he, strangely enough, makes (to the best of my belief) no allusion whatever to St. Luke's preface!

## Criticism of the Acts.

person¹; they maintain the same general character; and if we are to accept one of the theories most recently put forward they make use not only of similar documents but of one and the same document, of which there are large traces in the earlier treatise, but which also extends a long way into the later ².

I leave this theory and all other theories relating to the Acts an open question. It is with the Acts as it it is with the Gospels; I do not think that we can accept any theory as completely and satisfactorily proved. There is no book of the New Testament on which I more wish to see a Commentary undertaken by some really competent English or American scholar on the scale of those which we have on other books by Bishops Lightfoot and Westcott and Professor J. B. Mayor. The commentaries which exist in English already are wholly inadequate ³.

My reason for expressing this wish is that the work on the Acts has hitherto been almost entirely in the hands of the Germans; and although some progress has been made and more reasonable views

---

¹ Some would make 'Theophilus' an ideal personage, like Bp. Chr. Wordsworth's 'Theophilus Anglicanus.' Bp. Lightfoot seems to incline to this view (*Dict. of Bib.* i. 1. 25 f., ed. 2). But it hardly seems consistent with the epithet κράτιστε which is commonly applied to persons of high official rank.

² I refer to the theory of Feine, *Eine vorkanonische Quelle des Lukas in Evangelium u. Apostelgeschichte*, Gotha, 1891 : see below.

³ There is a scholarly little edition by Mr. T. E. Page (London, 1886), and the commentary of Dr. H. B. Hackett (Boston, U.S.A.) was good in its day, but it was first published in 1852 (new ed. 1863). Bp. Lightfoot's article in the new edition of the *Dictionary of the Bible* is a valuable addition to the list since the words in the text were written.

are beginning to prevail, even in Germany there is at present something like a deadlock, and I strongly suspect that with the methods on which the inquiry has been pursued a deadlock is inevitable.

I yield to no one in admiration for the Germans or in gratitude to them for their great services, of which I have continually availed myself both in these lectures and elsewhere. I am almost ashamed to mingle acknowledgment with what may seem to be depreciation of those who have borne the burden and heat of the day as they have done. But still it must be admitted that German criticism has its defects; and those defects seem to be specially prominent in their treatment of the Acts.

The fault seems to lie in the standard by which the writer of the book is judged. I mean not only that it is a severe standard—this is perhaps a natural survival of the time when every Biblical writer was expected to be not only veracious but infallible—but that it is an unreal and artificial standard, the standard of the nineteenth century rather than the first, of Germany rather than of Palestine, of the lamp and the study rather than of active life.

Let me illustrate what I mean by four of the leading charges which are brought against the author: (1) the charge that he does not understand the antagonisms of the Apostolic age; (2) the charge that his statements conflict with those in St. Paul's Epistles; (3) the charge that the histories of St. Peter and St. Paul are artificially balanced against each other; (4) the charge that the differences between St. Paul and the other Apostles have been ignored or glossed over. Every one of these charges I believe contains a large element of exaggeration.

(1) I greatly doubt if an Englishman would accuse the author of the Acts of not understanding the antagonisms of the Apostolic age. He is not himself too quick to understand the antagonisms, *i.e.* the hidden conflicting tendencies and movements of any age. He is too easily content with a simple straightforward narrative. To burrow beneath the surface is a specialty of the Germans. It is one which they have exercised with excellent results. But it is another thing to require the gifts of a German Professor in an early Christian situated like the author of the Acts.

Looking at the matter with such a measure of intelligence as I can command for myself, I should say that the Acts showed on the whole a very good understanding of the different opposing forces which brought the history to the point at which the author left it. It is not such an understanding as may be obtained from the writings of a leader of so much depth and originality as St. Paul. It is rather the understanding of an average, well-intentioned, painstaking man approaching things from without rather than from within. But as such I confess that it seems to me in many respects surprisingly good.

The first instance of any friction at all inside the Church is that between the widows of the Hellenistic Jews and those of the native-born Palestinians. This is exactly what we might expect. The division is just that which would be most prominent in the Church at Jerusalem, where Hellenistic Jews would be specially numerous and specially open to the preaching of Christianity. And the whole manner in which the dispute arose grows as naturally out of the circumstances of the early Church as possible. Every line of the story of St. Stephen bears verisimilitude upon the face of it—the arguments conducted in the synagogues specially constructed for the use of Hellenistic pilgrims; the accusations brought against St. Stephen; his spirited defence and martyrdom. Then we have the Pharisaic persecution, which was sure to come sooner or later, and which is thrown into relief by the friendly relations which are described as existing up to this point between the Christians and the mass of the populace. The comparatively easy terms on which throughout the Acts, except at certain definite crises, the Christians of Jerusalem are represented as living with the mass of their unbelieving neighbours, is a strikingly authentic touch, and in strong contrast to the state of things when the Acts was written.

Then we have, just in their proper place, certain tentative steps which show that another inevitable question was beginning to be raised, the question what was to be done first with proselytes and afterwards with direct converts from heathenism. When the Acts was written these questions had all long been settled, and it is to me surprising that the writer should have kept the proportions and order of development so well as he has.

The great controversy of the Apostolic age is no doubt the question of circumcision, which culminates in ch. xv. I do not see how this could be introduced more naturally than it is. The question first comes to a head at Antioch, and in connexion with St. Paul's first mission among the heathen. 'And certain men came down from Judaea and taught the brethren, saying, Except ye be circumcised after the custom of Moses, ye cannot be saved.' 'But there rose up certain of the sect of the Pharisees who believed, saying, It is needful to circumcise them, and to charge them to keep the law of Moses[1].' By the year 80 there would be not much question of converts from among the Pharisees; but the writer has hit exactly the class among whom the difficulty was sure to arise.

But then, it is said, the writer does not understand the deep theological teaching of St. Paul. To expect him fully to understand it is to expect too much. And to suppose that St. Paul was always in the frame of mind in which he was when he wrote the Epistle to the Galatians is an error. And yet I do not know that it would be easy to sum up St. Paul's teaching in a brief form more satisfactorily than is done in the speech at Antioch of Pisidia: 'Be it known unto you therefore, brethren, that through this Man is proclaimed unto you remission of sins: and by Him every one that believeth is justified from all things, from which ye could not be justified by the law of Moses' (Acts xiii. 38 f.).

But what of St. Peter and St. James? They are

[1] Acts xv. 1, 5.

represented as playing the kind of part which it is extremely probable that they did play as a matter of fact. The point which told decisively with them was just the point which was likely to tell with responsible leaders, the overwhelming actual success of St. Paul's preaching among the Gentiles. Every single document which we possess represents St. Peter as an impressible person, who would not take up any position too obstinately. And we see St. James anxiously mediating, as a good man in his place must have done, between St. Paul and the believing Jews who are zealous for the law (Acts xxi. 20). St. Paul it is impossible to doubt—in fact we have his own word for it [1]—met the Judaean Apostles half-way, and did all that he could to keep the Christian Church together [2].

[1] 1 Cor. ix. 20: a passage to which some of our German friends find it very hard to do justice (Schürer, however, is an exception; see his excellent remarks in *Theol. Literaturzeitung*, 1882, col. 348).

[2] The following are weighty words by one of the greatest scholars of our day: 'Both St. Paul's character and his work are grievously misjudged when they are interpreted exclusively by his zealous championship of Gentile liberties. This fidelity to the special trust which he had received was balanced by an anxiety to avert a breach between the Christians of Palestine, for whom the Law remained binding while the Temple was still standing, and the Gentile Christians of other lands; to promote kindly recognition on the one side and brotherly help on the other. Such a breach, he doubtless felt, would have cut Gentile Christianity away from its Divinely prepared base, and sent it adrift as a new religion founded by himself' (*The Sense and Service of Membership*, &c., a Sermon preached at the Consecration of Bp. Westcott by Dr. F. J. A. Hort, London, 1890, p. 5 f.). The context, which traces the development of this thought in the Epistles to the Romans and Ephesians, is well deserving of study.

## Criticism of the Acts.

The critics of the Acts, at least many of them, write like men who had never had any practical experience of affairs and whose one idea of action was that of a rigid theoretical consistency. How different the real course of public business is from this—whatever its nature, whether ecclesiastical or political—is a lesson which Englishmen at least do not need teaching.

(2) I must abridge what I have to say on so wide a field as the comparison of the Acts with St. Paul's Epistles. It is true that there are differences, and perhaps somewhat considerable differences. But for every such point of difference it would be easy to bring at least four of striking coincidence and harmony. Of the arguments which were put forward in Paley's *Horae Paulinae* and in Professor Blunt's *Undesigned Coincidences*, a great number still hold good[1]. They are ignored, partly because they are external, and partly because they are one-sided. No doubt they do not enable us to understand the principles at work in the Apostolic age—to do that would require different methods. And no doubt they are also apologetic and forensic. The writers do not profess to adduce all the instances they can on the

---

[1] See also the comparison of the Acts with St. Paul's Epistles in Lechler, *Das Apostolische Zeitalter*, p. 12 ff., ed. 3. 'Any writer ... who will take the pains to go carefully over Paley's discussion of the passages relating to the contributions for the Christian poor at Jerusalem, observing how they dovetail into one another, may satisfy himself of the validity of the argument. Yet it is plain that the writer of the Acts was unacquainted with these Epistles, or at all events that, if he had ever seen them, he made no use of them in compiling his history' (Lightfoot, *ut sup.* p. 34).

other side. But so far as they go, they are a perfectly sound vindication of the trustworthiness of the Apostolic history, which the instances on the contrary part would not avail to shatter. These instances only need to be judged in a human and reasonable spirit. It may be proved *ex abundanti* that St. Luke did not know everything that happened in the period which his history covers. His knowledge was naturally limited by his materials, and those materials collected in an age which had not telegraphic communication with every part of the globe, and daily papers delivered regularly every morning. He had something more to do than simply make cuttings of everything that interested him. He belonged to a society which was not naturally literary. He would often have to depend on a few rough notes or scraps of narrative, put together by an unpractised hand, and eked out by hearsay and personal recollections. And then his informants might be rather spectators from without than actors in the innermost circle of the events which they describe. When due allowance is made for such considerations as these, a study of St. Paul's Epistles may raise our opinion of the historical character of the Acts, but it certainly will not lower it.

(3) It used to be contended that the history of the Acts was a purely artificial construction in which every act or speech or miracle of St. Peter had its counterpart in some act or speech or miracle of St. Paul, with the inference that imagination bore a far larger part in both halves of the narrative than fact. This however is an argument which is now almost wholly

## Criticism of the Acts.

given up[1]. It is seen that on the one hand such complete correspondence can only be made out by much straining and exaggeration, and on the other hand that such real correspondence as remains was not more than might be expected in any age from simple parity of situation and conditions. There was nothing to cast valid suspicion on the historian's veracity.

(4) And in like manner as to the last of the objections which I enumerated. Granting that the differences between St. Paul and his opponents may have had their edge somewhat blunted, is not this just what must have happened from mere lapse of time if from nothing else? There is probably many a man who could write *sine ira et studio* about the Disestablishment of the Irish Church, whose feelings would be far more keenly moved by the threat of a like measure

---

[1] I may quote the following from a very disinterested writer: 'In Wahrheit freilich ist eine Abhängigkeit beider Erzählungskreise von einander nur auf ganz wenigen Punkten, namentlich in der Darstellung der Lahmenheilungen iii. 2 ff. and xiv. 8 ff., an vielen anderen Stellen aber, so zwischen der Verfluchung von Ananias und Sapphira v. 1 ff. und der Blendung des Elymas xiii. 6 ff., der Anbetung des Petrus durch Cornelius x. 25, und des Paulus in Lystra xiv. 11 ff., nicht einmal irgend eine nähere Beziehung vorhanden. Was aber die sonstigen Aehnlichkeiten, die von beiden Aposteln berichteten Dämonenaustreibungen und Wunderheilungen, Geistesmittheilungen und Verfolgungen "bei Leuten, die in demselben Beruf in derselben Zeit bei ähnlichen Begebenheiten unter denselben Verhältnissen wirken," irgend verfängliches haben soll, das ist in der That schwer einzusehen' (Dr. C. Clemen, *Prolegomena zur Chronologie der Paulinischen Briefe*, Halle, 1892, p. 17 f.; *cf.* also Meyer-Wendt, *Apostelgesch*. p. 6 f. ed. 5; Feine, *Eine vorkanonische Ueberlieferung d. Lukas*, p. 214).

aimed at the Church in Wales, or by the burning question of Home Rule. Happily wounds heal, and the moss grows over broken arch and battered wall.

But not only was there lapse of time; there may have been a touch of character at work as well. We naturally think of the beloved physician (if as I believe it were really he who wrote the Acts) as an amiable man who would not willingly aggravate any sore. It is an old story that the eye sees what it brings with it the power of seeing. So with the most perfect good faith the historian may have given a less agitated complexion to his annals than at the time they really wore. We feel the change at once when we leave the calm and even tenor of the narrative in the Acts and open a page of one of St. Paul's Epistles—without fightings, within fears. But so it is with all history, especially with history in sober, temperate, unimpassioned hands. We may admit all that can be said under this head, and yet see in it nothing to arouse distrust or suspicion.

I wish to take a just, not an optimist view of the Acts of the Apostles. I am willing to see every mistake, that can be proved to be a mistake, corrected[1]. But the sounder the critic the fewer mistakes

---

[1] There are some real difficulties. Of these the chief would be (i) the difference between the description of the speaking with tongues in Acts ii. 6–11 and that in 1 Cor. xiv, which it is difficult to explain entirely, though we remember that St. Paul recognises different kinds of tongues (γένη γλωσσῶν), and that some apparently are distinguishable as belonging to known languages (γλῶσσαι τῶν ἀνθρώπων); (ii) the case of Theudas (Acts v. 36), in regard to which it seems to me

he seems to find. I know nothing in German comparable for thoroughness and solidity of investigation to the parts which concern the Acts in Professor Ramsay's *Church in the Roman Empire*. That at least is not beating the air, but contributes data of real importance to criticism [1].

Of course it is true that the Acts is composite like the Gospel, and the question ultimately turns upon the discrimination and examination of sources. I have said that this has not led to any final result at present. It would be easy to put before you some of the latest theories [2]. But they all seem to be as yet in the tentative stage; and I do not wish to anticipate de-

equally wrong to assume that there is a mistake and to assert confidently that there is not (on this side see especially Lightfoot, p. 40); (iii) the omission of the journey, Acts xi. 30, in Gal. i. I cannot think that this journey, mentioned so incidentally, is unhistorical, and prefer to believe that the silence of St. Paul might be explained if we knew the circumstances; the journey may have synchronized with the persecution of Herod Agrippa I, when the leading Apostles were in prison or in hiding; (iv) the account of the reception of St. Paul by the Jews at Rome (Acts xxviii. 17-28), where however the indications which we get in Rom. xvi as to the way in which Christianity first established itself in Rome would be consistent with a considerable degree of ignorance on the part of official Judaism. I do not include among the number of serious difficulties the differences between Acts xv and Gal. ii. They are no doubt great, but not I think greater than can be satisfactorily accounted for by the difference in position between the two writers.

[1] Reference should also once more be specially made to Bishop Lightfoot's articles in the *Dictionary of the Bible* and the *Contemporary Review* for 1878.

[2] A comparative table of recent theories of the composition of Acts vi-xxviii is given by Clemen, *Die Chronologie d. paul. Briefe*, pp. 288-291.

cisions about which I am myself doubtful. The Acts presents upon the whole an easier problem than the Gospel. It is at least easier in the sense of being far less complex. At the same time it probably requires for its solution a wider and more varied knowledge, combined with independence of judgment. I could not name a book which possesses these qualities in a higher degree than Professor Ramsay's. Of course it touches only a limited section of the subject. But within that section its result is—what I believe would be in greater or less degree the result of investigations all along the line—to put the Acts on the same level with the Gospel as deriving its materials from those who were 'eyewitnesses and ministers of the word,' and as a sober unsophisticated historical record, from which we, as well as the generation for which it was first written, may 'learn the certainty' of the things wherein we have been instructed.

# LECTURE VII.

## THE GENESIS OF THE NEW TESTAMENT.
## THE EPISTLES AND APOCALYPSE.

'And I was with you in weakness, and in fear, and in much trembling. And my speech and my preaching were not in persuasive words of wisdom, but in demonstration of the Spirit and of power: that your faith should not stand in the wisdom of men, but in the power of God.'—1 *Corinthians* ii. 3–5.

'He that hath an ear, let him hear what the Spirit saith to the Churches.'—*Revelation* ii. 7, &c.

IF ever there was a manifestation of the supernatural, it was in the condition of things out of which arose the New Testament. We have only to take up the Epistles of St. Paul, and we find him surrounded, penetrated, permeated with the supernatural. It is as it were the very atmosphere which he breathes. He does not assert it. He has no need to assert it. Except in a few special cases there is none of that straining and emphasis which becomes necessary where a claim is made and resisted. A large proportion of the references to supernatural influence is indirect, thrown in by way of casual allusion. St. Paul assumes it as a fact everywhere present to the consciousness of his readers as much as to his own. In writing to the

Corinthians he reminds them of the circumstances of his first preaching among them. The contrast could not be more striking. On the one hand the Apostle, with his weak and nervous frame shattered by illness, conscious of the tremendous odds against him, with none of the arts of the rhetorician, none of the imposing phrases of the philosopher. But on the other hand, bursting masterfully through all obstacles, triumphing over every drawback, there was this 'demonstration of the Spirit' (*i.e.* demonstration borne by the Spirit) 'and of power.' Certainly from the lips of St. Paul this was no unmeaning or conventional phrase. He is evidently as sure as any of the Old Testament prophets was ever sure that the message which he delivered was no invention of his own, that it was not commended by ability and skill on his part, but that he was merely an instrument in the hand of God, that anything which he had to say came from God, and that it was God alone who gave it success. In that expressive figure which he uses in this same Epistle it was for him or for any other preacher only to plant and water, the seed was God's, all its germinative and expansive power was God's, and it was God who caused it to strike root and grow.

This Gospel which he was commissioned to preach, even if it were to some extent moulded by his own faculties, was not moulded by those faculties acting independently and spontaneously but only as the tools and instruments which God made use of to give intelligible shape to His own creation; the Gospel thus given to him was a new and wonderful force in the world, and the community which had grown up round it to be its earthly vehicle and to carry it far and wide had also a special endowment corresponding to the magnitude of its task. The universal name which the first Christians gave to this characteristic of their own time was the 'gift of the Spirit.' They dated it from the first Pentecost after the Ascension. From that time onwards a strange exaltation and enthusiasm pervaded the Church. It was not confined to any one locality; it was not confined to any one class or order, not even to the Apostles; but wherever there were Christians St. Paul assumes that the same mighty movement would be at work. It would take many different forms; now ecstatic utterance, now heightened and sharpened insight, now actual miracle, especially miracles of healing, now gifts of judgment, discrimination, organizing, governing. Some of these gifts if they occurred in our own day we should not call supernatural. 'Natural' and 'supernatural' are imperfect terms which we use to describe from the point of view of our human ignorance different modes, or what appear to us to be different modes, of the Divine action. The essential point is that the action is Divine; that whether transcending known laws or not transcending them, it does come direct from God. There can be no doubt that St. Paul regarded all the manifestations around him as having this origin. They all radiated from a single centre. And that centre was the Incarnation, and the forces which the Incarnation had set in motion.

The one permanent deposit left behind by this tidal

wave of God-given energy was the New Testament. The kernel of the New Testament considered as such a deposit is the Epistles of St. Paul. The Gospels too are part of the deposit, but in a sense they stand outside it. That which they enshrine and which gives them their value was not a product but the cause of the product, the original force which gave the impulse to the rest. Of the Gospels we have spoken, and it now becomes our duty in like manner to follow the course of the Epistles, first in their origin and then in their recognition as inspired Scripture. We start, as it is natural to do, from the Epistles of St. Paul.

I. It may at first sight seem a strange thing that so much of the New Testament should consist of Epistles. It is this which marks most clearly the difference between the New Testament and the Old. Christianity broke through the narrow limits of Judaism. It soon began to plant its colonies throughout the Roman Empire; and the needs of these scattered societies drew from the leaders of the Church letters of instruction and warning which have become the law of Christians for all time.

We may well think it surprising that a Sacred Book should be built up in a way so incidental—not to say, accidental—as this. The consequences are deeply impressed upon the character of Christian theology. It is due to this that the teaching of the New Testament is so unsystematic, and in some respects so incomplete. But it is due to it on the other hand that the same teaching is so real and so practical, in

## Origin of the Epistles. 335

such warm and vital contact with the human heart. The fabric of Christian doctrine was not elaborated in the study, but was struck out in the 'storm and stress' of actual life.

There was precedent in the past for conveying weighty religious instruction in the form of letters. Probably the oldest example which has come down to us is the letter of Jeremiah to the captives in Babylon (Jer. xxix). But the division of the nation into these two halves, one in Judaea and one in Babylonia, after the Restoration, and the founding of another large settlement in Alexandria and Egypt, caused this form to be adopted in more than one of the Apocryphal Books[1]. These are based, we need not doubt, upon real intercourse in which the several branches of the nation sought to strengthen and encourage each other in their loyalty to the faith of their fathers.

St. Paul therefore had before him models to follow. He was probably not thinking of any models when he began to write to the young communities which he had founded. His solicitude for them in the dangers to which they were exposed, and his keen desire to carry them on to the highest point of Christian perfection, was quite enough motive with him for writing. But the fact that the same literary form had been used for similar purposes before, probably suggested to him to throw into his letters such a carefully constructed body of teaching as is found for instance in the Epistles to the Romans and Ephesians.

[1] The so-called Epistles of Jeremiah and Baruch, and the Epistles at the beginning of 2 Maccabees.

Observe how easy and natural the whole process is. When St. Paul began to write, probably neither he himself nor his readers attached so much importance to his letters as they came to do. We can clearly see that not a few of his early letters must have been lost, simply we may suppose because no special care was taken to preserve them. The two Epistles to the Thessalonians, dating about the years 52, 53, are the earliest extant Epistles. Yet already in 2 Thessalonians he has to take precautions against forgery and to remind his readers that his autograph signature is the sign of genuineness in 'every Epistle[1].' '*Every* Epistle' would naturally imply that it had more than a single precursor. And the very idea of forgery shows that the correspondence must have attracted attention. In the next extant Epistle, the First to the Corinthians, there are clear indications of a previous letter[2], now lost; and in the Second Epistle to the same Church, probably the fourth in date of those referred to in our Bibles, we have proof that the letters of the Apostle had acquired a high reputation and were sometimes contrasted with his personal infirmities[3]. The Epistle to the Galatians was wrung from him by bitter controversy, which he could not conduct upon the spot; but by the time he came to write to the Romans it is evident that the Apostle knew that he would be listened to, and that even a lengthy composition addressed to a distant Church of which he was not the founder would not be thrown away.

---

[1] 2 Thess. iii. 17; *cf.* ii. 2.   [2] 1 Cor. v. 9.   [3] 2 Cor. x. 10.

The practice thus established St. Paul continued for the remainder of his life. For I must needs believe that all the Epistles which have come down to us as his are genuine. I cannot imagine that a conscientious opponent of these letters, who when he laid down his pen would turn round to look back over the arguments by which he had been led to deny their genuineness, could honestly say that they were conclusive. In the first place, we may put aside Philippians and 1 Thessalonians as practically acknowledged by all but a few extravagant Dutch and Swiss critics who furnish us with nothing but an instructive warning[1]. There remain 2 Thessalonians, Ephesians, Colossians, Philemon, and the Pastorals. There is however no tenable line between any of these. In fact nothing is more remarkable than the way in which each questioned letter is linked on to one or more that are unquestioned. The critic who accepts 1 Thessalonians cannot make out a good case against its companion Epistle. The critic who accepts Philippians is disarmed when he comes to attack the other Epistles of the Imprisonment. Most Englishmen will have a short and easy method for deciding the genuineness of Colossians; for it is inseparably bound up with that most winning little Epistle to Philemon, which only pedantry could ever think of doubting. And then Colossians and Ephesians are so intertwined that a highly artificial and laboured theory has to

---

[1] These have certainly received all the refutation which they need in Mr. Knowling's learned and able work, *The Witness of the Epistles*, pp. 133–243.

be invented to disunite them[1]. It may be mentioned by the way that a writer who had made a specially close and careful study of the Epistle to the Colossians, after beginning with the theory that it was interpolated, has quite recently given up that hypothesis, and now accepts the whole as genuine[2]. It is perhaps some set-off against this that a strong defender of the Epistle to the Colossians has now pronounced against Ephesians[3]. But in regard to this latter Epistle the point I think was touched by a remark made to me the last time we met by that profound Cambridge scholar who passed away at the end of last year, viz. that Ephesians was required to complete the argument of the fifteenth chapter of Romans. This thought he has indeed himself worked out in a page of the very striking sermon preached at the consecration of Bishop Westcott[4], the utterance of one who spoke but seldom, but when he did speak left behind matter which will well bear pondering.

No doubt of all the disputed Epistles the strongest case can be made out against the Pastorals. But how much of this case turns simply upon our ignorance! And even so the negative argument seems to have received a severe shock from Professor Ramsay's

---

[1] Colossians in part genuine, in part interpolated by a disciple of St. Paul, who also wrote Ephesians.

[2] Von Soden in the *Handcommentar*.

[3] Klöpper, *Der Brief an die Epheser*, Göttingen, 1891. On the whole question of the Epistle to the Ephesians, see especially the excellent article by Dr. Robertson in the new edition of the *Dictionary of the Bible*.

[4] *The Sense and Service of Membership*, &c., p. 6.

recent investigation of the legal status and early persecution of Christians. It is true that the hypothesis of the genuineness of the Pastoral Epistles requires the further hypothesis that the life of St. Paul was prolonged beyond the point reached by the narrative of the Acts. The Acts itself suggests as much, because if St. Paul had really met his tragic fate at the end of the two years of comparative freedom in his own hired house it must surely have been noticed. The one substantial argument was that the only known persecution about this date was that which followed the burning of Rome in 64 A.D. Here Professor Ramsay comes in and proves, as I cannot but think decisively, that the persecution begun then by Nero did not really cease, or, as Mommsen had put it before him, 'The persecution of the Christians was a standing matter as was that of robbers[1].' Christians were treated like pests of society which it was as much the duty of the police to put down as it was to suppress anything else which tended to the breach of decency and order. If they were left unmolested, it was only from indolence or connivance. Persecution would soon break out again all the more fiercely.

The bearing of the Pastoral Epistles upon this question has led Professor Ramsay to examine afresh the question of their genuineness, and his vigorous judgment has decided in their favour. Another important work which has appeared within the last few weeks, Godet's *Introduction to the Pauline Epistles*,

[1] *Ap.* Ramsay, *The Church in the Roman Empire*, p. 269.

also states the argument from a more professedly theological point of view, but in a very convincing form.

It may be asserted without fear of contradiction that nothing really un-Pauline has been proved in any of the disputed Epistles. A development and progress truly there is, but not such as is incompatible with unity of authorship or such as may not well come within the range of a single life. It is true that the development is rapid. But the acknowledged Epistles taken in connexion with the dates to which they belong and their place in the Apostle's career prepare us for rapidity of development. The writer of the Epistles to Corinthians, Galatians and Romans lived a life of extraordinary intellectual and moral intensity. The rate of thought-production in such a life must not be measured by commonplace standards. And what was true of the Apostle was true in a manner of the whole Church. It too, if we may say so, lived hard. Its vital energies had full play. And the spread of Christianity throughout the Empire brought it in contact with varied modes of thought, as well as with varied social conditions and practical necessities.

There is one landmark which stands out quite independently of the Epistles of St. Paul. The Epistle to the Hebrews is quoted unequivocally in the oldest post-Apostolic writing, the letter of the Roman Church to the Church at Corinth which goes by the name of St. Clement. That proves that it was in use by the year 97 A.D. But it deals with the spiritual condition of a community which was tempted

## The Pauline Epistles.

to relapse into Judaism. The rich Mosaic system still exercises its attractions, to which the readers of the Epistle seem likely to succumb. But can we think of such a state of things after the crushing blow which Judaism received by the fall of Jerusalem and the destruction of the temple? We date the Epistle then certainly before A.D. 97, and probably before A.D. 70. And in it we have a fixed point by which other books of the New Testament can be gauged. Does not this abundantly cover any progression that can be traced in the writings of St. Paul, or indeed in any of the New Testament writings? If the Epistle to the Romans could be reached by the year 58 and the Epistle to the Hebrews some ten years later, there certainly is not one of the New Testament Books to which we can point and say, Such an advanced stage of either doctrine or practice at such a date was impossible, or even in the least degree improbable[1]. We remember that if there is development it is natural and logical development. There is no violent change, no breach of continuity.

This holds good even of the point in which the difference between the earlier and later Epistles of St. Paul is perhaps most perceptible—the style and modes of expression. Here again there are a number of subtle links which attach the disputed Epistles to the undisputed. And the difference which remains over and above the common features and resemblances does not seem to be in any case greater than can fairly and naturally be accounted for by differences of

[1] The writer has used similar language in *Expositor*, 1892, i. 391.

circumstance, differences of object, differences of mood, and perhaps we should add the use of different amanuenses. There is, it is true, a somewhat peculiar relation between Epistles like Colossians and Ephesians and some of the other Epistles. The ideas are Pauline; the vocabulary is Pauline : it is mainly in the cast and structure of the sentences that difference is perceptible. I have sometimes asked myself whether this may not be due to the degree of expertness attained by the scribe in the art of shorthand. We know that this art was very largely practised ; and St. Paul's amanuenses may have had recourse to it somewhat unequally. One might take down the Apostle's words *verbatim*; then we should get a vivid, broken, natural style like that of Romans and 1, 2 Corinthians. Another might not succeed in getting down the exact words; and then when he came to work up his notes into a fair copy, the structure of the sentences would be his own, and it might naturally seem more laboured.

However this may be, even supposing that a margin has to be left for the operation of causes of which we are ignorant, I cannot think that that margin is large enough to interfere seriously with the conclusion to which the positive evidence points, that the Epistles which have come down to us in St. Paul's name are, both in whole and part, really his. I say 'both in whole and part,' because unless it has documentary support even the hypothesis of interpolation seems to me inadmissible. It should be remembered that the text of the New Testament is quite unique in the extent and excellence of its external attestation. Not only are the authorities for it (MSS., Versions, and quoations in the Fathers) earlier and more abundant than those for any other work in ancient literature (Virgil perhaps coming nearest to it), but when these authorities are arranged in groups and families and we argue from the readings dispersed throughout these groups to the readings of the common archetype of all the extant authorities, viz. the primitive original from which they must all have sprung, that primitive original carries us back so near to the Apostolic age itself, that the interval within which interpolation could have taken place must have been very short—if indeed there is any such interval at all. The New Testament is in this respect on a wholly different footing from the Old Testament or from classical writings which depend on some few comparatively recent copies; and the freedom of speculative reconstruction which may be permissible there is out of place here [1].

We take then the New Testament as it lies before us in a text like that of the Revised Version, or still better, because of its wider recognition of possible textual change, that of Drs. Westcott and Hort. Among the books are no less than thirteen which, although they certainly do not represent the whole of St. Paul's correspondence with the Churches, yet are at least a very weighty selection from that correspondence. When we consider what has just been said

[1] Compare what the writer has said on a typical instance of supposed interpolation in *The Classical Review*, 1890, p. 359 f.

about the gradual way in which the correspondence arose and acquired its reputation, is it not natural to infer that the other letters which the New Testament contains were suggested by this example, and composed upon this model? This would not indeed be the case if we could accept the date (40–50 A.D.) assigned to the Epistle of St. James by Dr. J. B. Mayor[1]. Dr. Mayor's edition of this Epistle is a monument of scholarship, a fruit of that alliance between classical studies and theology which it is to be hoped may long be characteristic of our English Universities. But on this point of the date of the Epistle of St. James I cannot think that Dr. Mayor is right. His view, which it is only fair to say is shared by a number of eminent writers—Neander, Ritschl, Weiss, Beyschlag, Mangold, Lechler, Paul Ewald—assumes that the writing of doctrinal Epistles would come to the first generation of Christians as a matter of course. To this I cannot agree. It seems to me to be a fact which needs to be accounted for. It can be accounted for easily and naturally if we believe that the practice began with St. Paul. The missionary Apostle went from city to city, founding Churches. He was sure to communicate with these Churches by letter. And we can see how his letters would grow from simple greetings and exhortations to elaborate theological treatises. Then when once the example had been set with such striking results it is easy to understand how the other Apostles would follow. But it is not so easy to believe that it was they who set the

---

[1] *Epistle of St. James*, p. cxxiv.

example, and that the Epistle of St. James was written before any extant Epistle of St. Paul's or even before he returned from his first missionary journey.

The character of the Epistle itself seems to me decidedly against this. It implies too settled a condition of things. It is too little concerned with laying foundations. The distinctive doctrines of Christianity are presupposed. For this reason it would seem that the Epistle should be put as late as it can be put. Its relation to the Epistle to the Romans I would explain as not so much direct as indirect. Much of the resemblance in subject between the two Epistles I believe to be due, as Bishop Lightfoot held, to their dealing with questions current in the Jewish Schools. But besides this, it is probable that St. James was influenced not by the actual text of an Epistle like that to the Romans, which I do not think that he had seen, but by hearsay reports of what St. Paul was teaching. If we suppose direct polemics between the two Apostles, then both seem strangely to miss the mark. Each would be arguing against something which the other did not hold. It seems more true to the situation to regard St. James as with a proper modesty not imputing to his brother Apostle erroneous teaching which he had not sufficient evidence to bring home to him, but taking a firm stand against dangers to which teaching such as that attributed to St. Paul seemed liable.

Dr. Mayor has done good service by the effective way in which he has disposed of the attacks upon the genuineness of the Epistle. The most significant proof that it really belongs to the Apostolic age is the description of the Church as a 'synagogue' in which it is assumed that all the members are not Christians. Such mixed communities, in which believing and unbelieving Jews worshipped side by side, are not likely to have existed after the Fall of Jerusalem, when the breach between Jew and Christian became irreparable.

The question as to the genuineness of the First Epistle of St. Peter has entered upon a new phase with the researches of Professor Ramsay. But on this I do not think that we have as yet heard quite the last word. In any case, Professor Ramsay has done more to determine the position of things implied in the Epistle than had ever been done before. He has made it impossible to argue, as many critics had done, that it must date from the time of Trajan. But I am expressing elsewhere [1] my reasons for dissenting from the view that it falls under the Flavian dynasty about the year 80 A.D. The question is too long and too technical to be argued here, and the conclusion would be only one-sided. I do not doubt that an understanding may soon be arrived at now that the question has been placed upon such healthy lines and brought to so near an issue [2].

No doubt the most crucial case for the validity of the New Testament Canon is that which is raised by the Second Epistle of St. Peter. With respect to

---

[1] *Expositor*, June 1893, p. 411 f.
[2] See Additional Note A: *A New Theory as to the Origin of the Catholic Epistles.*

this I hope to be forgiven if I return to my personal recollections of perhaps the greatest critic whom our Church has produced. I put the question to him about a year ago what he thought of this Epistle. He replied that if he were asked he should say that the balance of argument was against the Epistle—and the moment he had done so that he should begin to think that he might be wrong.

This is of course very different from the way in which critics of less scrupulous conscience dismiss the whole question as if it were not really arguable. I had myself not long before expressed in print a somewhat similar opinion [1], at least to the extent that the arguments commonly brought against the genuineness of the Epistle did not seem to me quite decisive. But here again a new element has been introduced within the last few months by the discovery, not of the Gospel, but of part of the so-called Apocalypse of Peter. It has been pointed out [2] that this presents many marked resemblances of style to the second Epistle. The resemblances are so marked as I think to prove that the two writings are nearly connected. But the question is, what is the nature of the connexion? It is no doubt possible that the writer of the Apocalypse may have imitated the Epistle or that both may be affected by some common influence. If there had been on the whole better reason than not for believing the Epistle to be the genuine work of St. Peter, it would be natural to fall back upon

---

[1] *The Oracles of God* (London, 1891), p. 73 n.
[2] *E.g.* by Mr. M. R. James, *The Revelation of Peter*, p. 52 f.

some such assumption. But as the balance of argument is really the other way[1], the question is forced upon us whether it is not on the whole more probable that the two writings are both by the same hand. This is at least the simplest of the different hypotheses which are open to us.

We must then, I think, distinctly contemplate the possibility, if not the probability, that we have in the New Testament a book which is not by the writer whose name it bears. What this would mean is that the New Testament is not upon a different footing to the Old; that there would be a real parallel to a case like that of Ecclesiastes, in which a book has found its way into the Canon under an assumed name.

There is indeed nothing new in the situation thus defined. The Epistle is not mentioned at all until the beginning of the third century[2], and as soon as it is mentioned it is also doubted. Many Syriac-speaking Christians were without it until far on into the Middle Ages. The Sixth Article of our own Church gives no list of the Books of the New Testament, and, apparently draws a distinction between those Canonical Books which have been doubted and those which have not. For some time past there has been a sort of tacit consent, wherever criticism is admitted, to use the Second Epistle of St. Peter with a certain reserve.

---

[1] See Additional Note B: *The Genuineness of 2 St. Peter.*

[2] See pp. 26, 382; also Salmon, *Introduction,* pp. 485–490, ed. 5.

## Inspiration of the Epistles. 349

I am not one of those who would depreciate the contents of the Epistle. In spite of its strained and turgid style it is written in a good spirit, in close contact with the currents of genuine inspiration; and more of the Epistle than we perhaps suppose has passed into the household speech of Christians. If the Epistle is not genuine, the writer would not mean any great harm when he took upon himself to write in the name of St. Peter. He would be like that Asian presbyter who confessed to the authorship of the *Acts of Paul and Thecla* and said that he had done it 'from love for Paul[1].' We remember that even then the presbyter in question upon his confession was degraded from his office. But now a still stricter view prevails, and to many modern readers the critical doubtfulness of the Epistle, combined with its claim to speak with the authority of St. Peter, is a more serious stumbling-block.

From the point of view of our present subject it will be chiefly important as showing that the boundary line of the New Testament, like that of the Old, perhaps has not been drawn with absolute accuracy. If we take our New Testament as a whole we may well believe that a Divine Providence has watched over it. It is a wonder that in such an age so little that is in any sense unworthy has found its way into it. But in this, as in other things, the Providence of God does not absolutely exclude the infirmities of men. In the best-tilled field other growths will come up beside those which the husbandman planted. All of these

[1] Tertullian, *De Bapt.* 17.

will not be noxious; some may be useful enough in their place. And although that place may not be where they are found, it would not be wise to attempt to remove them, lest peradventure the wheat should be uprooted with them.

In all parts of our subject alike the same phenomenon meets us—here a blaze of light, the central orb shining in its strength, there a *corona* of rays gradually fading away and melting into the darkness. It is thus, not only with the limits of the Canon of the Epistles, but also with their inspiration. St. Paul, as has been said, does not go out of his way to claim inspiration. It seems to be almost an accident that he says anything about it at all. And yet it is impossible to read the first few chapters of the First Epistle to the Corinthians or the first chapter of the Epistle to the Galatians without feeling that his own inspiration is an axiom of his thought, and not only an axiom of his own thought, but that the inspiration of himself and others is an axiom in the thought of Christians generally.

It is the Epistle to the Galatians which takes us back to the origin of the gift. We seem to be reading a description of the call of one of the prophets of the Old Testament. 'For I make known to you, brethren, as touching the Gospel that was preached by me, that it is not after man. For neither did I receive it from man, nor was I taught it, but it came to me through revelation of Jesus Christ. For ye have heard of my manner of life in time past in the Jews' religion, how that beyond measure I persecuted the Church of God,

## Inspiration of the Epistles.

and made havock of it: and I advanced in the Jews' religion (*lit.* Judaism, 'Ιουδαϊσμῷ) beyond many of mine own age among my countrymen, being more exceedingly zealous for the traditions of my fathers. But when it was the good pleasure of God, who separated me, even from my mother's womb, and called me through His grace, to reveal His Son in me, that I might preach Him among the Gentiles; immediately I conferred not with flesh and blood: neither went I up to Jerusalem to them which were Apostles before me: but I went away into Arabia; and again I returned unto Damascus' (Gal. i. 11–17). So great a crisis was not one for human intervention. The soul must wrestle out its own problems between itself and God.

What could be more explicit than this? If we may follow the consciousness of the Apostle, there cannot be the slightest doubt as to its testimony. And it is impossible not to notice the depth and largeness of the view which he takes. He seems to see the counsel of God fixed long before he was born and taking effect in spite of his own errant will as soon as the appointed moment was come. This counsel does not concern himself alone, but has to do with the opening of a new page in the great design. He himself is a mere instrument for the preaching of the Gospel among the Gentiles. So the old Particularism was to be broken down and the glad tidings were to be carried forth into all the world. The Apostle speaks with a certain awed but absolutely unshaken sense of the part which he was called upon to play in this vast making of history. The root of it all is that 'Gospel of Jesus Christ' so wonderfully revealed in his heart—'in me' is his phrase, 'in' and filling his consciousness, so that no other motive-power was left there.

Nor is it to be supposed that this was only an initial impetus, amplified to the imagination by that tension of soul in which the Apostle took up the pen to write to his recreant converts in Galatia. We turn to the opening chapters of 1 Corinthians. There again we have that loftiness of view which cannot help regarding the circumstances of the moment as part of the great stream—the Gulf Stream, we might call it—of events by which Christianity was introduced among the chilled waters of Paganism. How mean and insignificant were the instruments which God had chosen for such a mighty purpose! They were not scholars, not philosophers, not orators, or statesmen! Yet their preaching had a wonderful effect; and the contrast of this effect with the inadequacy of the cause was just to prove that it was really the work of God.

For, after all, though what had been offered to the Corinthians was not a philosophy in the common sense of the word, though it made none of those dazzling appeals to the intellect which philosophies usually made, it was not on that account without a deep and hidden wisdom. There was concealed within it a wisdom which was not human but Divine. This wisdom was derived from none other than the Holy Spirit, who being conversant with the deep things of God Himself was able also to communicate them to men.

'Which things also,' the Apostle continues, 'we speak, not in words which man's wisdom teacheth, but which the Spirit teacheth, comparing spiritual things with spiritual' (1 Cor. ii. 13[1]). This is the normal habitual level of inspiration. It is more sustained than the inspiration of the prophets in the Old Testament; it extends not merely to single truths revealed for a special object, but to a body of connected truths, a system of theology.

For this reason it would seem as if the inspiration of the Epistles had more direct relation to the written word than the inspiration of the Old Testament. No doubt the 'demonstration of the Spirit and of power' was primarily concerned with oral delivery. But the impulse came from the body of truth which lay behind, of which the spoken and written word were only alternating modes of expression. The inspiration of the New Testament was more that of an indwelling abiding Spirit than that of the Old[2]. It was one form of that great outpouring which flooded not an individual here and there but the whole society.

There were doubtless many in the Apostolic age who were qualified to write inspired books. The prophets of the New Dispensation must have had a gift similar in kind to that vouchsafed to the prophets

---

[1] Compare 1 Thess. ii. 13 : ἐδέξασθε οὐ λόγον ἀνθρώπων, ἀλλὰ (καθώς ἐστιν ἀληθῶς) λόγον Θεοῦ, ὃς καὶ ἐνεργεῖται ἐν ὑμῖν πιστεύουσιν.

[2] So Novatian, *De Trin.* 29 : *Unus ergo et idem Spiritus, qui in Prophetis et Apostolis ; nisi quoniam ibi ad momentum, heic semper. Ceterum ibi non ut semper in illis inesset: heic, ut in illis semper maneret : et ibi mediocriter distributus, heic totus effusus : ibi parce datus, heic large commodatus.* Compare Tertullian, *De Exhort. Cast.* 4 *ad fin.*

of the Old. As a matter of fact this gift does run over into the next age; there are traces of it in the writings of the Apostolic Fathers[1]. But above the prophets and above the more ordinary manifestations of the Spirit there was a yet higher grade of authority, that of Apostles. And it is the works of these Apostles which have come down to us and constitute this part of our Bibles.

There are many interesting indications of the more sustained character of the Apostolic inspiration. One would be the use every now and then by St. Paul of such phrases as ἀνθρώπινον λέγω, κατὰ ἄνθρωπον λέγω[2]. When the Apostle throws in apologetically that he is speaking 'after the manner of men,' he is clearly condescending from his usual level. He is meeting carnal persons with carnal weapons. It is the opposite of 'comparing spiritual things with spiritual.' In one place St. Paul appeals to those who have an inspiration to some extent like his own. 'If any man thinketh himself to be a prophet or spiritual, let him take knowledge of the things which I write unto you, that they are the commandment of the Lord' (1 Cor. xiv. 37). St. Paul is conscious of speaking really from the mind of Christ and with the authority of Christ. Those who have themselves the true gift of the Spirit he is sure will at once recognise this. And as to the rest, they must be left in their blindness.

And yet with all this impressive Divine background

---

[1] See Additional Note C: *The Claim to Inspiration in certain passages of the Apostolic Fathers*.

[2] Rom. vi. 19; 1 Cor. ix. 8; Gal. iii. 15.

## Inspiration of the Epistles.

there is also a strong human element in the Epistles of St. Paul. Not that Divine and human are really separable, except as an abstraction of thought. They are not otherwise separable [1]. The Divine *acts through* the human. The psychological processes through which it acts remain unaltered. They bear the stamp of an individual mind, subject to certain conditions of place and time, of race and circumstances, but with the strongly marked lineaments of the man superadded to them. The theology of St. Paul is a reasoned system. In spite of its fragmentary presentation to us, one part here and another part there, pushed to the surface by the stress of temporary and passing needs, behind these occasional utterances there lies what is really a system, marvellously knit and compacted together, a structure of closely articulated thought. I do not mean that it is a system without gaps—gaps in the mind of the Apostle, as well as in the way in which it has found expression in his extant writings. There were some things which even an Apostle could only 'know in part.' But there were no essential points in the principles of Christian belief and practice on which St. Paul was not prepared to give a judgment; and the various judgments which he has given hang together, so that in many cases we can see how they were reached. The centre of St. Paul's creed was the simple belief that Jesus

---

[1] 'The human and the divine are held together in an union which is organic and unanalyzable. They have not been mixed together, they have grown together.' (Rev. J. G. Richardson, quoted by Cheyne, *Aids to Devout Study*, p. 150.)

was the Messiah and Son of God. Given that, and the rest followed in due sequence, with only such additional assumptions as must have been made at the time by a pious Jew.

It was natural that some of the reasoning which had this Jewish character imprinted upon it, should not be according to our modern standards strictly valid reasoning. Some examples of this have been given in an earlier lecture. I do not think it can be said that the Rabbinical methods which St. Paul does employ from time to time really affect the essence of his teaching. His main propositions are arrived at independently of the formal proof which he alleges for them. Indeed it is often in the strict sense not meant as proof at all, but something between what we should call proof and illustration. Thus in that string of passages, culled from various contexts, some of them originally of far more limited application, by which in Romans iii. St. Paul supports his thesis of universal wickedness, he is doing little more than connect with the language of Scripture a proposition which really rested on the evidence of his own eyes and ears. Still in the logical sense the argument is defective.

And as there are defects of logic, so also there are defects of temper. It ill becomes one who has nothing to try him as St. Paul was tried to speak of these. Rather may he wonder how in the midst of pressure and distraction which might well tax the nerve and shake the balance of the strongest and most impassive, this most sensitively organized of men com-

## Inspiration of the Epistles.

bines firmness with conciliation, never yielding a point of principle, and yet meeting his refractory converts with such infinite tact and resource, such delicate courtesy and consideration, as to carry out his purpose with the smallest possible amount of friction. This lies upon the surface and is in fact the characteristic note of St. Paul's Epistles. And yet the strain is too great sometimes. The Epistle to the Galatians begins with rebukes which if severe are dignified, but towards the end the tone becomes less patient. As far back as the time of St. Jerome it was observed that the outbreak against the circumcision-party in Gal. v. 12 could not have been written under the immediate influence of the Spirit. St. Paul soon shakes off this, and draws that beautiful picture of what the fruit of the Spirit should be (Gal. v. 22, 23); but what he had just written rather reminds us of his fiery answer to the injustice of the high priest at his hearing before the Sanhedrin (Acts xxiii. 3).

From Tertullian onwards it has been pointed out that St. Paul is conscious of degrees in his own inspiration [1]. Sometimes he knows that it is not he who speaks but Christ who speaks in him [2]. At other times he speaks somewhat less confidently. After expressing an opinion of his own on the greater blessedness of the single life, he adds, 'and I think that I also have the Spirit of God [3].' He would not

---

[1] See Additional Note D: *Early Patristic Comments upon* 1 Cor. vii. 10, 12, 25, 40.

[2] 1 Cor. xiv. 37 (*ut sup.*); 2 Cor. xiii. 3, ii. 10.

[3] 1 Cor. vii. 40.

speak quite in this way if a direct revelation had been vouchsafed to him on the particular point. Still he believes that the judgment he has given is connected with other judgments in which he has a real inspiration. Sometimes he will not claim as much as this. A little earlier in the same chapter he says expressly that concerning virgins he has no commandment of the Lord, but gives his judgment like a good and loyal Christian[1]. And again he says plainly and without qualification, 'To the rest say I, not the Lord[2].'

We must take the facts as we find them, and give them the best name we can. At one end of the scale there is a strong unhesitating conviction of an impulse and guiding, nay of actual possession, from above. At the other end of the scale this conviction shades off into more ordinary conditions. That the conviction itself is real and no delusion, is confirmed by the power with which the products of the state of mind to which it relates still come home to us. We do right to call that state of mind 'Inspiration.' But in so calling it we must leave a place for the other phenomena as well.

If St. Paul had not had his authority resisted, we should have heard little or nothing about his inspiration. As it is, however much it is implied, the direct allusions to it are few and far between. The other Apostles met with no resistance, and therefore they have still less occasion to assert what no one questioned. At the same time it is impossible to read their Epistles without feeling that there is in them a

---

[1] 1 Cor. vii. 25.     [2] *Ibid.* ver. 12.

πληροφορία or fulness of assurance quite as great as with St. Paul. They expect to be obeyed; and even when they speak of mysteries, they expect to be believed. 'Peter, an Apostle of Jesus Christ, to the elect who are sojourners of the Dispersion'; 'James, a servant (δοῦλος) of God and of the Lord Jesus Christ, to the twelve tribes which are of the Dispersion'; 'Jude, a servant of Jesus Christ, and brother of James[1].' The modest self-suppression of the last two titles does not imply any weakness in the position of the writers. Their readers know who they are too well to need credentials. But most impressive of all is the opening of the First Epistle—the only public Epistle—of St. John : ' That which was from the beginning, that which we have heard, that which we have seen with our eyes, that which we beheld and our hands handled, concerning the Word of life . . . declare we unto you.' It is as if the Apostle came fresh from the presence of the Incarnate Word with plenipotentiary powers to announce the way of holiness and salvation to men. As compared with St. Paul the other Apostles place themselves less upon the same level with their readers. They teach, they command, they warn, they exhort; but there is less of argument and expostulation. Yet they make the same general postulate as St. Paul, that outpouring of the Spirit of which the Apostolic letters are a conspicuous product.

And now we have to trace the process by which this body of letters, St. Paul's Epistles and the

[1] 1 Pet. i. 1 ; James i. 1 ; Jude 1.

Catholic Epistles, took their place in the New Testament as sacred writings. Weighty as St. Paul's Epistles were, they were not composed in the first instance for such a place. When he sat down for instance to write his first extant Epistle to the Thessalonians, his only thought was one of mingled joy and anxiety over the newly founded Church. We may be sure that it never occurred to him that this letter of his to his converts would be written, as he himself described the histories of the Old Testament, 'for our admonition, upon whom the ends of the ages are come.' By what steps did the Epistles come to assume this new character?

One of the most important of these steps was public reading before the assembled Church. This first Epistle contains a strong injunction that it is to be read 'to all the brethren[1].' It was addressed in the first instance to certain leading individuals in the Church—not to call them by too formal a name—and they were to see that every one was made acquainted with its contents. It sometimes happened that an Epistle would be read to other Churches besides that to which it was addressed. Thus the Colossians are charged to send for a letter addressed to Laodicea, and they in turn are to send on their own letter to the Laodiceans; and the exchanged letters are each to be read in the neighbouring Church. This passing about from Church to Church would naturally help the idea that the Epistles possessed a general and permanent

---

[1] 1 Thess. v. 27: 'I adjure you by the Lord that this epistle be read unto all the brethren.'

*Early History of the Epistles.* 361

value. And the stress which St. Paul lays upon the public reading of his Epistles would suggest that the reading should be repeated. It was not long before the Apostolic letters began to be treasured in the archives of the Church, in the same chest or cupboard we may suppose with the copies of the Old Testament; and they would be brought out and read on special occasions, at first somewhat irregularly, but after a time in a certain order and system. It is of course very much a matter of accident when we first have positive evidence for the custom. We meet with this in Tertullian[1]. But a full generation before Tertullian we learn from Dionysius of Corinth that the Corinthian Church had kept up the primitive custom of having the letter written to it by Clement in the name of the Church of Rome[2] read at the Sunday services[3]. We may argue from this *à fortiori* to the letters of Apostles. Indeed it would seem as if any weighty letter from a leader of the Church or from one of the

---

[1] *De Praescr.* 36 : *apud quas* (sc. *ecclesias apostolicas*) *ipsae authenticae litterae recitantur*.

[2] Eus. *H. E.* vi. 23. 11 : Ἐν αὐτῇ δὲ ταύτῃ καὶ τῆς Κλήμεντος πρὸς Κορινθίους μέμνηται ἐπιστολῆς δηλῶν ἀνέκαθεν ἐξ ἀρχαίου ἔθους ἐπὶ τῆς ἐκκλησίας τὴν ἀνάγνωσιν αὐτῆς ποιεῖσθαι. Λέγει γοῦν· Τὴν σήμερον οὖν κυριακὴν ἁγίαν ἡμέραν διηγάγομεν, ἐν ᾗ ἀνέγνωμεν ὑμῶν τὴν ἐπιστολήν, ἣν ἕξομεν ἀεί ποτε ἀναγινώσκοντες νουθετεῖσθαι, ὡς καὶ τὴν προτέραν ἡμῖν διὰ Κλήμεντος γραφεῖσαν.

[3] The express mention of Sunday seems to negative the distinction which Weiss would draw: 'Es handelt sich also um eine gelegentliche Lesung solcher Gemeindebriefe, die mit der gottesdienstlichen Lesung heiliger Schriften gar nicht zu vergleichen ist' (*Einl.* p. 53). Weiss seems to me to understate the whole case as to the authoritative use of the Epistles.

greater Churches must have been made to serve the purpose of edification almost without a break from the time when it was first received.

The desire for edification goes back to the outskirts of the Apostolic age itself, and it can be satisfied by others besides Apostles. The remembrance is still fresh in men's minds of the time when the prophetic gift was widely diffused, and a 'word of exhortation' was easily obtained. 'These things, brethren,' says St. Polycarp, 'I write unto you concerning righteousness, not because I laid this charge upon myself, but because ye invited me[1].' But it is noticeable that Polycarp goes on to deprecate the distinction thus bestowed upon him, and to refer the Philippians rather to the letter (or letters?) which had been left them by the blessed and glorious Paul, who according to the wisdom given to him had taught the men of his day 'the word which concerneth truth carefully and surely' —significant language as to the esteem in which the Epistles were held and as to the way in which they were beginning to be marked off from other writings— even of one so famous as Polycarp. Ignatius just before had in like manner deprecated comparison between himself and the Apostles. 'I do not enjoin you,' he had said to the Romans, 'as Peter and Paul did. They were Apostles, I am a convict; they were free, but I am a slave to this very hour[2].'

There is another point of interest in Polycarp's letter. It shows what active communication went on

---

[1] Polyc. *ad Phil.* iii. 2 (tr. Lightfoot).
[2] Ign. *ad Rom.* iv. 3.

# Early History of the Epistles.

between the Churches at this date, and how eagerly the letters of distinguished men were sought after and cherished—the echo doubtless still reverberating of the effect produced by the Apostolic correspondence in the previous century. 'Ye wrote to me,' Polycarp says, ' both ye yourselves and Ignatius, asking that if any one should go to Syria he might carry thither the letters from you. And this I will do, if I get a fit opportunity, either I myself, or he whom I shall send to be ambassador on your behalf also. The letters of Ignatius which were sent to us by him, and others as many as we had by us, we sent unto you, according as ye gave charge; the which are subjoined to this letter; from which ye will be able to gain great advantage. For they comprise faith and endurance and every kind of edification, which pertaineth unto our Lord[1].'

The Philippians had asked for, and Polycarp sends, a collection as complete as he could make it of the letters of Ignatius. The idea of a collection it will be observed is 'in the air.' We note further that in his short Epistle of something under six octavo pages Polycarp quotes from or alludes to no less than nine out of thirteen of St. Paul's Epistles, including of the disputed Epistles, 2 Thessalonians, Ephesians, and 1, 2 Timothy. The letters of Ignatius in like manner contain clear indications of six Epistles, among which are 1 Timothy and Titus. It seems natural to infer with Holtzmann[2], a very unprejudiced judge, that Ignatius and Polycarp both had in their possession

[1] Polyc. *ad Phil.* xiii. 1, 2.  [2] *Einleitung*, p. 102, ed. 3.

the full collection of the Pauline Epistles[1]. This would be probably before the year 117 A.D.[2] We remember also that a little later, about 140 A.D., Marcion had a collection of ten Epistles, to which he refused to add the Pastorals. It would seem to be not quite certain, but on the whole probable, that Marcion knew and deliberately rejected these Epistles on the obvious ground that they were private letters, addressed to individuals and not to Churches[3]. Tertullian accuses him of inconsistency in rejecting them but accepting the Epistle to Philemon. It is remarkable that the external evidence for the Pastoral Epistles should be so good and so early as it is; because, apart from the question which seems to have been raised and debated during the second century whether letters to individuals could rightly have Canonical value assigned to them[4], it would be only natural to suppose

---

[1] Weiss goes so far as to say that the existence of a collection of Pauline Epistles before Marcion 'entbehrt jedes geschichtlichen Grundes' (*Einl.* p. 63 n.). Surely the arguments in the text afford a good presumption of it. Holtzmann is here the better critic.

[2] It is true that Holtzmann describes the Ignatian Epistles as dating 'at the latest' from 170 to 180 A.D. Most Englishmen consider that Bishop Lightfoot has proved their genuineness. Granting this, they must be at least earlier than the death of Polycarp in 156. Harnack's theory as to the list of the bishops of Antioch, though he still assumes it, has really broken down (Lightfoot, *Ignatius*, ii. 452 ff.).

[3] So Zahn, *Gesch. d. K.* i. 634 f.

[4] This is denied by Kuhn, *Mur. Fragm.* p. 80. Zahn contends with some reason (i. 267 f.) that the question might be raised and discussed as a matter of speculation without anywhere leading to the actual rejection of the letters. There is no proof of such rejection except by Marcion and some other Gnostics (reff. in Zahn, i. 266 n.).

that such letters would be later in getting into circulation than letters addressed to Churches and read in the public services. Their inclusion in the collection which was known both to Polycarp and to Ignatius must have gone far to secure their position.

Can we go back further than Ignatius and Polycarp for proof of the existence of a definite collection of Pauline Epistles [1]? Zahn thinks that we can; he would trace the use of the collection to Clement of Rome, but on grounds which seem to me of doubtful cogency. We must be content with the inference that the collection is older than the end of the reign of Trajan (117 A.D.): how much older, we cannot say. From the many traces of this one collection of thirteen letters, and from the complete absence of any like traces of smaller or divergent collections, we may justly conclude that the collection was made by one person at a definite time, and that it rapidly spread over the whole of Christendom.

It is more a matter of speculation where it was made. There seem to have been two competing lists of the order of St. Paul's Epistles. One, as old as Origen, has the letters arranged substantially as at present, the principle being doubtless to place them in the order of their length and importance. Other lists agree in putting the Epistles to the Corinthians first and that to the Romans last. It is argued that these represent the primitive collection, which on that ground is supposed to have been made at Corinth. The strength of the argument depends upon details;

[1] *Gesch. d. K.* i. 811 ff.

and it may retain its interest, without being exactly convincing [1].

In regard to the nature of the authority attaching to the Epistles, there can be no reasonable doubt that from the time of Irenaeus onwards they were treated as on the same footing with the Old Testament. This may be maintained for the East as well as for the West [2]. But to say that the Epistles are upon the same footing with the Old Testament is only a different way of describing an authority which they were felt to possess all along. We have seen with what respect Ignatius and Polycarp speak of the Apostolic letters. It is true that they do not use technical language; the idea present to their minds may have been rather vague; but there can have been no generation, from the first onwards, in which the Apostles did not carry special weight. Their written word would count for just as much as their spoken word. Among strictly Christian documents there can have been none so authoritative, except those which contained the 'Words of the Lord.' At first letters from other leaders of the Church might be treasured up beside them. But when at last the Church came consciously and deliberately to take the teaching of the Apostles for its standard, these would one by one be excluded.

The acknowledged Catholic Epistles, 1 St. Peter, 1 St. John, and in a less degree St. James, were quoted in precisely the same way as the Epistles of St. Paul, and no tenable distinction can be drawn

---

[1] See especially Zahn, *Gesch. d. K.* i. 835 ff.
[2] See above, pp. 20 f., 67 ff.

between them. The comparative slowness with which the other Epistles took their place has about it nothing surprising. There was not here the safeguard of a collection. Single Epistles, sent out to somewhat vague addresses, and received at a time when there was no difference between the written word of an Apostle and his spoken word; received at a time when every Church had its prophets, and was frequently visited by wandering Apostles and Evangelists, who besides their own words of exhortation and encouragement, would no doubt often bring messages or repeat what they had heard from members of the original Twelve, or the Seventy, or from the great Apostle of the Gentiles; received at a time, further, when the end of all things seemed at hand, and when the present was so full of intense and thrilling interest that men might be forgiven for losing sight of the future; single Epistles, we cannot but feel, received under circumstances such as these, even though it were from Apostles, needed something of a special Providence to secure their preservation at all. And when we think also of the fragile material (papyrus) on which they would be written, of the very disturbed times in which their recipients found themselves, and of the imperfect organization which in those early days must have connected the scattered Churches with each other; when we think of all this, our wonder is increased, not that they should have been somewhat slow in coming into general use and that their use should at first have been local and partial, but that so much of this literature should have been saved from destruction, and that it should have been brought together as completely as it has. Everything would depend on those first fifty years which are so dark to us. An Epistle lodged in the archives of a great and cultured Church like the Church of Rome would be one thing, and an Epistle straying about among the smaller communities of Bithynia or Pontus would be another; while an Epistle written to an individual like the Gaius of 3 St. John would have worse chances still. There were busy, careless, neglectful and unmethodical people in those days as well as now; and we can easily imagine one of these precious rolls found with glad surprise, covered with dust in some forgotten hiding-place, and brought out to the view of a generation which had learnt to be more careful of its treasures. But even then, once off the main roads, circulation was not rapid; an obscure provincial Church might take some time in making its voice heard; and the authorities at headquarters might receive the reported discovery with suspicion. They might, or they might not, as it happened. There would be few copyists available in a remote district[1], and there would be much delay and perhaps some flagging of enthusiasm, before any number of copies got into use. They would be welcomed here, suspected there; and so would grow up just such a

---

[1] St. Basil and his brother Gregory Nyssen complain of the difficulty of finding trained copyists in Cappadocia. Cf. Basil, *Ep.* cxxxv. *fin.* (Migne, *P. G.* xxxii. 573); Greg. Nyss. *Ep.* xii. (Zacagni, *Collect. Mon. Vet.* p. 382) πένητες οἱ Καππάδοκες ἡμεῖς, πλέον δὲ πάντων πένητες τῶν γράφειν δυναμένων: Wattenbach, *Schriftwesen im Mittelalter*, p. 267 f.

condition of things as our fragmentary records reveal to us. By degrees the usage of the different Churches was equalized. The smaller Churches one by one followed the example of the larger. The great leaders on the orthodox side in the fourth century compared notes together. And so, more by a sort of tacit consent than by public argument and discussion, there was gradually formed our present New Testament Canon.

II. Among the disputed books in this Canon was the Apocalypse. It was disputed not so much from doubts as to its authorship as from objections to its doctrine or to the inferences drawn from it. It is true that it was assigned to other authors than the Apostle—the Alogi assigned it to Cerinthus, Dionysius of Alexandria to John the Presbyter—but the motive was dislike of the book more or less freely acknowledged, and the critical difficulties which Dionysius raised, although skilfully conceived, were a second thought and had no historical tradition behind them.

The criticism of the Apocalypse, like that of the Synoptic Gospels and the Acts, is at the present moment in an interesting stage, but cannot be said to have reached finality[1]. Some twenty years ago there was nearly an agreement among the leading European scholars, including our own most trusted

---

[1] A scholarly account of the present position of the question is given by Prof. Milligan in his *Discussions on the Apocalypse*, London, 1893. But I regret to find myself often forming a different estimate of the value of an argument, especially in chap. iii.

Biblical theologians, Bishops Lightfoot and Westcott, that the Apocalypse was all the work of one hand, and that its date was shortly before the Fall of Jerusalem, about the year 69 A.D.

Within the last decade both these questions have been re-opened. Bishop Butler held that there were discoveries still to be made in the Scriptures by closer attention. And it is certainly the case that very many theories which seem to have the mass of the facts in their favour have yet some awkward little difficulty lurking away in the corner, which when it is brought to the front may throw out the balance of the whole.

Such a disturbance of almost accepted theories occurred when in 1886 Harnack and his pupil Vischer put forward the view that the Apocalypse could not be satisfactorily explained as a work of wholly Christian origin. Its mixed character had already given some trouble to commentators. One feature here seemed to imply an advanced Christian Universalism; another feature there seemed to breathe the narrower aspirations of Judaism. Hitherto the solution offered had been to describe the author as a Jewish Christian. But what if there were really two authors? What if the Judaism all came from one, the author of an original Apocalypse soon after the death of Nero, and the Christianity were added to this by the other, who worked over the older piece and issued it with a new face under Domitian?

There was at least one *primâ facie* argument which lent a certain attractiveness to this view besides the main grounds on which it had been propounded. This

# Origin of the Apocalypse.

was that by giving to the book a double authorship it was possible also to give it a double date. There had been always this drawback to the Neronian theory, that Irenaeus, a pupil of Polycarp, who was himself a pupil of St. John, said expressly that the vision of the Apocalypse had been seen at the end of the reign of Domitian[1] (c. 95 A.D.). Surely it would not be easy to have better evidence. For other points connected with the Apocalypse, Irenaeus appealed to those who had had actual personal contact with the Apostle. Why should not they be also his authorities here?

But then there were the many marks which seemed to require an earlier date, between the death of Nero and the Fall of Jerusalem. It was an obvious advantage of the Vischer-Harnack hypothesis that at one stroke it satisfied both these sets of conditions, by placing the original work under Nero and its revised and Christianized edition under Domitian.

The hypothesis when it was first started fell in with the tendencies of the time, and not only attracted considerable attention but made a certain number of converts. Now however a reaction seems to have set in. After all, the supposed dualism of the Apocalypse has an artificial look. The more it is examined the more it is felt that the Apocalypse will not really bear to be dismembered. The very peculiar style with its strange eccentricities of grammar runs through the whole; the historical situation implied in the parts supposed to be added is the same with that in those supposed to be original; and there are many other

[1] *Adv. Haer.* v. 30. 3.

cross-references from the one to the other. Besides, there are serious difficulties in the way of regarding the ground-stock of the book as Jewish. It is true that there was war between the Romans and Jews, but war is not persecution; and the Jews could never have been persecuted like the martyrs of the Apocalypse[1]. They were protected by laws which the Romans appear to have respected under great provocation to throw them over. We may ask, too, who were the prophets who play so prominent a part in the book? We hear little of prophets among the Jews at this period, while the Christian Church was full of them.

I think then that we may safely dismiss this idea of a Jewish base and Christianized redaction, as raising worse difficulties than it removes. It is indeed in many respects in direct contradiction to the facts.

There remains therefore the old question of date. And here again we may note a reaction. The traditional assignment of the Apocalypse to the reign of Domitian has been of late strongly reinforced. Last and most important of all, it has received the adhesion of Professor Ramsay, who has pronounced decidedly for it in his work on *The Church in the Roman Empire* (p. 301).

Yet Professor Ramsay's investigations, valuable as they are, have appeared too recently to command assent before they have been tested. I myself must confess to doubts as to the main premiss on which his argument in this particular case depends, and

[1] Cf. Ramsay, *The Church in the Roman Empire*, pp. 268, 301.

I am expressing my reason for these doubts elsewhere. If I do so it is only for the sake of truth and with every willingness to be convinced that the doubts are unfounded. I am prepared to admit beforehand that strong reasons may be alleged for the later date under Domitian. It increases the difficulties arising out of the relation of the Apocalypse to the Fourth Gospel. But those difficulties must not be allowed to stand in the way if direct and positive evidence leads to the conclusion which entails them. My hesitation is chiefly due to the fact that the arguments which induced so many excellent critics to prefer the earlier date are still unanswered[1]. If one group of phenomena points one way, other groups point another. Apart from details, I question if any other date fits in so well with the conditions implied in the Apocalypse as that between the death of Nero and the destruction of Jerusalem by Titus. On all hands there are wars and rumours of wars. There are the revolts of Vindex and Civilis in Gaul; the successive rise and fall of Galba and Otho; the hosts of Vitellius mustering for the final shock with the armies of the East under Vespasian; the dreaded Parthians beyond the Euphrates, and the rumour that the tyrant Nero was not really dead but had gone to join them; the horizon full of all these rumours of titanic conflict, and then at the point which for a Jew was still the centre of all, the legions of

[1] They are very clearly stated by Archdeacon Farrar in *Early Days of Christianity*, ii. 179–322. Among the supporters of the early date must be numbered both Bishop Lightfoot (*Galatians*, p. 343) and Bishop Westcott (*Gospel of St. John*, p. lxxxvi f.).

Titus drawing closer round Jerusalem and the fated city already enveloped in the horrors of the siege. It might well seem as if this crash of empires was a fit prelude to the crash of a world. Never was the expectation of the approaching end so keen; never were men's minds so highly strung. If this were the moment when St. John was exiled from a great mart of commerce like Ephesus, to which news would come pouring in from every quarter of the Empire, we could well understand the tension of mind to which every page of the Apocalypse bears witness. There were no such tremendous issues, no such clash of opposing forces, no such intense expectation of the end under Domitian. The background seems inadequate.

How grandly over all echoes the voice which borrows its tones straight from the prophets of the Older Covenant: 'Righteous art Thou, which art and which wast, Thou Holy One, because Thou didst thus judge.... Yea, O Lord God, the Almighty, true and righteous are Thy judgments[1].' Whenever it is, Christians are being persecuted; the Empire is making its hand heavy upon them; they are as incapable of offering resistance as a child. And yet the prophet's gaze hardly seems to dwell upon the sufferings of himself and his people. They are a school of steadfastness and courage. 'Be thou faithful unto death and I will give thee the crown of life,' is the chief moral to be drawn from them. But the prophet looks away beyond the persecution to the fate of the persecutors. 'Fallen, fallen is Babylon

---

[1] Rev. xvi. 5, 7.

the great. . . . Woe, woe, the great city, Babylon, the strong city! for in one hour is thy judgment come¹.' Rome did not fall quite so suddenly or so soon as the prophet expected; but the principle which underlies his words is true, that nations like individuals are absolutely in the hand of God, and that He will punish them for their misdeeds. Small, insignificant, helpless as it seemed, the Christian Church has outlived pagan Rome.

Properly to understand and appreciate the Apocalypse we must think of it just as we think of the prophecies of the Old Testament. It differs only in this, that it takes the special form of 'Apocalyptic'; it is concerned with the 'last things.' The author repeatedly describes himself as a prophet and his book as a prophecy². He also repeatedly speaks of being 'in the Spirit³.' The words which he addresses to the Churches are as if they were spoken by the Spirit⁴. Indeed there is no writer in the New Testament who makes such explicit claim to inspiration. The strongest language which is found in the older Scriptures he uses and applies to his own book. He makes the highest authority asseverate its truth, and he invokes blessings upon those who observe it: 'And He said unto me, These words are faithful and true: and the Lord, the God of the spirits of the prophets, sent His angel to show unto His servants

---

¹ Rev. xviii. 2, 10.
² *Ibid.* i. 3; x. 7, 11; xxii. 6, 7, 9, 18, 19.
³ *Ibid.* i. 10; iv. 2; xvii. 3; xxi. 10.
⁴ *Ibid.* ii. 7, 11, 17, 29; iii. 6, 13, 22; *cf.* xiv. 13; xxii. 17.

the things which must shortly come to pass. And behold, I come quickly. Blessed is he that keepeth the words of the prophecy of this book[1].' And the concluding words are obviously modelled upon passages which we have noticed in Deuteronomy and Proverbs[2]: 'I testify unto every man that heareth the words of the prophecy of this book, If any man shall add unto them, God shall add unto him the plagues which are written in this book: and if any man shall take away from the words of the book of this prophecy, God shall take away his part from the tree of life, and out of the holy city, which are written in this book. He which testifieth these things saith, Yea: I come quickly[3].'

It may be asked how this emphatic language can be reconciled with the fact that the main expectation of the prophet, that of the near approach of the Second Coming, has not been fulfilled. We may say that from the very first it was doomed to non-fulfilment. If the hour of His own Second Coming was not revealed to the Son Himself, far less could it be revealed to one of His servants. This was one of those things which the Father hath kept in His own power.

No doubt the Christians of the Apostolic age did live in immediate expectation of the Second Coming, and that expectation culminated at the crisis in which the Apocalypse was written. In the Apocalypse, as in every predictive prophecy, there is a double element,

---

[1] Rev. xxii. 6, 7.
[2] Deut. iv. 2; xii. 32; Prov. xxx. 6; *cf.* p. 267 *sup.*
[3] Rev. xxii. 18-20.

one part derived from the circumstances of the present and another pointing forwards to the future. It was the present which suggested to the mind of the Seer all that grandiose imagery, ultimately based upon the Book of Daniel, of the beast with the seven heads, of which five had fallen, and one though wounded to death was to recover from his wound[1]. It was the horrible present, the idolatrous worship of the Emperors, which had its headquarters in Pergamum 'where Satan's throne is[2],' which is reflected in the worship of the beast and his image[3]. From the present are drawn those pictures of the great river Euphrates with myriads of horsemen marshalled along its banks and its waters dried up for the kings of the East to pass over[4]. From the present too we get looming in the background that mighty Babylon, imperial Rome, drunk with the blood of saints and martyrs, of which the fall is to usher in the end[5]. The present runs into the immediate future when the prophet sees the temple with all but its innermost shrine given up to the Gentiles, and the holy city trodden underfoot by them; and it is in the same near future that he looks for the great and final outburst of wickedness and the short-lived triumph of the beast and of the false prophet, collective names for the powers in which it is embodied.

All these things, in an exact and literal sense, have fallen through with the postponement of that great event in which they centre. From the first they were

---

[1] Rev. xiii. 1, 3, 12; xvii. 10.  [2] Ibid. ii. 13.
[3] Ibid. xiii. 4, 14, 15; xiv. 9.  [4] Ibid. ix. 14, 16; xvi. 12.
[5] Ibid. xvii. 3, 4; xviii. 2, 24.

but meant as the imaginative pictorial and symbolical clothing of that event. What measure of real fulfilment the Apocalypse may yet be destined to receive we cannot tell. But in predictive prophecy, even when most closely verified, the essence lies less in the prediction as such than in the eternal laws of moral and religious truth which the fact predicted reveals or exemplifies. We can seldom see the whole of these laws until it is possible to place prophecy and fulfilment side by side. But we shall hardly be far wrong if we take as the central feature of the Apocalypse its intense longing for the Advent of Christ and His Kingdom, with its confident assertion of the ultimate victory of good over evil and of the dawning of a state of blissful perfection when sorrow and sighing shall flee away.

## NOTE A.

### *A new Theory of the Origin of the Catholic Epistles.*

WHEN the discovery of the *Didaché* threw a new and unexpected light upon the activity of the prophets and διδάσ-καλος and showed what an important part they had played along with the Apostles (in the wider and narrower sense) in the history of the Primitive Church, the idea occurred to Harnack that in this direction was to be sought the solution of the problem as to the origin of the so-called Catholic Epistles. Starting from the assumption that they could not be the work of the authors whose names they traditionally bear, and yet not seeing in them the marks of deliberate fiction, he hit upon the theory that they were originally the work of nameless prophets or teachers, which in the course of the second century, as the tendency grew to refer all the institutions of the Primitive Church to the Apostles, had the names of Apostles attached to them. This he believed was done in the case of the Epistles of St. James, St. Jude, and 1 St. Peter by interpolations in the opening words of address. In proof of the possibility of this, appeal was made to the textual phenomena of the end of the Gospels of St. Mark, St. Luke, and St. John, of the end of the Epistle to the Romans, and the beginning of the Epistle to the Ephesians. Overbeck's theory as to the Epistle to the Hebrews was referred to, and a like hypothesis was suggested for the Apocalypse and 1 Tim. vi. 17-21. Cases were also quoted such as that of the Epistle of Barnabas and the attempt to bring writers like Clement of Rome and Hermas into connexion with the Apostles.

The value of the theory must depend upon the strength of the objections to the traditional ascriptions. In case these should give way the hypothesis of anonymous authorship is certainly preferable to that of fiction. But the really valid support for the interpolation-theory shrinks into very small compass indeed.

The instances which rest upon pure conjecture may be left to themselves. I do not believe that they have any sort of probability. [As to Hebrews see p. 24 f. above; the ascription of the Apocalypse to St. John is guaranteed as early as Justin; the theory that 1 Tim. vi. 17–21 is interpolated is entirely 'in the air' and no reasons are alleged for it.] On the other hand, those which have some documentary basis are really wide of the mark, and present no parallel to the hypothesis which they are adduced to prove. The evidence against St. John xxi. 25 has been proved by Dr. Gwynn (in the current number of *Hermathena*) to be practically nil. The words which drop out of St. Luke xxiv. 53 (if these are what Harnack means, but there is nothing which really serves his purpose) are just a common case of conflation which has nothing to do with ascription of authorship. The same is true of the last twelve verses of St. Mark. The most probable view, I think, is that they were written to make good a loss through the frayed end of a roll. But in neither of its forms does the supplied ending even hint at the name of an author. If there is any tendency in the variants of Romans and Ephesians (Rom. i. 7, 15; Eph. i. 1) it is rather to make the address of the Epistles vaguer and not more definite; and the readings at the end of Romans (xiv. 23, xvi. 20, 24, 25–27) may affect the form in which the Epistle circulated, but do not affect its authorship.

The examples thus adduced really tell against and not for the thesis which they are called in to support. They show how sensitive the documentary evidence is to early changes of any kind, and they raise a presumption that if the text had been tampered with as Harnack supposes, traces of the fact would have been somewhere forthcoming.

Again, when we look at the history of the Catholic Epistles we see that interpolation was quite unnecessary. The Epistles of St. John were accepted as Apostolic without any name in their salutations at all.

If the object were to impress by the weight of authority it is strange that the interpolator should have been so modest in his procedure—that the author of the Epistle which bears the name of St. James should be called simply 'a servant of Jesus Christ' without any personal identification, and that the interpolator who inserted the name of Jude should only describe him as 'brother of James.'

But indeed we have nothing in any of our authorities to make it likely that an ordinary prophet or teacher, however general his commission, would have taken upon himself to write in so commanding a strain to such widely scattered communities as the 'twelve tribes of the dispersion,' or 'the dispersion of Pontus, Galatia, Cappadocia, Asia, and Bithynia.' Of course the data are defective. But whereas we have analogies for Apostles taking so large a sweep of the horizon, we have no analogies for lesser persons doing so.

Lastly, the number of Epistles which are supposed to have been interpolated in this manner is really reduced to three, St. James, 1 St. Peter, and St. Jude. As to 2 St. Peter, there can be no doubt that the whole Epistle was written in the name of St. Peter from the first. But 1 St. Peter also contains a number of personal greetings (1 Peter v. 12–14) which show that it was written by some one very high up in the ranks of the Church—by some one who calls St. Mark his 'son' and who makes use of Silas as a scribe. Or is all this too interpolation? And did the interpolator insert ἡ ἐν Βαβυλῶνι συνεκλεκτή?

There is therefore extremely little positive foundation for a theory which however possesses a certain interest, and is at least an improvement on the forms of negation hitherto current.

Harnack expounded his theory in a long note in his edition of the *Didaché*, p. 106 ff., and in *Dogmengeschichte*, i. 311 f., ed. 2.

## NOTE B.

### On the Genuineness of 2 St. Peter.

THE arguments commonly adduced in disproof of the genuineness of 2 St. Peter are as follows:—

(1) That the external evidence is insufficient.—I think we may consider that the clear evidence begins with Origen, who, however, also mentions that the Epistle was doubted. I cannot be sure that it was really commented upon by Clement of Alexandria. And the instances of the use of the Epistle by writers earlier than this date may perhaps rather be explained as coming from the common stock of Christian ideas and language and not specially from the Epistle. We should thus have a state of things which, though no doubt compatible with the spuriousness of the Epistle, by no means amounts to proof of it. The delay in the acceptance of the Epistle might well be due to other causes than defective credentials: see p. 367 f. above.

(2) That 2 St. Peter is based upon and borrows freely from the Epistle of St. Jude.—It has been contended with almost equal zeal that 2 St. Peter borrows from St. Jude and *vice versa*. The balance of authority, and perhaps it may be thought the balance of argument, is in favour of the priority of St. Jude, but in view more particularly of the elaborate work of Spitta mentioned below, I should not like to assert it too positively. Questions of this kind are hard to bring to a decision. But in fact either case, that 2 St. Peter borrows from St. Jude, or St. Jude from 2 St. Peter, would not exclude the Apostolic authorship of both Epistles. We must not throw back the literary habits of our own day to that of the Apostles.

## Note B.

(3) That the author of the Epistle borrowed not only from St. Jude but from the *Antiquities* of Josephus and the Epistle of Clement of Rome.—This would really be fatal. But the case does not seem to be made out. Again, as with the external evidence to the Epistle, the resemblances seem to be due rather to a common intellectual atmosphere than to direct borrowing.

(4) That, apart from this, the style is too forced and artificial to be worthy of an Apostle.—The facts have been somewhat exaggerated; but what there is of truth in them has too many parallels in the literature of the time to be at all decisive.

(5) That the author shows a too manifest anxiety to have his work attributed to St. Peter.—The question would be whether this anxiety was so great as to be suspicious. Perhaps it is slightly so. But there is no reason why St. Peter should avoid allusions to his own career. And a personator of St. Peter might easily have made his allusions in a cruder form than those in the Epistle.

(6) That the differences of style between 1 and 2 St. Peter prove that the two Epistles cannot have had the same author. —Resemblances also have been noticed, but on the whole differences preponderate. Spitta boldly turns them against the First Epistle, which he thinks was written by Silvanus (*cf.* 1 Pet. v. 12). And we cannot wholly put aside the hypothesis of St. Jerome (*Denique et duae epistolae quae feruntur Petri stilo inter se et charactere discrepant, structuraque verborum. Ex quo intelligimus, pro necessitate rerum, diversis eum usum interpretibus*). This hypothesis, however, does not seem to work out so well as in the case of St. Paul (see p. 342 above).

(7) That there are differences of idea between the two Epistles which are still more important.—Of these the most considerable is in regard to the expectation of the Second Coming. 1 Peter regards this as near at hand (1 Pet. iv. 7, 17, v. 1); in 2 Peter iii. 4, 8-10 there are apologies for its long delay. The language which is here used does not seem

to suit any part of the Apostolic age before the year 70. And even if we could, with Professor Ramsay and some others, prolong St. Peter's life beyond that date, we should still have to place the two Epistles near together at the end of it.

(8) That the well-known verses 2 Pet. iii. 15, 16 imply a collection of St. Paul's Epistles which is already treated as Scripture.—This I confess is the impression which the passage makes upon me, though Spitta protests energetically against it ('Von einer Sammlung paulinischer Briefe, von der uns erhaltenen Sammlung, von dieser Sammlung als einer kanonischen ist 2 Peter iii. 15 absolut gar nichts zu lesen,' p 527).

The arguments thus enumerated vary in strength. Some which are weak in themselves gain somewhat by combination. And the last two seem to me to be of considerable force. The natural inference from them seems to be that the Epistle belongs to an age later than that of the Apostles.

And then, to crown all, there are the coincidences of style with the Apocalypse of Peter. It may be true that these are not enough to prove identity of authorship: still they are favourable to it.

On the other hand, I confess that if we can get over the presumption in favour of the priority of St. Jude, Spitta has proposed a historical situation which would suit the two Epistles very well. He thinks that 2 St. Peter was written by the Apostle shortly before his death, and that the Epistle of St. Jude was written after that event to the same readers with the object of carrying out the intention expressed in 2 Pet. i. 15; and also that Jude 17, 18 refers back directly to 2 Pet. iii. 3. This last point is not a new one; but if it were not for the difficulties which it involves, it would be really attractive. While it is difficult to resist a total impression which is against the genuineness of the Epistle, every *primâ facie* view is not necessarily the true one; and if the writer of this were to commit himself definitely to the negative conclusion he would feel that he was leaving behind arguments on the other side which he had not fully answered, and combinations which he could not say were impossible.

Among recent discussions of the subject in English the following would be the most noteworthy : Dr. Lumby in The Speaker's Commentary (in favour of the genuineness and priority of 2 St. Peter); Dr. Edwin A. Abbott in The Expositor, 1882, i. 49 ff., 139 ff., 204 ff. (strongly against both genuineness and priority); Dr. B. B. Warfield in The Southern Presbyterian Review (U.S.A.), 1882, p. 45 ff., 1883, p. 390 ff. (the first article a very able defence of the Epistle, the second in reply to Dr. Abbott); Archdeacon Farrar in The Expositor, 1882, i. 401 ff., also Early Days of Christianity, i. 174-208 (in part accepting but also considerably qualifying Dr. Abbott's arguments, and summing up against the genuineness of the Epistle, but not certainly or decisively); Dr. Salmon, Introduction to the N. T., 5th ed., 1891, pp. 481-508 (a judicial and thorough examination of the arguments on both sides, especially controverting the arguments of Dr. Abbott); Dr. Plummer, in Comm. for Eng. Readers and in The Expositor's Bible (St. James and St. Jude), pp. 391-400 (in the earlier work inclining to affirm the genuineness and priority of 2 St. Peter, in the later work more doubtful).

Of recent foreign works, Holtzmann, Einleitung in d. N. T., 1892, ed. 3, and von Soden in the Handcommentar, pronounce decidedly against the Epistle; Weiss, Einleitung, 1886, is doubtful; Spitta, Der zweite Brief d. Petrus und der Brief d. Judas, 1885, warmly and in close detail defends both the genuineness and priority of 2 St. Peter. Spitta is not at all an apologist, and in this as in his other works fresh and original points which fully demand attention are found side by side with others which are quite untenable.

## NOTE C.

*The Claim to Inspiration in certain passages of the Apostolic Fathers.*

BOTH in the Epistle written by Clement in the name of the Church at Rome and in the Epistles of Ignatius there are passages which seem to make a claim to inspiration.

CLEM. ROM. *ad Cor.* lix. 1 : Ἐὰν δέ τινες ἀπειθήσωσιν τοῖς ὑπ' αὐτοῦ [*sc.* τοῦ Θεοῦ] δι' ἡμῶν εἰρημένοις, γινωσκέτωσαν ὅτι παραπτώσει καὶ κινδύνῳ οὐ μικρῷ ἑαυτοὺς ἐνδήσουσιν κ. τ. λ.

*Ibid.* lxiii. 2 : Χαρὰν γὰρ καὶ ἀγαλλίασιν ἡμῖν παρέξετε, ἐὰν ὑπήκοοι γενόμενοι τοῖς ὑφ' ἡμῶν γεγραμμένοις διὰ τοῦ ἁγίου Πνεύματος, ἐκκόψητε τὴν ἀθέμιτον τοῦ ζήλους ὑμῶν ὀργὴν κατὰ τὴν ἔντευξιν ἣν ἐποιησάμεθα περὶ εἰρήνης καὶ ὁμονοίας ἐν τῇδε τῇ ἐπιστολῇ.

IGNAT. *ad Philadelph.* vii. 1 : Εἰ γὰρ καὶ κατὰ σάρκα μέ τινες ἠθέλησαν πλανῆσαι, ἀλλὰ τὸ Πνεῦμα οὐ πλανᾶται, ἀπὸ Θεοῦ ὄν· οἶδεν γὰρ πόθεν ἔρχεται καὶ ποῦ ὑπάγει, καὶ τὰ κρυπτὰ ἐλέγχει· ἐκραύγασα μεταξὺ ὤν, ἐλάλουν μεγάλῃ φωνῇ, Θεοῦ φωνῇ· Τῷ ἐπισκόπῳ προσέχετε καὶ τῷ πρεσβυτερίῳ καὶ διακόνοις.

These passages naturally recall those which were quoted in a previous lecture from Ecclesiasticus and Wisdom. They represent the same sort of survival or overflow of the consciousness which is so strong in the authors of the Canonical Books of both Testaments. This is the less surprising in the case of the New Testament because there can be no doubt that the order of prophets went on for some little time after the close of the Apostolic Age strictly so called. Ignatius evidently felt himself to have spoken under an access of prophetic inspiration, of which he retains the remembrance in writing. The words of Clement are perhaps dictated rather by the strong assurance that he is applying inspired and scriptural principles to the particular case before him.

## NOTE D.

*Early Patristic Comments on* 1 *Cor. vii.* 10, 12, 25, 40.

IRENAEUS. The first Christian writer to comment on the places in 1 Cor. vii in which St. Paul seems to draw a distinction between the different degrees of authority with which he writes or speaks is Irenaeus. He makes use of the passages in question to show that in this respect the New Testament is on the same footing as the Old, and that St. Paul on the one hand and Moses on the other gave some commands which were not of absolute but relative validity for the 'hardness of heart' of those to whom they were given. After quoting Matt. xix. 7, 8, he goes on :—

'Et quid dicimus de veteri Testamento haec? quandoquidem et in novo apostoli hoc idem facientes inveniuntur propter praedictam caussam, statim dicente Paulo: *Haec autem ego dico, non Dominus.* Et iterum : *Hoc autem dico secundum indulgentiam, non secundum praeceptum.* Et iterum : *De virginibus autem praeceptum Domini non habeo ; consilium autem do, tanquam misericordiam consecutus a Domino, ut fidelis sim'* (*Adv. Haer.* iv. 15. 2).

TERTULLIAN evidently finds the chapter one of considerable difficulty. It appears to conflict with his views on the subject of second marriage. Accordingly he draws a broad distinction between the different ways in which the Apostle speaks : the laxer precepts he sets down to human prudence, the stricter to Divine inspiration :—

'Ceterum de secundo matrimonio scimus plane apostolum pronuntiasse : *Solutus es ab uxore, ne quaesieris uxorem, sed etsi duxeris non delinques.* Proinde tamen et huius sermonis ordinem de consilio suo, non de divino praecepto introducit. Multum autem interest inter Dei praeceptum et consilium hominis. *Praeceptum Dei,* inquit, *non habeo, sed consilium do, quasi misericordiam consecutus fidelis esse,* quoniam neque in evangelio neque in ipsius Pauli epistolis ex praecepto Dei invenias permissam matrimonii separationem.... Sed ecce rursus mulierem defuncto marito dicit nubere posse, si cui velit, tantum in domino. *At enim felicior erit*, inquit, *si sic perseveraverit secundum meum consilium. Puto autem, et ego Dei spiritum habeo.* Videmus duo consilia, quo supra nubendi veniam facit, et quo postmodum continentiam nubendi docet. Cui, ergo, inquis assentabimus? Inspice et lege. Cum veniam facit, hominis prudentis consilium allegat, cum continentiam indicit, Spiritus Sancti consilium affirmat. Sequere admonitionem cui divinitas patrocinatur' (*De Exhort. Cast.* 4). Then follows a passage, referred to above (p. 354), on the fuller indwelling of the Spirit vouchsafed to the Apostles as compared with others of the faithful.

The treatise *De Monogamia* contains expressions much to the same effect and not less explicit :—

'Denique conversus ad alteram speciem dicendo; *Nuptis autem denuntio, non ego sed Dominus*, ostendit illa quae supra dixerat non dominicae auctoritatis fuisse sed humanae aestimationis. At ubi ad continentiam reflectit animos, *Volo autem vos sic esse omnes*, *Puto autem*, inquit, *et ego spiritum Dei habeo*, ut si quid indulserat ex necessitate, id Spiritus Sancti auctoritate revocaret' (*De Monog.* 3 ; comp. 11).

ORIGEN in his keen way propounds as a problem for consideration whether when St. Paul says πᾶσα γραφὴ θεόπνευστος καὶ ὠφέλιμος, he includes his own writings and in particular κἀγὼ λέγω καὶ οὐχ ὁ Κύριος and other passages written by him with authority but not in the pure quintessence of Divine inspiration (τὸ εἰλικρινὲς τῶν ἐκ θείας ἐπιπνοίας λόγων). This is in the course of a discussion as to how far the Gospels can be rightly described as the 'first-fruits' of the New Testament. He decides that they can be so described though there is a sense in which the Acts and Epistles are all 'Gospel' (*Comm. in Ev. Jo.* i. 5 ; ed. Lommatzsch, i. 11 ff.).

The strongest expressions of Origen's are found in a fragment preserved in Cramer's *Catena*: οἱ νόμοι οἱ κατὰ Μωσέα (*sic*), οἱ μὲν Θεοῦ εἰσιν, οἱ δὲ Μωσέως· καὶ τοῦτο ἐπιστάμενος ὁ Κύριος

διαφορὰν νόμων Θεοῦ καὶ νόμου Μωσέως, εἶπεν ἐπὶ μὲν τῶν ὑπὸ Θεοῦ νενομοθετημένων· ὁ γὰρ Θεὸς εἶπεν, 'τίμα [τίνα Cram.] τὸν πατέρα καὶ τὴν μητέρα·' ἐπὶ δὲ τῶν ὑπὸ Μωσέως, 'Μωϋσῆς διὰ τὴν σκληροκαρδίαν ὑμῶν ἐπέτρεψεν ὑμῖν ἀπολῦσαι τὰς γυναῖκας'
... Μωϋσῆς μὲν οὖν ὑπηρετῶν Θεῷ, νόμους ἔδωκεν δευτέρους παρὰ τοὺς νόμους τοῦ Θεοῦ. Παῦλος δὲ ὑπηρετῶν τῷ Εὐαγγελίῳ, νόμους ἔδωκεν δευτέρους τοῖς ἐκκλησιαστικοῖς μετὰ τοὺς νόμους τοὺς [τοῖς Cram.] ἀπὸ [Cram., ἀτὲρ Cod.] Θεοῦ διὰ Ἰησοῦ Χριστοῦ. Καὶ καλόν ἐστιν ἀκούειν νόμου ἀπὸ Κυρίου, ἢ ἀκούειν νόμων Παύλου τοῦ Ἀποστόλου· κἂν γὰρ ἅγιος ᾖ, ἀλλὰ πολλῷ ὑποδεεστέρους [Cram., ὑπὸ δὲ ἑτέρους Cod.] ἔχει νόμους τῶν νόμων τοῦ Κυρίου (*Catena ad* 1 Cor. vii. 12).

Again later:—

Τῶν ἐντολῶν αἱ μὲν εἰσὶν ἐπιτεταγμέναι, αἱ δὲ οὐκ ἐπιτεταγμέναι, ἀλλ᾽ αὐτεξούσιοι καὶ τῇ προαιρέσει ἐπιτετραμμέναι ὑπὸ τοῦ Θεοῦ· αἱ μὲν γὰρ αὐτῶν ὧν οὐκ ἔστιν ἄνευ σωθῆναι, αὐταὶ εἰσὶν αἱ προστεταγμέναι· αἱ δὲ μείζονες τῶν προστεταγμένων, ἃς κἂν μὴ ποιήσωμεν, σωζόμεθα, οὐκ εἰσὶν ἐπίταγμα τοῦ Θεοῦ ... διὰ τοῦτο λέγει ὁ Ἀπόστολος, 'περὶ δὲ τῶν παρθένων ἐπιταγὴν Κυρίου οὐκ ἔχω· γνώμην δὲ δίδωμι, ὡς ἠλεημένος ὑπὸ Κυρίου πιστὸς εἶναι.' ἐν γὰρ τῷ λέγειν τοῖς μαθηταῖς τὸν Κύριον, 'οὐ πάντες χωροῦσι τὸν λόγον ἀλλ᾽ οἷς δέδοται,' καὶ ἐπιφέρει 'ὁ δυνάμενος χωρεῖν, χωρείτω,' οὐκ ἐπέταξεν ἀλλ᾽ αὐτεξούσιον εἴασεν· 'γνώμην' οὖν φησὶν ὁ Ἀπόστολος 'δίδωμι·' καὶ ἵνα παραστήσῃ ὅτι Κύριος ἐν αὐτῷ λέγει, εἶπεν, 'ὡς ἠλεημένος ὑπὸ Κυρίου πιστὸς εἶναι' (*ibid. ad* ver. 25).

The idea of one set of precepts as of universal obligation, and others as forming a sort of counsel of perfection, occurs elsewhere with reference to this passage: *e.g. Comm. in Ep. ad Rom.* iii. 3, x. 14 (Lomm. vi. 181, vii. 423). In several places Origen appeals to 1 Cor. vii. 40 in proof of St. Paul's inspiration: *e.g. Comm. in Ev. Jo.* xiii. 52, *in Ep. ad Rom.* i. 8 (Lomm. ii. 107, vi. 32).

CHRYSOSTOM, like Origen, distinguishes the two classes of commands, but he follows the second passage quoted from the *Catena* rather than the first in claiming that those which are spoken by the Apostle on his own authority are nevertheless inspired. His comment on ver. 10 is as follows:—

Ἐπειδὴ νόμον ῥητῶς ὑπὸ τοῦ Χριστοῦ τεθέντα ἀναγινώσκειν

## Notes to Lecture VII.

μέλλει περὶ τοῦ χωρὶς πορνείας μὴ ἀφιέναι γυναῖκα, διὰ τοῦτό φησιν, ' οὐκ ἐγώ.' Τὰ μὲν γὰρ εἰρημένα ἔμπροσθεν, εἰ καὶ μὴ ῥητῶς εἴρητο, ἀλλὰ καὶ αὐτῷ δοκεῖ ταῦτα· τοῦτο μέντοι καὶ ῥητῶς παρέδωκεν. Ὥστε τὸ ' ἐγώ,' καὶ ' οὐκ ἐγώ,' ταύτην ἔχει τὴν διαφοράν. Ἵνα γὰρ μηδὲ τὰ αὐτοῦ ἀνθρώπινα εἶναι νομίσῃς διὰ τοῦτο ἐπήγαγε· ' Δοκῶ γὰρ κἀγὼ πνεῦμα Θεοῦ ἔχειν ' (*Hom.* xix. *in Ep. I ad Cor.*).

These may be taken as specimens of early Patristic comments upon the chapter. On the whole they seem to follow the lines of natural exegesis.

# LECTURE VIII.

RETROSPECT AND RESULTS.
THE TRADITIONAL AND INDUCTIVE VIEWS OF
INSPIRATION COMPARED.

'I have yet many things to say unto you, but ye cannot bear them now.'—*St. John* xvi. 12.

FROM the discussions in which we have been engaged two conceptions of Inspiration seem to emerge, which we may call respectively the Traditional and the Inductive or Critical. And it now becomes our duty to compare these two conceptions, to see how they are related to each other and how far they are capable of being combined in a single resultant conception.

So far it may well seem that the object of these lectures has been only to state and advocate the inductive or critical theory in opposition to the traditional. And it is true that where the two come into direct collision, as in other matters of human thought, the more scientific statement is to be accepted. This is true, but it is not the whole truth, because the inductive or critical theory needs to be supplemented; and when it is supplemented the two theories will be found to approximate to each other more nearly, and even where they do not exactly meet, the gap between them is in a manner bridged over. We can see historically how it arose; and we can also see theoretically how by a slight change of definitions it may be diminished.

I. But before we can consider these approximations between the two theories we shall do well to pass rapidly over the ground we have traversed, in order to have them both presented to our minds as clearly as possible, and in order to see just how far the gap between them extends.

The traditional theory needs little description. Fifty years ago it may be said to have been the common belief of Christian men, at least in this country. It may have been held somewhat vaguely and indefinitely, and those who held it might, if pressed upon the subject, have made concessions which would have involved them in perplexities. But speaking broadly, the current view may be said to have been that the Bible as a whole and in all its parts was the Word of God, and as such that it was endowed with all the perfections of that Word. Not only did it disclose truths about the Divine nature and operation which were otherwise unattainable, but all parts of it were equally authoritative, and in history as well as in doctrine it was exempt from error. It was not quite a hard and fast view. Some kinds of error might be admitted, and there might be no clear dividing line where these possibilities of error were to stop, but it would be agreed that they could not extend to anything of importance. They would belong chiefly to the sphere of the text: it might be allowed that the true text could not always be discovered; but when once it had been discovered it could not be otherwise than infallible.

This was the view commonly held fifty years ago. And when it comes to be examined it is found to be substantially not very different from that which was held two centuries after the Birth of Christ. The chief difference would be as to the exact list of books which constituted the Bible. The properties ascribed to those which held an acknowledged position in it were much the same.

Nay more; it was possible to go further back still. Of course it was not until about the year 200 A.D. that there could be said to be a New Testament by the side of the Old. But the Old Testament existed at least two centuries earlier; and even then the same attributes were ascribed to it. The full conception of the Bible as a Sacred Book was already formed; and when the Books of the New Testament came to be added to those of the Old, both were included under the same general idea. Indeed the one proof which in all ages has been the simplest and most effective as to the validity of that idea was the extent to which it was recognised in the sayings of Christ Himself.

It is no doubt a great inversion of method when the Books of the two Testaments are interrogated without any assumption whatever beyond that of a

Personal God who might be conceived as capable of putting Himself into communication with men. Yet even when so interrogated, we found them speak with no uncertain sound in their claim to a real Divine inspiration.

We started from the Prophets, because in the Prophets not only the fact of Inspiration but the manner of it are most evident. The distinguishing characteristic of the prophets, first of their speech and action and afterwards of their writings, was the firm and unwavering belief that they were instruments or organs of the Most High, and that the thoughts which arose in their minds about Him and His Will, and the commands and exhortations which they issued in His Name, really came at His prompting, and were really invested with His authority. There is no alternative between accepting this belief as true and regarding it as a product of mental disease or delusion. But to bring such a charge, not against a few individuals but against the whole line of prophets from Moses or Samuel to Malachi, is a step from which most of us would shrink. And the charge is refuted in advance by the contents of the prophecies themselves, which, if once we allow that there is a God, make those affirmations about Him which the world has pronounced to be the best and truest, and which it has taken as the centre of its beliefs to this day.

A world-wide religion which for more than thirty centuries has been taking increasing hold on the most highly developed races could not have its origin in mere mental disease. It is not denied that a conviction such as that entertained by the prophets has its analogies among heathen and savage peoples. Neither would it be denied that there is some relative justification for these lower forms of the idea, however to all appearance rude and barbarous. They would be related to the higher forms as rudimentary structures in the physical organism are related to the corresponding developed and perfected structures. It must not be thought that God is present only in a single creed and that all others alike are destitute of Him. It is rather His method to lead men gradually, and sometimes by circuitous routes, to the better understanding of Himself.

There is also this further difference, that whereas in heathen and savage religions there is too often a mysterious infusion of evil affecting the heart's core of the religion itself, in the case of the religion of Israel this element was wonderfully kept away; not indeed so as to leave no traces in the mass of the nation, which always ran the risk of contagion from the surrounding heathenism, but so that the writings which have come down to us as authoritative are singularly free from it. They may show limitations of knowledge, they may show progressive stages of development, but the worship of Jehovah never was tainted as the other great religions of antiquity were tainted. It lived in a serener region and breathed a purer air.

Of this religion the prophets were the organs. It was they who made it what it was. And that which enabled them to impress this high stamp upon it was what we call their inspiration, the gift by which

God Himself spake through them and made them the channels of the communication of His Will to men.

The prophets let us see the workings of this inspiration. And having once realized what it is, we have a standard by which we can argue backwards and forwards. We can argue backwards to one like Moses, of whom the documents are too late to give us a perfectly adequate portraiture. We know however that he was a prophet himself and the founder of the prophetic religion, so that we cannot be wrong in ascribing to him the laying down of its most essential features.

And then we observe further that round the nucleus of prophetic and primary inspiration, embodied as much in the Law as in the works of the prophets properly so called, there gathered a sort of secondary inspiration, the products of which are often not inferior in permanent value. Religion consists not only in the knowledge of God and of His Will, but in the realization of that knowledge in the heart and conscience, in its effect upon conduct, and in its recognition by acts of worship and praise. It was therefore a matter of great importance that these forms of *applied revelation*, if we may so call it, should also receive classical expression, both as a model to after-ages and as a school of devout feeling. And that classical expression it is natural to seek at the hands of those who, if not immediately gifted with a new and special insight into the nature of God and His dealings with them, yet lived in close contact with those who were so gifted and were in a position really and vitally to assimilate their teaching. It is natural to seek along with the revelation for the practical commentary upon revelation, pressing it home into the chinks and crannies of daily life and responding to the gift by a worthy offering of thanks and praise to God, the Giver. We seek for this and we find it, as we should expect, when we approach most nearly to the fountain-head, the living well-spring, of the Divine self-communication. There were in Israel other classes, priests, psalmists, wise men, some of whom were by no means untouched with the direct gift of prophecy, but who were still more largely impregnated with the prophetic teaching to an extent which fitted them for applying it in new directions. They did so not as hirelings in the house of God, but as privileged members of the inner circle of His chosen ones. From the point of view of the manner of their inspiration, as compared with that of the prophets it must be described as secondary; but judged by the value of its results, the inspiration of priests, psalmists, and wise men is not inferior to that of the prophets themselves.

At the same time we cannot be surprised if, in this process of the application to life and worship of the central truths of the religion, there are some parts which are more distant from the centre than others, and proportionately influenced in less degree by the principles which are most fundamental. The glowing mass which sends forth light and heat loses both by radiation. So in the Old Testament, whereas there are on the one hand books, like the prophecies of Isaiah and Jeremiah, which are throughout the work of men strongly inspired and gifted with the faculty of not only applying old truths but creating new ones; and whereas there are other books, like the Psalms, the authors of which, while not exactly creating, do a work which is no less valuable by cultivating and giving adequate expression to religious feeling; there are on the other hand books, like Ecclesiastes, which, though grave and sincere and up to a certain point really religious, have not strength of faith enough to master the problems with which they wrestle; or again, like the Books of Chronicles, where there is a genuine warmth of religious feeling, but imperfect historical method and defective sense of historical accuracy; or lastly, like the Book of Esther, which probably never professed to be in the strict sense history, and which does not even point a very exalted moral. In other words, there are some books in which the Divine element is at the *maximum* and others in which it is at the *minimum*. When we come to reflect, it may be seen that the lower modes have a place in relation to the Divine purpose (which includes both high and low) that is not less appropriate than the higher, but from our present standpoint they must be described as lower.

In like manner as to the New Testament. Just as in the Old Testament the central phenomenon is Prophecy, so in the New the central phenomenon is the outpouring of the Spirit, and the special endowment conferred by it upon those who came under its influence, and more particularly upon the Apostles. And while there are some books in which the presence of this gift is as clear as the sun at noonday, there is one, and I do not myself think more than one, the Second Epistle of St. Peter, which is probably at least to this extent a counterfeit, that it appears under a name which is not that of its true author. We observe too that the Historical Books of the New Testament, like those of the Old, whatever the sanctity attaching to them from their contents, are yet in the first instance strictly histories, put together by ordinary historical methods, or in so far as the methods on which they are composed are not ordinary, due rather to the peculiar circumstances of the case and not to influences which need be specially described as supernatural.

To sum up then, we may compare the Traditional and Inductive theories of Inspiration thus. The inspiration implied by both is real and no fiction, a direct objective action of the Divine upon the human. Nay, in one sense, if the inductive conception of Inspiration is not more real than the other, it is at least more thoroughly realized, because it is not something which is simply taken for granted but comes freshly and spontaneously, in such a way that the mind can get a full and vigorous impression of it, from the study of the documents themselves. The danger of the traditional view is lest inspiration should be thought of as something dead and mechanical; when it is arrived at inductively it must needs be conceived as something vital and organic. It is a living product which falls naturally into its place in the development of the purpose of the Living God. It is not therefore in the least degree inferior in quality to traditional inspiration. So far as they differ it would be rather in quantity, inasmuch as on the inductive view inspiration is not inherent in the Bible as such, but is present in different books and parts of books in different degrees. More particularly on this view—and here is the point of greatest divergence—it belongs to the Historical Books rather as conveying a religious lesson than as histories, rather as interpreting than as narrating plain matter of fact. The crucial issue is that in this last respect they do not seem to be exempted from possibilities of error.

In the course of our inquiry we saw, or thought we saw, how the traditional theory of inspiration had been reached from a basis such as that which has been critically verified. It had been reached by a simple process of enlargement or extension, properties which the prophets and lawgivers of Israel claimed for themselves in their own proper spheres being applied to other writers in a different sphere or being applied to themselves otherwise than in their capacity as prophets and lawgivers. The prophets of Israel were also to a large extent its historians. But it did not follow that the same confidence and certainty of affirmation which attended the prophet speaking prophetically, also attended him as a writer of history. As to that we can only judge by a study of the facts. But the methods pursued in the writing of history were wholly different from those by which at some particular moral crisis the prophet became an organ for conveying the Divine Will. It cannot be said that the writing of history as practised by the Hebrews required, or that as a matter of fact it shows, signs of supernatural intervention. The Hebrew, like the Greek or Roman, made use of previously existing documents or of oral tradition. It is only when he stops to moralize that his true prophetic character comes out; and even then he does not write under the special *afflatus* by which he delivered his message as prophet, but only with the help of reflexion on the principles of the Divine action which by intermittent visitations were made known to him or other members of his order. But nothing could lie nearer at hand than to bracket the different activities of the prophet together, and in fact to bracket together as subject to precisely the same laws all the different activities which went to make up the Sacred Volume.

It is just the same with the New Testament. The preface to St. Luke's Gospel breathes a different spirit from that in which St. Paul wrote his Epistles. In the one authority speaks, in the other a patient collection of testimony. In the one we see the recipient of special revelations, who had been caught up into the third heaven, and who prophesied and spake with tongues more than all his contemporaries; in the other we see plain human care and research, dealing it is true with sacred things, but dealing with them on the side on which they become visible and tangible; setting down faithfully what had been heard and seen, and having its reward—but a reward appropriate to the gifts exercised and not one appropriate to a different set of gifts, to which the writer made no claim.

## VIII. Retrospect and Results.

II. But I began this lecture by saying that the inductive theory needs to be supplemented. How is this? We call the theory 'inductive' because it starts by examining the consciousness of the Biblical writers. It inquires what they say, or what they give us to understand, as to the nature of their own inspiration. It sets out from the mind of the individual writer.

But if we take a wider range, and look at the diversified products of this individual inspiration, and see how they combine together, so as to be no longer detached units but articulated members in a connected and coherent scheme, we must needs feel that there is something more than the individual minds at work; they are subsumed, as it were, in the operation of a larger Mind, that central Intelligence which directs and gives unity and purpose to the scattered movements and driftings of men. So much of these movements has been disclosed to us that we can see in part the objects to which they were tending—not of course the ultimate object, but such stepping-stones towards that ultimate object as history has revealed to us.

In the light so vouchsafed to us, we are no longer confined for our data to the consciousness of the individual writer, but we may take in the tendency of these isolated efforts as gravitating towards a common goal and as forming part of a larger scheme. We may study the operations not only of these individual minds but of the central Mind, and ask if they too have not something to tell us.

Now we have more than once had occasion to observe in the course of our inquiry how certain events which from the point of view of a contemporary must have seemed of very little importance, mere accidents almost as they might be called, which at the time made hardly any difference in the balance of active forces, yet proved in the sequel to have been of immense importance, in fact to have done little less than change the face of the world.

The committing of the prophets' discourses to writing was one such event. For the generation which it addressed the writing was probably less effective than the living speech; but it stereotyped that speech for all future generations; in fact it was the first step in a number of steps which gave to the world the Bible. How little can Amos and Hosea have seen of the significance of what they were doing!

Another event, no less momentous, was when St. Paul called one of his companions to his side to dictate to him what perhaps at first was meant to be a few lines of encouragement to one of the Churches which he had lately founded or recently visited in person. The letters by degrees get longer, and include teaching as well as encouragement, until they grow into elaborate treatises like the Epistle to the Romans. When the Christian remembers that the letters so written form the greater part of his *corpus* of authoritative theology, he cannot help seeing a marked disproportion between the circumstances of its origin and the magnitude of the result. Here too he may see the directing Mind at work with objects within its ken which no one saw of those more immediately concerned, neither writer nor scribes nor readers, nor (we may add) for some time to come those who were entrusted with the custody of the letters when written.

But when once we introduce this Providential disposition of events, we understand other things which apart from it would be dark to us. Take, for instance, that wonderful phenomenon of Messianic Prophecy. It is now seen that it is a mistake to suppose that the prophets who prophesied of the Messiah had definitely before them the Birth of Jesus at Bethlehem, and His Life in Galilee and Judaea, and His Death on Calvary. What they saw was something arising out of, suggested by, the circumstances of their own time, an ideal figure projected into the future, and, as probably they may have thought, the immediate future. No one of the figures thus imagined adequately corresponds to the real Birth and Life and Death of Christ. They need to be combined, and a key by which to combine them has to be sought. How are we to bring together those two parallel lines of prophecy, which exist side by side in the Old Testament but nowhere meet, the ideal King, the descendant of David, and the ideal Prophet, the suffering Servant of Jehovah [1]? What have two such different conceptions in common with each other? They seem to move in different planes, with nothing even to suggest their coalescence. We turn the page which separates the New Testament from the Old. We look at the Figure which is delineated there, and we find in it a marvellous meeting of traits derived from the most different and distant sources, from

[1] *Cf.* Driver, *Sermons*, p. 70.

Nathan, from Amos, from First Isaiah, from Second Isaiah, from Zechariah, from Daniel, from the Second Psalm, from the Twenty-second, from the Sixty-ninth, from the Hundred-and-tenth. And these traits do not meet, as we might expect them to do, in some laboured and artificial compound, but in the sweet and gracious figure of Jesus of Nazareth—King, but not as men count kingship; crowned, but with the crown of thorns; suffering for our redemption, but suffering only that He may reign.

There is yet another direction in which we may see a purpose at work in the Old Testament beyond any that was present to the minds of the writers. One whole book, the Song of Songs, and parts of other books, especially the Psalms, have long been applied in the Christian Church in a sense different from that which was originally intended. Are we called upon to throw over utterly all this secondary application? I think not, so long as we draw a clear distinction in our own minds between this secondary application and the primary. A book means in the strict sense what its writer intended, and nothing more. That is clearly all that we can press in the way of argument. If we go beyond it and are challenged, we have nothing to do but to give way. At the same time there are subtle analogies in things. The spiritual world and the material world are 'double, the one against the other.' Both proceed from the hand of the same Creator, and He has impressed similar laws upon them. Hence it is not an illegitimate process to make use of these analogies, to speak of the spiritual in terms of the not-spiritual, if by so doing spiritual things are brought home more closely to the apprehension. A twofold advantage results from this. Things not spiritual are refined and sanctified by their association with the spiritual, and spiritual things are made more intelligible by their translation into forms which are more level to the common understanding. Imagination has its proper field in religion, and the shapes which it has woven round the sterner realities are both innocent and beautiful, provided that they are not mistaken for something more substantial.

Here then there is added to the conclusions arrived at by strict and rigorous induction a wide expanse in which the devout mind may expatiate, not confining itself to those scientific propositions, which alone can be rightly pressed upon the unbeliever, and which alone the believer can take as his foundation; the devout mind, if it will, may soar above these and either dwell upon the traces of a higher teleology in the ways of Providence, or else delight itself by discovering the relations and affinities between things seen and things unseen. The follower of the older view of inspiration did this with more emphasis and with less caution; but if he clearly recognises the distinction between what can be verified and what cannot be verified, he is not called upon either to abandon all that a pious fancy has accumulated in the past or to desist from the employment of like methods in the future.

III. But now that we have done what we could to define the relations of the inductive theory to the traditional, and to show how even where they differ the former stretches out hands in the direction of the latter, we come at last to a branch of the argument which I have hitherto reserved, from no desire to minimize its importance, the argument from the usage of our Lord and the Apostles. How far does that usage sanction the one theory or the other?

Two preliminary remarks must be made before we attempt to answer this question. The first is, that whatever view our Lord Himself entertained as to the Scriptures of the Old Testament, the record of His words has certainly come down to us through the medium of persons who shared the current views on the subject. We must therefore be prepared for the possibility that His *dicta* in regard to it have not been reported with absolute accuracy. Some allowance should be made for this, but not I think very much allowance. The sayings which bear upon the subject of Inspiration, perhaps with just one or two exceptions, have every appearance of being faithfully preserved [1].

The other observation is, that the sayings on this subject partake, and that in a high degree, in the fragmentariness which is a general characteristic of the Gospels. Nowhere have we direct and express teaching on the Old Testament [2]. Our inferences in

---

[1] See Additional Note A: *On St. Matthew* xii. 40, 41, *and St. John* x. 35.

[2] 'Le Sauveur et les Apôtres ont cité un corps d'Écritures divines, et il ne paraît pas que dans leur enseignement ils aient voulu rien innover en ce qui convenait l'étendue et l'autorité de cette collection.

regard to it have to be pieced together from a number of side-allusions. There are few topics on which we have so much reason to wish that more had been told us. We feel that there is so much more behind the glimpses which are given us. How much easier our task might be, and what precious insight might we have obtained, if only a hint here and a word there had been more fully developed! There are some things which it was the Will of God that we should be left to make out for ourselves, and make out by slow degrees. And the hints which are given to us were not meant to supersede but only to stimulate efforts of our own.

There is the more reason to wish for greater light from the Gospels because the data which they contain do not seem to be all of one kind. They seem to point in different directions; and to the particular question which we have been led to ask they might seem to give different answers. One set of passages seems simply to fall in with the current view, which another set of passages conspicuously transcends.

The acceptance of the traditional estimate appears to be most complete in the region of criticism. It is not possible to point to any anticipation of modern theories in this respect. Moses is repeatedly spoken of

Ni les écrits apostoliques, ni la tradition de l'Église chrétienne ne portent la trace d'une décision expresse rendue par Jésus-Christ ou les Apôtres touchant le canon de l'Ancien Testament, et bien moins encore d'une décision qui aurait formellement rectifié les opinions reçues dans le monde juif' (Loisy, *Canon de l'A. T.* p. 97).

as the author of the Pentateuch [1]. A Psalm is quoted as David's which, whatever its true date, it seems difficult to believe really came from him [2]. The Book of Daniel is assumed to be really the work of the prophet of that name [3],—but this it is right to say is only in one Gospel, where the mention of Daniel may be an insertion of the Evangelist's. The stories of Noah [4] and of Jonah [5] are both referred to as literal history, though with some critical doubt attaching to a part of the last instance. In one passage of peculiar strangeness and difficulty [6] a parenthesis is thrown in which again may proceed from the Evangelist and not from our Lord Himself, 'and the Scripture cannot be broken' (καὶ οὐ δύναται λυθῆναι ἡ γραφή)—which seems to mean that its *dicta*, even where we should naturally take them as figurative, must be true. And to crown all, we have in the Sermon on the Mount that strong assertion, 'Verily I say unto you, Till heaven and earth pass away, one jot or one tittle shall in no wise pass away from the Law, till all things be accomplished. Whosoever therefore shall break one of these least commandments, and shall teach men so, shall be called least in the kingdom of heaven; but whosoever shall do and teach them, he shall be called great in the kingdom of heaven [7].'

---

[1] Matt. xix. 8 (*cf.* Mark x. 3, 5); Mark xii. 26 (=Luke xx. 37); Luke xvi. 29, 31; John v. 45, 46; vii. 19, 22, 23.
[2] Matt. xxii. 43, 45 (=Mark xii. 36, 37, Luke xx. 42, 44); *cf.* Driver, *Introd.*, p. 362 f.    [3] Matt. xxiv. 15.
[4] Matt. xxiv. 37-39 (=Luke xvii. 26, 27).
[5] Matt. xii. 40, 41; xvi. 4 (*cf.* Luke xi. 29, 30).
[6] John x. 34-36.    [7] Matt. v. 18, 19.

And yet on the other hand, almost in the same breath [1] with this affirmation of the inviolability of the Mosaic Law, we have a magisterial succession of new commands, each of them prefaced with a direct antithesis to some older command of like subject-matter: 'Ye have heard that it was said to them of old time . . . but I say unto you [2].' Side by side with the condemnation of those who break one of the least of the legal injunctions, we have a saying which sweeps away not one but a whole class of these injunctions: 'Hear Me all of you, and understand: there is nothing from without the man, that going into him can defile him: but the things which proceed out of the man are those that defile the man.' To which it is added in the correct text of the Second Gospel, 'This He said' [supplied from the preceding verse] 'making all meats clean [3]'; in other words, revoking in one sentence all the elaborate distinctions of clean and unclean contained in the Book of Leviticus. And in reference to another of these Levitical commands it is expressly said that it was given only for a time 'for the hardness of heart' of previous generations [4].

If the Son of Man was Lord over the Sabbath [5], it

---

[1] The critical question must be reserved as to the probability that the second series of sayings was really spoken in close juxtaposition with the first. Many critics treat them as incompatible with each other; but I believe them to be perfectly compatible. The moral laxity which seeks to evade an acknowledged duty is one thing, the deeper view of the nature of that duty is another.

[2] Matt. v. 21, 22; 27, 28; 33, 34; 43, 44.

[3] Mark vii. 14, 15, 19.    [4] Matt. xix. 8.    [5] Mark ii. 28.

## The Sanction of Christ.

is clear that He was Lord not only over the Fourth Commandment but over the whole of the Law, with plenary power to correct and repeal; nay more, with power not only to substitute new commandments for the old, but to substitute Himself as the way of righteousness and of life for the whole body of written law [1].

The key to a great part of the seeming discrepancy lies in the sovereign breadth of view and deep penetration of insight by which the Founder and Master of our faith was enabled to seize the spirit of the Old Testament legislation and to ensure that even the letter (at least of the moral commands) should be observed more effectively than it had been by striking down to the root of motive which the letter could not reach.

It is not only the Law which receives this drastic treatment, but all that is most authoritative in the Old Testament. The love, the sincere heart-felt love of God, and the love of our neighbour; on these two commandments, we are told, 'hang all the Law and the Prophets [2].' Therefore it is that where the love of God and of man are so powerfully reinforced, even in the very act of seeming abrogation, the Law and the Prophets are not abolished but fulfilled. In their essence they receive a new lease of life, and of life more vigorous than they had ever had before.

There is something deeply tragic in the thought that the Jews should have brought about the cruci-

---

[1] Rom. x. 4; John v. 40.  [2] Matt. xxii. 40.

fixion, as a transgressor and enemy of their Law, of Him Who was to cause the world-wide spread and triumph of all that was best in it. Their own fidelity to that Law is a most pathetic spectacle. It was not all mere formalism; and even where it was or is formalism, our Christian formalism is worse, because it involves less severe self-restraint, less sacrifice, and less suffering. But if only God's ancient people had known in that their day the things that belonged unto their peace! If only the eyes of their understanding had been opened to see, that the Law which they cherished was not being destroyed but transmuted, renewed as it were in a higher sphere, putting off the rudiments of the letter to reappear as a world-moving energy of the Spirit! If they could but have understood this, that splendid tenacity of theirs would have had a nobler object and a far richer and grander reward!

The Jews had the two commands[1], of love to God and man, which are simply extracted from their Law, and which it is still within their power to study and to practise. But one thing they cannot have, without taking a step which is harder for them to take. They cannot have the true key to the fulfilment of those commands. They cannot have the help and the repose which flow from the Person of Him Who said, 'Come unto Me, all ye that labour and are heavy laden, and I will give you rest[2].' There it was that they knew not the time of their visitation, and that

---

[1] Deut. vi. 5; Lev. xix. 18.     [2] Matt. xi. 28.

a blindness happened to them in part. Would that it might prove to have been only in part, and that the heart's desire of the Apostle who was driven against his will to turn to the Gentiles might be not too long before it is fulfilled. 'I say then, Did they stumble that they might fall ? God forbid : but by their fall salvation is come to the Gentiles, for to provoke them to jealousy. Now if their fall is the riches of the world, and their loss the riches of the Gentiles, how much more their fulness ? . . . As touching the Gospel, they are enemies for your sake: but as touching the election, they are beloved for the fathers' sake. For the gifts and the calling of God are without repentance [1].'

There is no real difficulty in reconciling the seemingly contradictory sayings in regard to the Law, though we cannot but observe that the procedure of Christ and His Apostles in reference to the Law was more revolutionary than anything that is involved in accepting the lessons of criticism. The question between the observance of the Law in the letter and the spirit was nothing less than a difference of dispensations. The question between a Bible construed critically and a Bible construed uncritically is far more a difference of process than of results. The Voice of God still speaks through it to man, and still speaks the same eternal truths in more intelligible and living tones.

It must however be frankly admitted that even

[1] Rom. xi. 11, 12, 28, 29.

when deductions have been made, as some deductions must be made, on critical grounds, there still remains evidence enough that our Lord while upon earth *did* use the common language of His contemporaries in regard to the Old Testament; that He did speak—if not of Daniel as the author of the book which bears his name, yet of Moses as the author of the Pentateuch, and of David as the author of one of the later Psalms; and that He did apply to His own day some part at least of the story of Jonah and the story of Noah as literal narrative.

What are we to say to this? May we not accept it as a fact, and let it enter simply as an element into our conceptions? Or must we, as some would have us, reverse the whole course of criticism and undo it to the beginning, like Penelope's web?

No doubt we may justly and rightly test the critical processes with all the care and caution we can command. No doubt we may suspend our judgment about them to the last moment. And if we exercise a deliberate delay and reserve in regard to them, that too will be pardonable; it will be only waiting to see how far they stand the test of other minds besides our own. But when the mind is made up, not to a single conclusion here or a single conclusion there, but to a whole network of conclusions which hang together and form a coherent body of thought, it would be an act of violence to the intellectual conscience to arrest the process and suppress its results even at the bidding of the highest authority.

But is there any such bidding? In other words, is

it inconsistent with our Christian belief to suppose that He Who called Himself the Son of Man along with the assumption of human flesh and a human mind should also have assumed the natural workings of such a mind, even in its limitations?

We may consider the question from two points of view, theologically, and (as the ancients would have said) economically, *i.e.* with reference to the methods of revelation.

Theologically I would rather that others should speak, who have approached the subject, not as I have approached it from the Biblical and inductive side, but rather from the side of formulated doctrine. Happily many of those who are best entitled to be heard have spoken. And although it cannot be said that there is complete agreement among them, many of the most reverent and most careful of our theologians, men of the most scrupulous and tender loyalty to the historical decisions both of the Undivided Church and of our own, have pronounced that there is no inconsistency, that limitations of knowledge might be and were assumed along with other limitations by Him Who was in all things made like unto His brethren, though without sin [1].

[1] Compare what is said in *The Oracles of God*, p. 103 (text and note). Since that was written a number of essays and books have appeared the conclusions of which are entirely consistent with the views here put forward. The following may be mentioned:—Mr. Gore, Preface to the 10th edition of *Lux Mundi*, p. xxxii. ff.; *Bampton Lectures* (London, 1891), pp. 147 ff., 267; Dr. Plummer, 'The Advance of Christ in ΣΟΦΙΑ,' *Expositor*, 1891. ii. 1 ff.; Mr. W. S. Swayne, *Our Lord's Knowledge as Man* (with a preface by the

## VIII. Retrospect and Results.

But when it is examined the theological question is found to run up into the economical. The limitations which the Son of God accepted when He became Man all had reference to the purpose of His Incarnation; and we have therefore to consider what came or what did not come within that purpose. I take a judicially weighed and balanced statement by one of the most trusted of my colleagues, Dr. Bright. He writes as follows: 'In regard to this latter point [the function of our Lord as the Prophet and Light of the world], His human mind could receive, through ordinary human media, real accessions of knowledge; even during His ministry He could humanly ask for information on points which in no sense touched His Messianic office; on the very eve of His glorification, He did not humanly "know" the appointed time of His Second Advent. Now it would be a strange inference that because He was in this sense non-cognisant of some matters on which He did not affirm, He was therefore capable of error, and could mislead His hearers, on matters on which He

---

Bishop of Salisbury), London, 1891; Canon Bodington, *Jesus the Christ*, Lichfield, 1892 (this very careful and thoughtful paper was brought to my notice by Dr. Gregory Smith). Mr. De Romestin's '*How knoweth this Man letters?*' (London and Oxford, 1891) is judicial and contains a useful collection of Patristic passages, but can hardly be reckoned as favourable in its results (see p. 43). A line of more decided opposition is taken by Mr. H. E. Clayton, '*The "Advancement" of our Lord's Humanity*' (Oxford, 1891); Mr. W. F. Hobson, *Some Aspects of the Incarnation* (London and Oxford, n.d.); the Bishop of Gloucester and Bristol, *Christus Comprobator* (London, n.d. [1891]).

did affirm. Whatever He explicitly or implicitly *taught*, whether as to the kingdom of God, or the will of the Father, or His own unique claims, or the Scriptures which testified of Him, must have been the expression of a knowledge which flooded His mind with Divine light; He could not, without self-contradiction, have been either peccable as Man or fallible as Teacher [1].'

Here it will be seen that everything turns upon the question, What Christ did *affirm* in the strict sense, what He did deliberately set Himself to teach, what was and what was not included in His Messianic office. Now it may be maintained that all those points on which there may seem to be any collision between the language used by Christ and modern inquiry are not of the nature of direct affirmation or explicit teaching and were in no way essential to His Messianic office, but that they all belong to the presuppositions of His humanity; like the Aramaic or Greek which He spoke with its peculiarities of vocabulary and grammar.

This however is a point on which I wish to enlarge somewhat, because for our present subject and for the particular line of argument which we have been following it seems to me of great importance.

And first, we observe that there is a law running through the whole of Revelation which, after the example of the logicians, we might call perhaps the Law of Parsimony; the law, I mean, that all

---

[1] *The Incarnation as a Motive Power*, p. 300, ed. 2.

revelation is suited to the condition of those who are to receive it, that it starts from the actual circumstances in which they are placed, and that it tells them what is essential for them to know and not really more—for although there may be a latent meaning which comes out in the wider survey of God's purposes, we certainly cannot lay down beforehand how far this meaning shall extend. Even predictive prophecy, which more than any other form of revelation has to do with the future, starts from the present and takes its whole cast and colour from the surroundings of the moment.

This I say is a law of God's Providence in general, and the revelation made to us through Jesus Christ is no exception to it. It is true that this revelation is the culmination of all revelation and that it has a surprising width of range, so as in some respects to look forward not only to our own time but beyond it into dim and distant futurity. But all this wonderful outlook starts from a certain well-defined historical situation. There are certain clearly prescribed limits which it does not overpass. It is as if the Son did not wish to hurry the counsels of the Father, but kept constantly saying, 'My times are in Thy hand.' One great example of this was the restriction of His mission to Israel. All was laid ready for the preaching of the Gospel to the Gentiles; such a Gospel could not help being preached both far and wide; within a generation it was so preached; and yet the three years of our Lord's own ministry were all but strictly confined to Jews, and to Jews of

Palestine [1]. The limitation was tolerated, even though it was so soon to be removed.

May we not discern something like this in other directions? Is there not what we might perhaps call a *neutral zone* among our Lord's sayings? Sayings, I mean, in which He takes up ideas and expressions current at the time and uses without really endorsing them. There were many matters which it was the will of God to have altered some day, but 'the time was not yet.' And the Son entered so far into the mind of the Father as to leave these matters where they were, and to forbear from making any change in regard to them.

Sometimes He does this with a kind of irony, having special reference to the persons with whom He is dealing. For instance, in regard to the very point of which we were just speaking, the restriction of His mission to Israel, He seems on one occasion to express this in terms of the narrowest Jewish particularism. It is in His answer to the Syro-Phoenician woman, ' It is not meet to take the children's bread and cast it to the dogs' (Matt. xv. 26). A severe, and as we might be tempted to think, a harsh and unfeeling answer; and yet it was only meant to prove its recipient, and to call forth an outburst of humble faith on her part, with a flow of love and compassion in return.

Of a kind different, and meant to prove in a different way but yet also meant to prove, was that question to

---

[1] The exceptions would be, the Centurion (Matt. viii. 5 ff.; Luke vii. 2 ff.), the Syro-Phoenician woman (Matt. xv. 21 ff.; Mark vii. 25 ff.), and the Greeks mentioned in John xii. 20 ff.

the Pharisees: 'If David then calleth Him Lord, how is He his Son' (Matt. xxii. 45)? It was not criticism or exegesis that were at issue. The true methods of these might well be left for discovery much later. The Pharisees were taken upon their own ground; and the fallacy of their conclusion was shown on their own premises. All we need say is that our Lord refrained from correcting these premises. They fell within His 'neutral zone.'

Few would hesitate to apply such an explanation to the details of that most graphic parable of the Rich Man and Lazarus. 'And it came to pass that the beggar died, and that he was carried away by the angels into Abraham's bosom: and the rich man also died, and was buried. And in Hades he lifted up his eyes, being in torments, and seeth Abraham afar off, and Lazarus in his bosom. And he cried and said, Father Abraham, have mercy on me, and send Lazarus, that he may dip the tip of his finger in water, and cool my tongue; for I am in anguish in this flame' (Luke xvi. 22–24). What impressive and terrible simplicity, like that of a tale told by the fire-side! But it would surely be a mistake to say that by this parable the Jewish notions of Hades and Abraham's bosom were fixed and made absolute for all time.

But it will be said that anything relating to the Scriptures touched a more central and fundamental point than these. Is that quite so clear? The doctrine of the future state is an important matter. And if the doctrine of Holy Scripture is also important, it must be shown that those details of it which are affected by critical inquiry are really of its essence. After all, the best way to tell what is essential and what is non-essential is to see where erroneous notions have been allowed to prevail as a matter of fact.

I suppose we should all be agreed that the method of allegory as practised by Origen was far in excess of what was right and reasonable. Yet Origen's method deeply influenced his successors and determined the character of a large part of the Patristic exegesis and of that in use throughout the Middle Ages. But can it be said that the difference between a sober and sound exegesis and the more unrestrained kinds of allegory is less than that between the Bible as it is understood ordinarily and by the best critical methods? If it was the will of God to permit so much fantastic and wasted interpretation as there certainly was between Origen and the Reformation, is it not conceivable that He may have allowed wrong ideas to prevail, *e.g.* as to the authorship of certain books, even down to our own day?

If we would but use the argument from Analogy a little more freely I do not think that we should find anything at which we need stumble. After all, the Author of Nature and the Author of Revelation are the same; and we cannot be surprised if we find written small here and there in a corner of Revelation some of the same characteristics which are already written large on the broad page of human history and development. When we think of the immense part which myth and legend and vague approximations at truth have borne in the thought and literatures of early peoples, and how very partial and imperfect history of all kinds has been, and in many of its departments still is, there can be nothing abnormal if similar elements enter to some extent into the Bible.

Of course it is urged that but few other literatures put forward the claim which the Bible puts forward to be a direct communication from God. And there are some who would absolutely deny this claim as made by any other religion, and absolutely affirm it for the Bible. But the one thing which history and criticism do disprove is this idea of absoluteness in all its forms. The methods of God's Providence are not of this character: This all white, that all black; here nothing but light, there nothing but darkness. Even in things evil there is a soul of good; and even upon things good there is a touch of imperfection. The true method by which Divine Providence has worked is indicated in that most pregnant phrase of St. Paul's, 'The purpose of God according to selection' ($\dot{\eta}$ κατ' ἐκλογὴν πρόθεσις τοῦ Θεοῦ). The universal law of the Divine order is 'selection'—not always 'natural selection,' for in the sphere of revelation we believe that the selection is supernatural, or due to more direct Divine action—but everywhere selection. Certain peoples are chosen; and certain classes within those peoples; and certain individuals within those classes, to be in a special sense and for special purposes instruments or organs of the Most High. But this very idea of selection implies also infinite gradation and variety of tone and shade. Every higher phenomenon has its roots in something lower; the superior grows out of the inferior. But they must needs bear some traces of their origin : the plant which is rooted in the earth will of necessity have some earth cling to its roots. So the very grandest and sublimest of Divine revelations have been made through human *media*; and from time to time we are reminded that the *media* are human.

The only question between the very strictest form of the traditional theory and that which has been put forward in these lectures is as to the extent of the human element. And the contention which underlies the whole of the lectures is that the extent of it cannot rightly be determined by any *à priori* methods, by any deduction from such a postulate as that Revelation is a self-communication from God, but only by an inductive and critical inquiry as to the course which that self-communication has as a matter of fact taken.

The results of such an inquiry seem to fit in wonderfully with all that we know from other sources as to the laws of that great Kingdom of God, the plan which is gradually being unfolded of His operation in the universe. Nothing violent, nothing mechanical, nothing really sudden, however much it may appear so, but a long concatenation and subtlest interweaving of causes, all knit together as if in a living organism ; bursting, sprouting, pushing its growth upwards ; first the blade, then the ear, then the full corn in the ear. Truly there is a *scala coeli*, a ladder of ascent for the soul of man ; and though its top is in heaven its foot is on earth, and though its foot is on earth its top is in heaven.

In this vast ascending scale, which seems to stretch

from the one end of the universe to the other, there is a place, a natural and appropriate place, for the history of the idea of Inspiration. If I am right in supposing that the present age will see a transition from the traditional conception to one which is more strictly accurate and scientific, that too would be only in accord with what God has willed to be the method and manner of progress in regard to many other like conceptions. We have seen how the idea of the Bible as the Word of God invested with all the attributes of the Divine Word, arose out of the fact that the different parts of the Bible each contained a number of Words of God with the attributes proper to them. This aggregation of Words and the one Word was not quite the same thing, because in the interstices between the Words there was a considerable human element binding them together[1]. And in the conception of the one Word this human element was apt to be, and was, lost sight of. It could hardly be otherwise, and human things being what they are, it would hardly have been well for it to be otherwise. The idea of the One Word was a plain idea, adapted to the simplest understandings. It secured a proper respect and reverence for those great truths and great commands which were really Divine Words. The larger idea included and protected the narrower. It

---

[1] Yet there was justification for the idea of the One Word in what has been said above (p. 402 ff.) as to the traces of a directing Will or Providence presiding over the whole. We need to realize more completely that human instruments even in their weakness and imperfections can yet be carrying forward a Divine design.

was like what the Rabbis called 'setting up a hedge or fence round the Law.'

It would have been most dangerous at that day to attempt to discriminate between Divine and human. The Divine would have gone with the human; wheat and tares would have been rooted up together. If the authority of the Bible had been broken down upon any one point, it would soon have been broken down upon all. One age can bear what another age cannot; and Divine Wisdom has never put upon any age a burden too great for it.

When the Saviour said, ' I have yet many things to say unto you, but ye cannot bear them now,' we may well believe that these truths which are now coming out about the nature of the Bible were potentially at least included. Nothing that He said or refrained from saying on this subject ought to cause us any difficulty, because it is only a repetition in miniature of the broad outlines of God's Providential working. When we think of it there is really a peculiar fitness and harmony in all the different parts of the Divine operation. It was through the Eternal Word that God made the worlds and impressed upon them that character which they have been unfolding ever since. Yet in some inscrutable way the Divine Omnipotence, if we may say so, limited itself, leaving a place for free-will, and with free-will of necessity also for evil. The Word became incarnate; and then too It voluntarily assumed limitations, limitations strictly in accordance with the plan which Divine Wisdom was working out, and adapted to the conditions of human ignorance and weakness by which Its ministry on earth was to be surrounded. Lastly, there is the Revealed or Written Word; and that again had its limitations, corresponding to the progressive stages of moral development in man through which it was to pass, and of which it was to be the informing principle [1]. It was given 'in divers portions and in divers manners,' with its several parts all conditioned by the time and circumstances in which they appeared, and yet so looking beyond them and so inter-related as to combine to form a Bible or Sacred Book, not only for the generations to which it was given but so long as the moral and spiritual nature of man remains the same. And in like manner as the Word itself varied in the successive stages by which it grew into the complete Volume, so also has the estimate and interpretation of it varied progressively, until there is reserved for us a new stage, which, if one of greater freedom—not than all but than the last of the preceding stages—is yet also we may hope one of greater depth and reality, more fully harmonized and assimilated with the whole body of contemporary thought. Thus we have first the personal Divine Word, the Agent in Creation, by whom the world was formed such as we see it; then we have the same personal Word, Divine and also human, moving amongst men and adapting Itself to them; and thirdly, we have the Written Word, along

---

[1] This comparison of the λόγος ἔνσαρκος and the λόγος γραπτός was suggested to me by Koelling, *Prolegomena zur Lehre von der Theopneustie* (Breslau, 1890), p. 9 ff., where however it is used for a wholly different purpose. The idea is an old one.

with the interpretation of the Written Word; all so many successive expressions or manifestations of the Godhead, yet all partaking of the same character; all revealing the Godhead, not in Its pure unmixed essence, which no man hath seen or can see, but under such qualifications and conditions as make It intelligible by man, and intelligible by man in different ratios according as his own power of understanding develops.

Is there not unity in such a conception? Has it not indeed the best kind of unity, which is not merely *à priori* and metaphysical, but in touch with, or rather growing spontaneously out of, the facts of history? Does it not in particular fall in with that noble conception of Bishop Butler's, which I hope may long be the fundamental conception of English theology, of Christianity as 'a scheme or system imperfectly comprehended'—imperfectly comprehended, and yet so far disclosed as to let us see that it is a scheme, with analogies between its several parts?

I call this a noble conception because of its profound humility. It is often objected to the argument which makes so large a use of analogy that it is 'a *poor* argument,' by which it is meant that it does not have recourse to ideal constructions, that instead of professing to solve the riddles which beset one part of the Divine operation, it contents itself with pointing out that there are like riddles inherent in other parts of the same operation.

Let us admit that this is a poor argument[1], which we

[1] In defending the argument from Analogy I do not of course claim for it that it is either the sole key or the best key, or indeed in

might paraphrase by saying that it is not an ambitious argument, that it does not profess to solve more than it does solve, and that it keeps near the ground of fact and reality. We will leave it to others to strike out the negative from the description of the dealings of God with men as 'a scheme imperfectly comprehended'; we will leave it to others to boast of their superior *gnosis*, and we will be content to say with St. Paul, ' O the depth of the riches both of the wisdom and knowledge of God! how unsearchable are His judgments, and His ways past tracing out [1] !'

There are two classes which will be impatient of the kind of result at which we seem to arrive in these lectures; the classes which are always making play with the dilemma, ' All or Nothing,' and which for themselves take one or other of its two limbs.

One class will have ' All ' of some little system, whether as is most often the case descended from the past, or an invention of the present. This is perfectly clear-cut and sharp in its outlines, and it fits compactly together like a piece of mechanism. With it they drive

itself a key at all, for unlocking the secrets of religion. It assumes the belief in a Central Personal Cause for the phenomena of the universe as a reasonable belief. It assumes that this Central Personality is capable of self-communication or revelation, and that there are certain writings which profess to embody such a revelation. It only steps in to rebut the objections which are taken to these writings as if they were inconsistent with the character of Him from Whom they are said to come. The value of the argument is not direct but indirect, inasmuch as it gives free play to the Bible by permitting us to accept what it tells us about itself, and so opening our hearts to the influences which flow from it.

[1] Rom. xi. 33.

## Conclusion. 429

a straight furrow through the world of phenomena, regarding neither to right nor left, and not heeding what delicate flowers or what subtle interlacing growths their ploughshare overturns and buries.

The other class will have 'Nothing.' 'This argument,' they say, 'breaks down; and that argument breaks down; and there is nothing left except that blank materialism which is the modern version of the old "Let us eat and drink, for to-morrow we die."' Because there is such a thing as error in the Scriptures, because there are prophecies which have not been fulfilled and history which is not strictly accurate, because there are perplexities which are not removed both as to the nature and dealings of God and as to the duty of man, therefore God has not given any revelation of Himself at all; no Voice from the Unseen has ever spoken; no Hand from the Unseen has ever been stretched out; it is pure delusion and self-projection of human fancies from beginning to end.

But there is yet a third class who argue that beliefs which are so widely spread and so deeply rooted, and which have been proved by experience to form such excellent nuclei for other ideas to group themselves round as to the morals of life and conduct, cannot be mere delusion. They go back to the documents and look at them again; and they find that, admitting all that can be said as to mistakes both in the Scriptures themselves and in the early estimate of them, yet the former do not touch any of the essential features of Revelation and the latter does not need any great modification to bring it into accordance with the facts. They find also that there is a multitude of phenomena which point towards the positive reality of Revelation, and which are far better explained on that hypothesis than upon any other. What has come down to us is Revelation, *i.e.* a number of concrete truths contained in written books on the subject of God and religion. And they are truths because these books are the work of inspired men, so that even through the printed page there speaks the Spirit of God.

This is the kind of view which will naturally commend itself to those who have a rooted disbelief in the formula 'All or Nothing,' who think that no such drastic theories can ever correspond to the complexity of phenomena, who do not expect to be able to drive a straight furrow through the world of thought without losing far more than they gain. Those who constitute this class are quite aware that they do not look down upon existence from above with a rigid theory in their hands which they are prepared to impose upon all that is presented to them. They look not down but up, their hearts filled with awe and wonder at the mystery —which is not wholly mystery—around them. They are conscious of 'moving about in worlds not realized' —that is not fully realized, for some firm standing-ground is theirs which is not bare and barren, but rich with flower and fruit and with gleams upon it from heaven.

Such will cling to their Bible; they will clasp it all the more closely to their breasts, because there breathes beneath it a genuine human life, the life of men who though illuminated from on high were yet of like passions with themselves. And if they note how He who is the centre of all this illumination, the Light which lighteth every man, coming into the world, touched gently, or forbore to touch, some of the simpler features in the faith of His contemporaries, they will remember that it was written, 'Blessed is he whosoever shall not be offended in Me.'

## NOTE A.

### On St. Matthew xii. 40, and St. John x. 35.

WHEN we compare the parallel narratives in St. Luke xi. 29-32 and St. Matthew xii. 39-42, the question naturally arises whether the First Evangelist has not mixed up an interpretation of his own with the words as originally spoken. The text of the two Gospels runs thus :—

St. Luke xi. 29–32.

29. Ἡ γενεὰ αὕτη γενεὰ πονηρά ἐστιν· σημεῖον ζητεῖ, καὶ σημεῖον οὐ δοθήσεται αὐτῇ εἰ μὴ τὸ σημεῖον Ἰωνᾶ.

30. Καθὼς γὰρ ἐγένετο Ἰωνᾶς τοῖς Νινευείταις σημεῖον, οὕτως ἔσται καὶ ὁ υἱὸς τοῦ ἀνθρώπου τῇ γενεᾷ ταύτῃ.

. . . .

32. Ἄνδρες Νινευεῖται ἀναστήσονται κρίσει μετὰ τῆς γενεᾶς καὶ κατακρινοῦσιν αὐτήν· ὅτι μετενόησαν εἰς τὸ κήρυγμα Ἰωνᾶ, καὶ ἰδοὺ πλεῖον Ἰωνᾶ ὧδε.

St. Matthew xii. 39–41.

39. Γενεὰ πονηρὰ καὶ μοιχαλὶς σημεῖον ἐπιζητεῖ, καὶ σημεῖον οὐ δοθήσεται αὐτῇ εἰ μὴ τὸ σημεῖον Ἰωνᾶ τοῦ προφήτου.

40. Ὥσπερ γὰρ ἦν Ἰωνᾶς ἐν τῇ κοιλίᾳ τοῦ κήτους τρεῖς ἡμέρας καὶ τρεῖς νύκτας, οὕτως ἔσται ὁ υἱὸς τοῦ ἀνθρώπου ἐν τῇ καρδίᾳ τῆς γῆς τρεῖς ἡμέρας καὶ τρεῖς νύκτας.

41. Ἄνδρες Νινευεῖται ἀναστήσονται ἐν τῇ κρίσει μετὰ τῆς γενεᾶς ταύτης καὶ κατακρινοῦσιν αὐτήν· ὅτι μετενόησαν εἰς τὸ κήρυγμα Ἰωνᾶ, καὶ ἰδοὺ πλεῖον Ἰωνᾶ ὧδε.

It will be seen that the reference in Matt. xii. 40 to the sign of the 'three days in the whale's belly' has nothing to correspond to it in St. Luke; and as the whole context turns on repentance aroused by preaching and in no way upon the

Resurrection, it is highly probable that the allusion to this is a gloss which formed no part of the original saying, but was introduced, very naturally though erroneously, by the author of our present Gospel. It is true that as the repentance of the Ninevites is accepted as historical, the incident of the whale would probably have been treated in the same manner; but in neither case was the presence or absence of historical foundation essential to the application of the narrative as a 'sign.' Our Lord's use of it starts from the way in which it was understood by His hearers: behind this He does not go.

Similarly in St. John x. 34-36, the argument is strictly hypothetical and *ad hominem*. Its object is to show the inconsistency of the Jews' conduct with their own premises, and it does not raise the question how far those premises were justified. The mode of argument is so peculiar and so well suited to the historical situation (it is not an argument which would have occurred to a Gentile Christian, or even to a Jewish Christian who had no personal knowledge of the controversies which gathered round our Lord in His lifetime), that we may be sure that *something like* it really happened. At the same time the memory of this had lain for some sixty years in the mind of one who was himself a thorough Jew, and we cannot be equally certain that it came out precisely as it went in.

# APPENDIX.

## CHRONOLOGICAL TABLE OF DATA FOR THE HISTORY OF THE CANON.

IN constructing the following tables my chief object has been to bring out the fixed points, or those which may be taken as relatively fixed, in the history of the Canon—the pivots, so to speak, on which other points must turn. I have therefore not hesitated simply to abstain from any attempt to indicate the position of certain books (such as the Song of Songs, or Jonah) where I did not feel that I had an opinion which was sufficiently well founded to be worth expressing. The whole of this book, so far as it deals with the Old Testament, aims at representing only so much of the conclusions of criticism as the writer feels that he can honestly and fairly assimilate. There is much on which he waits for further light which must come through the discussions of those who are specially equipped for the study and who can speak with greater authority.

The chronology of the Kings of Israel and Judah is taken from Kittel, *Gesch. d. Hebräer*, ii. 200-206, which in its turn is based upon a monograph by Kamphausen, *Die Chronologie d. Hebr. Könige*, Bonn, 1883. There are several points in the dating of the early Christian writings which must be taken as provisional. In particular the group Barnabas—*Didaché*—Hermas has not, I think, as yet had its place finally determined. The date assigned to Barnabas is Bishop Lightfoot's, which seems to me to satisfy best the conditions of § iv. But to obtain so early a date as this we must assume that Barnabas makes use of an earlier Jewish document, the 'Two Ways,' and not of the *Didaché*. Then comes in the difficulty of the coincidence of *Did.* xvi. 2 with Barn. iv. 9, in regard to which I can see no other way than to suppose with Mr. Vernon Bartlet, in a paper recently read in Oxford, that the subject of this section also belonged to the 'Two Ways.' But this supposition too is not without its difficulties. I must also confess to not being clear as to the date commonly assigned to Hermas. It has not been thought worth while to pursue the traces of use of New Testament Books beyond Origen; and the lists which are given for the fourth century are only a selection; others are easily accessible.

## Chronological Table of Data

#### EVENTS IN GENERAL HISTORY.

|  | B.C. |
|---|---|
| Tell-el-Amarna tablets | 15th cent. |
| The Exodus | c. 1320? |

| | |
|---|---|
| Saul | 1037–1017 |
| David | 1017–977 |
| Solomon | 977–937 |

| Kings of Israel. | B.C. | Kings of Judah. | B.C. |
|---|---|---|---|
| Jeroboam I. | 937–915 | Rehoboam | 937–920 |
| [Invasion of Shishak, 932.] | | | |
| Nadab | 915–914 | Abijam | 920–917 |
| Baasha | 914–890 | Asa | 917–876 |
| Elah | 890–889 | | |
| Zimri | 889 | | |
| Omri | 889–877 | | |
| Ahab | 877–855 | Jehoshaphat | 876–851 |
| Ahaziah | 855–854 | Joram | 851–843 |
| Jehoram | 854–842 | Ahaziah | 843–842 |

[Battle of Karkar (Ahab and Benhadad II or Hadadezer of Syria, with other allied kings, defeated by Shalmaneser II; Assyrian power advancing westwards), 854.]

[The Moabite Stone, c. 850.]

## History of the Canon.

B.C.

Indeterminate element in the Pentateuch derived from Moses, but if committed to writing probably not preserved exactly in its original form.
Song of Deborah.

David's Elegy (2 Sam. i. 19–27), and possibly some Psalms not to be certainly identified.

The Book of the Wars of the Lord.
The Book of Jasher.

Historical material relating to the period of the Judges, Samuel, Saul, and David.
From this time historical records become fairly continuous.

The Book of the Covenant (Ex. xx. 23—xxiii. 33).

# Chronological Table of Data

## EVENTS IN GENERAL HISTORY.

| Kings of Israel. | B.C. | Kings of Judah. | B.C. |
|---|---|---|---|
| Jehu | 842–814 | Athaliah | 842–836 |
| Jehoahaz | 814–797 | Joash | 836–796 |
| Jehoash | 797–781 | Amaziah | 796–78? |
| Jeroboam II | 781–740 | Azariah (Uzziah) | 78?–737 |

[Israel hard pressed by Hazael and Benhadad III of Syria under Jehu and Jehoahaz, but reaches the height of its prosperity under Jeroboam II.]

| | | | |
|---|---|---|---|
| Zechariah | 740 | Jotham (sole ruler) | 737–735 |
| Shallum | 740 | | |
| Menahem | 740–737 | | |
| Pekahiah | 737–735 | | |
| Pekah | 735–733 | Ahaz | 735–715 |
| Hoshea | 733–725 | | |

| | |
|---|---|
| Syro-Ephraimite War | 735–734 |
| Tiglath-Pileser III (= Pul) | 745–727 |
| Shalmaneser IV | 727–722 |
| Fall of Damascus | 732 |
| Fall of Samaria | 722 |
| Hezekiah | 715–686 |
| Manasseh | 686–641 |
| Amon | 641–639 |

| Kings of Egypt. | | Kings of Assyria. | |
|---|---|---|---|
| (Dynasty XXV, Ethiopian.) | | | |
| Sabaco | 728–717 | Sargon | 722–705 |
| Sabataka | 717–705 | Sennacherib | 705–681 |
| Tirhaka | 704–664 | Esarhaddon | 681–669 |
| (Ebers 694–668) | | Assurbanipal (Sardanapalus) | 669–625 |

## History of the Canon.

B.C.

The historical works of the Jehovist (Southern kingdom) and Elohist (Northern kingdom), afterwards incorporated in the Pentateuch, are earlier, and may be considerably earlier, than 760.
[*Some place the prophecy of Obadiah* 848–844, *and that of Joel* 837–817 B.C.]

Prophecies of Amos . . . . . . . *c.* 760
Prophecies of Hosea . . . . . . . *c.* 740
[These prophecies imply if not the actual works of the Jehovist and Elohist at least a conception of the history similar to theirs, and a long previous religious development.]

Prophecies of Isaiah . . . . . . . 737–*c.* 700
[Is. xv, xvi are thought to be older than Isaiah, perhaps older even than Amos, *c.* 780; it is probable that other portions of Is. i–xxxix do not belong to Isaiah.]

Prophecies of Micah.
[Younger contemp. of Isaiah; capp. vi, vii perhaps later, under Manasseh.]
The 'Men of Hezekiah' make a small collection of Proverbs (Prov. xxv. 1).

## Events in General History.

|  | B.C. |
|---|---|
| Merodach-Baladan, King of Babylon 721–710, and at intervals till | c. 694 |
| Sabaco and Hanno of Gaza defeated at Raphia | 720 |
| Great campaign of Sennacherib, defeat of Tirhaka at Altaku and destruction of Sennacherib's army | 701 |
| Invasion of Egypt by Esarhaddon and capture of Memphis | 671 |
| Invasion by Assurbanipal and capture of Thebes | 662 |
| Egypt mainly in Assyrian possession | 671–650 |

### Kings of Judah.

| | |
|---|---|
| Josiah | 639–608 |
| Jehoahaz | 608 |
| Jehoiakim | 608–597 |
| Jehoiachin | 597 |
| Zedekiah | 597–586 |

| Kings of Egypt. (Dynasty XXVI.) | | Kings of Babylon. | |
|---|---|---|---|
| Psammetichus I | 663–610 | Nabopolassar | 625–604 |
| Necho II | 610–595 | Nebuchadnezzar | 604–561 |
| Psammetichus II | 595–588 | Evil-Merodach | 561–560 |
| Hophra (Apries) | 588–569 | Neriglissar | 560–556 |
| Amasis (usurper) | 569–525 | Nabonidus | 556–538 |

| | |
|---|---|
| Inroads of the Scythians (checked by Alyattes, King of Lydia, 617) and break-up of Assyrian power | 625–606 |
| Destruction of Nineveh by Medes and Babylonians | 608 |
| Battle of Megiddo and death of Josiah | 608 |
| Battle of Carchemish and defeat of Necho | 604 |
| Taking of Jerusalem and first deportation | 597 |
| Second siege and destruction of Jerusalem and second deportation | 586 |

## HISTORY OF THE CANON.

B.C.

Prophecy of Nahum . . . . *c.* 624
Prophecy of Zephaniah, before . . 621
Promulgation of main part of Deuteronomy . . . 621
[The influence of this book is strongly marked in the succeeding literature, prophetic and historical: see p. 242 f.]
Prophecy of Habakkuk . . . . . *c.* 608
Prophecies of Jeremiah . . . . . . 627–*c.* 580
[Jeremiah's prophecies are none of them committed to writing until 604.]
Substantial completion of Books of Kings (Cornill) . . *c.* 600

Prophecies of Ezekiel . . . . . . . 592–572

Isaiah xl–lxvi (if, or so far as, by the same hand) 546–538

# Chronological Table of Data

## EVENTS IN GENERAL HISTORY.

### Persian Period.

|  |  | B.C. |
|---|---|---|
| Cyrus, King of Medes and Persians | 550–530 | |
| Cyrus, King of Babylonia | 538–530 | |
| Cambyses | 530–522 | |
| Pseudo-Smerdis | 522–521 | |
| Darius I (Hystaspes) | 521–486 | |
| Xerxes | 486–465 | |
| Artaxerxes I (Longimanus) | | 465–425 |
| Xerxes II } Sogdianos } | | 425 |
| Darius II | | 424–404 |
| Artaxerxes II (Mnemon) | | 404–361 |
| Artaxerxes III (Ochus) | | 361–336 |
| Darius Codomannus | | 336–330 |

| | B.C. |
|---|---|
| Defeat of Croesus and conquest of Lydia | 546 |
| Decree of Cyrus | 537 |
| First return of the Jews | 536 |
| Conquest of Egypt by Cambyses | 525 |
| Rebuilding of the Temple | 520–516 |
| Battle of Marathon | 490 |
| Invasion of Greece by Xerxes | 480–479 |
| Mission of Ezra | 458 |
| Nehemiah appointed governor | 445 |
| Nehemiah's second visit to Jerusalem | 432 |
| Peloponnesian War | 431–404 |
| Battle of Chaeroncia | 338 |
| Accession of Alexander | 336 |
| [Beginning of Samaritan schism soon afterwards.] | |
| Jaddua, high priest | 351–331 |

### Greek Period.

| | B.C. |
|---|---|
| Alexander the Great | 330–323 |
| Battle of Ipsus (defeat of Antigonus and Demetrius) | 301 |
| [Palestine falls to Egypt | 301–198 |
| Palestine falls to Seleucidae | 198–167 |
| Syria to Seleucidae | 301–64] |

N.B.—Seleucid era dates from 312.

## HISTORY OF THE CANON.

| | B.C. |
|---|---|
| Book of Job? | |
| Prophecies of Haggai | 520 |
| Zechariah i–viii | 520–518 |

[Implies portions of both parts of Isaiah, Jeremiah, and Ezekiel.]

Malachi, shortly before 458 (Cornill) or 432 (Driver).

Promulgation of the Pentateuch by Ezra and Nehemiah . . 444

[Must there not be some interval between the composition and the promulgation of this work? It was composed as a Hexateuch, published as Law, *i.e.* as Pentateuch.]

### Canon of the Law.

The Memoirs of Ezra and Nehemiah are the foundation of the present books, which date from about B.C. 300 (see below).

Many of the Psalms were probably composed at this period.

Final collection and arrangement of the Book of Proverbs perhaps also about this time.
If the Book of Jonah belongs to this date it contains reminiscences of a number of Psalms.

| | |
|---|---|
| Chronicles | *c.* 300 |

[Note that Chronicles was originally one work with Ezra and Nehemiah, so that a distinct stage in the history of these books is marked by their separation, as in the Jewish Canon. This was accomplished by B.C. 180.

Note also that Chronicles implies some of the later Psalms: *e.g.* 1 Chron. xvi. 7–36 works up parts of Pss. cv. 1–15, xcvi. 1–13ª, cvi. 1, 47, 48, and 2 Chron. vi. 41, 42 works up parts of Ps. cxxxii (*cf.* Driver, *Introd.* p. 361).

It has been inferred, and the inference denied, that the doxology in 1 Chron. xvi. 36 (= Ps. cvi. 48) proves

## Chronological Table of Data

### Events in General History.

| Kings of Syria. | | Kings of Egypt. | B.C. |
|---|---|---|---|
| Seleucus I (Nicator) | 306–281 | Ptolemy I (Soter) | 306–283 |
| Antiochus I (Soter) | 281–261 | Ptolemy II (Philadelphus) | 285–247 |
| Antiochus II (Theos) | 261–246 | | |
| Seleucus II (Callinicus) | 246–226 | Ptolemy III (Euergetes) | 247–221 |
| Seleucus III (Ceraunus) | 226–222 | Ptolemy IV (Philopator) | 221–205 |
| Antiochus the Great | 222–187 | | |
| | | Ptolemy V (Epiphanes) | 205–181 |

Battle of Raphia (defeat of Antiochus by Ptolemy IV, who retains Palestine) . . . . . . 217
Conquest of Coele-Syria and Palestine by Antiochus . 198–197
Battle of Magnesia (defeat of Antiochus by the Romans) 190

### Succession of Jewish High-Priests.

Onias I (*temp.* Ptolemy I).
Simon I (the Just).
Eleazar, brother of Simon (*temp.* Ptolemy II).
Manasseh, uncle of Eleazar.
Onias II, son of Simon I (*temp.* Ptolemy III).
Simon II, son of Onias II.
Onias III, son of Simon II (*temp.* Seleucus IV and Antiochus Epiphanes).
[The dates cannot be fixed more exactly (Schürer, *Zeitgesch.* i. 140).]

| King of Egypt. | | Kings of Syria. | B.C. |
|---|---|---|---|
| Ptolemy VI (Philometor) | 181–146 | Seleucus IV (Philopator) | 187–175 |
| | | Antiochus IV (Epiphanes) | 175–164 |
| | | Antiochus V (Eupator) | 164–162 |
| | | Demetrius (Soter) | 162–150 |

Desecration of the Temple by Antiochus Epiphanes 168
Persecution . . . . . . . 167–166

## History of the Canon.

that the Chronicler used the complete Psalter in Five Books (*cf.* Cheyne, *B. L.* p. 457; Robertson Smith, *O. T. J. C.* p. 202); but the coincidence is somewhat remarkable.]

B.C.

Canon of the Prophets.     *c.* 250

Ecclesiastes?

Original Book of Ecclesiasticus . . . . . *c.* 180
  [Implies Prophetic Canon; see p. 247 *sup.*]

Numerous copies of the Law in private possession, 1 Macc.
  i. 56–58 . . . . . . . . .  167
  On the question of Maccabaean Psalms, see pp. 256 f., 270 ff.

The Book of Daniel . . . . . . .  *c.* 164
  [Dan. ix. 2 implies Prophetic Canon. The Book of Daniel is itself implied in *Orac. Sibyll.* iii. 396–400, dating about 140 B.C.; see p. 102.]

Greek Version of Ecclus. by the grandson of the author,
  soon after . . . . . . . .  132
  [Prologue implies Canon of Law and Prophets, with beginnings of Canon of *Hagiographa*; *cf.* p. 98 f.]

## Events in General History.

|  | B.C. |
|---|---|
| Victories of Judas Maccabaeus and re-dedication of the Temple | 166–165 |
| Death of Judas | 161 |
| Jonathan Maccabaeus (high-priest, 153) | 158–142 |
| Simon Maccabaeus | 142–135 |
| John Hyrcanus | 135–105 |
| Aristobulus I (king) | 105–104 |
| Alexander Jannaeus | 104–78 |
| Alexandra (Salome) | 78–69 |
| Aristobulus II | 69–63 |
| Hyrcanus II | 63–40 |
| Antigonus | 40–37 |

### Roman Period.

|  |  |
|---|---|
| Taking of Jerusalem by Pompey | 63 |
| [Roman supremacy dates from this time.] | |
| Battle of Pharsalia, followed by death of Pompey | 48 |
| Assassination of Julius Caesar | 44 |
| Defeat of Brutus and Cassius at Philippi | 42 |
| Herod the Great | 37–4 |
| Archelaus | 4 B.C.–6 A.D. |
| Battle of Actium and founding of the Roman Empire | 31 B.C. |
| Rebuilding of Temple by Herod begins | 20–19 B.C. |
| [Completed under Albinus, 62–64 A.D.] | |
| Nativity of our Lord Jesus Christ | 4 B.C. |

### Emperors of Rome.

| | | | A.D. |
|---|---|---|---|
| Augustus | B.C. 31–A.D. 14 | Claudius | 41–54 |
| Tiberius | A.D. 14–37 | Nero | 54–68 |
| Caligula | 37–41 | Galba | 68–69 |

[Nero, *ob.* June 9, 68; Galba, *ob.* Jan. 15, 69; Otho, *ob.* Apr. 17, 69; Vitellius, *ob.* Dec. 4, 69.]

## History of the Canon.

B.C.

First Book of Maccabees . . . . . .    *c.* 100
[Implies Book of Daniel (p. 102 *sup.*), and quotes Ps. lxxix. 2, 3 as Scripture (p. 256).]
We may perhaps place about this time

### The Canon of the Hagiographa.
[Apocryphal additions go on being composed and find their way into the collection, esp. at Alexandria.]
Ecclesiastes quoted as Scripture by Simon ben Shetach (p. 102 *sup.*) . . . . . . . . . 105-79

Psalms of Solomon . . . . . . . . *c.* 63-48

Old Testament systematically expounded by Shemaiah and Abtalion . . . . . . . . . . *c.* 50-40

Hillel expounds Ecclesiastes and puts forth seven rules of interpretation (pp. 81, 82 *sup.*) . . . . . 37-4

A.D.

Writings of Philo imply Jewish Canon, though his conception of Inspiration extends beyond it (p. 93 f. *sup.*), for the most part before . . . . . . 40
Book of Jubilees . . . . . . . . *c.* 50-60
[A Midrash on Genesis.]
Pauline Epistles . . . . . . . . 52-67
Catholic Epistles . . . . . . . . *c.* 57-90
Epistle to Hebrews . . . . . . . *c.* 68
Apocalypse . . . . . . . . . . 69? (or 95?)

## Chronological Table of Data

### Events in General History.
#### Emperors of Rome.

|  | A.D. |  | A.D. |
|---|---|---|---|
| Vespasian | 69–79 | Domitian | 81–96 |
| Titus | 79–81 | | |

| | |
|---|---|
| Herod Philip, Tetrarch of Ituraea, Trachonitis, &c. | 4 B.C.–34 A.D. |
| Herod Antipas, Tetrarch of Galilee and Peraea | 4 B.C.–39 A.D. |

#### Roman Procurators of Judaea.

|  | A.D. |  | A.D. |
|---|---|---|---|
| Coponius | 6–9 | Pontius Pilatus | 26–36 |
| Marcus Ambivius | 9–12 | Marcellus | 36–37 |
| Annius Rufus | 12–15 | Marullus | 37–41 |
| Valerius Gratus | 15–26 | | |

Herod Agrippa I receives from Caligula the tetrarchies of Philip and Lysanias, A.D. 37; to this is added the tetrarchy of Herod Antipas, A.D. 40; King of Judaea . 41–44

Herod Agrippa II . . . . . . . . . 50–100

#### Roman Procurators again, 44–66.

| | | | |
|---|---|---|---|
| Cuspius Fadus | 44–? | Porcius Festus | 60–62 |
| Tiberius Alexander | ?–48 | Albinus | 62–64 |
| Ventidius Cumanus | 48–52 | Gessius Florus | 64–66 |
| Felix | 52–60 | | |

| | |
|---|---|
| Affair of Caligula's statue (Petronius legate of Syria.) | 40 |
| Outbreak of the Jewish War | 66 |
| Subjugation of Galilee | 67 |
| Internal strife in Jerusalem | 67–69 |
| Siege of Jerusalem by Titus from shortly before Passover to Sept. 8 | 70 |
| Destruction of the Temple, 9, 10 Ab (August) | 70 |
| Conclusion of the War | 70–73 |

## HISTORY OF THE CANON.

|  | A.D. |
|---|---|
| Composition of Synoptic Gospels in stages spread over the years | 60-80 |
| [Perhaps beginning earlier.] | |

Acts . . . . . . . . . .     *c.* 80

Gospel of St. John. . . . . . . .     *c.* 90
[The New Testament implies the Jewish Canon with full conception of Inspiration, but also bears traces of some use of Apocrypha.]

Josephus, *Antiq.* and *Contr. Apion.* . . . . .     *c.* 94
[Reckons 22 Books of Jewish Canon, with full conception of Inspiration, which however extends beyond these books.]

4 Ezra, after . . . . . . . . .     70
[Implies twenty-four Canonical Books of the Old Testament, with others which are also inspired.]

Epistle of Barnabas . . . . . . .     70-79?
[Quotes Matthew, or possibly some earlier Synoptic document, as Scripture.]

Clem. Rom. *ad Cor.* . . . . . . .     *c.* 97
[Uses some Synoptic matter, 1 Corinthians by name, Romans, Hebrews certainly, Ephesians, 1 Peter, James possibly; Old Testament with Apocrypha.]

## Chronological Table of Data

### Events in General History.

*Rabbinic Succession.*

|  | B.C. |
|---|---|
| The Five Pairs dating from (Schürer, *Zeitgesch.* ii. 293) | c. 150 |
| Simon ben Shetach | c. 90–70 |
| Shemaiah and Abtalion (perhaps = Polio and Sameas) | c. 50–20 |
| Hillel and Shammai | c. 37–4 |

|  | A.D. |
|---|---|
| Gamaliel I | c. 30–40 |
| Hananiah ben Hezekiah | c. 50–60 |
| Simon ben Gamaliel | c. 60–70 |

*School of Jamnia, A.D. 70–135.*

| Johanan ben Zakkai | *fl.* c. 70–90 |
|---|---|
| Gamaliel II, Eliezer ben Hyrkanos, Joshua ben Hananiah | c. 90–110 |
| Eleazar of Modiim, Eleazar ben Azariah. | |
| Ishmael ben Elisha (locally separate from the School of Jamnia and opposed to Akiba) | c. 100–120 |
| Akiba | c. 100–135 |
| The second Jewish War under Bar-Cochba | 132–135 |
| Formation of the Mishna, esp. by the Patriarch Jehuda I (Rabbi) carrying on the work of Akiba, completed | c. 220 |

[The leading Rabbis of the earlier period, from Hillel, are called *Tannaim*, those of the later period to the completion of the Talmud *Amoraim*.]

| Jerusalem Talmud finished c. 425, Babylonian | c. 500 |
|---|---|

*Roman Emperors.*

| Nerva | 96–98 |
|---|---|
| Trajan | 98–117 |
| Hadrian | 117–138 |
| Antoninus Pius | 138–161 |

## History of the Canon.

|  | A.D. |
|---|---|
| Rabbinical discussions at Jamnia, resulting in full ratification of the Jewish Canon . . . . . . | 70–130 |
| Διδαχὴ τῶν ιβ´ ἀποστόλων . . . . . . . | c. 100–110 |

[Uses some Synoptic and Johannean matter.]

| Collection of Pauline Epistles, before . . | 117 |
|---|---|
| Ignatius, *Epistles*, before. . . . . . . | 117? |

[Uses some Synoptic and Johannean matter (perhaps Matthew, John), 1 Corinthians, Galatians, Ephesians, Colossians, 1 Timothy, Titus.]

Polycarp, *Ep. ad Phil.* (soon after Ignat. *Epp.*).
[Uses Synoptic matter, 1 Corinthians (as St. Paul's), Ephesians (perhaps as Scripture), also clearly Romans, Galatians, Philippians, 2 Thessalonians, 1 and 2 Timothy, 1 Peter, 1 John, Acts.]

| Papias makes express statements respecting λόγια of St. Matthew and Notes of St. Peter's Teaching put together by St. Mark; also used 1 Peter, 1 John | c. 125–130 |
|---|---|
| Apocryphal Gospel of Peter . . . . . | c. 125–130 |

[Probably based on Four Canonical Gospels, see p. 310 f., *sup.*]

| Basilides . . . . . . . . . | c. 130 |
|---|---|

[Probably himself used Luke, John; see p. 307 *sup.*]

| Massoretic Text of O.T. dates from . . . | c. 135 |
|---|---|
| 'Presbyters' quoted by Irenaeus . . . . | c. 140–160 |

Expound Ev. Jo., Epp. Paul., and recognise Apocalypse.

| Ποιμήν of Hermas . . . . . . . | c. 140? |
|---|---|

[Perhaps implies Four Gospels, also 1 Corinthians, Hebrews, James, Old Testament Apocrypha.]

| Marcion . . . . . . . . . | c. 140 |
|---|---|

[Acknowledges Luke, and ten Epp. Paul.]

| Writings of Justin Martyr . . c. 150–165 or perhaps 138–165 |
|---|

[Use Four Gospels + Ev. Pet. and Apocalypse by name.]

## Chronological Table of Data

### Events in General History.

A.D.

M. Aurelius . . . . . . . . . 161–180

Commodus . . . . . . . . 180–192

Dynasty of Severus . . . . . . 193–235

Period of disturbance and dissolution . . . . 235–268
  [Persecutions under Decius, 250, 251; under Valerian, 257, 258.]

## History of the Canon.

|  | A.D. |
|---|---|
| Clem. Rom. *Ep. II* (Pseudepigraphal Homily) . | *c.* 150 |
| [Quotes Synopt. and Apocr. Gospels.] | |
| Tatian, *Diatessaron* . . . . . . . | *c.* 170 |
| [Harmony of Four Gospels.] | |
| Ptolemaeus } . . . . . . . . | *c.* 170 |
| Heracleon } | |
| [Use freely Four Gospels and Epp. Paul.; Heracleon writes allegorical commentary on St. John.] | |
| Melito . . . . . . . . . . | *c.* 170 |
| Makes list of twenty-two Books of Old Testament (implying conception of New Testament) and comments on Apocalypse.] | |
| Athenagoras . . . . . . . . . | *c.* 177 |
| [Evv., Romans, 1 and 2 Corinthians, Galatians, 1 Timothy.] | |
| *Ep. Eccles. Vienn. et Lugd.* . . . . . . | *c.* 177 |
| [Luke, John, Acts, Epp. Paul., 1 Peter, Apocalypse.] | |
| Theophilus of Antioch . . . . . . . | *c.* 181 |
| [Quotes St. John by name and as inspired, also Matthew as Scripture, Epp. Paul. (including Past.), Hebrews, 1 Peter.] | |
| Irenaeus . . . . . . . . . . | *c.* 180–190 |
| [Quotes, mostly by name and as Scripture, Four Gospels, Acts, twelve Epp. Paul., 1 Peter, 1 and 2 John, Apocalypse.] | |
| Clement of Alexandria . . . . . . . | *c.* 190–210 |
| [= Irenaeus with addition of Jude, and some Apocrypha —with a distinction.] | |
| Muratorian Fragment . . . . . . . | *c.* 200 |
| [Four Gospels, Acts, thirteen Epp. Paul., 1 and 2 John, Jude, Apocalypse, to which some add Apoc. Petr.] | |
| **Provisional Canon of New Testament** . . | 200 |
| Includes Four Gospels, Acts, thirteen Epp. Paul., and (except in Syria) 1 Peter, 1 John. | |
| Tertullian . . . . . . . . . | *c.* 194–221 |
| [Adds to the above Jude, Apocalypse, Hebrews as work of Barnabas.] | |
| Hippolytus . . . . . . . . . | *c.* 200–235 |
| [Adds Apocalypse, not Hebrews.] | |
| Julius Africanus . . . . . . . . | *c.* 240 |
| [Maintains stricter Jewish Canon against LXX additions.] | |

## Events in General History.

A.D.

The Illyrian Emperors . . . . . . . 268–283
[Recovery of the Empire.]
Diocletian and his colleagues, with their successors . . 283–323
[The Great Persecution, 303–313.]
Constantine sole emperor . . . . . . 323–337
[Council of Nicaea, 325.]

Sons of Constantine (Constantine to 340, Constans to 350,
    Constantius to 361) . . . . . . . 337–361

Julian . . . . . . . . . . 361–363
Jovian . . . . . . . . . . 363–364
Valens 364–378, Valentinian I and his sons . . . 364–392

Theodosius . . . . . . . . . 379–395
Arcadius 395–408, Honorius . . . . . . 395–423

## History of the Canon.

| | A.D. |
|---|---|
| Origen . . . . . . . . . | 185-253 |

[Has complete Canon of Old and New Testaments, the Twelve Minor Prophets being omitted, probably by accident, and doubts noted as to 2 Peter, and 2 and 3 John. Origen's list of books corresponds to the Hebrew Canon, though he defends the use of LXX additions.]

Eusebius . . . . . . . . .     *c.* 324

[Classes Four Gospels, Acts, Epp. Paul., 1 John, 1 Peter as acknowledged; James, Jude, 2 Peter, 2 and 3 John as disputed by a minority; Apocalypse as wavering between complete acceptance and rejection.]

Cyril of Jerusalem . . . . . . . .     *c.* 348
[Complete Canon, except Apocalypse.]

Mommsen's List . . . . . . . .     *c.* 359
[Complete Canon except James, Jude, and note of doubt as to 2 Peter, 2 and 3 John.]

Council of Laodicea . . . . . . .     *c.* 363
[Complete Canon, except Apocalypse.]

Athanasius . . . . . . . .     367
[Complete Canon.]

Amphilochius of Iconium. . . . . . .     *c.* 380
[Complete Canon of Old Testament, Epp. Cath. three or seven, Apocalypse omitted.]

Gregory Nazianzen, before . . . . . .     391
[Complete Canon, except Apocalypse.]

Epiphanius, before . . . . . . . .     403
[Complete Canon.]

Council of Carthage III . . . . . .     397
[Complete Canon.]

Council of Carthage IV . . . . . . .     419
[Ratifies list of previous Council.]

The Syrian Canon at this date, however, still recognises only three Epp. Cath. (Chrysostom) or two (Theodore of Mopsuestia).

Quinisextine or Trullan Council . . . . .     692
Sanctions previous lists (see pp. 6 f., 59 *sup.*).
[For other lists reference may be made to works on the Canon, or *Stud. Bibl.* iii. 227 ff., 254 ff.]

# INDEX.

[References are given to the names of living or recent writers only where they are introduced with some comment, and in cases of special indebtedness.]

Abbott, Dr. Edwin A., p. 385.
— Dr. T. K., 310.
Abtalion, 81, 447, 450.
Acts of the Apostles, 12, 17 f., 66 f., 265, 278, 318 ff., 339, 449, 451, 453, 455; Commentaries on the, 319; Criticism of the, 320 ff.
Addis, Mr. W. E., 134, 234.
Africanus, Julius, 92, 105, 453.
Age, The Apostolic, 321 ff., 327 f., 331 ff.; The Subapostolic, 14, 298 ff., 360 ff.
Akiba, 90, 108 f., 450.
Alexander, bp. of Jerusalem, 9.
*Alexandrinus, Cod.*, 11.
Allegory, 39, 68 f., 79 f., 405 f., 421.
Alogi, The, 14 f., 55, 369.
*Amoraim*, 450.
Amos, 155, 227, 229 ff., 403, 439; Book of, 118, 143, 229 f., 405, 439.
Amphilochius, 7, 92, 455.
Analogy, Argument from, 421 ff., 425 ff.
Anonymous writings, 240 f., 379.
Apocalypse, The, 8 f., 23 f., 27, 369 ff., 379 f., 447, 451, 453, 455; Inspiration of the, 375 ff.
— of Peter, 347, 384.
Apocalypses, Apocryphal, 27, 91, 107, 347.
Apocalyptic, 375.
Apocrypha of the N. T., 27 f., 451, 453; of the O. T., 91 ff., 447, 451.
Apocryphal, Double sense of the word, 106 ff.
Apostles, Authority of the, 48 ff., 67, 305, 354, 358 f., 362, 366, 379 ff.; Memoirs of the, 304 ff.
Apostolic authorship, 47 ff.

Archelaus, bp. of Caschara, 36.
Aristeas (Pseudo-), 86.
Arnold, Matthew, 153.
Article, The Sixth, 258, 348.
Athanasius, 8, 92, 113, 455.
Athenagoras, 453.
Augustine, 6 f., 46, 51 f.
ἅγιος, 28, 73, 289.
ἀδελφός, 289.
ἀνθρώπινον λέγω, 354.

*Baba Bathra*: see 'Talmud.'
Bacher, Dr. W., 81 f.
Bäthgen, Dr. F., 256.
Balaam, 77, 131, 139, 268.
Ball, Mr. C. J., 261.
Barnabas, Epistle of, 27, 301, 379, 449.
Baruch, 237 ff.; Apocalyse of, 91, 284; Epistle of, 335.
Basil, 368.
Basilides, 38, 308, 451.
Baudissin, Graf von, 121.
Bel and the Dragon, 262.
Bennett, Mr. E. N., 311, 313.
Bevan, Prof. A. A., 215.
Bible: *see* 'Canon,' 'New Testament,' 'Old Testament,' 'Scriptures,' &c.; Beginnings of the, 226 ff.
Blunt, Dr. J. J., 325.
Bodington, Canon, 416.
Book-production, Modes of, 157, 297.
Briggs, Dr. C. A., 191.
Bright, Dr. W., 416 f.
Budde, Dr. K., 270.
Buhl, Dr. F., xi, 102, 107 f., 121.
Butler, Bp., 370.
βιβλία, βίβλοι, 28, 72, 73.

## Index. 457

Caius, 15.
Callistus, 53.
Campe, Dr. W., 243.
Canon: see 'Bible,' 'Inspiration,' 'New Testament,' 'Old Testament,' 'Scriptures'; also *Hagiographa*, 'Law,' 'Prophets,' &c.; Conception of a, 4 f., 71, 234, 393; The Jewish, 92, 96 ff., 257 f., 447, 449, 451, 453; Divisions of the Jewish, 98 ff.; Eastern, 8, 257, 366; Western, 8, 257, 366; The Alexandrian, 91 ff.; The Palestinian, 91 ff.; The *maximum*, 257 ff.; The *minimum*, 257 ff.; Roman Catholic view of the, 257 f., 273 ff.; Lutheran view of the, 257.
Canons, The Apostolic, 7.
Carthage, Councils of: see 'Councils.'
Catechesis, 300, 302 f.
Catholic Epistles (*see* 'James, Epistle of,' &c.), 8 f., 10, 56, 344 ff., 358 ff., 366 ff., 379 ff., 447; Collection of the, 8 f.
Catholicity, 53 ff.
Cheyne, Dr. T. K., 116, 121, 190, 195, 198 f., 243, 355.
Chiliasm, 64.
'Christ,' The name, 289.
Chronicles, Books of, 102, 163, 244, 253 ff., 398, 443, 445.
Chrysostom, 10, 389 f., 455.
Church, Dean, 198.
Churches, Reception by the, 51, 368 f.
Circumcision, Controversy on, 323.
Clayton, Mr. H. E., 416.
Clemen, Dr. C., 278, 327, 329.
Clement of Alexandria, 17, 21, 26, 28 f., 31 ff., 37 ff., 49, 53, 65 ff., 299, 315, 382, 453.
Clement of Rome, First Epistle of, 27, 50, 299 ff., 340, 361, 365, 380, 386, 449; Second Epistle of (so-called), 17, 27, 453.
Colossians, Epistle to the, 337 f., 342, 360, 451.
*Computus de Pascha*, 35.
Constantine, The Emperor, 33.
Cooke, Mr. G. A., 235.
Corinth, Church of, 361.
Corinthians, Epistles to the, 332, 340, 342, 350, 352 ff., 357 f., 387 ff., 451, 453.

Cornill, Dr. C. H., xi, 101, 159, 201, 210, 242, 443.
Cosmas Indicopleustes, 11.
Councils, 6 f.; of Carthage, iii, 6 f., 60, 455; of Carthage, iv, 6, 8, 59, 455; of Laodicea, 7, 60 f., 455; Quinisextine or Trullan, 6, 59, 455; of Trent, 274 ff.; Vatican, 274.
Covenant, Book of the, 180 ff., 233 f., 437.
Criticism, Modern, 2, 115 ff., 408 f., 413.
Cultus: see 'Law, The ceremonial.'
Cyprian, 29 f.
Cyril of Jerusalem, 8, 92, 113, 455.
χρησμός (*see* 'Mantic'), 72, 75.

Daniel, Book of, 85, 100, 102, 143, 215 ff., 247, 253 ff., 377, 409, 414, 445, 447.
Darmesteter, M. James, 152.
Davidson, Dr. A. B., 118, 199, 201, 205, 230.
*De Aleatoribus*, 20.
Deborah, Song of, 229, 235, 437.
'Defile the hands,' 78, 111.
Demetrius, bp. of Alexandria, 53.
Deuterocanonical, Conception implied by the term, 261, 273 ff.; Inspiration, 259 ff.
Deuteronomic Code, Promulgation of the, 121, 231 ff.
Deuteronomy, Book of, 121, 170, 177, 236, 242 f., 245, 376, 441.
Development, 14, 205, 340, 395.
*De Vita Contemplativa*, 99.
*Diatessaron*, The, 302, 307.
*Didaché*, The, 27, 301 f., 379, 451.
Dienstfertig, Dr. M., 73, 76 f.
Dillmann, Dr. A., 121.
Dionysius of Alexandria, 36.
Dionysius of Corinth, 361.
Disciples, 239; Synonyms for the name, 288.
Distinctions, Method of, 269.
Docetism, 313 f.
Dreams, 131.
Driver, Dr. S. R., xi, 87, 116 f., 139, 199, 201, 215, 230, 234, 243, 256, 443.
Drummond, Dr. James, 308.
Duhm, Dr. B., 101, 242.
*deificus*, 29.
*divinus*, 29.
διαθήκη, 30, 65 f.

Ebed Jesu, 11.
Ecclesiastes, Book of, 82, 97, 102 f., 208 ff., 253 ff., 258; Inspiration of, 208, 249, 398, 445, 447.
Ecclesiasticus, Book of, 94, 98 f., 168, 247, 254 f., 259 ff., 386, 445.
Ecstasy, 74 f., 131.
Edersheim, Dr. A., 114 f.
Egyptians, Gospel according to the, 27.
Eichhorn, J. G., 72.
Eleazar ben Azariah, 450.
Eleazar of Modiim, 450.
Election (or Selection), The principle of, 126, 140, 163, 422 f.
Eliezer ben Hyrkanos, 82.
Elijah, 227, 231.
Elisha, 227.
Ellicott, Bp., 119, 416.
Elohist, 158 f., 439.
Elohistic redaction of Psalms, 271.
Emperors, Worship of the, 377.
Engelhardt, Dr. M. von, 301.
Enoch, Book of, 91.
Ephesians, Epistle to the, 19, 337 f., 342, 363, 379 f., 453.
Ephod, 132, 143.
Epiphanius, 8, 64, 104, 113, 455.
Epistles, The Canonical (*see also* 'Catholic Epistles,' 'Paul, Epistles of St.'), 334 ff., 359 ff.
Esdras, Books of, 262 f.
Esoteric, 107.
Esther, Book of, 82, 97 f., 213 f., 222 f., 254, 262, 398.
Ethnic Religions, 126 ff., 139 f., 179, 201 f., 395.
Eusebius of Caesarea, 33, 46, 51, 293, 455.
*Excerpta Theodoti*, 308.
Exegesis, 39 ff., 80 ff., 85 ff.
Exile, Influence of the, 244 f.
Exodus, Book of, 164, 176, 180 ff.
Extensions, Principle of, 264 ff., 400 f.
Ezekiel, 177, 243; Book of, 97, 103, 242, 247, 441, 443.
Ezra, 101, 235, 246; Book of, 96, 164, 253, 262, 265 f., 443; Fourth Book of, 91, 106 f., 113, 449.
ἐκκλησιαστικός (*ecclesiasticus*), 52 f.
ἐνθουσιᾶν, 75.
ἐπιθειάζειν, 75.
εὐαγγέλιον, 317 (*cf.* 304, 306).

Fairbairn, Dr. A. M., 125, 198.
Farrar, Archdeacon F. W., 373, 385.
Feine, Dr. P., 319.
First Century, 71 f.
Fourth Century, 6 ff.
Future State, Doctrine of the, 420.

Galatians, Epistle to the, 83, 336, 340, 350 f., 357, 451, 453.
Gamaliel I, 450.
Gamaliel II, 450.
Genesis, Book of, 164, 170, 221 f.
Gnosticism, 13, 15, 62, 64.
God, Idea of, 124 ff., 152 ff., 394.
Godet, Dr. F., 339.
Gore, Mr. C., 415.
Gospels: *see* 'New Testament,' 'Scriptures,' 'Matthew, Gospel of St.,' &c.; The Four Canonical, 12, 14 ff., 36, 277 ff., 303 ff., 307 ff., 449, 451, 453, 455; Uncanonical, 27, 290, 300, 310 ff., 453; Precanonical, 279 ff., 300, 303 f., 449, 451; Criticism of the, 281 ff.; Harmony of the, 301 f., 453; Text of the, 295 ff.; Inspiration of the, 298, 316 ff.; History of the name, 304, 306, 316 f.
Grafe, Dr. E., 94.
Gregory Nazianzen, 8, 92, 455.
Gregory Nyssen, 368.
Gwynn, Dr. J., 10.
γράμματα, 28, 73.
γραφή, 28 f., 67, 72 f.

Habakkuk, Prophecy of, 441.
Hackett, Dr. H. B., 319.
Haggai, Prophecies of, 443.
*Hagiographa* (*see also* 'Psalms,' 'Job,' &c.), 188 ff., 247 ff.; Canon of the, 100 ff., 253, 445, 447; Inspiration of the, 189 ff., 207, 249.
Hananiah ben Hezekiah, 97, 450.
Harclean Version, 10.
Harnack, Dr. A., xi, 12 ff., 18, 20 f., 28, 61 ff., 64 ff., 311 ff., 364, 370, 379 ff.
Harris, Prof. J. Rendel, 296, 301.
Headlam, Mr. A. C., xiii, 188, 305.
Heathen: *see* 'Ethnic.'
Hebrew language, 256.
Hebrews, Epistle to the, 23 ff., 27, 51, 106, 287, 340 f., 379 f., 447, 451, 453; Gospel according to the, 27, 307.

*Index.* 459

Heracleon, 37, 39, 267, 307 f., 453.
Hermas, 26 f., 309 f., 380, 451.
Hezekiah, Men of, 247 f., 439.
Hilary of Poitiers, 113.
Hilkiah, 121, 180.
Hillel, 78, 81 f., 97, 103, 447, 450.
Hippolytus, 27, 29 f., 33, 53, 308, 453.
Historical Books, 155 ff., 399 ff.; Inspiration of the, 162 ff.
Hitzig, Dr. F., 243.
Hobson, Mr. W. F., 416.
Holtzmann, Dr. H. J., xi, 278, 293, 300, 310, 363 f., 385.
Hooker, Richard, 209.
Hort, Dr. F. J. A., 19, 41, 324, 338, 343, 347.
Hosea, 155, 227, 229 f., 403; Book of, 118, 229 f.
Huxley, Prof. T. H., 129, 181.

Ignatius, 50, 362, 365 f.; Epistles of, 50, 301, 362 ff., 386, 451.
Immortality, Doctrine of, 205.
Individual scholars, Influence of, 8, 53.
Inspiration: *see* 'Canon,' 'Scriptures,' 'Spirit,' 'New (Old) Testament,' 'Gospels,' 'Law,' 'Prophets,' &c.; Conception of, 31 ff., 74 ff., 263 ff., (see also the different 'Views of' below); Psychology of, 127 f., 144, 146 f., 355 ff.; Postulates of the doctrine of, 124 ff.; proceeds from the Holy Spirit, 31 ff., 127, 333 f.; proceeds from Christ, 33; Degrees of, 42 ff., 259, 350, 357 f., 385 ff., 397 f.; Criteria of, 47 ff., 110 ff., 260; of Apocrypha, 359 ff. (cp. 386); Formative period of doctrine of, 3; Verbal, 34 ff., 85 ff., 303, 306, 313 f.; Philo's view of, 72 ff., 84, 93 f., 447; New Testament view of, 76 f., 83, 87 ff., 407 ff., 449; Josephus' view of, 76 f., 84 f., 89 f., 110 f., 449; Traditional view of, 391 ff., 399 ff.; Inductive or critical view of, 391 ff., 399 ff.
Interpolation, 159, 342 f., 379 ff., 409.
Irenaeus, 12, 33 ff., 38, 41 f., 49, 53, 56 f., 115, 309, 315, 371, 387, 453.
Irony of Christ, 419.
Isaiah, 84, 106, 155, 179, 239, 241;
Book of, 84, 103, 137, 170, 241 f., 247, 405, 439; Second, 164, 405, 441, 443.
Ishmael ben Elisha, 82, 450.
ἱεραί (γραφαί, βίβλοι, &c.), 28, 72 f.
ἱεροφαντεῖν, ἱεροφάντης, 72, 75.

James, Mr. M. R., 347.
James, St., 8, 359, 381; Epistle of (see also 'Catholic Epistles'), 9, 23 ff., 344 ff., 359, 366, 379, 381, 451, 453, 455; Terminology of, 287.
Jamnia, School of, 71, 82, 93, 96 ff., 107 ff., 123, 451.
Jasher, Book of, 229, 437.
Jehoiakim, 238.
Jehovist, 158 f., 163, 439.
Jeremiah, 84, 155, 177, 180, 237 ff., 242 f.; Book of, 96, 103, 113, 142, 164, 237 ff., 245 f., 247, 441, 443; Epistle of, 335.
Jerome, 43 f., 47, 51, 92, 100, 113, 214 f., 230, 383.
Jerusalem, Church of, 9; Fall of, 279, 283 ff., 291 ff., 370, 374.
Jesus Christ, Use of the Old Testament by, 407 ff., 414 ff.; Teaching of, 417 ff.; Irony of, 419.
Joash, 232 f.
Job, Book of, 102, 204 ff., 243, 443; Inspiration of the, 206 f.
Joel, Book of, 229, 439.
Johanan ben Zakkai, 82, 450.
John, St., 67, 359; Writings of, 14 ff.; Gospel of (see also ' Gospels, Four Canonical '), 14 ff., 83, 203, 265, 287, 289 f., 294, 307 ff., 311, 379 f., 433, 449, 451, 453; First Epistle of, 9, 11, 359, 366, 451, 453, 455; Second Epistle of, 25, 453, 455; Third Epistle of, 25, 368, 455; Terminology of, 287.
Jonah, Book of, 97, 137, 409, 414, 443.
Josephus, 72, 76 ff., 84 f., 89 f., 94, 100, 113 f., 267, 278, 383, 449.
Joshua, 243.
Joshua ben Hananiah, 450.
Josiah, 121, 232.
Jubilees, Book of, 91.
Judaism, Hellenistic, 91, 95, 321 f.; The later, 185, 255, 411 ff.
Jude, St., 359, 381; Epistle of, 26, 359, 379 ff., 382 ff., 453, 455.

Judges, Book of, 96, 113, 229, 243.
Judith, Book of, 254 f.
Junilius, 10.
Justin Martyr, 12 f., 50, 301, 304 ff., 451.

Kamphausen, Dr. A., 215.
Keim, Dr. Th., 278.
*Kethubim: see Hagiographa.*
King, The ideal, 404.
'Kingdom of God' (or 'of heaven'), The phrase, 288.
Kings, Books of, 96, 104, 155, 164, 201, 229, 243, 265.
Kirkpatrick, Dr. A. F., 229, 266.
Kittel, Dr. R., 121.
Klöpper, Dr. A., 338.
Knowling, Mr. R. J., 303, 337.
Köhler, Dr. A., 138.
König, Dr. E., xi, 106, 130, 138, 141 f., 146, 256.
*Koheleth: see* 'Ecclesiastes.'
Kuenen, Dr. A., 101, 116 ff., 249.
Kuhn, Dr. G., 364.
κατὰ ἄνθρωπον λέγω, 354.

Lagarde, Dr. P. de, 92, 101.
Lamentations, Book of, 96, 112, 253.
Laodicea, Epistle to, 360; Council of, *see* 'Councils.'
Law: *see* 'Pentateuch'; Jewish estimate of the, 168 ff.; Christian estimate of the, 170 f.; Critical estimate of the, 171 f.; Origin of the, 178 f.; Religious Character of the, 180; Humanity of the, 181 f.; The ceremonial, 182 ff.; Written, 231 ff.; Reading of the, 244 ff.; Promulgation of the, 227, 231 f., 443; Stages in the history of the, 235 f.; Abrogation of the, 410 f.; Canon of the, 100 f., 170, 228, 236, 246; Inspiration of the, 173 ff., 183 ff., 264 ff., 396; Use of the term, 170.
Lazarus, Parable of, 420.
Lechler, Dr. G. V., 344.
Leontius, 113.
Leucius Charinus, 27.
Libraries, Influence of, 9.
Lightfoot, Bp. J. B., 278, 300, 319, 329, 345, 370, 373.
Lock, Mr. Walter, xiii, 56, 222 f.
Lods, Mons. A., 313.

*Logia*, The, 281, 300, 304.
*Logos*, The, 204, 289 f., 425 ff.
Loisy, Prof. A., 273 ff.
Luke, St., 279 f., 328; Gospel of (see also 'Gospels, The Four Canonical'), 18, 51, 99 f., 277 ff., 293, 301, 379 f., 401, 432, 451, 453.
Lumby, Dr. J. R., 385.
λόγιον, 72 f., 75.
λόγος (θεῖος, ἱερός), 28, 72.

Maccabees, Books of, 102, 109 f., 254, 256 f., 335, 445, 447.
Malachi, 443.
Manasseh, Prayer of, 262.
Mangold, Dr. W. J., 344.
Mantic, 75, 132, 143.
Marcion, 15, 19, 364 f., 451.
Mark, St., 280 f., 294, 451; Gospel of, 51, 280 ff., 291 ff., 301, 311, 379 f.
Massebieau, Prof. L., 99.
Matthew, St., 280 f., 300; Gospel of, 83, 265, 280 ff., 291 ff., 301, 311, 432, 451, 453.
Mayor, Dr. J. B., 24, 344 f.
*Megilloth*, 252 f.
Melito, 30, 92, 132 f., 453.
Mesha, 135 ff.
Messianic office, The, 417.
Messianic Prophecy: *see* 'Prophecy.'
Metaphysics, 153.
Method, *A priori*, 423; of the inquiry, 3 ff.
Methodius, 37.
Micah, Book of, 142, 241, 439.
Mill, J. S., 144.
Milligan, Dr. W., 369.
Moabite Religion, 135 ff., 151.
— Stone, The, 135 ff., 228, 436.
Mommsen, Prof. Th., 339.
Mommsen's List, 113, 455.
Monarchians, 41, 64.
Monks, as historians, 158.
Montanism, 13, 15, 62, 64.
Montefiore, Mr. C. G., 116, 119, 121, 141 f., 144, 163, 185, 249.
Mosaic element in the Pentateuch, 172 ff., 177.
Moses, 175, 177 ff., 408, 414; Assumption of, 91.
Müller, Dr. K., 21 f.
Muratorian Fragment, The, 12, 19, 23, 26, 32, 45, 48, 56, 453.

*Index.* 461

μαθητής, 288 ff.
μακάριος, 67.
μανία, 75.

Nahum, 84, 441.
Narrative, Historical, 160.
Nathan, 231, 405.
Naturalism, 2, 116 f.
Neander, August, 344.
Nehemiah, 101, 235, 246; Book of, 96, 164, 253, 443.
Neopythagoreanism, 56, 75.
Nero *redivivus*, 373.
Neubauer, Dr. A., 256.
Neutral zone in our Lord's teaching, A, 419.
New Testament, The: see 'Canon,' 'Scriptures,' 'Gospels,' 'Acts,' 'Epistles,' &c.; on the same footing with O. T., 30 f., 65 f., 316, 366, 375; Use of O. T. Apocrypha in, 94 f.; Text of, 295 ff., 342 ff.; Criticism of, xii f.; Canon of, 6, 12, 22 f., 57, 63, 348, 369, 453, 455; Inspiration of, 31 ff., 333 f., 350 ff., 353.
Nicephorus, 113.
Noah, 409, 414.
Novatian, 30, 38.
Numbers, Book of, 229.
— Symbolical use of, 56 ff., 112 ff.
νόμος, ὁ, 265.

Obadiah, Book of, 229, 242, 439.
Old Testament, The: see 'Canon,' 'Scriptures,' 'Law,' 'Prophets,' *Hagiographa*, 'Pentateuch,' 'Genesis,' 'Exodus,' &c.; Criticism of, xii, 115 ff.; Text of, 262 f.; Canon of, 4 f., 91 f., 257, 447, 449, 455; Inspiration of, 74 ff., 353.
Origen, 26, 28, 31 ff., 37 ff., 46, 51, 53, 55, 92, 105, 113, 115, 267, 310, 382, 388 f., 421, 455.
Overbeck, Dr. F., 24 f., 379 f.

Page, Mr. T. E., 319.
Paley, William, 325.
Papias, 23, 45, 280 ff., 451.
Parsimony, Law of, 417 ff.
Parthians, The, 373, 377.
Particularism, 351, 370.
Pastoral Epistles, 19, 25, 337 ff., 363 ff., 379 f., 451, 453.

Paul, St., 331 f., 339 f., 350 ff., 355 ff., 359; Epistles of, 12, 18 ff., 68 f., 229, 325 f., 335 ff., 360 f., 363 ff., 403, 447, 451, 453, 455; Inspiration of, 42 ff., 323 f., 326 f., 331 ff., 401; Terminology of, 287; Acts of, 11; and Thecla, Acts of, 17.
Pauline Epistles, Collection of the, 19, 363 ff., 384; Order of the, 365 f.
Pentateuch, The: see 'Law'; Structure of, 172, 443; Mosaic element in, 172 ff., 177, 437; Prophetical element in, 177 ff.; Priestly element in, 179 ff., 397; Authorship of, 172 ff., 409.
Pentateuchs, 104.
Persecution of Christians, 339, 372, 374 f.
Peshitto Version, Influence of the, 10.
Peter, St., 67, 323 f., 326 f., 359; First Epistle of, 9, 12, 56, 346, 359, 366, 379 ff., 451, 453, 455; Second Epistle of, 26, 346 ff., 381, 382 ff., 399, 455; Terminology of, 287; Apocryphal Gospel of, 16, 290, 310 ff., 451; Apocalypse of, 27, 347 f., 384; Preaching of, 27.
Philemon, Epistle to, 43, 223, 337, 364.
Philippians, Epistle to the, 337, 451.
Philo, 72 ff., 79 ff., 84 ff., 93 f., 99, 447.
Philoxenian Version, 10.
Physical excitement, 130, 143.
Plummer, Dr. A., xiii, 385, 415.
Pörtner, Dr. B., 273.
Polycarp, 299, 362, 365 f.; Epistle of, 362 f., 451.
'Presbyters' quoted by Irenaeus, 451.
Priests, 157, 179, 183 ff., 224, 236, 397.
Prophecy, 76, 82 ff., 132 f., 231, 254; Predictive, 78, 83 ff.; Fulfilment of, 82 ff., 265 f., 376 ff.; Conditional character of, 266; Messianic, 154, 219 f., 404 f.
Prophet, The ideal, 404.
Prophets, 129 ff., 224, 394 f.; Communities of, 133; False, 134,

141 f.; Professional, 133 ff., 140 ff.; Writing, 227 ff., 237 ff., 403; As historians, 155 ff., 164, 268 f., 400 f.; The Former, 155, 164; The Latter, 155, 164; The Major, 102, 143, 157; the Minor, 96, 143, 157, 247; The higher, 143 ff.; Transmission of the writings of the, 239 ff.; Canon of the, 100 f., 228, 231, 247; in the New Testament, 353 f., 362, 372, 375 ff.; Authority of the, 231, 245; Inspiration of the, 128 ff., 146 ff., 264 ff., 268, 353, 375 ff., 394 ff., 400 f.; Modern, 166 f.
Proverbs, Book of (*see* 'Wise Men'), 102, 200 ff., 247 ff., 276, 443; Structure of the, 200 ff.
Providence, Traces of a Higher, 212, 226 f., 231, 237, 239, 244 ff., 402 ff.
Psalms, 170, 185, 191 ff., 243 f., 250 ff., 398, 405, 409, 414, 443; Smaller collections included in the Book of, 193 ff., 250 ff., 271; Date of the, 192 f., 251 f., 270 ff., 443, 447; Maccabaean, 256 f., 270 ff.; Inspiration of the, 195 ff., 397.
Pseudonymous authorship, 217 f., 224 f., 348.
Ptolemaeus, 308, 453.
Public Worship, Reading or Use in, 244 f., 252, 315 f., 360 f.
*principalis*, 32.
*providentia* (*Sancti Spiritus*), 35 (*cf.* 83).
περιοδοι τῶν ἀποστόλων, 27.
πνευματοφόρος, 31.

Quartodecimans, 55.
Quinisextine or Trullan Council: *see* 'Councils.'
Quotation, Formulae of, 76, 301, 304; Freedom of, 298 ff.

Rabbinical exegesis, 80 ff., 87 f., 356.
Rahlfs, Dr. A., 192.
Ramsay, Prof. W. M., 329 f., 338 f., 346, 372 f., 384.
Reading in public worship: *see* 'Public.'

Reading public, A, 241 f.
Resch, Dr. A., 296, 299 f., 303 f.
Revelation, 124 f., 164 f., 430; Applied, 396 ff.
Richardson, Mr. J. G., 355.
Riehm, Dr. E., 144, 146.
Ritschl, Dr. A., 344.
Robertson, Prof. James, 118 f., 130, 230.
Romans, Epistle to the, 336, 340 ff., 345, 356, 379 f., 403, 413, 451.
Rome, Church of, 368; Imperial, 375 f., 377.
Romestin, Mr. de, 416.
Routh, Dr. M. J., 28.
Rufinus, 92, 113.
Ruth, Book of, 96, 112 f., 155, 223, 252 f.
Ryle, Prof. H. E., xi, 73, 130, 227 f.

Sacrificial system, The, 186 f.
Salmon, Dr. G., 15, 309.
Samaritans, 246 f.
Samuel, 131 f., 140 f., 231; Books of, 96, 129, 164, 239, 243.
Schools, 242; of the Prophets, 133.
Schürer, Dr. E., 81, 94, 278, 301, 312 f., 324, 444.
Schultz, Dr. H., 130.
Scillitan Martyrs, 20 f.
Scribes, 240, 246, 249, 253, 256.
Scriptures, The: *see* 'Bible,' 'Canon,' 'New (Old) Testament,' 'Law,' 'Prophets,' &c.; Names applied to the, 28 f., 72 f.; Doctrine of, 420 f.; infallible, 37 f., 88, 265 f., 393; authoritative, 38, 79, 264 f., 392 f.; not discordant, 37, 55; Interpretation of, 39, 42, 85 ff., 447; Perversion of, 40 f.; Mutilation of, 40; Sacredness of, 28 f., 39, 72 f., 78; Perfection of, 36 f., 85 f., 90; Finality of, 37, 89, 267, 376.
Second Century, 12, 27, 48, 393.
Seer, 129, 131 f.
Sellin, Dr. E., 192.
Septuagint, 92, 262, 453, 455.
Serapion, 16, 33, 48, 315.
Servant of Jehovah, 404.
Severianus, 10.
Shammai, 78, 81, 97, 450.
Shemaiah, 81, 447, 450.

Shorthand, 342.
Sibylline Oracles, 102, 445.
Siegfried, Dr. K., 86.
Silvanus, 383.
Simon ben Gamaliel, 450.
Simon ben Shetach, 102, 447, 450.
Sinaitic legislation, 234 f.
*Sinaiticus, Cod.*, 11.
Smith, Dr. I. Gregory, 416.
Smith, Dr. W. Robertson, 119, 194, 256.
Socin, Dr. A., 234.
Soden, Freiherr von, 288, 311 f., 317 f., 338, 385.
Solomon, 248; Psalms of, 91, 447.
'Son of Man,' The title, 288.
Song of Songs, 82, 97, 211 ff., 252 f., 405, 435.
Song of the Three Children, 262.
Spirit, Gift of the, 332 ff., 352 ff., 359, 375, 398.
Spitta, Dr. F., 382 ff.
Stade, Dr. B., 130.
Stephen, St., 322.
Sunday, 361.
Supernatural, The, 117, 331 ff., 333.
*Supernatural Religion*, 300, 307.
Surenhusius, 79.
Susanna, Story of, 362.
Synagogue, The Great, 253.
Synagogues, 244 ff., 346.
Synoptic problem, The, 281 f.
Syria, Church of, 9 ff., 21, 348, 453, 455.
Syro-Phoenician Woman, The, 419.
*sacrosanctus*, 29.
*scriptura*, 29.

Talmud, The, 73, 80, 87, 103 f., 113 ff., 450.
*Tannaim*, 450.
Tatian, 301 f., 307, 453.
Taylor, Dr. C., 309 f.
Tell-el-Amarna tablets, The, xii, 221, 228, 436.
Tertullian, 26, 29, 31, 34 f., 38, 41 f., 48 f., 51, 112, 315, 357, 361, 364, 387 f., 453.
Theodore of Mopsuestia, 10, 455.
Theodoret, 10.
Theophany, 235.
Theophilus, 319.
Theophilus of Antioch, 28, 302, 453.

Thessalonians, Epistles to the, 336 f., 353, 360, 363, 461.
Theudas, 328 f.
Timothy, Epistles to: *see* 'Pastoral Epistles.'
Titus, Epistle to: *see* 'Pastoral Epistles.'
Tobit, Book of, 255.
Tongues, Speaking with, 328.
Tradition, Jewish, 98 ff., 103, 155, 216.
Turpie, Mr. M<sup>c</sup>Calman, 79.
θαυμάσιος, 67.
θεϊκός, 29.
θεῖος, 28 f., 67.
θεόπνευστος, 33, 88.
θεοφορηθείς, θεοφόρητος, 32, 75.

Uncanonical Writings (*see* 'Apocrypha'), 11, 16 f., 27, 91 ff., 105 ff., 447.

Valentinians, 41, 308.
Valentinus, 15, 38, 308.
Version, The Harclean, 10; The Old Latin, 18; The Peshitto, 10; The Philoxenian, 10; The Vulgate, 8; Monophysite, 11.
Victorinus of Pettau, 113.
Virgil, Text of, 343.
Vischer, Herr E., 370.

Warfield, Dr. B. B., 385.
Wars of the Lord, Book of the, 229, 437.
Wattenbach, Dr. W., 368.
Weiffenbach, Dr. W., 292.
Weiss, Dr. B., 303, 344, 361, 364, 385.
Weizsäcker, Dr. C., 288.
Wellhausen, Dr. Julius, 116 ff., 130, 173, 178, 180, 227.
Westcott, Bp. B. F., 7, 28, 128, 191, 343, 370, 373.
Wildeboer, Dr. G., xi, 102, 107 f.
Wisdom, Book of, 94, 254, 256, 258 ff., 262, 386.
— of the Son of Sirach, Book of: *see* 'Ecclesiasticus.'
— Conception of, 202 ff.
Wisdom-Books, 199 ff., 247.
Wise Men, 199 ff., 224, 249, 255, 397.

Word of God (*see Logos*), 392, 424, 426 f.
'Words of the Lord,' 303 f.
Writing, 228 f., 248; Transition from Speech to, 226 ff., 394, 403.

Zahn, Dr. Th., xi, 7, 19, 28, 64 f., 106, 309 ff., 364 ff.
Zechariah, Book of, 243, 405, 443.
Zephaniah, 242; Book of, 441.
Zephyrinus, 53.

THE END.